The Discipline of Western Supremacy

Also available by Kees van der Pijl from Pluto Press

Nomads, Empires, States:
Modes of Foreign Relations and Political Economy, Volume I

The Foreign Encounter in Myth and Religion:
Modes of Foreign Relations and Political Economy, Volume II

Global Rivalries from the Cold War to Iraq

The Discipline of Western Supremacy

Modes of Foreign Relations and Political Economy

Volume III

KEES VAN DER PIJL

PlutoPress
www.plutobooks.com

First published 2014 by Pluto Press
345 Archway Road, London N6 5AA

www.plutobooks.com

Distributed in the United States of America exclusively by
Palgrave Macmillan, a division of St Martin's Press LLC,
175 Fifth Avenue, New York, NY 10010

British Library Cataloguing in Publication Data
A catalogue record for this book is available from the British Library

ISBN   978 0 7453 2318 3   Hardback
ISBN   978 1 8496 4888 2   PDF eBook
ISBN   978 1 8496 4890 5   Kindle eBook
ISBN   978 1 8496 4889 9   EPUB eBook

Library of Congress Cataloging in Publication Data applied for

10   9   8   7   6   5   4   3   2   1

Typeset from disk by Stanford DTP Services, Northampton, England
Simultaneously printed digitally by CPI Antony Rowe, Chippenham, UK and
Edwards Bros in the United States of America

Contents

Preface

This volume concludes the trilogy in which I redefine world politics as an evolving composite of modes of foreign relations. Foreign relations are about communities occupying separate social spaces and considering each other as outsiders. Occupation, its protection, and the regulation of exchange with others are universal attributes of human communities; they date back to the dawn of anthropogenesis and have evolved with the ongoing transformation of nature. Hence, as we have seen in Volume II, all human groups, communities and societies rely on mythologies and religious imaginaries to make sense of the foreign encounter. They originate in the tribal and empire/nomad modes and continue to run through contemporary foreign relations. Indeed in our contemporary epoch, such primordial imaginaries are resurgent on a grand scale.

International relations as we understand them today constitute a historical mode of foreign relations too. The grid of sovereign states under the guidance of a self-styled 'international community' headquartered in Washington and London not only remains imbricated with modes of older parentage; at some point it will make way for other patterns – if, that is, we live to see it. With the faltering ability of the liberal West and capitalism to develop the productive forces in ways conducive to the improvement of life chances, the very idea of a future is being eclipsed by proliferating violence and the spectre of ecological disaster.

Along with the need to dissect and discard economic theories of the self-regulating market which brought us to where we are today, Western supremacy in the global political economy must be challenged in the name of human survival too. In the present volume, I take the critique of foreign relations developed in Volumes I and II to its logical conclusion as a critique of the mainstream discipline of International Relations (IR). Along with adjacent fields dealing with foreign relations, such as comparative politics, area studies, and anthropology, IR serves to discipline thinking about foreign relations in terms of the pre-eminence of the Western way of life. It turns the alienated consciousness that underpins the idea of foreignness into a body of thought that denies validity to other ways of life and other political systems, whilst naturalising Western supremacy and obscuring the relations of dominance and exploitation that IR codifies.

Social science originally dealt with 'domestic' challenges. It crystallised in its present disciplinary form when the labour movement in the nineteenth century began to embrace socialist ideas. This triggered an epochal, across-the-board retreat from the most advanced social philosophy of the age – not just from historical materialism, but also from Hegel and others without whom Marx's quantum leap would not have been possible. The first stage of the process saw the formulation of utilitarian economics in Britain, French sociology, and the German *Staatswissenschaften*. Their common inspiration was to create the conditions for authoritative class compromise – scientific advance was at best secondary to this task. Parcelling out knowledge across a number of different fields would allow adjustments in each whilst leaving the core structures of class society intact. For as the Anglo-Irish parliamentarian and writer Edmund Burke warned at the time of the French Revolution (*Works*, iii: 259, emphasis added), 'a state without the means of *some change* is without the means of its conservation'.

The modern academic division of labour translates this insight into a series of teaching and research programmes in the service of the existing order (Wallerstein 2001: 20). It achieved its contemporary form in North America, where the aforementioned reformulations of social theory were further differentiated, with a common grounding in the agnostic, empirical theory of knowledge that John Locke developed in the seventeenth century. When control of the universities in the United States around the turn of the last century passed from the Protestant clergy to the business world, academic discipline mutated into a straightforward continuation of class discipline by different means, subject to methods of scientific management. The process was well advanced when the Russian empire collapsed in revolution in 1917, with the Bolsheviks emerging victorious from civil war and foreign intervention. The US president at the time, Woodrow Wilson, projected what would become the implicit programme of IR till the present day – the creation of a world of formally sovereign nation-states under liberal, Anglo-American supervision, arrayed against the spread of social revolution and open for business. Or as Ikenberry summarises the project (2011: 4), 'The "problems of Hobbes," that is, anarchy and power insecurities ... had to be solved in order to take advantage of the "opportunities of Locke," that is, the construction of open and rule-based relations'.

Wilson's entourage at Versailles created the framework for the one remaining specialisation needed to complete the academic infrastructure developed in the United States – international politics. Every branch of science, writes Bourdieu (1984: 90), at some point changes from obeying a scientific necessity that is socially arbitrary, to obeying a social necessity that is scientifically arbitrary. The Russian Revolution was that moment in the study of world affairs. Thus, in the decades following the First World War, discipline was imposed on a terrain captured by Marxist writers on imperialism and national self-determination. IR instead focuses on global governance and (subordinate) sovereign equality, two modes of foreign relations which owe their specific form to the rise of a transnational, Anglophone society and ruling class. Rival principles of world order, be they atavistic ones such as empire, or alternatives looking to equitable global governance such as socialist internationalism, are disregarded, as are tribal and other pre-modern foreign relations and their ideational forms. Hence it comes as no surprise that the academic discipline of IR, as Schmidt reminds us (1998: 13), is 'marked by British, and especially, American parochialism'.

For Marx, historical change originates in class formation and struggle. We can analyse these in terms of a contradiction between an existing social order (including its ideational superstructures) and the vision of a different one arising from new possibilities. In the transformation of nature through the social labour process, this works out as a contradiction between forces and relations of production; in foreign relations, in which class relations are mediated by ethno-political difference, the contradiction is between human community and common humanity. Global governance, enabled by the development of the exploitation of nature and society on a world scale, would appear to be in contradiction with sovereign equality in this sense; but the contradiction is overcome in practice by making the states of the Lockean heartland 'more equal' than others. Since this cannot be the official introduction to a teaching programme, the discipline rests on a presumed foundational debate between Wilsonian 'idealism' and 1930s *Realpolitik*. Caught in a pre-Hegelian understanding of static antinomies conceived from the vantage point of the unconstrained 'actor', and confining itself to politics, this supposed 'first debate' in IR invites students and scholars to a partisan appreciation of either position.

Yet even by plain logic, a real or imagined global governance (imperial, Western liberal, or socialist) is always prior to any resistance to it; they are aspects of an evolving combination. Walker captures this when he writes (1993: 42) that

if it is necessary to identify a tradition of international relations theory, then the most appropriate candidate is not 'realism' but 'idealism'. For what is systematically obscured by the reifying claims about political realism as a tradition is that realism has been constituted historically through the negation and displacement of a prior understanding of political life understood in the context of universalist aspirations ... The tradition of political realism as we have come to know it is unthinkable without the priority ascribed to universalist claims within political theory.

As in social science generally, however, IR's foundation in a Kantian antinomy leads to endless pirouettes on the threshold of a dialectical understanding. The same theoretical positions are reinvented over and over again under new labels, a process spawning its own clichés: 'bringing x back in', 'the y turn', 'z matters', and so on (Abbott 2001: 32). Instead of moving forward on the basis of historical materialism (like music after Wagner, or physics after Einstein and Planck), English-speaking social thought, which today dominates academic life the world over, remains locked into the antinomy between (materialist) empiricism and (religious–idealist) moral judgement, 'positive' and 'normative' theory. But that of course is inherent in a social discipline that is scientifically arbitrary. As long as capitalist property relations are safe from critical questioning, any economics will do; as long as liberal global governance and open nation-states remain the norm, IR can be left to self-regulate, from Angell to Krasner.

Now if social science suffers from having turned its back on classical thought once Marx transformed it into a challenge to the existing order, the historical materialist tradition has not survived its exclusion from academia unscathed either. Unlike the Nazi attempt to remove Einstein from physics (documented by Poliakov and Wulf 1989: 102–3), which was too short-lived to produce an 'Einsteinism' reproducing itself in isolation, the century-long exile of Marx has engendered sectarianism and formulaic retrogression. Marxism after Marx largely failed to assimilate his philosophical revolution, lapsing into a positive–materialist theory of economic causation again, a 'Marxist economics' (Desai 2013: 12–14; cf. my vol. i, 2007: viii–ix) removed from class struggle and consciousness.

Lenin in his notes on Hegel's *Logic* began the process of rediscovering the Marxist method, and Gramsci and others were to follow. In this spirit the present volume develops a critique of Anglo-American IR, its social determinants, and its practical role in sustaining Western supremacy in the world.

The English ruling class pioneered reflection on the conditions under which an Atlantic society uses maritime supremacy as a road to global dominion, whilst playing off continental contenders against each other. In Chapter 1, I address how from Elizabethan times, the dilemma between empire and liberty was recognised in ways prefiguring the eventual project of Western supremacy. By encouraging client nation-state formation against illiberal, multi-ethnic constellations, freedom could be projected abroad as informal empire; the Congress of Vienna, the Greek revolt and the emancipation of Latin America mark the beginnings of the process in practice. Of course nationality was conceptualised from two different angles – the Lockean doctrine of the property-owning citizen is incompatible with Rousseau's and Herder's understanding of a historic, organic community. In the second half of the nineteenth century, Anglophone ideologues from J.S. Mill to Mackinder and Hobson then articulated global governance and nationality in a form prefiguring the eventual disciplinary programme of IR. In the chapter's final section, I summarise the Marxist theses on national autonomy and imperialism to which the discipline would constitute the response in the twentieth century.

In Chapter 2, I recapitulate how Woodrow Wilson, himself a political scientist and academic politician before he became president of the United States, through his strategy of encircling revolutionary Russia also inaugurated the establishment of a dedicated IR. Wilson entrusted the think tank 'The Inquiry' with the task of identifying potential client states to stem the spread of revolution. Its secretary, Walter Lippmann, in turn recommended that the universities be made an adjunct of policymaking by the federal government, as an academic intelligence base. The Council on Foreign Relations and the Royal Institute of International Affairs that emerged from this episode, the large foundations spun off from the big capitalist dynasties, and the US university system were thus mobilised as a research and training infrastructure for the policy sciences, including IR. Paradoxically, it took until the collapse into fascist dictatorship of the states 'made safe for democracy' before a flow of refugees fleeing Nazi persecution and racism breathed life into this skeleton academic complex. Their quasi-tribal concept of existential foreignness, borrowed from the Third Reich's crown jurist Carl Schmitt, merged with the Lockean antagonism towards illiberal societies into the Atlantic synthesis that is at the root of modern IR.

The atomic bombardment of Japan in 1945 marks a watershed in the conduct of world politics. Once various projects for equitable global governance had been sidelined, Western supremacy became premised on maintaining nuclear superiority. In Chapter 3, I discuss how the collective fear of atomic annihilation in the United States underpinned the communist witch-hunt of Senator Joe McCarthy. Besides intimidating the liberal intelligentsia into submission to the new national security state, McCarthyism also engendered, through the medium of IR realism and its tribal concept of the foreign, an essentially autistic understanding of world politics. With the doomsday assumption of a nuclear Pearl Harbour given, war strategists in the RAND Corporation substituted game theory for political analysis as they calculated the equilibrium point in an atomic standoff. As IR mobilised behind a 'pugnacious Christianity', the national security state crystallised into what the dean of post-war US realists, Hans Morgenthau, afterwards identified as the 'dual state'. In a dual state, he writes (1962: 400; cf. Tunander 2009),

the power of making decisions remains with the authorities charged by law with making them while, as a matter of fact, by virtue of their power over life and death, the agents of the secret policy – co-ordinated to, but independent from, the official makers of decisions – at the very least exert an effective veto over the decisions.

This dual state, which Morgenthau saw as a spillover from totalitarian practice that in the United States might still be contained, has in fact remained at the heart of the Western power structure. Within the dual state, the shadow structures operating behind the scenes (or the 'deep state', to use a term coined in Turkey) are the ones that can impose emergency rule – thus revealing, by Schmitt's definition, who is the ultimate sovereign. This is not a matter of saying, for example, that the CIA secretly governs. It is, by definition, the ruling class that rules; but it necessarily does so through a range of intermediate governing structures with which its different fractions are connected differentially. Intelligence agencies are key instruments, but they are not exempt from being disciplined by deep politics themselves – as in the 1970s 'Team B' episode in the case of the CIA (see Chapter 5). Equally when the US military failed to produce evidence of weapons of mass destruction after the invasion of Iraq, this proved once again that 'the' military, or even the military–industrial complex, are not monolithic entities in the service of imperialism. Yet when academics work for the CIA or the Pentagon, it is usually not to assist those who, like Private Bradley Manning when he released evidence of US war crimes in Iraq that ended up on the WikiLeaks website, resist abuse and secrecy, but as members of the academic intelligence base of US and NATO policy – more often than not assisting its covert operations, as in the case of the 'Marshall Plan for the social sciences' discussed in this chapter.

Post-war decolonisation posed the greatest challenge to the continued supremacy of the West since the Bolshevik Revolution. This time, a vast academic infrastructure was in place to provide expert intelligence. In Chapter 4, I discuss first how the open nation-state form emerged from colonial rule as a class compromise between the British ruling class and local bourgeois elements, with India and Pakistan as the examples. Once the United States assumed leadership in handling the decolonisation process in order to prevent progressive forces from pushing beyond liberalism, its academic intelligence base was mobilised to develop theories of political development. Since Cold War IR was largely irrelevant in the process, comparative politics and area studies took up the task of projecting how a decolonised, pre-industrial or even tribal society could begin the supposedly natural process of moving towards the American way of life, or at least, a pro-Western stance against state socialism. By the mid 1960s, modernisation theory had given way to a security concern articulated by the single most important ideologue of post-war US imperialism, Samuel Huntington, in his work on the role of the military in the new nations. Thus the concerns of IR merged again with those of its sister disciplines. Together, the academics involved in them (very often the same people) functioned as what Noam Chomsky famously called the 'new mandarins', assisting the US government in Vietnam and other contested arenas. Indonesia in this respect occupies a place of its own as a testing ground for how the grooming of an alternative governing class followed by violent regime change secured the country for exploitation by the West. Paradoxically, Soviet theory as well as Third World national liberation ideology did not stray from positing the sovereign nation-state as the endpoint of historical development.

In Volume I, I drew the contours of the class coalition which will be centrally involved in any attempt to move beyond Western supremacy and globalising capitalism. Such a coalition must also revive and take forward the intellectual diversity which the May 1968 students' and workers' movement brought back to academia. In Chapter 5, I argue that the upsurge in international studies and the rediscovery of the themes of imperialism and militarism sidelined by mainstream debates proved short-lived. With a new ethics to bolster Lockean liberalism and key issues such as transnational corporations absorbed into a sub-discipline of international political economy, IR geared itself towards specifying actual global governance and the need to discipline the remaining non-compliant states under its regime. Wars of dispossession dressed up as humanitarian intervention and coups choreographed as velvet revolutions after the script of Harvard scholar Gene Sharp all owe their efficacy (at least in their launching) to the work of contemporary IR scholars training new generations of cadre. After the collapse of the Soviet Union, the 'clash of civilisations' thesis was formulated to justify continued military outlays, this time against the new contender state, China, and 'Islam' was demonised as a hotbed of terrorism. As I document in this chapter, the outlines of a 'war on terror', complemented by a domestic surveillance state, were already drawn at dedicated conferences in Jerusalem and Washington in the early 1980s. Yet once the new Pearl Harbour, announced for more than a decade, actually happened, the event and its consequences have remained taboo as IR subjects. The discipline has instead assumed a mercenary quality and scholars have become 'embedded intellectuals' sustaining Western supremacy in the face of mounting challenges. Clearly the various undercurrents of critical theory will have to be bolstered well beyond their present impact if intellectual integrity and social relevance to international studies are to be restored – a task that in the light of the threats to human existence can no longer be postponed.

Acknowledgements

This is a book about the IR discipline, not about its representatives as humans. This must be borne in mind when I write about those of my own generation, some of whom I have met and who have given me no reason to be adversarial – on the contrary. I should in fact thank them for the chance to check my ideas about an academic intelligence base at first hand. Yet even the mainstream is only selectively represented here; the planned size of this volume rules out a comprehensive overview of the discipline. This is also why I have not discussed any progressive currents, whilst economising as much as possible on references and omitting biographical sources, both in print and online. Neither are there any learned or courtesy references to 'further reading', 'see also', etc.; the list of references is already much larger than in Volumes I and II. More extensive works on the history of international thought (1996, 2009) cover those deficits to some extent, just as they prefigure some of the arguments made here.

For the current volume I owe a debt to Alex Colás, who organised a panel on the Modes of Foreign Relations project at the Stockholm SGIR Conference in September 2010, with Klaus-Gerd Giesen, Heide Gerstenberger and Mauro di Meglio as discussants. I further thank Pınar Bedirhanoglu and her colleagues at METU in Ankara, who kindly invited me to give the keynote speech to the June 2011 IR conference where nine years earlier I had first presented the modes of foreign relations idea. I also wish to express my deep appreciation to those who attended the farewell seminar in my honour at Sussex in September 2012, especially Peter Newell for organising the event and Nadya Herrera Catalán, Benno Teschke and Christopher Eves for making the seminar and related festivities a success. Finally, I owe a debt to the organisers of a conference on the Political Science of the South at the University of Havana, Cuba, for giving me a special slot to present the argument of this work in November 2012.

Of those others who helped me with materials and suggestions for the present volume, I thank Alex Anievas, Marco Arafat Garrido, Erkki Berndtson, Ian Bruff, Alan Cafruny, William Carroll, Antonio Cerella, Marlies Glasius, Don Kalb, Peter Katzenstein, Gabriel

Kolko, Richard Lane, Raffaele Marchetti, James Mittelman, George Moody, Bhabani Nayak, Patricia Owens, Ronen Palan, Leo Panitch, Fabio Petito, Frédéric Ramel, Ben Selwyn, Dimitris Sotiropoulos, Benno Teschke, Srdjan Vucetic and Steffan Wynn-Jones. Roger van Zwanenberg has now retired from Pluto, but he has been an indispensable support and an occasionally tough critic. The team at Pluto have done their usual first-rate job on this book, as have Anthony Winder, whom I was again fortunate to have as copy-editor, and Sue Stanford, who proofread the final text.

The Leverhulme Trust, on the recommendation of Thomas Ferguson, Andrew Linklater, and Jan Nederveen Pieterse, supported the writing of Volumes I and II. In 2008 the British Academy awarded a small grant (SG-50186) to conduct a pilot study on the spread of Anglo-American IR theory into the former Soviet space (Moody 2010). After that my attempts to obtain funding were unsuccessful. In at least two cases (one with the Economic and Social Research Council in England, one with the European Research Council) this served as a stark reminder of how discipline is maintained through funding policy. For young scholars, already working under unprecedented pressure, this has become a real nightmare, of which I have witnessed some shocking results.

Indeed as our society is moving well past its expiry date, discipline is being tightened in every respect and basic freedoms are being curtailed in ways I would not have thought possible 40 years ago. When Daniel Ellsberg made public the Pentagon Papers, exposing the motivations behind the US war in Vietnam, he also initially feared for his safety, but then became a public hero; Private Bradley Manning, Julian Assange, the founder of WikiLeaks, and others who have exposed US war crimes in Iraq and Afghanistan are being mercilessly hounded down by US and UK authorities. Aaron Swartz, an activist against Internet censorship, hanged himself when faced with disproportionate prosecution over downloading academic papers from JSTOR and other unduly copyrighted material; Edward Snowden, who exposed the National Security Agency's secret PRISM surveillance programme and its British GCHQ equivalent, had to seek refuge in China and has just been granted asylum in Russia as I write. It is to those who are not intimidated by the heavy hand of 'the law' and who continue to work for transparency and democracy that I dedicate this book.

1
Empire and Nationality in the Pax Britannica

In the closing decades of the eighteenth century, Edmund Burke (1729–97) articulated the fracture in world affairs that still today underlies the discipline of International Relations – between what I call the Lockean heartland, freely uniting sovereign nations respectful of property, family and (our) religion, and illiberal contenders trampling on all of these. Burke had no difficulty with the revolt of the North American settlers; on the contrary. In a speech in the Commons on 22 March 1775 (*Works*, ii: 120), he praised their 'fierce spirit of liberty … stronger in the English colonies, probably, than in any other people of the earth'. For 'the people of the colonies are descendants of Englishmen'.

England, Sir, is a nation which still, I hope, respects, and formerly adored, her freedom. The colonists emigrated from you when this part of your character was most predominant; and they took this bias and direction the moment they parted from your hands. They are therefore not only devoted to liberty, but to liberty according to English ideas and on English principles.

Revolutionary France instead intended to abrogate 'the public law of Europe, the ancient conventions of its *several* states', Burke wrote in the *Third Letter on a Regicide Peace* of 1795 (*Works*, v: 443, emphasis added). It projected an empire 'which is not grounded on any balance, but forms a sort of impious hierarchy, of which France is to be the head and the guardian'. As we will see, this notion of a plurality of states would remain key in the concept of Western supremacy.

In this chapter I discuss the ideological divide between an English-speaking, Protestant practice of sovereign foreign relations premised on commerce, and a contender counterpoint developed on the European Continent. After the downfall of Napoleon, Britain, enjoying a commercial primacy unchallenged until 1860, adopted the French policy of sponsored nation-building, casting itself as the champion, in Bauer's words (1907: 474–5), of 'the freedom of other countries – those without factories'. Towards the end of the nineteenth century this was again challenged by contenders, for whom Hegel's organic understanding of the state served as a guiding principle. By then, the two lineages of European social thought, agnostic–practical in the liberal West, theoretical–comprehensive on the Continent, had crystallised. I conclude with the Marxist theses on national self-determination and imperialism that would eventually be responded to by the formulation of an Anglo-American discipline of IR.

THE COLLECTIVE MIND OF ANGLOPHONE DOMINION

English overseas expansion, Neil Smith writes (2004: 15), 'as early as the sixteenth century represented an almost seamless extension of the concurrent struggle to establish and delineate the still weak nation-state'. Shakespeare made his name as the ideologue of Tudor state building at home. Like many of his contemporaries the playwright valued the Welsh dynasty for providing the robust authority that brought peace and stability, a message communicated to the lower folk in a language they understood. Spicing his dramas with what Rowse calls (1998: 279), the 'naïve jingoism ... of the years immediately succeeding the Armada', Shakespeare painted his favourites in glowing colours – in contrast to their opponents, who relied on court intrigue and 'set the murderous Machiavel to school' (*3 Henry VI*, III, ii).

Overseas expansion followed the often-cited maxim of Elizabeth's favourite, Walter Raleigh, that 'whosoever commands the sea commands the trade; whosoever commands the trade of the world commands the riches of the world, and consequently the world itself'. This, he inferred, would entail settlement across the Atlantic, from which arose the heartland that still today occupies the commanding heights of the global political economy. Raleigh's protégé Richard Hakluyt (c.1552–1616), an Anglican priest and chaplain to Robert Cecil, the principal secretary of state, elaborated his patron's argument into a series of works beginning with *A Discourse of Western Planting* of 1584. In this tract Hakluyt speaks (1993: 2) of the 'greate necessitie and manifolde commodyties that are likely to growe to the Realme of Englande by the westerne discouveries'. He adds, though, that only settlement would insulate the new possessions from the vacillations of a purely commercial interest. In a subsequent work, *The Principal Navigations, Voiages and Discoveries of the English Nation* of 1589 (as in Gollwitzer 1972: 131) Hakluyt advocated a 'more perfect league and amity of such countrys ... so to be possessed ... with our Realms of England and Ireland'. The *Discourse* also recommends (Hakluyt 1993: 28) that 'idle and mutynous persons' the country wants to get rid of anyway should settle in North America. That the natives across the Atlantic were supposedly 'crying out to us ... to come and help', as Ferguson (2003: 64) cites Hakluyt, highlights how expansion was already in those days sold as 'humanitarian assistance'.

Formal Equivalence and the Bourgeoisie

From a bourgeois viewpoint a key problem of the Tudor age was how to reconcile overseas expansion with the idea of innate freedom, 'English birthright' (vol. i, 2007: 136). Classical writers from Polybius to Machiavelli had contrasted Roman imperial expansion and its loss of civic freedom with Spartan (and Rome's original) republican virtue. Elizabethan commentators, speaking to an outward-looking middle class as much as to the Court, took up the theme. In 1594 an Irish county official (as in Armitage 2000: 132–3) contrasted Sparta's concern with ethnic purity and lack of territorial ambitions with imperial Rome's generosity towards foreigners, which bequeathed a legacy of 'true glory' – although it too perished in the end. Francis Bacon (1561–1626) rather saw the difference in the perennial shortage of manpower of Sparta against Rome's readiness to extend citizenship irrespective of ethnic considerations. As he put it in the essay on 'The True Greatness of Kingdoms and Estates' of 1612 (1942: 127):

Their manner was to grant naturalisation (which they called *ius civitatis*), and to grant it in the highest degree ... Add to this their custom of plantation of colonies, whereby the Roman plant was removed into the soil of other nations ... It was not the Romans that spread upon the world, but it was the world that spread upon the Romans; and that was the sure way of greatness.

Thus the threat to civic freedom could be neutralised and the frictions inherent in national–territorial identities avoided. Hence in the Anglophone tradition, W.R. Brubaker writes (as in Stewart 1995: 66), 'legal and political status were conceived ... in terms of allegiance – in terms of the vertical ties between individual subjects and the king. The ties of allegiance knit together the British empire, not the British nation.' Although differentiated across the English-speaking West later, this concept of imperial citizenship continues to run through it.

Bacon was the last of the English court philosophers. He was Hakluyt's contemporary but of superior social station (his father was Elizabeth's Lord Chancellor, his uncle the aforementioned Robert Cecil). Upon his return from a junior diplomatic assignment in Paris, Bacon became what Wolfers and Martin call (1956: 12) 'an important link in Elizabeth's elaborate foreign intelligence service' during her remaining years. Indeed if Hakluyt's ideological anchorage is in the world of commerce (he hailed from a merchant family and remained close to the Merchant Adventurers throughout), Bacon is connected to the state and its coercive powers. Under James Stuart, the king of Scotland who succeeded Elizabeth in 1603, Bacon rose to great prominence amidst continuing court intrigue, eventually himself becoming Lord Chancellor in 1618.

Bacon's legacy is that of the founder of modern naturalistic materialism, but he was raised as a strict Calvinist. He solved the dilemma by seeing God as the demiurge–engineer of the universe; humans in turn can decipher the rationality of Creation and compose 'the second great book of God's wisdom' (in addition to the Bible; Gammon 2008: 267). Thus 'the bounds of human empire' are enlarged, he argues in New Atlantis (written briefly before his disgrace in 1621; 1942: 288), 'to the effecting of all things possible'. With respect to foreign relations, Bacon elaborated his rival Raleigh's maxim of maritime pre-eminence: 'he that commands the sea is at great liberty, and may take as much and as little of the war as he will' ('The True Greatness of Kingdoms and Estates', 1942: 131–2). In one of his last speeches to Parliament, Bacon explained that England should concentrate on naval pre-eminence and leave the Spanish threat on land to the United Provinces and France – although as Kleinschmidt comments (2000: 118–20), this was not yet the balance of power as a hierarchical principle that grants the 'balancer' a structural advantage.

The 'Society of Solomon's House' in New Atlantis, a 'house or college ... [which] is the very eye of this kingdom', served as the model for the Royal Society, established in 1660 (Haight, in Bacon 1942: xvi; Gollwitzer 1972: 171). Here God's 'second great book' was studied under a special licence from the Church of England (cf. vol. ii, 2010: 179). Materialism henceforth became the silent assumption of the agnostic, empiricist approach that continues to characterise Anglophone social science. Thomas Hobbes was Bacon's assistant and helped translate a few of the *Essays* into Latin; he also removed his patron's subtle observations concerning ideological distortion when he took political analysis further into the realm of the study of nature. Seeking to apply to society Galileo's insight that everything is caused by motion, Hobbes' *Leviathan* of 1651 posits that authority is needed, not on moral or religious grounds, but because self-interest, prudence, fear, and, ultimately, reason dictate it. Thus, Macpherson argues (1962: 79), 'The postulate of opposed motion ... enabled him to treat all individuals as equally insecure, and hence as equally in need of a system of political obligations.' Although the work's actual recommendations concerning foreign relations are slight, its implications for sovereign equality are obvious.

Formal equivalence is the bourgeois organising principle for all social relations. Hence sovereign equality arises with the bourgeoisie as a class, although pre-bourgeois formations may participate in its historical constitution, as in 1648 (Teschke 2003). But then equivalence is formal only. As Marx writes (1973: 247, emphasis added), it is '*a surface process, beneath which, in the depths, entirely different processes go on, in which this apparent individual equality and liberty disappear*'. Lefebvre (1977: 55–6) generalises this into a *chain* of formal equivalences which have their anchorage in the nation-state. All equivalences (market exchange, the social contract, and sovereign equality) are a matter of principle; the preoccupation with *form* (for example, in science, with method) has been a telltale sign of bourgeois thought ever since. If the trader, the citizen, and the nation-state enter into relations with counterparts endowed with equal rights, this is their entitlement as subjects – a historical claim developed against, respectively, tribute, absolute rule, and empire. Since equality is only formal, the underlying social reality from a bourgeois perspective is approached agnostically, by quantitative measurement and mathematics. Indeed in the empirical tradition that begins with Hobbes, Engels writes (*MEW*, xxii: 293), 'the physical movement is sacrificed to the mechanical and the mathematical'.

In the Renaissance, mathematics was reintegrated into craftsmanship (famously when Brunelleschi built the dome of the cathedral of Florence; Sohn-Rethel 1970: 123). Galileo then brought mathematics, workmanship, and experiment together in a single method. However, the same sorts of shortcut that facilitate the study of nature also work to obfuscate essential qualities of social reality. John Locke (1632–1704) was conscious of this implication, and he welcomed it. Mathematics not only is real knowledge, he emphasises in his *Essay Concerning Human Understanding* of 1689 (1995, bk.iv, ch.iv, §6), but it also leaves untouched the 'two great rules, religion and justice' (iii, x, §12). Thus Locke pays heed to the Anglican ruling not to touch on God and the soul, whilst adding material social relations ('justice') to the taboo subjects. For as Bourdieu explains (2001: 98–9), an epistemology that relies on mathematics no longer needs to adopt a position on the reality of the world. In Locke's words (still iii, x, §12), 'real things are no further concerned, nor intended to be meant by any such propositions, than as things really agree to those archetypes in [the] mind' (the archetypes being mathematical principles).

Locke, a medical doctor by training, was no longer a court scholar, but the organic intellectual of the Whig aristocracy that triumphed in the English Civil War. He first served as physician and adviser to the Earl of Shaftesbury (a minister of Cromwell's and the architect of the Restoration of 1660) and, from 1683, to Lord Somers, Lord Chancellor after the Glorious Revolution and president of the Royal Society until 1703. In the latter capacity Somers was succeeded, on Locke's recommendation, by Isaac Newton. Newton, whose *Principia Mathematica* dates from 1687, was brought to London in the 1690s to help with reorganising English state finances (Struik 1977: 135). That he remained deeply religious (Locke actually helped him with the publication of some of his theological writings) is testimony to the radical separation of quantitative science from metaphysics.

Unlike Bacon, Locke thought of a governing class as men of property and practical statecraft, not as scholars. 'It was to the unscholastic statesman that the governments of the world owed their peace, defence, and liberties', he writes in the *Essay* (1995, iii, x, §9). The priority of practice over principle allows Locke to invert the Hobbesian notion of the state confiscating the social sphere, and to assign sovereignty to society. Charles Taylor calls this the Grotian–Lockean tradition, because Grotius already assumes an impersonal order, a society that obeys laws of its own (anchored in natural law). The political order, the king's 'body politic', operates on a different plane. Locke takes this further in the *Two Treatises of Government* (also published in 1689, following the Glorious Revolution). Importantly, though, he drops the idea that a self-regulating society is ultimately subsumed under an undivided sovereign rule, as Grotius and Pufendorf still assumed (Taylor 2004: 127). Locke also casts his notion of civil society much wider, to include the Anglophone West as a whole. As the editor of the *Treatises* notes (in Locke 1965: 277n.), the concept of social self-regulation was in fact modelled on the way of life of the North American planters' families. Locke also looks beyond market exchange and theorises money as interest-bearing money – capital. By noting, in the *Second Treatise* (ch.v, §28, 1965: 330), that the enclosing landlord may consider the labour of his servants his property too, Locke provides a justification for the process of original expropriation.

Wage labour makes it possible (Locke argues in *Some Considerations of the Consequences of the Lowering of Interest and Raising the Value of Money* of 1691, as in Macpherson 1962: 206) to transfer the reward of one man's labour into another man's pocket, and thus start the cycle of capital accumulation. Of course, this only works if private property is anchored constitutionally. 'The great and chief end therefore, of Men uniting into Commonwealths, and putting themselves under Government,' Locke writes (*Second Treatise*, ix, §124; 1965: 395), 'is the Preservation of their Property.' Those without property cannot actually be responsible citizens. Again, in the words of Macpherson (1962: 234), 'at the point where labouring and appropriating became separable, full rationality went with appropriating rather than with labouring'.

This is a disjunction that also pertains to foreign relations. Not only did Locke reject royal absolutism as in France. As Laslett notes (in Locke 1965: 75), the working manuscript of the *Treatises* was entitled 'on the Gallic illness'. Societies not organised on the basis of private appropriation are generally irrational. The priority of property over everything else even applies in the case of slavery following on a war of conquest, because as a slave a man loses his freedom (although not the right, as Locke puts it nicely, 'to draw on himself the Death he desires'; 1995, ii, iv, §23; 1965: 325), but not his property. These contradictions point to the utopian aspect of the Lockean concept of a property-owning civil society. Stapelfeldt (2001: 283) traces the punitive and vindictive reflexes of the liberal West, with its harsh and partisan practice of justice at home and abroad, to the disjunction between a property-owning ideal and exploitative reality. In fact Locke himself already kept open that the state must be able to intervene in an emergency: ''Tis fit that the Laws themselves should in some Cases give way to the Executive Power', he writes (1995, ii, xiv, §159; 1965: 421), a 'Prerogative [which] is nothing but the Power of doing publick good without a

Rule' (1995: ii, xiv, §166; 1965: 425). So behind and above 'the laws' there looms another social force.

Ideologues of the Lockean Heartland

It fell to Henry St John, Viscount Bolingbroke (1678–1751), to translate Locke's explorations into a coherent class and international practice. With Bolingbroke the idea of empire achieves the status of what Armitage (2000: 102) calls 'a pan-British conception ... as an oceanic entity, equipped with its own historical foundations and destiny'. Bolingbroke was Britain's chief negotiator at Utrecht in 1713, where the initial round of wars with the rival contender for world power, absolutist France, was settled. Elaborating the maxims of Raleigh and Bacon into a doctrine of selective engagement (Wolfers and Martin 1956: 57), Bolingbroke ensured that the peace treaty in its Article vi formally established the balance of power as the regulative principle of European affairs. Britain held the balance – a cost-effective means of keeping continental rivals busy with each other, whilst it was itself engaged in overseas expansion. At home Bolingbroke also presided over an epochal homogenisation of bourgeois daily life into a 'civil society' in the sense we use the term today. Habermas (1971: 59–60) traces its formation to the popular coffee houses in the cities and to the newspapers, especially their op-ed columns, which supplied the themes for discussion. Thus emerged the phenomenon of a 'public opinion'.

This opens up a new era of politics. No longer do periods of rule end by dynastic succession, court intrigue or popular revolt. Instead a fluid alternation of government and opposition, a 'political business cycle', emerges through which the property regime can reproduce itself relatively smoothly. Will and compulsion blend in a concept of control through which social discipline is maintained – rule takes the modern form of gaining the consent of the ruled. Gramsci's notion of hegemony (protected by the 'armour of coercion'; 1971: 263) applies here. Anglophone civil society played the pioneer role in the process because its ruling class was unified behind a general capitalist interest. This interest is pursued from the alternating vantage points of landed property and money capital, or manufacturing and trade. In the political business cycle, leadership circulates between these two fractions; each draws on its own mass base and the drift of public opinion as it fluctuates with the conjuncture of profit distribution. As I have shown elsewhere

(2012), this can be seen to have operated transnationally across the North Atlantic heartland from the late nineteenth century on.

Bolingbroke's role in this epochal transition began in the aftermath of Utrecht. Welding together a loose bloc of defeated Jacobites, disaffected Whigs and urban radicals into what became known as the 'Country Opposition', he attacked the centralisation of the state by his rival in the Tory party, Walpole. As Lazare writes (2004: 12), Bolingbroke claimed to speak for the 'Country', a transcendent entity presumably held together by a spiritual bond traceable to an ancient constitution. This vindicates the Lockean principle of self-regulating society against the encroaching state, or the older still prerogative of freeborn Englishmen against the 'Court' potentially beset by corruption. Yet Bolingbroke was not a democrat. He held on to Locke's idea of the diminished rationality of the lower classes, but saw it as an opportunity to conduct a popular politics. For as he put it himself (as in Habermas 1971: 116), even if 'all men cannot reason, all men can feel'. That feeling should be focused on the novel concept of *patriotism*, based on 'the first good principles on which [the Country] was founded'. It would neutralise sectional interests dysfunctional to the operation of the political business cycle and also fill the spiritual void now that God, according to the Deism ascendant in the period, no longer administered people's lives directly.

In the *Craftsman* articles of 1730 Bolingbroke celebrated the supposed 'Spirit of Liberty' alive in the people. His essay *The Idea of a Patriot King* (which began its career as a bestseller in 1749) is its classic statement. The Patriot King was to take his distance from the Court and follow the Country's instinct, a 'panacea for corruption, the solvent of party division, and the herald of commercial greatness' (Armitage 1997: 405) – in brief, a symbol of national unity fostering capitalist development. It was ideas like these that attracted continental visitors such as Voltaire and Montesquieu to England, making Bolingbroke's circle in London the centre of European intellectual networks, the springboard of the Enlightenment. However, Bolingbroke's programme also included the reassertion of Lockean agnosticism against the potentially dangerous materialism of Bacon, resurgent in France. Not only did the anti-materialist, anti-scientific crusade led by the Anglican bishop George Berkeley reaffirm English empiricism and make epistemology, in Collins' words (1998: 612) 'into the central region of philosophy in its own right'. It also resonated in Jonathan Swift's mockery of science in the closing part of *Gulliver's Travels* of 1726, a satire directly inspired by Bolingbroke (Habermas 1971: 79). Even the commercial advantages of playing the balance of power find their place here (in the account of Gulliver's mediation between Lilliput and Blefescu and the goodwill gained from both).

English liberalism in the Enlightenment was celebrated as the most advanced form of society. Its key transmission belt abroad was freemasonry. As I argue elsewhere (1998: 99–108), the lodges enabled the class compromise between the aristocracy and the ascendant bourgeoisie along the lines of the Country Opposition. Gramsci (1977: 12) calls the Enlightenment a 'bourgeois spiritual International in the form of a unified consciousness'; but whilst the Lockean principles were absorbed very much in their original spirit in the Anglosphere, they often worked out rather differently elsewhere. Voltaire, admitted into a Paris Masonic lodge late in life, gave the ideas he was exposed to in Bolingbroke's circle a twist relevant primarily to absolutist France, where progress implied radical opposition. Thus the translation into French of Locke's *Treatises* (which according to Margaret Jacob, may well have been the one used by Rousseau; Jacob 1991: 111) was doctored by translating 'commonwealth' and 'community' as 'republic'; a translation arranged by Dutch Freemasons to bolster the opposition against absolutism and ward off a feared invasion of the Low Countries.

The Scottish Enlightenment on the other hand proved a largely truthful relay in the spread of liberal ideas through David Hume (1711–76) and Adam Smith (1723–90). Hume's *Treatise on Human Nature* (1739–40) (popularised in the abbreviated *Inquiry into Human Understanding* of 1748) radicalised Locke's epistemology by claiming that people arrive at ideas by association, which they then turn into habits of thought. In 1742 Hume published the *Essays Moral, Political and Literary*, with a second volume in 1752; two years later he began the publication of the *History of England*. This made him a fortune; no longer was it necessary for a thinker to serve a powerful patron as in Locke's days. As Therborn relates (1976: 157), both Smith and Hume were members of the Select Society, an illustrious association of intellectuals, aristocrats and businessmen set up in the 1750s. Hume also held diplomatic posts on the Continent, including three years in Paris. He was received with great enthusiasm and Rousseau even travelled back with him to London, although they soon fell out. Hume also helped Smith to obtain a chair in Glasgow; the Scottish universities were close to the thriving manufactures north of the border and already experimented with academic division of labour. Smith and his colleague Adam Ferguson 'turned chairs of moral philosophy into bases for economics, political theory, and sociology' (Collins 1998: 616).

Hume was a patriot in the spirit of the Country Opposition. 'Let us cherish and improve our ancient government as much as possible,' he wrote in one of his *Essays* (1875, i: 113), 'without encouraging a passion for ... dangerous novelties'. He classically formulated sovereign equality among open societies from a Deist perspective. In one *Essay* (1875, ii: 343) he writes that 'the Author of the world has intended, by giving [neighbouring nations] soils, climates, and geniuses, so different from each other', that they engage in 'free communication and exchange'. According to Gammon (2010: 225), Smith's understanding of the 'invisible hand' in the *Wealth of Nations* of 1776 likewise 'shows self-interest as an instrument of Providence, [so that] "vain and insatiable desires" lead to the most opportune distribution of the "necessaries of life"'. Barker (1982: 63) interprets Hume's ideas about sympathy, 'relations of contiguity' (family and acquaintance), and 'creatures ... related by resemblance' as a prelude to the racism of the Thatcher era. Yet from the *Essays* one is rather left with the idea that nationality and national character arise through cumulative class compromise (cf. 1875, i: 248), from which Hume significantly excepts the English, whom he claims have no peculiar national character because of their individual liberty and religious diversity (1875, i: 252).

The projection of a global governance over separate, open nation-states, or as Hume puts it in *Essay* xiv of Part I (1875, i: 181), 'a number of neighbouring and independent states, connected together by commerce and policy', is elaborated in some detail. Even those states closest to each other should not forget about independence and guard against state encroachment. 'The emulation, which naturally arises among [them], is an obvious source of improvement: but what I would chiefly insist on is the stop, which such limited territories give to both *power* and to *authority*.' Indeed Hume's understanding of global political economy prefigures the 'English School' in IR – from Edinburgh, that is. *First*, the states 'under civil government' constitute a family, under the rule of law and open for business. 'When civil government has been establish'd over the greatest part of mankind, and different societies have been form'd contiguous to each other, there arises a new set of duties among the neighbouring states, suitable to the nature of that commerce, which they carry on with each other' (1739–40, iii, pt.ii, sect.xi: 567). *Secondly*, the principles governing this core group of states will spread. 'The advantages ... of peace, commerce, and mutual succour, make us extend to different kingdoms the same notions of justice, which take place among individuals' (ibid.: 567–8). *Thirdly*, however (1875, ii: 215–16, as in Wolfers and Martin 1956: 71), 'were a civilised nation engaged with barbarians', the moral obligations it has imposed on itself can be abrogated, because they serve no purpose any longer. In their handling of the barbarian threat 'they should instead render every action or encounter as bloody and pernicious as possible' – a reminder certainly of the punitive and vindictive implications of the Lockean utopia.

The patriotism espoused by Bolingbroke struck deep roots in North America too. Initially, as discontent with British mercantilist trade restrictions grew, the attempt to avoid a rupture included projecting an Anglophone commonwealth as the solution to the dilemma of empire and freedom. In 1768 a former colonial governor (Pownall 1971: xvi) warned that 'A general and intire [sic] union of the British dominions, is the only measure by which Great Britain can be continued in its political liberty, and commercial prosperity, perhaps in its existence'. Even when separate statehood seemed the only way forward, the ethno-constitutional bond remained the reference. 'Providence has been pleased to give this once connected country to one united people,' John Jay, US Chief Justice and governor of New York wrote in *The Federalist*, no. 2 (Hamilton, Madison and Jay 1992: 6), 'a people descended from the same ancestors ... attached to the same principles of government.' Indeed as Lazare explains (2004: 13, emphasis added), 'the American Revolution was very much in the Country mould – a revolution fought not only against British imperial power, but against power per se'. Hence it developed in a direction opposite from the French Revolution.

Where popular sovereignty in the latter was securely wedded to the concept of the nation-state 'one and indivisible', the dominance of Country ideology in America meant that it was married to a *concept of the polity as something almost endlessly divisible*.

Montesquieu's *On the Spirit of the Laws* of 1748, on which the US Constitution is based, itself suffers from 'translation problems'. The French baron, who frequented the meetings of Country Opposition during his stay in Britain from 1729 to 1731, mistook the way in which Bolingbroke's circle thought the powers of the state *should* be limited for how British institutions actually worked. The Federalist Papers were also influenced by the Scottish Enlightenment. Fosl maintains (1999: 173) that they are imbued with Hume's political philosophy throughout. Alexander Hamilton, like Jay a prominent member of the New York–Philadelphia secessionist fraction led by his father-in-law, Philip Schuyler, had been exposed to Smith's teachings during his studies in New York; the Schuyler bloc's emissary to France, Benjamin Franklin, was close to Hume. James Madison, future secretary of state to President Thomas Jefferson, had been taught by John Witherspoon, the Presbyterian president of what is today Princeton University, for whom the Scottish thinkers were anathema because of their Deism. Yet Brock claims (in Hamilton, Madison and Jay 1992: xiv, xvii) that Madison too absorbed Hume's ideas.

This brings us back to Edmund Burke. Marx calls him (*MEW*, xxiii: 788n.) a sycophant who played the liberal against the English oligarchy whilst in the pay of the North American colonies, before playing the romantic against the French Revolution whilst in the pay of the same oligarchy. Yet, as we saw at the beginning of this chapter, these choices were perfectly consistent. Not only did Burke identify the foundations of the Lockean heartland as a collection of independent nation-states committed to 'English liberty' on account of their 'common stock'. He also specifically denounced the ambition of revolutionary France to establish a universal empire, just as he understood the need for 'some change' to maintain the existing order, as cited in our Preface. In his *Reflections* of 1790 (*Works*, iii: 275) Burke speaks of 'the method of nature in the conduct of the state'. This is the logic underlying the development of the contemporary social sciences; but, even more importantly for our argument, Burke was also the first to identify national state formation in the context of a projection, tentative at first, of liberal imperial governance on the part of Britain. Such a strategy rests on an appreciation of how authoritative class compromise sustains stable communities over time, a process he considered the British should actively manipulate for their own ends.

Burke made his reputation in the 1750s with an anonymous persiflage of Bolingbroke's writings against revealed religion. These were so well received that he had to clarify, in a second edition under his own name, that they were intended as a critique of the atheistic undercurrent in Bolingbroke's thinking. As a Freemason,

Burke's religious views were in fact Deistic too. Boucher (1998: 316) cites his references to the 'Governor of the Universe', 'the mysterious Governor', etc. Still amidst the furore over the Bolingbroke satire, Burke in 1758 co-founded the influential *Annual Register*, a chronicle of international politics of which he remained the chief editor until 1789. This marks his sustained interest in foreign relations. A Whig MP from 1765, he used the *Register* to back up his interventions in the House of Commons, as when he denounced (in the issue of July 1773) the partition of Poland, an early instance of supporting nationality against illiberal empire.

For Burke, the consolidation of the ideological community that is civil society proceeds through measured reform. The fluctuation of political fortunes must never exceed this limit. In the *Reflections* he expounds (*Works*, iii: 277) on how the need for constant deliberation turns 'all change into a subject of *compromise*, which naturally begets moderation; they produce *temperaments*, preventing the sore evil of harsh, crude, unqualified reformations; and [render] all the headlong exertions of arbitrary power ... for ever impracticable'. The priority, Wallerstein comments (2001: 16), lay with the preservation of 'the structures which ... could serve as brakes on any and all precipitate reformers and revolutionaries' – family, church, monarchy. The 'community', through a cumulative series of compromises, thus obtains its specific national character (i.e. 'temperament'), which alone allows rule along consensual lines, whilst obfuscating class divisions. The implication that the sense of community is then transmitted to the young by the education system is only one step away. The 'disciplinary' implications are highlighted in Burke's definition of nationality in *An Appeal from the New to the Old Whigs* (1791, in *Works*, iv: 174, emphasis added):

To enable men to act with the weight and character of a people, we must suppose them to be in that state of *habitual social discipline*, in which the wiser, the more expert, and the more opulent conduct ... the weaker, the less knowing, and the less provided with the goods of fortune. When the multitude are not under this discipline, they can scarcely be said to be in civil society.

Burke also saw that such national communities could then be made subject to diplomatic manoeuvre by Britain. Ever since Utrecht, the balance of power had been the 'common law' of Europe. 'This general balance was regarded in four principal points of view: the great middle balance, which comprehended Great Britain, France, and Spain; the balance of the north; the balance, external and internal, of Germany; and the balance of Italy', he writes in the *Third Letter on a Regicide Peace* of 1795 (*Works*, v: 441–2). 'In all those systems of balance, England was the power to whose custody it was thought it might be most safely committed.' So if, as Boucher says (1998: 320), Burke 'shared the widespread belief that Europe constitutes something like one large state or society of nations' (a view held also by his friend Hume), he was in no doubt about English supremacy over this constellation. This was to inspire British diplomacy in the process of national state formation henceforth.

NATIONAL STATE FORMATION AND INFORMAL IMPERIALISM

British international thought echoed on the continent in the writings of Prussian-born Friedrich von Gentz (1764–1832), confidant of Austria's chancellor, Count Metternich, and secretary of the Congress of Vienna. Gentz studied with Kant at the University of Königsberg but turned against the French Revolution after translating Burke's critique of it into German in 1794. In *Fragments on the Balance of Power in Europe* of 1806, when still a Prussian diplomat, Gentz expands on Burke's concept of a complex balance including the internal relations in foreign countries. Six years earlier he had defended the North American secession as follows (2009: 15):

No nation governed its colonies upon more liberal and equitable principles than England; but the unnatural system, which chained the growth of a great people to the exclusive commercial interest of a country, distant from them a thousand leagues, even with the most liberal organization of which it was capable, could not have lasted forever.

As a Prussian, Gentz had no sentimental attachment to colonies and considered (ibid.: 38) the right to their possession a temporary matter – 'a wavering, insecure, undefined, and often undefinable right'. This was not a matter of a recognition of nationality, and certainly not of democracy as it had triumphed in the French Revolution. 'The word *right* would have vanished from the French language,' he writes (ibid.: 49–50), 'had not an imaginary right of the *nation*, to do whatever they, or their representatives should please, appeared as a sort of substitute for all other rights.' Indeed 'in their system, all was right, which they resolved upon in the name of the *people*, or in the name of mankind'.

Both the Austrian empire and Britain rewarded Gentz liberally for his writings against the Revolution. Talleyrand, Napoleon's foreign minister, who after 1807 conspired with Russia and Austria against the Emperor (the British imposed him as foreign minister again under the restored Bourbon monarchy) also paid him generously for his services (Nicolson 1961: 232; Parkinson 1977: 52). Gentz therefore was the ideal mediator between Lockean liberalism and the continental reaction of which Metternich was the Grand Inquisitor. For the chancellor was deeply distrustful of liberalism, which he reproached among other things for failing to see the danger of nationalism. 'One of the sentiments *most natural* to man,' he wrote (as in Liebich 2008: 253, emphasis added), 'that of nationality, is itself erased from the liberal catechism.'

The Concept of Organic Nationality

Sovereign equivalence was a preoccupation of commercial societies wresting themselves free from illiberal empire – England from Rome, Holland from the Spanish Habsburgs, the United States from Britain. It is bound up with other bourgeois equivalences, as explained earlier. Now the Continent obtained its political topography through imperial conquest too, but the peasant societies subject to rule by distant administrative centres were usually more backward and often ethnically different. Hence in Europe east of the Rhine, as in the rest of the world, 'freedom' does not (or not to the same degree) denote the demands for property and citizenship of an ascendant bourgeoisie, but the unity of land, lineage and community. Indeed in all episodes of (post-)imperial reorganisation of the territorial distribution into nation-states, from the Congress of Vienna to the dissolution of Yugoslavia and the breakup of the USSR, Western designs to entrust client governing classes with the keys of new or reconstituted nation-states have stumbled on an organic concept of nationality alien to 'the liberal catechism'.

France occupies a middle position in this respect as in so many others. On the one hand, as Habermas highlights (1971: 48–9), there were the exclusive Paris salons where the satires of Voltaire provided the topics for discussion, not the practical matters debated by men of all walks of life in the coffee houses across the Channel. The Encyclopaedists on the other hand wanted to raise the level of French civilisation in a material sense and set free the country's productive forces. Since the world of work was hemmed in by webs of feudal–absolutist restrictions, 'English freedoms' had to be switched onto a different track too. Denis Diderot began the *Encyclopédie* in 1747 as a translation of an English lexicon, but soon recast it into an inventory of all the known arts and sciences then in existence (many still under the control of the guilds). The effort took him and his co-editor, the mathematician d'Alembert, 20 years to complete.

Diderot's friend Jean-Jacques Rousseau (1712–78) was also a craftsman. Trained as an engraver and a musician and composer in his native Geneva, he wrote the entries on music for the *Encyclopédie*. For Rousseau, private property is not the cause of freedom but of inequality. In the *Discourse* of 1755 he gives the example of the privatisation of free forests into cultivated countryside, 'watered by the sweat of men' (1969: 101). Instead Rousseau proposes to understand a community as a complex, living organism, close to nature. 'It is men who make the state, and it is the land that feeds the men', he writes in the *Social Contract* of 1762 (1966: 85–6). Imbalances and disproportionalities in these equations make foreign involvement necessary and ultimately lead to war. For Rousseau, sovereignty in foreign relations means independence (read autarky). As he seeks to demonstrate in his commentary on the design of a European peace treaty, written at the time of the Peace of Utrecht by the Abbott of Saint-Pierre, C.I. Castel, there cannot be a common interest among different states. Like Hobbes, Rousseau believes in the all-encompassing state, which must not tolerate any 'partial societies' (Lefebvre 1977: 49–50). Unlike Hobbes, though, Rousseau held that sovereignty always remains vested in the people; it is not alienated in the social contract.

The romantic, organic idea of nationality was further developed and made explicit (Rousseau does not yet use the term 'nation') by Johann Gottfried Herder (1744–1803), a vicar and author in Riga (then in the Russian empire). Herder took an interest in folk culture, both German and Slavic. He admired Rousseau, as did his teacher Immanuel Kant, but could not stomach Kant's metaphysics. 'My soul could not enjoy this realm of the dead, inhabited by lifeless, unfounded concepts', Herder later recalled (as in Kantzenbach 1970: 20). Like Rousseau, he wrote a treatise (of 1769) on the origin of languages, from which he concludes (2001: 105) that the mind obtains its characteristics in the process of ethnogenesis, not from innate reason. In *Another Contribution to the Philosophy of History for the Education of Humanity* of 1774, Herder repeats his thesis (1997: 32) that 'every human perfection is national, secular, and if observed most carefully, individual. Nothing is created which is not occasioned by time, climate, needs, the world and fate.' His exhortations to the Slav peoples to throw off their chattels would be reciprocated in due course by Russian and other East European nationalists – one only has to think of Gogol's impassioned prophesy, in the closing lines of Part I of his *Dead Souls* (of 1837), of how his beloved Russia would one day 'force all nations, all empires to stand aside, to give you way'.

The (professed) love of real humans, of work, land, and community, thus characterises organic nationalism. Different emphases then decide on its political orientation – 'work' draws it to the left, 'land' (territory, soil) to the right. But it never shies from naming a supposed 'essence', and this sets it apart from English agnosticism. In this respect, Kant stayed much closer to the Enlightenment ideal. As Sohn-Rethel explains (1970: 42–4), Kant's *Critique of Pure Reason* of 1781 has a logical structure comparable to Smith's *Wealth of Nations*. Both assume that social harmony is the result of not interfering with the processes that totalise the subjective concerns of the bourgeoisie (in Kant, the educated, civilised class, the *Bildungsbürgertum*). Just as the free market mediates and equilibrates self-interest, Kant suggests that by accepting the limits of subjective reason, morality and religion can play their beneficial roles undisturbed. However, in his 1795 design for a peace treaty, based on a rereading of Rousseau's summary of St Pierre, Kant speaks of a historical process, explained by an objective contradiction – the advancing commercial spirit and the republican state form, which in combination transcend the natural separation of peoples according to language and religion. The same 'nature' here is credited both with driving humans and societies towards conflict *and* with averting war (Kant 1953: 48–9). This is not the peace of the graveyard imposed by a universal despotism (so much feared by liberals; just think of Burke's remark on France's 'impious hierarchy' cited at the beginning of this chapter), but one based on a dynamic, forward-looking complex of forces.

Hegel would take this to a new plane altogether. I have briefly outlined his philosophical critique of Kant's subjective idealism in Volume I (2007: 14–15). In the *Philosophy of Right* of 1827 he also dismisses (1972: 220n.), not without malice, Kant's draft peace treaty. Hegel's revolutionary understanding of a world-historical process, in which different states struggle with each other as embodiments of advancing human civilisation, rules out that the process would ever be contained by Kant's commercial spirit and republican state form (or by Herder's Christian brotherly love for that matter). Hegel rejects both, mocking the bourgeois concept of sovereign equality (only love is between equals; Kojève 1968: 260). Wars in his perspective serve to secure the better right of those states which represent world-historic progress (the World Spirit) at a given juncture. As he puts it in his *Lectures on the Philosophy of History*, published posthumously in 1839 (1961: 86), 'Against this absolute right to be the bearer of the present phase of development of the World Spirit, the spirits of other peoples are without right.' If we remove the mystical imagery, cast in the language of Lutheran Protestantism but in fact referring to what we now call globalisation, we have here a theory of the material hierarchy of state power, in which one state exercises what we now call global governance as rationality incarnate.

The French Revolution and the Napoleonic wars had a profound effect on how foreign relations were conceptualised. Between the cosmopolitan Enlightenment ideal that inspired Kant and the French conquests which influenced Hegel, a momentous historical transformation occurred that not only changed philosophy but also shaped the educational structures that would guide its further evolution. The names of Johann Gottlieb Fichte (1762–1814), a Saxon by birth before he came to the Prussian capital, and his contemporary Wilhelm von Humboldt, mark the transition. In *The Closed Trading State* of 1800 Fichte identifies English liberalism and free trade as the world-historic force against which a German nationality will have to defend itself. His recommendations for the abolition of world trade and the prohibition of foreign travel except for scholars and artists of excellence are less important than his conviction (as in Nicolson 1961: 22–3) that such a Spartan civilisation would then be able to dedicate itself entirely to 'the "nation" as the one continuous reality to which each individual should devote his soul, his body and his life'. This is the first explicit argument for a contender-state posture.

After the rout of the Prussian army at Jena in 1806, Fichte began a series of *Addresses to the German Nation* to gain adherents for his project. Humboldt, who attended one of them, founded the University of Berlin two years later (Collins 1998: 647–8). It was to be a self-governing corporation with no restrictions on the topics of learning; as Humboldt explains in his sketch for Prussian education reform of 1810 (as in Kuczynski 1979: 101, cf. 110), the unity of the sciences would allow separate objects to be studied in light of the whole. Although watered down by the Prussian authorities, Humboldt's design corroborated the fact that in Germany academic degrees were awarded in philosophy ('Ph.D.'). Fichte became the first rector of the new university; upon his death, Hegel succeeded him in the chair of philosophy.

Hegel bases his concept of the nation-state not on a social contract, but on the organic imbrication of family and society, which is 'civil' because the state leaves the bourgeoisie a measure of economic freedom – without, as in the liberal West, subordinating itself to it. 'If the state is confused with civil society and its determination is seen in the security and protection of property and personal freedom,' Hegel writes in the *Philosophy of Right* (1972: 215), 'then the interest of the individual as such is the ultimate goal for which they are united and it follows that it is a matter of coincidence whether to be a member of the state at all.' That would violate the organic aspect of citizenship. In Hegel's Prussia, Fichte's German nation merged with the consummation of historical Reason; yet, as McCarney claims (2000: 145–8), this was not chauvinism, but the conclusion of a historical comparison of how individual freedom and state prerogative reached their final constitutional synthesis – in the passage of the *Philosophy of Right* cited, 'the one finding satisfaction and realisation in the other'. Such a state cannot bow to either property or public opinion: it must look beyond momentary concerns. One only has to think of the crisis of the biosphere today to see the wisdom of this insight, although an authoritarian interpretation is equally possible.

The latter tendency was still strong in the German princely states. Thus Friedrich List (1789–1846) got into trouble as the spokesman of an association clamouring for a German customs union and trade protection. List, a journalist and, from 1816, professor in the new department of socio-economics (founded at his own suggestion at the University of Tübingen), failed to get a hearing in any of the German capitals, least of all imperial Vienna. As Wendler (1989: 29–31) relates, the commercial and manufacturing interests that would subscribe to his economic nationalism were still too weak. When he also had a petition printed on civic rights in Württemberg, criminal proceedings were initiated that led to his imprisonment and exile to the United States in 1825. I return to List in the next chapter.

Opening Up Illiberal Empire Through Sovereign Equality

Britain's aspiration to become the sponsor of national state formation passed three major tests in the first half of the nineteenth century – the Congress of Vienna that reorganised post-Napoleonic Europe; Greek independence from Ottoman rule; and, jointly with the United States, the emancipation of Latin America. In all three, there was an effort to turn bourgeois class formation into an extension of Anglophone supremacy. Of course the lineage that runs from Rousseau to Hegel fundamentally contradicts such a subordination, because here the community, *as state*, prevails over the bourgeoisie. But then, the process of sponsored nation-building was still tentative and 'undisciplined'. At Vienna, nationality was not even recognised, notwithstanding Metternich's comments on the issue. Certainly the Allies, in order to counter French claims to have freed Germans, Italians, Poles and others from superstition and tyranny, 'ended by claiming that they also, and more truly, were the liberators of the nationalities from the newer tyranny of Napoleon' (Seaman 1964: 42). But in the reactionary climate of 1815, the Congress did not admit nationality issues on its agenda. In the Statistical Committee, established on British initiative to count the populations involved in territorial adjustments, Talleyrand failed to convince Hardenberg, the Prussian negotiator, that different levels of civilisation should be factored in. Hence, Nicolson writes (1961: 146), 'purely quantitative standards for the "transference of souls" became the yard-stick which the Congress adopted'.

In a treatise on the Congress of Vienna, D.-G.-F. Dufour de Pradt (1759–1837), Napoleon's chaplain and ambassador in Warsaw, held Britain responsible for this outcome. After he had been removed from his diplomatic post for incompetence, de Pradt secretly worked with Talleyrand to prepare the restoration of the Bourbon monarchy. Since he believed (as in Gollwitzer 1972: 379) that economic penetration made it possible 'to separate from one's colonies without losing them', de Pradt thought Britain's preoccupation with its overseas empire was short-sighted. After the Treaty of Paris of 1814 recognised the United Kingdom as the arbitrator and guarantor of all *extra*-European agreements, with the express right to settle outstanding naval and colonial questions, the Holy Alliance concluded that the Continent was for them. De Pradt therefore proposed a World Congress, but then not with Gentz, but with himself as its secretary.

Vienna was a reactionary exercise as far as nationality was concerned, de Pradt argues in *Europe and America* (1821: 80). It forced together again peoples and countries previously separated: Piedmont and Genoa, Austria and Italy, Russia and Poland, Holland and Belgium, Prussia and the new West Prussia, Sweden and Norway. Poland (the Grand Duchy of Warsaw) had forfeited its chances to become a sovereign nation-state by allowing Napoleon to raise an 80,000-strong auxiliary army for the presumed 'Second Polish War' against Russia in 1812, which placed it at the mercy of Tsar Alexander. Castlereagh, the British foreign secretary, in vain tried to persuade the Russian monarch to grant the Poles the constitution that Jeremy Bentham had drafted for them. His stipulation (as in Liebich 2008: 254) that the imperial monarchs 'treat as Poles ... the portions of the nation that may be placed under their respective sovereignties' was the best he could obtain, and neither could he play off the crowned heads of the Holy Alliance against each other. In the case of the Austrian Netherlands, attached to the north under British tutelage, the UK prime minister, Lord Liverpool, stipulated that the consent of 'the people of Brabant', through 'clauses guaranteeing to the Belgian populations complete religious toleration and commercial equality', was a precondition for the merger. These provisions, according to Nicolson (1961: 207), 'represent the first Minority Treaties to figure in diplomatic practice' – although the term itself was not yet used in this connection.

Minority provisions are a footnote to Anglophone liberalism. 'The true function of constitutionalism', writes Seaman (1964: 39) 'was to protect the bourgeoisie from the princes, who rejected the revolutionary slogans, and from the masses, who accepted [them]'. From a liberal perspective a nation-state is ideally ethnically homogeneous. Where ethno-territorial incongruities remain nevertheless, a nation-state can still function as a container holding democratic aspirations in check if at least the client governing class is homogeneous; minority protection then works to defuse potential separatism and prevent it from gaining a mass base. With this provision, support for constitutionality (in the sense of political class formation of a national bourgeoisie) in the words of Nicolson (1961: 272, emphasis added) allowed the United Kingdom to 'once again *lead the world along the middle path between despotism and revolution.*' This was still more art than science, an intuitive embrace of nationality where it offered itself; just as Britain would for another full century and a half turn a blind eye to demands for sovereign equality made by its colonial subjects. Yet when Canning took over from Castlereagh in the autumn of 1822, British diplomacy did begin to wrest itself free, albeit tentatively, from the Holy Alliance. The Greek breakaway from the Ottoman empire was the first stage of this transition, because it put Britain against Russia.

Hellenic independence was the project of the orthodox Patriarchate and the Constantinople Greek merchant elite, on which the Sultan had come to depend financially (Halperin 1997: 74–5). De Pradt also mentions (1824: 187) the exposure of the commercial Greek diaspora along the Black Sea to foreign culture, which kindled a desire to recover their own ancient civilisation. Under the Ottoman capitulations regime (cf. vol. i, 2007: 86–7), Russia had the right to 'protect' orthodox Christians (just as Austria had the right to protect the Catholics, and Britain the Protestants – as there were none, this devolved to the Druze sect). When the Ottoman *millets* in the nineteenth century were turned into 'nationalist and economic forward positions of the Western powers' (Rajewsky 1980: 40), Russia's connections to Serbs and Greeks therefore gave it a strong position, although as Özdemir explains (2009a: 56–7, 61), there was also a tendency within the Eastern Orthodox tradition championing a new Greek kingdom and a national church.

In 1822, one year into the Greek revolt, Canning granted the rebels the status of belligerents, but no further support. Suspected by Metternich to be a Jacobin in disguise, the new foreign secretary in fact subscribed to Burke's philosophy of blending property and other rights into 'national' bundles of compromise. But to rely on the Greeks to balance Russia, with the Ottoman empire still in place, was premature. The UK ambassador in Constantinople in the 1820s, Lord Stratford de Redcliffe (a cousin of Canning's) held on to the idea of a strong Ottoman state as a bulwark to keep both Russia and France in check; opportunities to exploit it through free trade agreements also remained alive, as the Baltalimani Agreement of 1838 would testify. Hence assistance to the Greek revolutionaries was left to private interests, none more famous than the poet George Gordon Noel, Lord Byron (1788–1824). Byron, the Che Guevara of his day, was mistrusted at home for his radicalism. Abroad, Russell writes (1961: 716), his views 'were developed and transmuted until they became so widespread as to be factors in great events'. Byron privately pioneered the diplomacy that would lock local bourgeois class formation into a British liberal design. His pride in his crusading ancestors and proverbial love of Mediterranean women made him a celebrity in his day and a quasi-citizen of Athens by 1810 (1981: 157 and passim). After a sojourn with the Italian *Carbonari*, Byron joined the Greek uprising, but found it mired in factional struggles. He aligned his brigade with Prince Mavrokordatos, a leader 'of the stature of Washington or Kosciusko', but warned him (1981: 71) that Greece should aim for a sovereign state and not exchange one colonial master for another (Russia) – to which the European powers including Russia finally consented in 1830. Of course this very sovereignty has kept Greece under Western governance ever since.

The dissolution of the Iberian empires in the Western hemisphere, finally, was to provide the prototype of imposing liberal governance over open nation-states. Britain initiated the project, but in the end acknowledged Washington's regional primacy. This left it to the United States to formally guarantee, under the Monroe Doctrine of 1823, the sovereignty of the new states and thus dispel any imperial designs from the Holy Alliance and France. Canning's famous comment a year later (as in Gallagher and Robinson 1967: 241) that 'Spanish America is free and if we do not mismanage our affairs sadly she is English', underscores Britain's commercial interests though. This then was what G. Grandin calls (as in Desai 2007: 444), a 'sophisticated imperial project, ... suited for a world in which rising nationalism was making formal colonialism unworkable'. To act as 'the arbiter of Europe in America, and ... incline the balance of European competitions in this part of the world', Hamilton had argued in 1788 (in Hamilton, Madison and Jay 1992: 50), a federal United States must speak with one voice; otherwise the Western hemisphere would remain exposed to meddling by Europe, which still 'plume(d) herself as Mistress of the World'. Latin America on the other hand should remain parcelled up in separate states. Thomas Jefferson, the leader of the North American expansionists, in a letter of 1803 (as in Gollwitzer 1972: 407) advocated Pan-Americanism as the format best suited to allow the United States to play the role of balancer in the Americas. Britain did the same in Europe and in the year of the Monroe Doctrine actually broke with the Holy Alliance and France when they sought to restore the Spanish monarchy. Instead the United Kingdom openly extended its patronage to the constitutionalist bourgeoisie in Spain, as the United States did in Latin America.

De Pradt was among the first to recognise the momentous importance of the break-up of the alliance against Napoleon. In so many words he analyses the role of the United Kingdom and the

United States as a combination capable of leading a transnational bourgeoisie. 'What has formed itself, with respect to the Continent,' he writes (1824: 48–9, emphasis added), 'is a party of democratic opposition [*opposition de sociabilité*] of which *England is the head, America the body, and all the enlightened men of Europe, the extended limbs.*' A comparable conclusion was drawn in 1827 by Alexander Hill Everett in *America, a General Survey*. With the Monroe Doctrine, Everett wrote (as in Gollwitzer 1972: 420–1), Britain had left its conservative political role behind and had gone over to the party of movement in world affairs, jointly with the United States. Everett had accompanied the US secretary of state, John Quincy Adams, on his mission to Russia and became US ambassador to Spain when Adams assumed the presidency in 1825. Tocqueville stayed with him on his visit to the United States. But if Everett saw a future world divided between Russia, the British Empire and the United States (controlling the Americas), the Frenchman rather thought, like de Pradt, in terms of Anglophone unity. The 'great Anglo-American family', he predicted in 1835 (1990, i: 431, 433), '... will preserve at least a similar social condition and will hold in common the customs and opinions to which that social condition has given birth.'

De Pradt's advocacy of colonial emancipation earned him honorary citizenships of Mexico and Colombia and a pension from Bolívar, with whom he corresponded. That he thought a break-up of the United States would preserve the hemispheric balance (1821: 68–9), at a time when Bolívar and San Martín still thought in terms of large federations in South America, highlights that de Pradt recognises the importance of the size and number of states even if he misread the balance of forces already established. Indeed as early as 1824 John Quincy Adams made it clear to Bolívar that further moves against the remaining Spanish colonies, Cuba and Puerto Rico, would not be tolerated. The Monroe Doctrine, Adams told the hero of the Latin American liberation struggle (as in Gerassi 1965: 226), 'must not be interpreted as authorization for the weak to be insolent with the strong'. This weakness was consolidated by the fragmentation into open nation-states – something which, as Milios and Sotiropoulos explain (2009: 33–53), the *dependencia* school has insufficiently recognised. Hence the attempts by Hugo Chávez of Venezuela and like-minded leaders of the continent to foster progressive bloc formation in the face of US imperialism, a process that in the case of the ALBA group blends with a resurgence of indigenous traditions in the political culture. Only by reversing the retrograde impact of the original colonisation on the indigenous peoples *across* the different societies will the exploitation of 'the sentiments and formalities of the national sovereignty of these states' dear to the white bourgeoisie be neutralised, as Mariátegui prophesied in 1929 (2011: 267). I will return to this in Chapter 4. Here we should ask: why were the federal projects of Bolívar and San Martín defeated in the first place?

The fact that colonial society was steeped in clerical and militaristic values of Iberian provenance (referred to in vol. i, 2007: 126–31), distances between the urban centres, and the topography with its forbidding natural obstacles all played a role (Bolton 1933: 459). But what really made the difference was that the urban nodes of state formation faced different class and ethnic balances in their hinterlands. So when Napoleon's conquest of Spain raised the issue of independence, each city responded differently, and the unevenly balanced class and ethnic structures and differently timed transitions to independence profoundly affected the demarcation of 'national' boundaries. Where the majority of the rural population was Amerindian (in Mexico, Central America, Ecuador, Peru and Bolivia) there was initially little interest in independence among Creole elites. As Perry Anderson notes (1990: 102), they above all feared a real revolution. The much stronger white bourgeoisie of Montevideo (which had a history of its own as a frontier formation resisting Brazilian settler pressure in the *Banda Oriental*) and that of its rival, Buenos Aires, on the opposite side of the Rio de la Plata estuary, on the other hand were able to take this risk, as did Venezuela. Everywhere though, the incomplete colonisation of Latin America left in existence large uncontrolled frontier zones populated by mestizos, Amerindians, free blacks or runaway African slaves involved in cattle-ranching and smuggling. Armed bands on the frontier often made the difference in fighting off the Spanish, but in the end all governing classes somehow had to complete the colonisation process under their own steam through new class compromises.

Frontiers have typically been non-national structures, whether in the ancient land empires or in the Americas. As I argue in Volume I (2007: 76–89), the frontier way of life is necessarily eclectic and exploratory. In South America too, 'individuals developed economic, kinship, and friendship connections with people "on the other side"', Duncan Baretta and Markoff write (1978: 608), so that loyalties and interests became split 'to the point at which they could (conveniently) identify with either nationality'. This was unthinkable on the North American frontier. Here a Lockean state–society complex confronted a quintessentially foreign, indigenous population with which no significant exchange or exogamy occurred. Certainly the murderous Civil War in the United States had to settle the nature of *its* incomplete colonisation, but that proceeded on the basis of a shared civilisation on one side of the frontier. In Latin America, internal foreign relations blended into different class compromises on either side as frontier conflict spilled over into fratricidal wars over contested boundaries. As López Alves notes (2000: 36), 'most of Latin America experienced almost constant war during the entire nineteenth century'. Through these wars the nation-states consolidated themselves separately, as containers of class conflict and compromise under Anglo-American tutelage.

Liberalism and the Nation-State

The break-up of illiberal empires into nation-states, precipitated by the dissolution of the first British Atlantic Empire and the French Revolution, heralded a new epoch of sovereign equality. It coincided with important departures in science and its emancipation from religion. A new, evolutionary geology and, eventually, Darwin's *Origin of Species* would also affect the understanding of how sovereign equality could be made part of Anglophone global dominion.

Britain's victory over Napoleon in 1815, according to Wallerstein (2001: 191), was followed by 'a thrust to consolidate and justify this hegemony in the domains of culture and ideology'. A religious crisis in the 1820s and 1830s necessitated what Gammon calls (2008: 267–9) 'an aggressive pursuit of new technologies of truth', from which Utilitarianism emerged triumphant. Jeremy Bentham's calculus of pleasure and pain allows a view of the self-regulating market 'as a mechanism of rewards and punishments that would ensure effective order in social relations' (ibid.: 273). 'From the utilitarian point of view', Polanyi infers (1957: 117), 'the task of the government was to increase want in order to make the physical sanction of hunger effective.' In addition Bentham designed a surveillance infrastructure (the Panopticon) which jointly with the market enables comprehensive social discipline – a combination, as Gill highlights (2003: 183–5) and as recent revelations dramatically underscore, still in full force today.

John Stuart Mill (1806–73) played a key role in shaping ideological discipline as a complementary structure of control. He worked with Auguste Comte, but in *On Liberty* of 1859 (1929: 16) dismisses Comte's positivist future as 'a despotism of society over the individual surpassing anything contemplated [by] the most rigid disciplinarian among the ancient philosophers' (the reference is of course to Plato). The 'individual' would typically be a member of the middle classes; below it was the mob, 'the many and the mediocre', whose irrationality Mill greatly feared (and which he thought his own father, James Mill, had overlooked). What was needed was a return to authoritative class compromise, which according to Gammon (2010: 234) Mill thought should be the work of intellectuals 'leading the masses beyond the metaphysical stage' whilst substituting 'an ideal of humanity' for the belief in God. From this perspective he also codified the liberal concept of knowledge as we know it today.

In his epistemology, Mill argues that the reliance on quantitative analysis, although it helps to obfuscate deeper social reality, may carry its own risks after all. 'The peculiarity of the evidence of mathematical truths is that all the argument is on one side', he writes (1929: 43, emphasis added). 'But on every subject on which difference of opinion is possible *the truth depends on a balance to be struck between two sets of conflicting reasons*.' Indeed in the social sciences, the idea of a single truth is incompatible with individualism and democracy. These, as Bourdieu observes (2001: 145), demand that truth is plural. Any unwanted progress, 'discovery', hence is met with denial or indifference, ultimately leaving everyone entitled to his or her own truth. This consummates the rupture with the continental tradition. Hegel discarded the idea of 'truth' as a category distinct from the real totality, to which Marx adds practice, the realm of the possible. But the notion of 'totality' is enough to make a true liberal shiver. Isn't the Anglophone embrace of French postmodernism also a sign of this hunger for hyper-individualised plurality?

Mill cleared the way for the marginal revolution in economics by replacing the labour theory of value by a theory of distribution. Thus a compensatory class compromise might be achieved whilst leaving capitalist production for what it is. Marx calls him (*MEW*, xxv: 825) one of the 'vulgar economists' who translated the class perspective of the capitalist into theoretical language. In addition Mill codified the liberal concept of the nation-state. Liberals have no developed theory of historical change, Mayall argues (1990: 31), so progress for them 'manifests itself through the rational development of society'. Hence they 'tend to be armchair nationalists'. Unlike the theorists of organic nationality, Western liberals usually are pragmatic about it. Mill for one thought that having more than one ethnicity in a state would produce (as in Peleg 2007: 75) 'mutual antipathies' and prevent 'liberty' – in other words, the role of the nation-state as a container and vehicle of class compromise might be undermined by it.

With respect to Britain's imperial domain, Mill had other concerns. Ever since his father got him a job in the East India Company as a youth, India had been the area of his particular interest. Of course its economy should be run on free-trade principles; in this respect he did not depart from the doctrines propagated at the Company's Haileybury college that made the colony, in Davis' words (2002: 31), 'a Utilitarian laboratory where millions of lives were wagered against dogmatic faith in omnipotent markets'. However, unlike his contemporaries Richard Cobden, the cotton textiles manufacturer and exporter, and John Bright, the Radical MP, who earned a reputation as pacifists from their free-trade convictions (although J.M. Hobson notes their disdain for non-European peoples, 2012: 36–9), Mill was an interventionist. Not observing individual liberty for him was a ground for intervention, indeed a 'sacred duty' (as in Manokha 2008: 102). This inclined him to the policy of Palmerston, who held that 'the decrepit Chinese and Ottoman empires could be transformed by commercial penetration but [who] unlike Cobden … would not flinch from the use of force in order to achieve this object' (Parkinson 1977: 97). Indeed, writing during the second Opium War, Mill (1929: 118) saw China's attempt to restrict access for narcotics as 'an interference', 'objectionable not as [an] infringement on the liberty of the producer or seller, but on that of the buyer'.

Once an illiberal empire had been opened up by commercial penetration or force of arms, it would have to be governed, however. And if a client governing class was to be won over for British tutelage, a country's educated elite in Mill's view should therefore not be alienated. As he put it in the 1830s, 'the lettered classes are still held by the people of India in high estimation, and their degradation and extinction cannot be received with indifference by their countrymen nor submitted to without resentment by themselves'. Zastoupil (1994: 40) detects in this passage Mill's reading of European romantics such as Herder, but it also reflects the practical need not to discard the class through which 'indirect rule' must be exercised. This prospect was of course dealt a severe blow by the Mutiny of 1857–58. The surprise indigenous revolt prompted Palmerston, the British prime minister, to dissolve the East India Company, placing the colony under direct British rule. Bright, a cabinet minister under Palmerston's rival Gladstone, proposed a different response: that India be broken up and parts of it be placed under Muslim rule now that the Hindu army had proved unreliable. As Sarila relates (2006: 75), the Anglo-Oriental College at Aligarh, southeast of Delhi, had the stated aim 'to produce an educated upper class of Muslims who might lead their people out of despair and ignorance towards humanism and intelligent government'.

Upon the dissolution of the East India Company, Mill declined the offer of an advisory post in the new India Office, but his interest in India did not diminish. Among other things he reflected on the degree of sovereignty to be granted to the Indian states, with a keen eye for actual ethnicity. In a letter of 1866, he contrasts (as in Zastoupil 1994: 153–4), 'really native states, with a nationality, & historical traditions and feelings, which is emphatically the case (for example) with the Rajpoot states', from 'modern states created by conquest', such as the Muslim and Maratha kingdoms or what he called 'foreign dynasties' in central India. The former (those 'with a nationality') should be exempt from British intervention. For the latter, on the other hand, Mill prefers to 'make the continuance of the dynasty by adoption not a right nor a general rule, but a reward to be earned by good government' – on which the India Office would then pass judgement of course, as do the Anglophone powers today.

Towards the close of the century, Britain, in response to encroachments by the German and Russian empires, began to adopt an overtly imperialist and racist perspective too. Herbert Spencer's argument that society evolves like an organism, first argued in *Social Statics* (eight years before the publication of Darwin's *Origin of Species*), did not get the resonance at home that it would have in the United States. His concept of the 'survival of the fittest', the phrase that, as Wolfers and Martin remind us (1956: 222), sums up Social Darwinism and is often mistakenly attributed to Darwin, did better (in *Man Versus the State* of 1884 Spencer links it to Darwin's 'natural selection'; 1982: 109). The notion was taken up by Charles W. Dilke in *Greater Britain*, an epic of the Anglo-Saxon stock published in

1868. Dilke argued (as in Gollwitzer 1982: 88–9) that wherever they went, Anglophone settlers demonstrated their 'fitness' relative to indigenous peoples – Amerindians, Aborigines, Maoris, and so on. Like Spencer, Dilke rejects formal imperialism; peaceful competition was enough to demonstrate Anglo-Saxon superiority.

Britain's empire-building reached its limits around the turn of the century. In South Asia the occupation, in 1880, of the North West Frontier Province, home to Pashtun (Pathan) tribes, marked the limit of its colonisation there. Thirteen years later the Durand Line settled the Indo-Afghan border, making Afghanistan a buffer against the advance of Russia (it also divided the Pashtun population, which the Amir of Kabul warned might turn the tribal areas in today's Pakistan into a future source of trouble; Sarila 2006: 244). Empire remained popular (John R. Seeley's *The Expansion of England* was reprinted 18 times between 1883 and 1914), but Cecil Rhodes' forays into southern Africa and the 'Great Game' with Russia prompted a series of revisions of the imperialist project. The geographer Halford Mackinder (1861–1947) and the pioneer critic of imperialism John A. Hobson (1858–1940) were the most prominent among those recognising that a new age had dawned. Mackinder argued that a world of nation-states was terminating the epoch of empire; Hobson took the next step (from our perspective – his book appeared first), by projecting a global governance over that world again.

Mackinder's 1904 paper 'The Geographical Pivot of History', presented to the Royal Geographical Society, identifies what I call an empire/nomad mode of foreign relations prior to sovereign equality. Mackinder also links the growth of land empires and their foreign relations with nomads to geography. Sovereign equality in Mackinder's view creates a new intensity of foreign, now inter-national relations. In the empire/nomad mode, he writes, 'every explosion of social forces ... [is] dissipated in a surrounding circuit of unknown space and barbaric chaos'. Under sovereign equality, however, states must be strong rather than extensive, since Mackinder expects (1904: 422) that every social movement

will be sharply re-echoed from the far side of the globe, and weak elements in the political and economic organism of the world will be shattered in consequence ... Probably some half-consciousness of this fact is at last diverting much of the attention of statesmen in all parts of the world from territorial expansion to the struggle for relative efficiency.

Certainly Mackinder, like his US counterpart, Captain Alfred Mahan, can be accused of 'geo-historical reductionism' (Davis 2002: 227). Yet his concept of 'heartland', for him the Eurasian continent, can also be understood as a concept of political economy rather than geography. In fact Mackinder points to such a reconceptualisation himself when he writes (1904: 432) that the discoveries and overseas settlement 'endowed Christendom with the widest possible mobility of power, short of a winged mobility'. Britain with the 'new Europes' (Canada, the United States, South Africa, Australia) and Japan 'are now *a ring of outer and insular bases for sea-power and commerce, inaccessible to the land-power of Euro-Asia*' (emphasis added). It was the anchoring of capital in the 'ring of outer and insular bases' that I would argue shifted to them the structural advantage associated with the heartland notion.

Eurasia instead was relegated to a staging ground for a series of contender states, including Japan after the 1868 Meiji revolution from above. Mackinder's fear that the powers controlling the Eurasian heartland could overwhelm the sea-powers by using railways can be dismissed as a temporary panic (Smith 2004: 16–17). The original, continental heartland thesis retained its validity only in a subordinate sense, i.e. as a cautionary note that Germany and Russia should never be allowed to link up in a challenge to the West (Mackinder 1904: 436). Preventing this from happening has been a key principle of Western policy in distributing nationality rights across the globe. But this leaves the question as to the larger organisation of the world of nation-states, and here Hobson comes in.

In *Imperialism: A Study*, originally of 1902, Hobson advocates putting a stop to imperial adventures like Rhodes' push to the Cape. He bases this on a fundamental distinction between colonialism (conceived as a policy of emigration and overseas settlement) and imperialism. The former amounts to a transplantation of nationality and civilisation; but what had been successful in Canada, Australia and New Zealand, in the absence of a comparably favourable proportion of settlers to indigenous inhabitants, had run into trouble in South Africa. It therefore degenerated into imperialism, Hobson claims (1968: 6–7), territorial greed reaching beyond what it can actually give 'colonial' substance to (French and German expansion, incidentally, in his view belonged to this imperialist category entirely). And where Cobden already posed the old question (as in Armitage 2000: 11) whether imperial conquest would not threaten liberties at home by importing the East's 'arbitrary political maxims', Hobson knows the answer and in *Imperialism* draws a compelling picture of the corruption of domestic life caused by expansion without settlement, driven by greed and adventure instead – a picture still relevant for understanding the 'homeland security' excesses of the War on Terror.

Hobson's alternative is *internationalism*, integration allowing peaceful economic competition (Arrighi 1978: 41). He argues that transnational civil society, as it developed under the hegemony of liberal internationalism in the Pax Britannica, offered perspectives far better than a straight confrontation with contender states. 'Direct intercommunication of persons, goods, and information' (what we would call today 'globalisation'), he writes (1968: 167–9, emphasis added) was spreading at great speed and 'this growth of the common experience necessary to found a common life *beyond the area of nationality* is surely the most mark-worthy feature of the age.' Hence, the quest should not be for national independence or conquest of weaker nations, but for

experimental and progressive federation, which, proceeding on the line of the greatest common experience, shall weave formal bonds of political attachment between the most 'like-minded' nations, extending them to others as common experience grows wider, until an effective political federation is established, comprising the whole of 'the civilized world,' i.e. all those nations which have attained a considerable fund of the 'common experience' comprised under the head of civilization.

As his distant relative J.M. Hobson highlights (2012: 48), there is no doubt where for the elder Hobson 'civilization' has its epicentre. In this respect he too (J.A.) subscribes to the idea of an expanding, Anglophone liberal heartland that runs through all English-speaking thinking about foreign relations, and which still today underpins mainstream IR. For whilst it is true that liberal global governance of open nation-states, as a complementary political form to capitalist universalism, crystallised only under US leadership (Colás 2008: 630), and its disciplinary expression too had to wait for North American guidance, the basic ideas were all developed in the Pax Britannica. The proximity of the contender imperialisms prompted atavistic reflexes in Britain too, but the underlying thrust was towards informal rule. Hence the relative ease of granting sovereign equality. 'Responsible government,' Gallagher and Robinson write (1967: 235), 'far from being a separatist device, was simply a change

from direct to indirect methods of maintaining British interests.'
Ultimately, therefore, 'liberal empire ... should preside over its own
eventual elimination' (Mayall 1990: 46), and that is what it did –
replacing formal by informal empire, today's 'good governance'.

INTERNATIONALISM AND NATIONAL SELF-DETERMINATION

To understand why a discipline of International Relations
prescribing , liberal, Anglo-American governance over a world
of open nation-states was part of the response to the Russian
Revolution, we must briefly assess the socialist alternative. Without
it we cannot fully appreciate the final instalment of the mainstream
academic division of labour. National self-determination and internationalism from the mid nineteenth century became part of a
progressive body of thought which in 1917 assumed the quality of
a real utopia, prefiguring a future not yet made actual. As argued in
Volume II (2010: 12–14), such a forward movement of collective
consciousness is an aspect of 'three-dimensional' human–historical
time – as was, under different circumstances, the regression to a
tribal concept of the foreign in post-Versailles Germany to which
we turn in the next chapter.

The socialist complex of internationalism and national autonomy,
in combination with the critique of capitalist imperialism,
challenged the idea of nationality sponsored by the great powers,
liberal or imperial. The French Revolution inaugurated the practice
of encouraging nationality for (as it turned out) imperial ends –
in Poland, but also in Egypt and elsewhere. Even under Napoleon,
however, nationalities like the Italians continued to place their
hopes in French patronage. Upon hearing the news that Napoleon
has escaped from Elba and has landed in southern France, the
youthful protagonist of Stendhal's *The Convent of Parma* of 1839
through his tears spots an eagle high up in the sky over Lake Como.
'I have seen this great image of Italy rising up from the cesspool in
which the Germans keep it submerged', he confesses. 'It stretched
out its mutilated arms still half locked in chains to its king and its
liberator.'

After the Congress of Vienna, Britain, restoration France as well
as Russia (on account of its Slav and Orthodox credentials) sought
to mobilise such sentiments for their own ends. With the Monroe
Doctrine, the United States joined in for the Western hemisphere. In
1917, Anglo-America proclaimed national self-determination as part

of its liberal design for the world, a counter-revolutionary copy of the Bolshevik programme. In the end, though, its internationalism remains different from the Marxist original.

From Marx to Austro-Marxism

Sovereign equality is a marker of bourgeois class formation; the revolts of 1848 were inspired by a wish (also on the part of the craft workers and proletarians drawn into them) to apply it universally. This internationalism goes back to the radical democratic thinking of Tom Paine and the Enlightenment (Halliday 1999: 69–72). Hence also the famous slogan of the *Communist Manifesto*, 'the workers have no fatherland' (*MEW*, iv: 479). But whilst some nationalities in 1848 behaved heroically, others were less courageous (if not actually supplying mercenaries for the ensuing repression). This in turn raised the question of the determinants of progressive nationality. That nation-building in the nineteenth century inevitably proceeded under great-power tutelage was recognised also by Marx and Engels. Thus they note (*MEW*, xi: 585) how both sides in the Crimean War appealed to national sentiment – the Anglo-French coalition by supporting the Hungarians, Poles, Italians and, to a degree, the Germans; Russia by supporting the unity of the Slav peoples – Pan-Slavism. They also congratulate Mazzini and Garibaldi for wresting Italy free from Napoleon III, 'the crowned impostor' (*MEW*, xiii: 365). But from their historical vantage point it was not yet obvious that bourgeois nation-building was increasingly directed by the Anglophone West.

Multinational contender states like Austria–Hungary or Russia, as noted above and argued in Volume I (2007: 179–82), often had urban and landed populations of different ethnicity. In these countries, Michael Mann writes (1987: 348), 'socialism was trapped in its urban-industrial enclaves, outvoted by the bourgeois-agrarian classes, and repressed by peasant soldiers and aristocratic officers'. Marx and Engels therefore played with the idea of 'agrarian democracy', in which the landed nobility of Poland and Hungary would play a progressive role. Wouldn't this neutralise the counter-revolutionary mobilisation of the peasants? In the early 1850s, Marx in his correspondence with Engels (as in Molnár 1975: 71) conceded that the answer was no. Engels in his assessment of '1848' (*MEW*, vi: 168) concluded that 'the participants in the struggle divided themselves into two big camps' – Germans, Poles and Magyars on the side of revolution, the combined Slavs minus the Poles, the

Rumanians and the Saxons in the north of today's Rumania on the other. Ultimately, as Marx had argued before (*MEW*, iv: 417), socialist revolution could not be achieved in pre-industrial societies. 'Poland must be liberated not in Poland, but in England.'

Limited industrialisation in many countries left the workers' movement saddled with the essentially bourgeois idea of the nation-state and sovereign equality as progressive forms, and empire as the backward counterpart. In its resolution of 27 September 1865, for example, the London Conference of the First International stated that 'it is imperative to annihilate the invading influence of Russia in Europe by applying to Poland "the right of every people to dispose of itself", and re-establishing that country on a social and democratic basis' (General Council n.d.: 246); and Marx and Engels called Poland the 'cosmopolitan warrior of the revolution' (*MEW*, xviii: 574). But assigning progressive or reactionary qualities to entire peoples inevitably led them back to the Hegelian idea of the state as the embodiment of historical reason, and of peoples destined (or not) to play a role in history as bearers of the World Spirit. From there it was only a small step towards drawing up lists of 'nations with history' and 'nations without history'. Engels, with whom this tendency is strongest, concludes on the basis of what he calls a tribal history (*MEW*, vi: 168; cf. Herod 1976: 4) that there were only three nations in central Europe that were bearers of progress, nations 'which have actively intervened in history, and which still today are capable of life – the Germans, the Poles, and the Magyars'. At the other extreme stood what he called 'national debris' (*Völkerabfälle*) (*MEW*, xvi: 158–9), remnants of old peoples such as the Croats, Ruthenians, and Slovaks, who were only mobilised behind the nationality principle by Russian design and not out of inner strength. The Czechs had played a historical role until 1848, but after that fell back. And so on and so forth.

As Germans, Marx and Engels were obviously interested in German unification as a precondition of socialism. Thus Marx criticises the liberal workers' leader, Ferdinand Lassalle, who preferred Prussia as the architect of German unity over Austria (*MEW*, xxix: 432). Yet Marx and Engels believed that in 1859, Austria should have been supported against France. Bismarck then wrested leadership over the process from Austria in the war of 1866. As Engels wrote in retrospect (*MEW*, xxi: 431), the Iron Chancellor resisted the parliamentary demands of the bourgeoisie (whilst taming the German working class with the Socialist Law), but was only too eager to execute its national–territorial objectives. The militarisation of German national unification was finally sealed in the Franco-Prussian war. Writing in September 1870 (*MEW*, xvii: 105), Engels identifies that war as inaugurating 'the new German imperialism'. With special licence from Bismarck, the defeated French government, holed up in Bordeaux, launched a war against the Paris Commune that sealed the fate of the First International. With 'a new Holy Alliance' (Marx in *MEW*, xviii: 135) facing them, the workers from now on would have to form a 'Sixth Great Power' against the unified ruling classes of Europe. Codified in Stuttgart in 1907 and Basel in 1912 in solemn agreements not to allow the imperialist ruling classes to turn their working classes against each other and destroy them in the trenches, this position obviously overlooked the material aspect of national class compromises. It gave socialist nationality policy the tactical, idealist tendency that has continued to characterise it (cf. vol. i, 2007: 169).

The second-generation Marxist approach to national self-determination was formulated from the vantage points of the two multinational empires struggling to adopt a contender-state posture – Austria–Hungary and Russia. The Austro-Marxists clung to the idea of the large state as a precondition for socialism; the Bolsheviks thought in terms of a radical break-up followed by voluntary reunion. Otto Bauer (1882–1938), the leading Austro-Marxist theorist of nationality, in his chief work, *The National Question and Social Democracy* of 1907, theorises the nation in historical materialist terms (1907: 16–17). It arises out of struggles over conditions of existence (he mentions nomads and warriors in connection with grassland, and makes a reference to Darwin). Internal class conflict and compromise shape a national character over time; through endogamy this in turn acquires a quasi-biological aspect. Now to preserve the multinational state, Bauer stresses (1907: 112, with a reference to Kant), the larger community must be a matter of access and interaction, not of uniformity. This was a sentiment shared with cosmopolitan strands in the bourgeoisie. Thus in Robert Musil's unfinished novel, *The Man Without Qualities* of 1942, a fictional group of pre-First World War notables discuss an appropriate present for the jubilee of the Emperor of the Dual Monarchy, only to decide on offering him … multinational Austria itself. The noble lady Diotima, obviously knowing her Hegel, claims that the presence on the committee of Dr Paul Arnheim, a German industrialist and politician (modelled on Walter Rathenau), 'proved that the Spirit as such had made Austria its home'. Did the empire not contain within itself the blueprint of a bright future? 'The world, she explained, would never find rest until the nations in it lived in an elevated unity as did the Austrian tribes in her fatherland. A Greater Austria, a World Austria …That was the crowning idea.'

That was not far from how the empire's socialists hoped to turn Austria into a model society of worldwide significance. By rejecting nationalism as a bourgeois creed, Michael Mann observes (1987: 247), the Austro-Marxists paradoxically became 'the major de facto supporter of the transnational monarchy'. Just before the turn of the century, Victor Adler, the socialist leader, indeed spoke (as in Talmon 1981: 133) of 'the experimental laboratory of world history', whilst Karl Renner, another leading Austrian socialist and a future chancellor, in 1918 argued (as in Kloss 1969: 493) that it might have been worthwhile to have an independent Bohemia, Hungary or Serbia in 1850, but that meanwhile 'states whose diameter is no more than a day's fast train ride, can no longer be effective pillars of a world political order'. Of course this overlooks that for a large, controlling power or bloc, the smaller the size of its nominally sovereign dependencies, the better – hence the Slovenia's and Montenegros, Kosovos and South Sudans of our time. Would a unified Yugoslavia have acted as a NATO proxy supplying arms to the Syrian uprising, as Croatia did in 2013, prior to joining the EU?

The solution proposed by Bauer (basing himself in part on Rudolf Springer's *The Struggle of the Austrian Nations over the State* of 1902) is as follows. Liberalism, the argument goes (Bauer 1907: 274–83, 326–59), only recognises individual citizens. It ignores the desire of nationalities to pursue their own cultural development, provoking a struggle of all component nationalities against each other. The organic approach to nationality on the other hand proceeds from either the *territorial principle* or the *personality principle*. Territoriality however is undermined by labour migration and shifting language boundaries, including language 'islands'. This would lead to endless further dissolution, with nation-states becoming smaller and smaller. Thus in Hungary in 1900 actual Magyar-speaking inhabitants were a minority of 45.5 per cent (ibid.: 427). Yet the personality principle is not satisfactory either, because the autonomy of a community is not secure without some sort of territorial administrative aspect. Springer solves this by the establishment of districts (*Kreise*), which as national and autonomous entities are entrusted with public administration. If a district is mixed, the different nationalities will have their own bodies to manage issues that the *Kreis* cannot handle, such as education in one's own language (Bauer 1907: 359, 371–81). Intermarriage between nationalities can only increase the need for flexibility, as does the case of the Jews, who in response to anti-Semitism were showing signs of a new national consciousness too, although Zionists were a negligible minority (cf. vol. ii, 2010: 193).

The bourgeois concept of national minority, intended as we saw to settle ethno-territorial incongruities from a great-power perspective (Özdemir 2009b: 153; Liebich 2008: 257), is no solution either. It only leads to further territorial adjustments under the motto, 'Why should we be a minority in your state if you can be one in ours?'. Hence for Bauer and the Austro-Marxists an active policy, based on combining territoriality (Springer's *Kreise*) with cultural autonomy rights attached to personal nationality, was the solution to keep the large state intact. *Autonomy* thus is made the core component of practical internationalism. This would become the actual model for state socialist nationality policy – paradoxical because Lenin and Stalin vehemently attacked the Austro-Marxist proposals as unhistorical.

Nationality Between Imperialism and Revolution

The attack by Lenin and Stalin on the Austro-Marxist proposals, referred to in Volume I (2007: 180–1), proceeded from the strand of Marxist thought that sees imperialism as an integral, constitutive aspect of the capitalism. National self-determination thus is explicitly formulated against empire, but also against the premature cosmopolitanism of the 'Workers have no Fatherland' kind. As Marx warned in a letter to Engels of 1866 (as in Löwy 1998: 13), that sort of celebratory fraternisation could easily turn into the silent supremacy of a dominant nationality over others. Around 1869–70 they therefore developed the view that a ruling class like the British drew its strength in part from suppressing autonomy in its overseas possessions (Anderson 2010: 144–5). Hence it would not be defeated before these foreign bases were liberated from foreign dominion. Just as the International had supported Poland against reactionary Russia, the Irish should therefore be encouraged to organise themselves as an autonomous workers' party. True internationalism, wrote Engels (*MEW*, xviii: 80), 'must necessarily be based on an autonomous national organisation; the Irish as well as other oppressed nationalities can only enter the [International] with the same rights as the representatives of the conquering nation and in protest against the conquest'.

The Russian Bolsheviks took up this line of thought in the attack against the Austro-Marxist concept. Lenin claimed that Springer and Bauer insufficiently recognised that nationality plays out differently at particular historic junctures; it arises with bourgeois class formation, but weakens again later. Enshrining it in a constitution eternalises something which is in reality a transient, historical phenomenon. The issue became acute when the Russian Mensheviks (who favoured a federal solution in a socialist Russia), the Jewish *Bund*, and Polish and Baltic socialists, along with socialists from the Caucasus, under the leadership of Trotsky, in 1912 formed an anti-Bolshevik bloc which among other things adopted the Austro-Marxist theses on cultural autonomy. Lenin then recruited Stalin, who as a Georgian was thought to have the right credentials for the undertaking, to go to Vienna and demolish the Austro-Marxist theses. Shaheen (1956: 38–9) believes that Stalin, who did not know German, was assisted by his fellow Bolshevik Nikolai Bukharin, who lived in Vienna at the time. The resulting tract of 1913, *Marxism and the National Question*, explicitly attacks Springer and Bauer. It was practically written on Lenin's dictate, albeit that Stalin's simplistic materialism and crude polemics are in evidence too.

A key element in the Lenin–Stalin approach was a nationality's right to a territorial state of its own, as was implied already in Engels' remarks on the Irish. They were less interested in the spiritual side; Stalin (*Werke*, ii: 276) actually denounces Bauer for 'mysticism'. For the Bolsheviks, given that nationality in the phase of bourgeois class formation is a progressive category (the examples are always from the Russian empire), a nation must have the right to secede. Lenin in his writings on the topic of 1913 and 1914 (*Critical Remarks on the National Question* and *The Right of Nations to Self-Determination*), also attacked Rosa Luxemburg, whose article 'The National Question and Autonomy' of 1908–09 supported Bauer's idea that a large state is an asset not to be squandered. Luxemburg was born in Poland, then a Russian province, and had emigrated at the age of 16. By the turn of the century she was one of the most prominent activists and theoreticians of the revolutionary wing of the German SPD. Her Jewish background may have made her averse to nationalism, of which the Jews in that part of the world had only seen the worst features. But also, wouldn't Poland develop faster within Russia with its large market, than outside it? In reply, Lenin argues (*Coll. Works*, xx: 451–4) that the reactionary nationalism of the Great Russians is strengthened by their oppression of the non-Russian nationalities. Hence the first nationalism that the proletariat must combat is that of the Great Russians, not of the oppressed nationalities like the Polish (as Luxemburg advocated in order not to strengthen the Polish bourgeoisie).

This argument links national self-determination to the transformation of empire and the struggle against imperialism. It sees the right to secede, paradoxically, as the precondition for the unity of the proletarian struggle. Otherwise imperialism will be reproduced under nominally socialist conditions. Wouldn't it be far better for the workers in the nations locked up in the Russian empire, Lenin asked in June 1917 (referring to Ukraine; *Coll. Works*, xxv: 91–2) to take the lead of the movement for a separate state, and then voluntarily join a revolutionary federation with their Russian brethren later – instead of remaining 'inside' and negotiating rights that would inevitably be limited? What he detects in the positions of Luxemburg and Trotsky is a quest to make a revolution only with the certified internationalist working class. But that is an illusion (*Coll. Works*, xxii: 355):

> To imagine that social revolution is conceivable without revolts by small nations in the colonies and in Europe, without revolutionary outbursts by a section of the petty bourgeoisie with all its prejudices, without a movement of the politically non-conscious proletarian masses and semi-proletarian masses against oppression by the landowners, the church, and the monarchy, against national oppression, etc. – to imagine all this is to repudiate social revolution.

One of Luxemburg's arguments against independence of small nations was that it exposed them to imperialist oppression. The critique of imperialism however was hostage to the regression to a theory of economic causation, 'Marxist economics' (Desai 2013: 12–14). This slide back into bourgeois materialism also invited positivist influences. Thus Rudolf Hilferding's *Finance Capital* of 1910, praised by Kautsky as the 'fourth volume' of *Capital*, was, rather, a historical update on phenomena not yet fully evident in Marx's days. Hilferding, the acknowledged 'economist' among the Austro-Marxists (Deppe 2003: 287–8), made his name with a series of articles in 1904 attacking the marginal utility theory of Böhm-Bawerk. He builds his analysis of imperialism around the interpenetration of bank and industrial capital typical of the late-industrialising contender state entrenching against British liberal internationalism. Highlighting the power struggle along national lines, he actually refers (1973: 246n.) to Hobbes to underscore the existential nature of the contest. In 1925 Hilferding specified his historical perspective with the thesis of 'organised capitalism' (as in Fülberth 1991: 19–20), which he claimed could be transformed into socialism under conditions of civil parliamentarian government with a socialist majority. He took his life in a French prison in 1941 waiting to be handed over to the Gestapo, knowing what was waiting for him as the hated 'negroid Jew' who twice served as minister of finance in the Weimar Republic (Deppe 2003: 287).

Rosa Luxemburg owed her rise to prominence in the SPD to her polemic with Eduard Bernstein, the ideologue of the reformist wing. In that debate Luxemburg attacks Bernstein's thesis that social self-regulation and the liberal state were also taking hold in Germany. Imperialism, she argued in 1899 (1970: 38–9), mobilises retrograde ruling classes, reinvesting the state with feudal interests. 'Tariff policy actually has become a means to give feudal interests a capitalist form and expression.' In *The Accumulation of Capital* of 1913, Luxemburg too sought to present an 'update' of Marx's *Capital*. Like Hilferding she analyses imperialism in the economistic, positivist–materialist mould prevalent in the Second International. It is hard to disagree with her key argument (1966: 289) that 'capitalism comes into the world and develops historically in a non-capitalist social milieu', or that imperialism marks the final 'competitive struggle of capital on the world stage over the remaining conditions for accumulation'. To make her point, however, as Fülberth highlights (1991: 9), Luxemburg revisits Marx's figures in *Capital* Volume II, treating them as empirical data. Since this volume, like Volume III, had been left as a manuscript at its author's death (to be edited by Engels), Luxemburg felt entitled to correct its figures and demonstrate that only by including a non-capitalist sector (both within and outside modern countries) did the sums add up.

Lenin too initially adopted an economistic, materialist position under the influence of his mentor, Georgy Plekhanov. Plekhanov's position transpires in *Fundamental Problems of Marxism* of 1908, in which he argues (1969: 31) that Marx and Engels 'completed' Feuerbach's materialism. In the same year, Lenin in *Materialism and Empirio-Criticism* placed Plekhanov, Engels, and Feuerbach in a single tradition (*Coll. Works*, xiv: 27). However, as the Dutch astronomer and prominent Marxist Anton Pannekoek, a contemporary of Lenin and Luxemburg, shows in his critique of this work (n.d.: 8, 65), Lenin's polemic against Ernst Mach and other neo-positivists defends not historical materialism, but the materialism of Feuerbach. As a scientist, Pannekoek had no difficulty demonstrating that Lenin strayed well beyond his competence in this book, confusing key concepts such as matter, energy, nature, and so on. However, Lenin undertook a fundamental rethink after August 1914. The decision of the main European socialist parties not to oppose their governments' decision to go to war, in spite of their solemn promises at the Stuttgart and Basel congresses, came as a great shock to him. When the news reached him in his Swiss exile that Plekhanov too had called on the Russian workers to defend the motherland, he actually refused to believe it. 'It was probably the trauma of these events', writes Löwy (1981: 59), 'that moved Lenin to seek a critical revision of "orthodox" Marxism from its very foundations.' These studies, crucially including a reading of Hegel's *Science of Logic*, led to what later became known as the *Philosophical Notebooks*. The result was a radically different approach to the materialism and positivism of the Second International. Here Lenin really begins to exploit the potential of the Marxist method, which relies on Hegel to overcome the limits of naturalistic materialism and hence cannot possibly 'complete it'. In the USSR, however, it was Lenin's *Materialism*, not the Notebooks, that became the officially sanctioned position – which is why Pannekoek in 1927 decided to write his booklet.

In Lenin's work written during the First World War, the effect of his studies on the dialectical method transpires clearly, in none more so than in *Imperialism, the Highest Stage of Capitalism* of 1916–17. His rupture with the theoretical tradition and patriotism of the Second International made Karl Kautsky (1854–1938), the grand old man of the SPD after the death of Engels, his natural target. Kautsky in 1914 published an article on imperialism that summed up the degree to which bourgeois thinking had penetrated the workers' movement. Kautsky's area of expertise was agriculture, and where Luxemburg had argued that the reproduction of capital relies on external markets, Kautsky claimed that it was dependent on 'the steady progress of the necessary agrarian inputs for industry' (1914: 911). Hence it was only a matter of time before the imperialists would conclude that it was much more economical to look beyond imperialism ('ultra-imperialism') and exploit the periphery collectively (ibid.: 920). 'Every enlightened capitalist today must shout at his comrades: capitalists of the world, unite!' The political absurdity of Kautsky's intervention (the article came out simultaneously with the outbreak of the war, which over four years of protracted slaughter, destroyed the core of the European socialist movement and much else), should not obscure the methodological issue at the heart of the subsequent debates. Thus in the view of Milios and Sotiropoulos (2009: 82–3), Kautsky's and many comparable analyses of imperialism fail to conceptualise social capital as a totality, a structure determining the mode of operation of particular capitals. Instead, individual capitals are seen as objects external to each other, so that the systemic nature of imperialism is lost sight of and classes and states are assigned a freedom of action they do not actually possess.

Lenin did not criticise Luxemburg's 1913 study and neither does he challenge the conclusions of Bukharin, for whose *Imperialism and World Economy* of 1917 he wrote a preface. Praising the work of his young friend for bringing together all the necessary materials for a thorough study, and so on (somewhat disingenuously because he pays no further attention to any of it), Lenin immediately switches to attacking Kautsky. Indeed Bukharin's thesis (1972: 106) of *global* production versus *national appropriation* has no bearing on Lenin's own analysis. For Bukharin, war follows from state rivalry in appropriating the spoils of globalised production. For Lenin (*Coll. Works*, xxii: 275–6), it is the result of a three-step process. First, the division of the world between states is complete, with no unoccupied territories left for further expansion; secondly, capital continues to develop unevenly; and thirdly, as a result, the only means for the inevitable redistribution is war. But precisely because of the wide-ranging webs of transnational capitalist interconnections, the separate states have become tied together into 'imperialist chains'; war exposes the weakest links in these chains to revolution by a committed proletarian party, etc.

This is not to suggest that Lenin's pamphlet is a model of scholarship. Thus he draws heavily on Hilferding's *Finance Capital*, adopting the notion that finance capital (and the related phenomena of capital markets, cartels, etc.) signified the 'latest', monopolistic–imperialist stage of capitalism – as if capitalism has ever existed without imperialism (Desai 2013: 48). But he equally relies on Hobson's pioneering *Imperialism: A Study*, which as we saw articulates a liberal, British perspective. As Arrighi highlights (1978: 25), when Hobson speaks of capital exports and the financiers, he means 'a supranational entity which had almost no links with any productive apparatus; whereas for Hilferding, it referred to an entity of a national character whose ties with the productive apparatus tended to be extremely close'.

The essential argument for Lenin is the continuous destabilisation by transnational capital movements of the existing distribution of state power (territory, population and resources, not only at home but obtained also through annexations and from colonies and other dependencies). Hence a transnational class structure comprising the owners and their related state bureaucracies may at certain points (the weak links) become exposed to revolutionary breakthroughs. Here Trotsky's theory of uneven and combined development (as in *The Permanent Revolution* of 1906 and *History of the Russian Revolution* of 1936), must be recognised as a precursor of Lenin's own. Eventually the two men would come to personify the Russian Revolution in the eyes of the world; but in fact Trotsky's idea of the self-organisation of the workers in councils (*soviets*) and Lenin's trust in the vanguard party are incompatible, as Stalin's rise to power would testify once the revolutionary conjuncture ended.

Lenin's reading of Hegel made him particularly aware of the idea of history as a complex whole, something which he felt was missing from so much writing on imperialism. Thus in his notebooks on imperialism he dismisses a particular study as having 'absolutely no scientific interest in an analysis of the *relations* of the world economy in their *totality*' (*Werke*, xxxix: 158). For our purposes, what is most striking in Lenin's analysis, however, is how it demonstrates the strengths of a dialectical analysis of the global political economy, of states and capital mediated by transnational class formation – over one cast in terms of Kantian antinomies and confined to either economics or politics. IR of course would first discard 'capitalism' or any other understanding of the world economy (the term is also absent from an economics approach, because mainstream economics is internal to a capitalist class perspective). But let us take the 'foundational' IR debate between (world order) idealism and (power) realism and see how Lenin, always in attack mode against Kautsky, treats the two.

'In the reality of the capitalist system,' he writes in *Imperialism* (*Coll. Works*, xxii: 295–6), '"inter-imperialist" or "ultra-imperialist" alliances, no matter what form they may assume, whether of one imperialist coalition against another, or of a general alliance embracing *all* the imperialist powers, are *inevitably* nothing more than a "truce" in periods between wars.'

Peaceful alliances prepare the ground for wars, and in their turn grow out of wars; the one conditions the other, producing alternating forms of peaceful and non-peaceful struggle on *one and the same* basis of imperialist connections and relations within world economics and world politics ... Kautsky *separates* one link of a single chain from another, separates the present peaceful (and ultra-imperialist, nay, ultra-ultra-imperialist) alliance of *all* the powers for the 'pacification' of China ... from the non-peaceful conflict of tomorrow, which will prepare the ground for another 'peaceful' general alliance for the partition, say, of Turkey.

One sees here how by disconnecting political phenomena from the integral political–economic process through which they are linked as instances of class struggle, separate 'idealist' peaceful and 'realist' warlike narratives of international relations become possible. Both are dismissed by Lenin as 'lifeless abstractions' which fail to recognise the 'living connection between periods of imperialist peace and periods of imperialist war' (ibid.).

The impact of Lenin's analysis, dramatically amplified by the successful seizure of power in the Russian Revolution (for which he did not fail to credit his critique of imperialism in subsequent editions, *Coll. Works*, xxii: 194), was momentous. At a juncture when the social sciences were in the process of nationalising and specialising, it cut through the complexities of the imperialist age, whilst adding (in its unrelenting polemic against Kautsky) an activist perspective that chimed with the widespread revulsion against those responsible for the four years of unprecedented slaughter and destruction then drawing to a close. As we see in the next chapter, this was a challenge that neither in theory nor in practice could be left unanswered. Just as economics and sociology had been shaped in response to the Marxism of the workers' movement in the late nineteenth century, IR crystallised as a separate discipline in response to the critique of imperialism, against the background of socialist revolution.

2
The Crusade for Democracy and World Politics

The modern academic specialisation of International Relations was a by-product of the victory over the Central Powers and the siege laid on the Russian Revolution. As Gramsci wrote in 1919 (1977: 81), 'During the war … the states making up the Entente formed a reactionary coalition with its economic functions powerfully centralized in London and its demagogy choreographed in Paris.'

The enormous administrative and political apparatus that was set up at that time is still in existence: it has been further strengthened and perfected, and is now effectively the instrument of Anglo-Saxon world hegemony. With Imperial Germany prostrated, and the Social-Democratic *Reich* incorporated into the global politico-economic system controlled by Anglo-Saxon capitalism, capitalism has now forged its own unity and turned all its forces to the destruction of the Communist Republics.

Emile Dillon, the correspondent of the *Daily Telegraph* at Versailles, a year later (2004: 21) compared the missionary spirit of the Anglophone states to the Catholic Counter-Reformation. This time the counter-revolution included the codification into academic discipline of the principles of liberal governance over a world of open nation-states, as worked out in the Pax Britannica.

The ostracism of the theory of imperialism did not wait for the formal establishment of a dedicated IR. Key proponents perished in the counter-revolution: in early 1919 Rosa Luxemburg was lynched by a fascist militia; Bukharin fell victim to the Stalinist repression in the 1930s. Hilferding's fate was noted in the last chapter. Also in 1919, Burch relates (1981, ii: 227), the leader of the American Socialist Party, Eugene Debs, was sentenced to ten years imprisonment for a speech in which he characterised the 1914–18 struggle as a 'capitalist war'. This was of course not lost on US academics. Given funding opportunities from the large foundations spun off from dominant steel, oil and auto capital – Carnegie, Rockefeller, and after the Second World War, Ford – it made a lot more sense to submit to the discipline of a narrowly circumscribed academic field and build a university career in peace. How social science was restructured to make this possible is the first concern of this chapter. I then turn to Woodrow Wilson's Crusade for Democracy, which drew on expert advice subsequently institutionalised into a capillary system providing the West with the academic intelligence base it needed in order to sustain its supremacy. Finally, I recapitulate how, after the collapse in the 1930s of the 'Social-Democratic Reich', the Weimar Republic, intellectual refugees inserted the Nietzsche–Weber–Schmitt lineage into the evolving IR discipline.

THE MAKING OF DISCIPLINARY SOCIAL SCIENCE

Disciplinary social science emerged in a direct line from the surveillance of the working classes. From public health surveys to the monitoring of working conditions (Derber 1967: 21), it elaborated Burke's adage, referred to in the Preface, that 'a state without the means of some change is without the means of its conservation'. Social discipline aims at keeping people in a passive condition, for which the nation-state historically has provided the 'normal' spatial confines (Foucault 2004). Its reproductive apparatus centrally involves education. Universities in particular produce those who apply discipline and at the same time, submit to it. They provide 'both a means for the selection of managerial staff and an ideological apparatus well suited to naturalizing social divisions "technically" and "scientifically"', Balibar writes (1991: 12). 'Through a network of apparatuses and daily practices, the individual is instituted as *homo nationalis* from cradle to grave, at the same time as he or she is instituted as *homo œconomicus, politicus, religiosus*' (ibid.: 93). Academia as we know it today emerged from this multiple mission, first in response to the political awakening of the working classes in Europe.

European Departures

Burke's reflections on the French Revolution highlight the profound differences between Anglophone liberal society and its continental contenders; in education and social theory, the divide is as profound as any. On the British Isles, the Utilitarians, as noted in Chapter 1, thought that prisons and churches would provide the complement to the regimentation of the worker in the factory. The middle classes meanwhile would be engaged with the individual pursuit of self-interest, 'utility'. The shift from a focus on production and the labour theory of value to distribution as the field in which that pursuit is arbitrated had been prepared by John Stuart Mill. It was taken further by W. Stanley Jevons (1835–82). Jevons, an engineer by training, declared utility, *marginal* utility, measured by the last item added, to be the source of value and elaborated the axiom of self-interest into a deductive system. After taking up the chair in political economy at the University of London in 1876, Jevons also re-baptised the field as 'economics', in order to neutralise the association with politics. So complete was the ideological hegemony of this economics that even the progressive Fabians who founded the London School of Economics and Political Science (LSE) in 1895 (Sydney and Beatrice Webb and the playwright George Bernard Shaw) 'had, and were proud of having, no economic theory of their own' (Bernal 1969, iv: 1099). 'Instead they accepted "scientific" economics, that is, the marginal theory.'

On the Continent, the surveillance of populations was not left to factories and Sunday schools. The contender-state perspective instead fostered secular social statistics and sociology. The Belgian astronomer Adolphe Quêtelet, author of *Social Physics* of 1835, pioneered social statistics and chaired its first international conference in 1853. By that time Auguste Comte, the secretary of Saint-Simon, had formalised his master's progressive doctrine into a scientistic philosophy of history, positivism. As we saw, for Mill this was a bridge too far; in France, however, restoring social cohesion in the aftermath of the country's traumatic revolutions was mandatory (Zeisel 1975: 122–3). In 1855, Frédéric Le Play's *The European Workers*, based on family histories gathered in 15 countries, was written to repair the damage of 1848; Émile Durkheim's sociology was intended to achieve the same in the wake of the Paris Commune. In *The Division of Labour* of 1893 (1964: 379) Durkheim urges the state to rein in social inequality and thus defuse class struggle. It took until the late nineteenth century before French universities began to accommodate the new social science. At the *École libre des sciences politiques* in Paris, founded in 1871, academics still freely engaged with trade unionists, women's rights advocates and other non-academics, whilst fields were not sharply demarcated (Giesen 2006: 22). Le Play was an amateur scholar who entertained a circle of acquaintances at his home; Comte had no academic basis either. Clark (1974: 111–13) notes how both Le Play's coterie and Comte's positivists degenerated into intolerant sects, inward-looking in the absence of career prospects for their members. Durkheim on the other hand taught social science at the University of Bordeaux before going to Paris in 1902 (holding one of the four chairs in social science in France at the time).

The state obtained in sociology a method in which it could train a dedicated cadre to enforce flexible social discipline. Therborn (1976: 225) calls sociology 'an investigative instead of a dogmatic guardian of the ideological community'. This remit implied that it had to make the quest for understanding society secondary to studying the conditions of class compromise and social control. This takes it one step away from historicising social philosophy, to what Gramsci (1971: 426) characterises as a 'philosophy of non-philosophers, an attempt to provide a schematic description and classification of historical and political facts, according to criteria built up on the model of natural science'. In Britain, the regression from classical thinking proceeded by abandoning Smith and Ricardo for a doctrine of subjective preferences combined with religion; on the European continent it relied on systematic state monitoring of the working classes. This rules out generalising from self-interest. The chief French representative of marginalist economics, Léon Walras (who taught in Lausanne), based his approach on scarcity and equilibrium; his work, Watson notes (2005: 59),'bears none of the Benthamite underpinnings of Jevons's *Theory of Political Economy'*.

The contender-state perspective was even more pronounced in Germany. Here social science was inscribed in what Wallerstein labels (2001: 192) a 'current of resistance' to liberal universalism, the *Staatswissenschaften*. German universities were not as directly geared to the recruitment of state personnel as were the *grandes écoles* established by Napoleon; even so, the privileged status of the civil service helped sustain the attraction of public employment for graduates and enshrine the central role of the state. If Humboldt's commitment to the unity of the sciences predisposed him to philosophy as the bedrock of all knowledge, the philosophy underlying the *Staatswissenschaften* in the course of the nineteenth century slipped back to pre-Hegelian thought as it resurrected the antinomies between subject and object (as in neo-Kantianism) and between materialism and idealism. German political economists like Friedrich List, whom we met in the previous chapter, dismissed the idea that the country would ever be able to industrialise by following the British free-trade model and hence were not amenable to liberal ideas. Heinrich von Treitschke, Ranke's successor as historiographer of Prussia, in 1864 argued (as in Kuczynski 1977: 171) that an ascendant country cannot afford to weaken its executive power and settle for what he called 'a state of the English/Belgian type'. When Bismarck united north Germany through the series of victorious wars that culminated in the triumph over the French in 1870, the new state was authoritarian, selectively extending citizenship and political rights to the population. The bourgeoisie, fearful of the workers and lacking a political culture of its own, modelled itself in the mirror of the antiquated feudalism of the Junkers.

The incomplete transition to a bourgeois society in countries like Germany and Italy engendered theories that would eventually re-emerge at the heart of Anglophone political science – the discipline entrusted with finding out how a majority, once enfranchised, can be held in check. The Italian conservative Gaetano Mosca in 1896 recommended developing a 'political formula' – a set of ideas and principles drawing on what he calls (1939: 71) 'one of [the] "great superstitions"' characteristic for a particular people, its 'social type'. Friedrich Nietzsche (1844–1900), who developed just such an aesthetics of politics, put war at the heart of it. He also grafts it onto ancient mythology, tapping into the regressive potential of belated ethnogenesis. In his posthumous *The Will to Power* he attributes to Manu, the legendary first king of the Aryans (1959: 484; cf. vol. ii, 2010: 91), the insight that 'we must consider all empires bordering on ours, as well as their allies, as enemies'. Naturalising the drive to power as 'inherent to the concept of life', Nietzsche (1959: 489–90) considered a society that rejects war and conquest as being in decline. 'The military state is the ultimate means ... of absorbing or retaining the supreme type of human, the strong type.'

When the working-class movement in Germany entered the political scene, the celebration of violence was modified by a social-science perspective. Like Durkheim in France, the *Katheder-sozialisten* ('socialists of the lectern') advocated a policy of class compromise. Gustav Schmoller, the first president of the *Verein für Sozialpolitik* that was dedicated to this task, developed a descriptive economics, baptised the 'historical school' on account of its evolutionary perspective. Max Weber (1864–1920) on the other hand sought to anchor class compromise in an explicitly neo-Kantian, hermeneutic theory to combat the (materialist version of) Marxism of the German-speaking labour movement. Today we label Weber a sociologist, but he is better classified under the *Staatswissenschaften* umbrella. In the *Protestant Ethic and the Spirit of Capitalism* of

1904–05 and *Economy and Society* (published posthumously in 1921), Weber sought to explain why Germany had entered the contest with the Lockean heartland so late, which remedies might help it to catch up, and how the working class was to be integrated into the state. Although he held several chairs, his last in Munich, Weber was not prominent in university life. Returning from a trip to the United States in 1904 he became one of the first European scholars to recognise that an American century was in the making; but as Rehmann highlights (1998: 20–8), the experience also left him deeply ambivalent about the prospect.

To obtain mass consent for an accelerated social modernisation, Weber puts his hope in a charismatic leader, a *Führer*. Charisma relies on magic; it operates on a different plane from the economy. It is a revolutionary force which alone is able to achieve a complete change in the mental and practical make-up of a traditional society. The Führer must be endowed with supernatural or superhuman abilities ('or at least, specifically extraordinary forces or characteristics not at the disposal of anyone else'; 1976: 140). Like Nietzsche and many other German thinkers of the epoch, Weber thought in terms of how Germany could make up for its failure to match the achievements of the liberal West by resorting to power politics. 'Weber's identification of politics with conflict', Radhika Desai writes (2001: 399), 'was also owed to Nietzsche …[in that it] exceeded the possibilities contained within … social contractarian models of politics.' The realism of Anglo-American IR is already in evidence in Weber. First he repeats the Nietzschean claim that *reality is irrational*. The dynamics of power, fed by the ubiquitous quest for prestige, triggers competition (Weber mentions France versus Germany) 'and this shows the eminent workings of the irrational element of all political foreign relations' (1976: 521).

Secondly, he posits the identity between nation(-state) and power (briefly referred to in vol. i, 2007: 12) when he writes (1976: 244):

In connection with the concept of 'nation' we always find ourselves directed to political 'power'. What is equally obviously 'national' – if it is anything unitary to begin with – is a particular kind of pathos, which binds a human group held together by a community of language, confession, habit or fate, to the thought of their own, already existing or desired organisational edifice of political power.

Hence, 'inherent in any "power" of political structures is a specific dynamic: it can develop into the basis for a specific claim to "prestige" of its members, which influences its foreign relations' (ibid.: 520). Certainly, as Giddens notes (1985: 27), the attempt to reconcile materialism and Nietzsche prevented Weber from developing a satisfactory definition of the national state or of its relation with capitalism. Perhaps that is also why his idea of a value-neutral social science lacks a social context apart from a nationalist ethics (Giesen 1992: 41n.).

Thirdly and finally, the realist 'prudence' of avoiding grand commitments (usually identified as the ground on which to posit the antinomy with IR 'idealism'), can be traced to Weber's 'ethics of responsibility'. A political decision maker should not only act on the basis of grand principles (the ethics of conviction) but should also consider the precise context of a decision, its possibilities and limits; politics as the art of the possible (Giesen 1992: 44). I shall return to Carl Schmitt's elaboration of the Nietzsche–Weber lineage below, but first look at the emergence of disciplinary academia in the United States.

The Academic Division of Labour in North America

The nineteenth-century departures from Enlightenment thought in Europe mark the beginning of the 'socially necessary' retreat from historicising social philosophy – from Hegel, Feuerbach and Marx. It was completed in the United States, where the mutations of the second half of the nineteenth century mixed with agnostic empiricism, under the supervision first of the Protestant clergy and then of business. The result was a strict disciplinary division of labour that we take for granted today, but which owes its emergence to exceptional circumstances. As Abbott concludes (2001: 123), 'The departmental structure appeared only in American universities'.

From the days of early English settlement the purpose of North American higher education had been to transmit the Protestant ethic and avoid 'rationalism'. With a curriculum consisting of the three biblical languages, grammar, logic and rhetoric, as well as arithmetic, geometry, astronomy and music (Barrow 1990: 39), the clergy in control of higher education felt confident that no godless digressions would occur. Looking beyond the original strongholds such as Harvard, Yale and Princeton, Protestant churches after independence also founded denominational colleges on the frontier. As Szasz records (2004: 15, cf. 17–18), it was felt that the diversity of immigrant populations might otherwise remain outside the WASP civic culture of New England. Such was the taboo on non-religious reflection, in combination with the practical pioneer mindset, that Tocqueville in 1840 concluded (1990, ii: 3) that 'in no country in the civilised world is less attention paid to philosophy than in the United States'.

The beginnings of social science in North America very much relied on German immigrants. Francis Lieber, an exile from Prussia in the 1820s, assimilated the Lockean creed and sang its praise in *Civil Liberty and Self-Government* of 1853. He was one of Tocqueville's principal informants on the latter's 1831 tour, but did not share the Frenchman's pessimism about mass society. Instead he felt (as in Ross 1991: 41) that 'the popular governments of England and America, with their interconnected system of institutions and their "articulated liberty", were the highest forms achieved by history'. Lieber's fellow exile, Friedrich List, did not share this appreciation. He was homesick for Germany and as early as the 1830s found out that in the United States, without 'some venture which will insure [one's] existence and future' (as in Wendler 1989: 88, cf. 79–83), one cannot be an intellectual. List's own business failed in 1837, but his critique of Smithian liberalism had meanwhile been embraced by spokesmen of the Pennsylvania manufacturers' society and advocates of protectionism such as Matthew Carey. It would become hegemonic after the Northern victory in the Civil War, when Atlantic capital accumulation came to rely on high tariff walls protecting a crash programme of railway and industrial development in the United States.

The restructuring of the US ruling class after the Civil War also entailed the reorganisation of higher education. As the original settler dynasties blended with ascendant capitalist wealth, control of the universities by the Protestant churches receded too. Clergymen had been the organic intellectuals of the mercantile elite; but as Barrow documents (1990: 39–40), the new heavy-industry bloc created by the railway boom relied on engineers and lawyers, soon to be joined by the financiers of the Atlantic economy like J.P. Morgan. Daniel C. Gilman (1831–1908, the son of a mill owner of old settler background) emerged in this transition as the key architect of the restructuring of post-Civil War academia. He relied for the task on a network largely drawn from a Yale student fraternity, Skull and Bones. Founded in 1833 by Alphonso Taft (secretary of war in the Grant administration and father of the later US president) and General William H. Russell, Skull and Bones, like other elite fraternities at the time, allowed the descendants of old

Puritan settler families to mingle with the offspring of new rich entrepreneurs. Among these, the Harrimans, Morgan's rivals in railway finance, were the most conspicuous at Yale (Sutton 1986: 17, 19; cf. my 2012: 42–3).

Ruling-class networks like the Yale 'Bonesmen' were able to play public roles of such importance because the US federal state still lacked an executive capacity in this domain. The American Social Science Association (ASSA), established in 1865 to help restore an ideological community in the wake of the traumatic Civil War, was the work of a broad coalition of reform-minded activists; it was still ecumenical, and as Fisher documents (1983: 207), academics in the ASSA freely mixed with social workers and other practitioners. Gilman however was in favour of separate disciplines, which he thought (as in Barrow 1990: 82) would avoid the duplication that plagued the railways. In 1872 Gilman became the first president of the University of California; from 1875 to 1901 he was president of Johns Hopkins, and then, until 1905, of the Carnegie Institution (devoted to basic science). He was further involved in the founding of the Peabody, Slater, and Russell Sage Foundations. His Yale classmate and fellow Bonesman Andrew White, the son of a director and stockholder of the New York Central Railroad and a board member himself, moved into university management as president of Cornell and founding president of the first professional organisation after the ecumenical ASSA, the American Historical Association (AHA) of 1884.

Gilman attached great importance to the Yale network. In 1856, upon his return from studies in Berlin, he incorporated Skull and Bones as The Russell Trust, appointing himself as treasurer (General Russell became president; Sutton 1986: 5, 66).[1] Yet Skull and Bones was not the secret conspiracy of popular folklore. Like parallel university fraternities at this juncture it was dedicated, in the words

---

1. The Russell Trust was legally closed down on 14 April 1961, two hours before the start of the Bay of Pigs operation against revolutionary Cuba (in which key roles were played by Bonesmen, notably the Bundy brothers, McGeorge in the White House and William at the State Department) and was reincorporated as RTA Inc. (Phillips 2004: 206; Rosenbaum 2000). This perhaps illustrates the degeneration of the Skull and Bones network from a progressivist ruling-class vanguard to a deep politics conduit. Especially once the membership of George W. Bush, a Bonesman like his father, became known, this fuelled a buoyant conspiracy literature. Sutton 1986 is an example, and whilst indispensable for its detail, should be consulted with due care.

of one journalist (Rosenbaum 1977, as in Sutton 1986: 201), to 'converting the progeny of the ruling class into morally serious leaders of the establishment', and this responsibility was bound to be interpreted in a variety of different ways. When a year after the founding of the AHA (which still covered history and politics) a truly disciplinary professional association was established (the American Economic Association, AEA), the conflicts surrounding it saw Bonesmen on both sides. Thus Richard T. Ely, hired by Gilman to teach political economy at Johns Hopkins, was an exponent of the *Staatswissenschaften* he had studied in Germany and of Schmoller's historical school, rebaptised 'institutionalism' in the United States. Ely's role in launching the AEA was reflected in its original commitment (as in Derber 1967: 24) to 'the State as an agency whose positive assistance is one of the indispensable conditions of human progress'. The opponents of this orientation were led by William Graham Sumner, a Protestant theologian converted to liberalism and Yale's chair in Political and Social Science from 1872. Although a Bonesman too, Sumner and his partisans stayed out of the AEA in protest.

In 1886 the Haymarket riot in Chicago (to which we owe the annual May Day) evoked widespread fear of the working class. The universities were not exempt from the rapidly changing mood. 'Academic men in the social sciences', writes Hofstadter (1955: 155), 'found themselves under pressure to trim their sails ideologically.' AHA president White warned (as in Ross 1991: 61) that the time was not far off 'when disheartened populations will hear brilliant preaching subversive of the whole system of social order'. 'The only safeguard', he claimed, 'is in a thorough provision for the checking of popular unreason, and for the spreading of right reason.' A series of dismissals of critical academics was the first step. Henry Carter Adams angered Russell Sage, benefactor of Cornell, by defending the railway strike of 1886, and after moving to the University of Michigan came under fire again for advocating socialism. Ely was forced by his AEA colleagues to 'moderate' his views and eventually resigned as secretary. Dismissed from Johns Hopkins, he was censured again for 'siding with labour' at the University of Wisconsin. Thorstein Veblen and John Commons, who further developed Ely's institutionalism (now a heterodox minority approach alongside marginalism) were both fired several times. And so on and so forth. Only when the Populist movement led by the Democrat William Jennings Bryan declined and Bryan was defeated by McKinley in the election of 1896, did the witch-hunt subside – until a new one flared up in 1918–19.

The effect was to emphasise factual expertise and academic discipline. 'In case after case of university pressure brought against social scientists in the 1880s and 1890s, the conservative and moderate professional leaders ... [made] clear the limited range of academic freedom', Ross writes (1991: 118, emphasis added). '*A degree of professional autonomy was achieved by narrowing its range.*' Discipline, in Foucault's phrase (2004: 46), is centripetal: 'it isolates, it concentrates, it encloses' – in this case, by creating new disciplinary structures to monopolise access to expert knowledge. The American Political Science Association (APSA) in 1903 was followed by the American Sociological Society (ASS) three years later; anthropology got its association much later because it first operated out of the Bureau of Ethnology at the Smithsonian Institution, established in 1897. Thus the disciplines were turned, in Abbott's words (2001: 126), into supply lines of a national academic labour market, with jobs traded at annual conventions.

Philosophical agnosticism in this setting had to be formalised to allow *inter*disciplinarity, the 'sovereign equality' between disciplines. This was achieved by pragmatism, which made the 'method' in which the common foundation of social research resides as thin as possible. Tocqueville (1990, ii: 16–17) already spoke with some disdain of scientific practice in North America as consisting of 'a brief and inattentive investigation', from which is derived 'a common relation between certain objects', only to 'hastily arrange these under one formula, in order to pass to another subject'. What the Frenchman captures is that phenomena are typically not seen as in any way intrinsically related, but as stand-alone, *externally* connected objects and practices. Behavioural psychology, which discards the notion of a substantive consciousness, in this respect prefigures pragmatism. It was picked up by Gilman again when during his stay in Germany he came across the work of Wilhelm Wundt, the founder of psychology as a separate discipline (from philosophy). Wundt's work focuses on experimentally establishing stimulus–response sequences. One of the many US students who worked in his Leipzig laboratory was G. Stanley Hall, who as Sutton relates (1986: 84–6, 90–1; cf. O'Neill 1968: 91), upon his return to the United States was hired by Gilman to teach psychology at Johns Hopkins. Hall, William James, and John Dewey, a student of Hall's, developed Wundt's ideas into so-called functional psychology, which sees the mind as an organ of adaptation; James and Dewey, along with Charles Peirce, elevated it into pragmatism as a general method. James and Peirce were members of the Cambridge Metaphysical Club in the 1870s, which declared itself opposed not just to the Paris Commune and socialism, but also to Cartesian rationalism and materialism (Shibata 1973: 18). Out of it evolved, as Collins relates (1998: 531), the Harvard philosophy department that lent pragmatism its academic credentials.

As James puts it in *Pragmatism: A New Name for Some Old Ways of Thinking* of 1907, pragmatism considers an idea true 'if it works'. With its publication, 'the intellectual horizon suddenly seemed to clear', writes Hughes (1958: 112). 'Everything became simple, direct, unequivocal. No longer was it necessary to break one's head over Kantian metaphysics and Teutonic hair-splitting'. One does not need extensive familiarity with the mainstream Anglo-American appreciation of 'Teutonic hair-splitting' (e.g. on Hegel; Russell 1961: 714–15) to understand what a relief this must have been. Of course there is a metaphysics to pragmatism too. But this has no philosophical basis, only a moral one, as expressed in the Social Gospel movement. Its protagonists included the foremost pragmatists (James, Dewey and George Herbert Mead), thinkers whom Joan Bethke Elsthain compliments (2001: 44) for refusing to traffic 'in a totalizing ideology on the Marxist model of so many European intellectuals' – as if their universalistic, missionary moralism was any less totalising (Elsthain in fact calls it a 'civil religion').

The 'vulgar evolutionism' that Gramsci (1971: 426) sees as a key characteristic of the 'philosophy for non-philosophers' underpinning the new social sciences profoundly influenced pragmatist thought. It reached North America from Britain through Henry Maine's claims concerning the 'Aryan connection' between village life in India, Germany and the Anglophone Atlantic states (and to which I refer in vol. i, 2007: 38). Along came the Darwinist interpretation of history of the London banker and editor of the *Economist* Walter Bagehot (author of *Physics and Politics* of 1872). In addition to the evolutionary continuity between the historical school and institutionalism in economics, these narratives saw Western liberty as originating in Indo-Germanic ethnogenesis, passed on (substituting an ethnic for a linguistic lineage) through the 'Teutonic chain'. With such a pedigree, Spencer's concept of the survival of the fittest made it obvious why the Lockean West had prevailed in all foreign encounters. At Yale, Sumner blended the Protestant ethic, liberal economics and social Darwinism into a single doctrine; he considered men like John D. Rockefeller and Theodore Roosevelt living proof of natural selection (Löwy 2004: 99–101). Henry Adams at Harvard and Herbert Baxter Adams at Johns Hopkins both embraced a political science which according to Ross (1991: 69) intended 'to verify, strengthen, and preach those Teutonic principles of civil liberty that now seemed threatened by change'.

Lieber too subscribed to the idea of the 'Teutonic chain' to explain Lockean liberty. His vision was endorsed by Gilman in his introduction to the posthumous fourth edition of *Civil Liberty and Self-Government* (Ross 1991: 67). By then, the legacy of the *Staatswissenschaften* was expiring and men like John W. Burgess, a Hegelian and head of the School of Political Science at Columbia established in 1880, were being censured for their pro-German leanings by colleagues such as Frank Goodnow, the first APSA president (Berndtson 1987: 88; Schmidt 1998: 48–50, 56). The Boer War and German interference in Venezuela, challenging the Monroe Doctrine, at that point worked to discredit the German link in the Teutonic chain (Vucetic 2011: 42–3; cf. vol. i, 2007: 158).

Higher education was now under the control of businessmen and corporate lawyers. The synchronisation of academic discipline and the discipline of capital over labour and society proceeded apace too. Henry S. Pritchett, president of MIT and a railway director in the Morgan group, in 1904 presented his ideas to President Theodore Roosevelt; as president of the influential Carnegie Foundation for the Advancement of Teaching, Pritchett in 1909 commissioned Frederick Taylor, the father of scientific management, to produce a blueprint for reorganising US universities. The report, by an associate of Taylor's, advised breaking up the 'guild structure' of academic life and creating a labour market for academics, with competition fostering 'greater research and teaching specialisation by faculty as a condition for promoting more intensive mass production' (Barrow 1990: 71–3). Bratsis' verdict (2006: 113n.) captures the transition: the disciplinary division of labour is a matter of 'Taylorising' it with an eye to 'standardising curricula so as to increase the "efficiency" of higher education and decrease the power of faculty by making them much more interchangeable'.

The supervision of the universities by capital and the new ruling class was accompanied by a rapprochement between the English-speaking peoples, of which Andrew Carnegie (1835–1919) made himself the most powerful advocate. Having emigrated to the United States as a boy in 1848, Carnegie used the proceeds of the sale of his iron and steel interests to J.P. Morgan, the architect of US corporate restructuring in the 'Gilded Age' to erect a series of foundations which until the end of the Second World War remained the largest group of philanthropic institutions in the United States. Dedicating his vast fortune to the propagation and dissemination of knowledge and understanding 'among the peoples of the United States and the British Dominions and colonies' (as in Nielsen 1985: 136), Carnegie too embraced Spencer's teachings, arguing (as in Parmar 2012: 62) for a 'race alliance' of the white English-speaking peoples. Starting with a public-library programme in the United States, Britain, and the settler colonies, Carnegie's first institutional establishment was the Carnegie Institute of Pittsburgh of 1896. The Carnegie Institute of Technology (today's Carnegie-Mellon University) followed in 1900. I have already mentioned the Carnegie Institution under Gilman and the Carnegie Foundation for the Advancement of Teaching under Pritchett. On the latter's board of trustees were Nicholas Murray Butler, president of Columbia University and a trustee of New York Life Insurance, and Woodrow Wilson, then still president of Princeton and a board member of Mutual Life, an insurance concern closely linked to Morgan (Tournès 2010: 14; Burch 1981, ii: 207). The final building block of the Carnegie empire was the Carnegie Corporation of 1911, set up to manage the founder's vast remaining wealth. It was administered by Carnegie himself until his death.

With the Carnegie Endowment for International Peace established in 1910 we move into the realm of world politics. Carnegie conceived foreign relations in the terms that would eventually constitute the groundwork of the discipline of IR – a global governance exercised by the white Anglophone states, combined with open nation-states modelled after them. The 'Teutonic nations' from this perspective were the true nation builders, Schmidt records (1998: 69): 'American Indians, Asiatics and Africans … can only receive, learn, follow Aryan example.' Already in 1887 Carnegie introduced a British parliamentary delegation to President Cleveland to plead for an arbitration treaty between Britain and the United States. It was signed two years later, but the Senate failed to ratify it by three votes, after which it took until 1911 before a treaty was finally put into effect. Two years later, Tournès relates (2010: 32), Carnegie in a lecture at St Andrews in his native Scotland proposed to create a League of Peace, with a court of arbitration guaranteed by the great powers – the United States, Russia, Britain, France and Germany, but without Japan, victorious in that year's war against Russia but not white or Christian.

The arbitration movement emerged from the Hague Peace Conferences of 1899 and 1907 – the period in which the labour movement committed itself to its own peace. To house a Permanent Court of Arbitration, Carnegie had the Peace Palace built in The Hague; it was completed in 1913 and eventually became the seat of the International Court of Justice. Back in the United States, William H. Taft was the chairman of the American Society for the International Settlement of Disputes (the forerunner of the League to Enforce the Peace, which in turn laid the groundwork for the League of Nations); its president was Theodore Marburg, like Taft a Yale Bonesman (Sutton 1986: 27, 32). At the State Department, Columbia law scholar and assistant secretary J.B. Moore worked to help prepare the US role in shaping the international arbitration machinery (Schmidt 1998: 65–7). Taft followed in the footsteps of Roosevelt in developing a policy of expansion when he had his run as US president from 1909 to 1913. Both presidents embraced the ideas of Captain Mahan, the advocate of sea power, and combined a classical gunboat attitude towards the Western hemisphere with a liberal 'open door' imperialism for the rest of the world, alongside Britain (Hofstadter 1955: 91). Taft consolidated the Carnegie connection when he appointed Philander Knox, legal counsel to the Scotsman's steel interests, as his secretary of state. Elihu Root, secretary of war under McKinley and promoted to the State Department by Roosevelt after McKinley's assassination, became the first president of the Carnegie Endowment for International Peace.

By then Taft had taken his progressivist credentials beyond the point Theodore Roosevelt deemed proper (by filing antitrust suits against key Morgan group corporations such as US Steel and International Harvester; Burch 1981, ii: 173–4). The ensuing feud split the Republican Party, opening the way for Woodrow Wilson's victory in 1912.

A WORLD MADE SAFE FOR DEMOCRACY

The Russian Revolution posed a momentous challenge to the ruling classes on both sides of the Atlantic. In his response to the challenge of socialist internationalism Woodrow Wilson reactivated the liberal imperial tradition developed by Britain in the eighteenth and nineteenth centuries. 'Just as Bentham, a century earlier, had taken the eighteenth-century doctrine of reason and refashioned it to the needs of the coming age,' Carr famously phrased it (1964: 27), 'so now Woodrow Wilson, the impassioned admirer of Bright and Gladstone, transplanted the nineteenth-century rationalist faith to the almost virgin soil of international politics.' In the process, exploratory, intuitive statesmanship and scholarship would be socialised into academic discipline dedicated to the preservation of Western supremacy.

The opportunities for creating client nation-states cut off from illiberal empires this time were vastly larger than after Napoleon's demise. If in 1814–15 only territorial issues were on the table because the peacemakers represented solidly conservative ruling classes, in 1918–19 revolution was spreading in Germany, along the Danube (with a focus in Budapest), in the Balkans and in Turkey. The 'souls' of old had become claimants to sovereignty. A statistical committee like the one active at Vienna, to cite Mayer (1967: 372), 'could not instantly have provided the political intelligence required for lasting decisions'. In the words of Neil Smith (2004: 177), 'a new assertion of global rights was filtered into the lexicon of territorial settlement … ethnic difference became the crucial political language of the [Versailles] conference' – although the final minority provisions were still labelled 'racial', 'linguistic' or 'religious', not 'national' (Liebich 2008: 245).

Nation-Building Against Revolution

Wilson early on recognised that the Anglophone heartland would have to guide the process of bourgeois emancipation in the great land empires. 'The East is to be opened and transformed whether we will or no; the standards of the West are to be imposed upon it', he explained in a piece for the *Atlantic Monthly* in 1901. 'Nations and peoples which had stood still the centuries through are to be quickened, and made part of the universal world of commerce and of ideas which has so steadily been a-making by the advance of European power from age to age'.

It is our particular duty, as it is also England's, to moderate the process in the interests of liberty; to impart to the peoples thus driven out upon the road of change … the habit of law … which we long ago got out of the strenuous processes of English history; secure for them, when we may, the free intercourse and the natural development which shall make them at last equal members of the family of nations (Wilson 1901).

By envisioning a League of Nations to govern a global political economy of open nation-states, Wilson created a factual identity between Western supremacy and transnational capitalism. The League idea had been around for some time, and issues like arbitration, collective security, and periodic international conferences assigned with the task of codifying international law had already been discussed in depth. Wilson committed himself to this package in May 1916, solemnly rejecting US involvement in the European war. Once re-elected, however, he immediately began preparing for a European intervention by replacing the Populist Bryan by the pro-British lawyer Robert Lansing at the State Department. In January 1917 Wilson then consulted Congress on the issue, characteristically placing the war aims in a universalistic context. Although the principles he had expounded were American principles, the president explained that 'they are also the principles and policies of forward looking men and women everywhere, of every modern nation, of every enlightened community. *They are the principles of mankind and must prevail'* (Wilson 1919: 14, emphasis added).

He then added the principle of national self-determination, taking Anglo-American dominion over Latin America as his model. As he put it in his address to the Senate on 22 January 1917 (1919: 12, 14):

I am proposing, as it were, that the nations should with one accord adopt the doctrine of President Monroe as the doctrine of the world: that no nation should seek to extend its polity over any other nation or people, but that every people should be left free to determine its own polity, its own way of development, unhindered, unthreatened, unafraid, the little along with the great and powerful.

The October Revolution later in the year dissipated any hopes for an equitable application of the Wilson project. The Bolsheviks demanded an immediate end to the war and called for world socialist revolution. Where necessary, socialists should concede a prior national autonomy and secession along the lines of the programme Lenin and Stalin had worked out. In early December the two men (Stalin meanwhile as People's Commissar for the Nationalities) issued an appeal to the 'labouring Moslems of Russia and the East' and annulled the pre-war agreement between Britain and Russia to partition Persia, along with comparable designs against Turkey and Armenia. At the opening of the peace conference at Brest-Litovsk on the 22nd of the month, Trotsky, the People's Commissar for Foreign Affairs, issued an appeal (as in Fischer 1960: 15) to the 'Oppressed and Bled Peoples of Europe'; but by now the counter-revolutionary implications of national state formation were all too evident. The imperial German delegation promptly subscribed to the demand for national self-determination; it legitimated their occupation of Poland, Lithuania and Ukraine, 18 provinces of pre-war Russia in all. The German foreign ministry in November 1918 acknowledged (as in Mayer 1967: 229) that 'encouragement of the formation of border states' would serve German security and weaken Russia – a policy that still resonates today.

Wilson's 'Fourteen Points' pronounced on 8 January 1918 combined national self-determination with liberal global governance (economic liberty and the League). In practice, this worked to create a *cordon sanitaire* in Eastern Europe against the spread of revolution; twelve countries including the United States simultaneously sent troops and money to strangle it in Russia. The revolutionary leadership in Russia certainly had no difficulty recognising that the American president applied national self-determination selectively. 'You demand the independence of Poland, Serbia, Belgium, and freedom for the people of Austro-Hungary', Karl Radek wrote in an exchange of notes between the Bolsheviks and Wilson later in the year (as in Fischer 1960: 102). 'But strangely we do not notice in your demands any mention of freedom for Ireland, Egypt, India, or even the Philippine Islands.' Social Democrats on the other hand joined the Wilson crusade unreservedly. As a result, 'European Socialism was fast becoming an integral part of the bourgeois, capitalist, and counterrevolutionary amalgam which, frightened by Bolshevism, proposed to fight it' (Mayer 1967: 409).

Both the Western liberal and the revolutionary socialist concepts of national self-determination were tactical, ancillary to the strategic goal of class formation from either angle. What Wilson added was the tremendous power of the society he represented. Once the president arrived in Paris, Dillon reported (2004: 38), 'The war-weary masses judged him not by what he had achieved or attempted in the past, but by what he proposed to do in the future. And measured by this standard, his spiritual stature grew to legendary proportions.' Essentially, Wilson's projection of liberal global governance over an 'international community' was inspired by the Lockean rights doctrine against encroaching authority. His entourage was still uncertain which entities he actually had in mind when speaking about self-determination – the existing states, or the constituent nationalities (Sluga 2005: 1-2). Given that rights are innate, and hence universal, they can be upheld against any power deemed illegitimate – in 1917, against the empires holding the nations captive, but equally against socialist internationalism, or, today, against any state not submitting to Western dominion. Yet the subject executing that right was ideally the property-owning individual, not a collective.

The quest was therefore for a client governing class capable of consolidating bourgeois class formation and 'good governance'. That class could then be entrusted with the keys of new or reconstituted states on the condition it leave the door open. The State Department (as in Mayer 1967: 34) urged the president to invest power in centrist liberals, whom the Department held were nationalists; but nationalists 'who insist that every nation has a right to be treated as an end in itself ... and [who] therefore hope to see established a supernational authority as justiciar between peoples'. Adhering to the 'benign national patriotism' of the Anglophone world (Sluga 2005: 7, 8), they would, according to a memorandum to Wilson (as in my 2012: 55), 'rapidly accept the leadership of the President if he undertakes a liberal diplomatic offensive'. However, as Keynes, who resigned from the British delegation at Versailles in protest over the punitive reparations imposed on Germany, wrote of the experience, this leadership proved less formidable once deployed in the conference room. 'It was commonly believed ... that the President had thought out, with the aid of a large body of advisers, a comprehensive scheme', he observed (1920: 39). 'In fact the President had thought out nothing ... his ideas were nebulous and incomplete ... he was in many respects, perhaps inevitably, ill-informed as to European conditions.' Only by tying it to a peace treaty could Wilson secure his League Covenant (Dillon 2004: 39); other themes such as the freedom of the seas were dismissed.

The British and French effectively guided the discussions (Clemenceau was the only leader speaking both languages used at the conference). They resisted not only the application of self-determination to the colonies but also threw into doubt the durability of new governments in East and Central Europe. Of course as Joseph

Grew, secretary to the US delegation at Versailles, observed at the time (1953, i: 339), 'America can fight for two more years while they cannot.' But whilst 'Wilson and his advisers did their best to press the Allies into helping the "receiver" and successor governments ... to consolidate themselves' (Mayer 1967: 9), Jan Smuts, the South African general on the Imperial War Council, spoke for the conservative European governments when he considered (as in Seaman 1964: 209) 'the people left behind by the decomposition of Russia, Austria and Turkey mostly untried politically'. On another occasion he proposed (as in Mayer 1967: 8) that the mandate system be extended to make the League 'the trustee of the politically untrained peoples', i.e. also of the new states carved off imperial Russia and Austria–Hungary. The insistence of having Western-style nation-states here wreaked its first round of havoc. 'The two Anglo-Saxon governments by enforcing their theories about the protection of minorities and other political conceptions in various states of Europe helped to loosen the cement of the politico-social structure there', ran the contemporary verdict of Dillon (2004: 21, cf. 3). As a result, 'Europe [was transformed] into a seething mass of mutually hostile states powerless to face the economic competition of their overseas rivals' – the English-speaking West.

From the Milner Group to the Inquiry

Bringing discipline to the idea of liberal governance over a world of open nation-states was critically inflected by the outbreak of the Bolshevik Revolution that threatened to undermine Western supremacy. The 'demagogy choreographed in Paris' of which Gramsci speaks could not under these circumstances be relied on to withstand the appeal of the theories of imperialism that plausibly explained the unprecedented massacre of the Great War as the result of intersecting circuits of transnational capital, dragging states into their conflicts of interest – states often actively pursuing chauvinist campaigns to undercut working-class internationalism. But as Krippendorff writes (1982: 27), accepting the world order as imperialist implied calling into question the bourgeois order itself.

The Anglo-American ruling classes from the turn of the century had geared up intellectual preparations for dealing with the challenge of mass democracy. In Britain, the Milner Group provided the focus to this process. There is no need to rehearse again the origins of this group in the secret society launched by the imperialist adventurer and financier Cecil Rhodes, with the journalist William T. Stead and

Lord Esher (Reginald Baliol Brett), a confidant of Queen Victoria and two subsequent monarchs. Mindful of Rhodes' warning to Stead that only imperialism could avert revolution (famously cited by Lenin in *Imperialism, the Highest Stage of Capitalism, Coll. Works*, xxii: 256–7), Alfred Milner, the executor of Rhodes' will, became the guiding spirit of the group that took over the leading role in the British ruling class from the defunct 'Cecil Bloc' (the extended family lineage going back to Elizabethan times and culminating in the government of Lord Salisbury). As Quigley documents (1981), the Milner Group elaborated the class compromise suggested by Rhodes into an imperialist mythology in which the 'English-speaking idea' warrants the global spread of its civilisation. The Group held key positions in the empire and, during the war, in the Lloyd George government (with Lord Milner as secretary of war, Philip Kerr, the future Lord Lothian, as secretary to the prime minister, and Smuts as a member of the Imperial War Cabinet, to name but a few). In the 1930s and 1940s the group would be transformed from within by new money, notably the Beit Trust, the Astors, and City merchant banks such as Lazard's. By then ascendant industries were in the process of separating from the imperialists and worked for appeasement with Nazi Germany, tearing apart the Milner Group eventually.

The original Milner Group drew up its programme in response to the rise of Germany as the new contender. Recruiting members from Oxford colleges such as All Souls, the Group's focus was on finding ways to strengthen the Anglophone bond, first by organising the so-called colonial conferences to draw the dominions closer together again. A Committee of Imperial Defence from 1902 set the agenda for these conferences and provided continuity. As Jordan writes (1971: 29), this crystallised the British tradition of a permanent secretariat, transmitted to the League and later to the United Nations. The Esher Report of 1904 defined the tasks of such a secretariat as comprehensive and anticipatory, intended to make vital strategic commitments immune from changes in the governing class and shifting public moods. Lord Esher also made an effort to propagate the idea of liberal global governance over a world of open nation-states, as when he launched a foundation to disseminate the ideas of the journalist and Labour MP Norman Angell (1872–1967).

Angell as a young man emigrated to the United States and after many odd jobs became a newspaper reporter. Having returned to Europe towards the turn of the century, he made his name in 1910 with *The Great Illusion*, a pacifist manifesto that would earn him a Nobel Peace Prize after the war. Angell shared Hobson's opposition to the Boer War but dismissed the association with capitalism, appealing to common sense instead. As he put it in the foreword of his magnum opus (1913: x–xi):

For a modern nation to add to its territory no more adds to the wealth of the people of such a nation than it would add to the wealth of Londoners if the City of London were to annex the county of Hertford.

Since the people were easily aroused in foreign relations, Angell in the spirit of Esher (as in de Wilde 1991: 88) recommended informal policy planning to avoid being drawn along on a wave of religious or nationalist emotions, which might propel the government into the wrong conflict from a ruling-class point of view. 'It is the business of those outside politics to prepare the ground for the wiser politician'.

This was exactly how Wilson in the United States had come to view the operation of politics. In his studies with Herbert Baxter Adams and Ely at Johns Hopkins, Wilson had still imbibed the *Staatswissenschaft* perspective (Schmidt 1998: 59–60), but like Bagehot in Britain, Wilson later 'found that around the formal structure of political offices and institutions there were all kinds of informal behaviour and organizations in which power over decision making might lie' (Easton 1985: 134). The National Civic Foundation (NCF), established in 1900 by progressivist businessmen ready to work with organised labour, and of which Wilson was a member (like his predecessor Taft, but also Franklin Roosevelt and many other corporate liberals), was different from exclusive, elitist networks like the Yale Bonesmen. Like the Cecil bloc in England, these would not have been equipped to meet the challenge of the growing working class, which in the United States was responsive to Bryan's Populism, to anarchism and socialism. But whereas the Milner Group in Britain projected a class compromise in the context of imperialism, the NCF situated it in industry and did not develop a foreign policy programme.

So when Wilson took the United States into the European war, the absence of policy planning was acutely felt. His chief of staff, Colonel Edward House, had confidentially urged the British government as early as 1915 to take post-war planning seriously (Nielson 1992: 230), but little had been done. The US State Department belatedly suggested to Secretary Lansing to set up a planning body, but the president already took that step himself. 'Dilatory in planning for war,' O'Toole writes (1991: 310), 'Wilson (who so often had made up foreign policy out of his hat), had grasped the necessity of planning for peace.' This was then given shape as the 'Inquiry', a body composed eventually of 126 academics. Colonel House put his brother-in-law, Sydney E. Mezes, a philosopher of religion and president of City College of New York, at its head, but Wilson instructed that Mezes be assisted by Walter Lippmann (1899–1974). Lippmann was a Harvard graduate, former socialist and journalist, whose advocacy of an English-speaking Atlantic community in the *New Republic* (see my 2012: 53–5) had won the confidence of the president's inner circle. Importantly he was a member of the American Round Table group, the US branch of a network named after a British imperial magazine started by the Milner Group in 1910 (Shoup and Minter 1977: 13). With the Inquiry in place in September 1917, Neil Smith writes (2004: 135), 'For the first time, rather than simply responding to events, the government attempted to provide a systematic worldview ahead of time.'

When the Bolsheviks on the eve of the Brest negotiations issued their calls for world revolution, House summoned Lippmann 'to get the Inquiry busy on preparing a policy proposal for the president'. As O'Toole relates (1991: 306), its report was ready on the day the peace conference began. Using maps, demographic and economic statistics, and studies of European national political movements, the team redrew the frontiers of Europe and the president's Points 6 to 13 of January 1918 on national self-determination were 'taken almost verbatim from the Inquiry report'. Lippmann was then sent to Britain to explain the Fourteen Points – essentially the work of his own outfit. Indeed to get to the origins and orientation of the IR discipline, what counted was the Wilsonian inspiration of the Inquiry, not so much the disappointing performance of the president in Paris, where his contribution in Keynes' estimate (1920: 38), proved 'essentially theological not intellectual'.

The Inquiry's Wilsonian perspective transpires in the views of Isaiah Bowman, the director of the American Geographical Society. With Harvard's Charles H. Haskins and two international historians from Columbia University, the Canadian-born James T. Shotwell and George L. Beer (US correspondent of *The Round Table*), Bowman guided the work of the Inquiry, a task he considered to be aimed at moderating the revolutionary tide. 'In a sense the whole world is in revolt all the time', he would note a few years later (as in Smith 2004: 206). 'All that we care about is that it shall be a thoughtful revolt and a gradual one.' To guide this process, the Inquiry's tasks in September 1918 were listed in the Preliminary Survey for the Paris Peace Conference as 'drawing boundaries, setting up governments, safeguarding minorities, providing equal economic opportunity, [and] writing international law and diplomatic history' (Nielson 1992: 234). In addition, it provided a number of experts for the American Commission to Negotiate Peace, whilst linking up with the Milner Group to plan for a joint Anglo-American international affairs institute.

The work of the Inquiry was marred by continuous friction. Groups working for the State Department were often at loggerheads with those working for Colonel House directly (Nielson 1992: 231). Upon their arrival in Paris, Bowman had secured for the group the official title, 'Territorial, Economic, and Political Intelligence Section', but Grew in his memoirs (1953, i: 383) calls it just 'the Intelligence Section (Dr. Mezes' Committee)', mentioning future CIA director Allen W. Dulles and other section heads with their respective areas of responsibility (Dulles' was Austria–Hungary). The subordination of US scholarship to the state as providers of 'intelligence' has remained a characteristic of the discipline of IR for which the Inquiry paved the way. In this respect it was different from the only earlier example of a 'brains trust' – the one assembled by Wisconsin Governor La Follette from the state university at Madison (Hofstadter 1955: 155). The experience also gave a foretaste of the mindset of the foreign policy intellectual in the United States, for whom the frontier to explore is a practical, not a scholarly one. Thus in Nielson's words (1992: 237),

The historians ... were in positions for which few had experience or training ... Even so, an elated [Yale historian Charles] Seymour could boast, for example, 'I am now running the entire show as far as Austria–Hungary is concerned', and he seemed undaunted that he now had 'the entire responsibility for seeing that the Commissioners get the right facts as well as advice on policy'.

In February 1919, the 'black books' and 'red books' with the Inquiry's recommendations were passed on to Wilson. Its specialists were then distributed over more than 60 committees set up by the Paris conference, diluting the Inquiry's collective impact. Beer, according to Nielson (1992: 248), was one of the most influential scholars of the Inquiry in Paris, because he came up with the idea of the mandates system, although he shared credit with Smuts for it. Otherwise 'Mr. Lloyd George and Mr. Wilson made short work of the reports of the expert commissions whenever these put forward reasoned views differing from their own', Dillon reported at the time (2004: 51). 'They became the world's supreme and secret arbiters without ceasing to be the official champions of the freedom of the lesser states and of "open covenants openly arrived at".'

Foundations of the IR Discipline

As a political scientist, having been president of the APSA and of Princeton, Wilson looked upon the social sciences as crucial in providing the framework for a reform-oriented, empirical policy. 'Wilson's Burkean historicism ratified gradual change, organically linked to the past' (Ross 1991: 265). His interest in the study of opinion rather than institutions led him to accept a position as vice-president of the International Sociology Institute in 1920 under the Czechoslovak president, Tomas Masaryk (Therborn 1976: 142). With respect to international relations, 'gradual change organically linked to the past' hinged on nationality and the nation-state; but in the absence of a disciplinary lineage comparable to sociology or economics, the step from constitutional and international law to social science was less easily made. For Wilson, nationality was the aspiration to have a bourgeois civil society. 'The Anglo-Saxon essence of English and American nationality attested to the abilities of these heterogeneous states to unify their disparate national and racial selves' (Sluga 2005: 8–10). For a man like Masaryk on the other hand, who spent the war exiled in London, nationality was a world away from Lockean liberalism or a Burkean concept of civic compromise – otherwise he might as well have remained in Austria. In Masaryk's journal *The New Europe* (edited by R.W. Seton-Watson), nationhood was defined in the organic tradition of Rousseau and Herder, as 'will' and 'self'. This exposed *The New Europe* to criticism by Angell, Hobson, and others who doubted the idea of national identity in the first place. That the journal denied the colonies, as well as Ireland, the right to sovereignty because they had no 'self' was not enough to convince Anglophone liberals that continental statesmen would be inclined to subordinate their nation-states to Western governance. Yet that was the premise of the Wilson project.

On 30 May 1919, Lippmann, along with Shotwell, Thomas Lamont, chief banker of the J.P. Morgan firm, and Whitney Shepardson, secretary of the American Round Table Group, met Lionel Curtis, secretary of the Round Table, in a hotel in Paris to discuss a joint Institute of International Affairs (on Curtis, cf. vol. ii,

2010: 116, 183, 193–4). As Shoup and Minter document (1977: 16), the Institute failed to materialise in its original, transatlantic format when the mood in the United States turned away from Wilson's universalism. The US branch merged into the wartime Council on Foreign Relations (CFR) and the British settled for a Royal Institute for International Affairs (RIIA, Chatham House). Elihu Root, former president of the Carnegie Endowment, became honorary president of the CFR; the president was John W. Davis, chief legal counsel to J.P. Morgan, Wilson's ambassador in London and Democratic presidential candidate in 1924 (Burch 1981, ii: 222). The RIIA in 1925 was placed under the directorship of the historian and Milner Group member Arnold J. Toynbee, who had worked at the Foreign Office during the war and would remain at the helm of the RIIA until 1955. The question then was how these policy-planning bodies would function as channels linking actual policymaking and the academic intelligence base.

This itself is a moment of modern state formation. As the example of the Skull and Bones network illustrates, the socialisation of individual knowledge into collective intelligence requires a dedicated social agency; at a particular level of socialisation it is the state that takes on this role. Hence Neil Smith (2004: 121) correctly interprets the beginnings of a scientific approach to foreign policy, exemplified by the Inquiry episode, as part of the evolution of the United States into a 'politically coherent nation-state'. Lippmann played a crucial role in the process. At Harvard he had studied with William James and he was a close friend of Graham Wallas, the LSE political scientist whose writings stress the importance of a psychological approach to politics (Sluga 2005: 6). Lippmann feared that the Lockean West, with its individualism and self-government, would not be able to meet the challenge of the contender states in the field of science. Like Elihu Root, who in a lecture for the Carnegie Institution in 1918 argued (as in Jenkins 2002: 15) that 'the effective number of a great number of scientific men may be increased by organization just as the effective power of labourers may be increased by military discipline', Lippmann believed that knowledge production should be socialised under state auspices. This would generate a system in which intelligence percolates from academia into the halls of power and back. In such a structure, he explains in his seminal *Public Opinion* of 1922 (2010: 246), a new type of social scientist would emerge, no longer puzzled by historical riddles but 'tak[ing] his place in front of decision instead of behind'.

Thus if the State Department wants to know the extent of Mexican oil reserves, it should be able to turn to a 'central clearing house', and this, Lippmann specifies (2010: 257, in the chapter entitled 'Intelligence Work'), should be constituted by the social sciences. Relevant government information in turn 'would traverse concretely the whole gamut of the social sciences'.

It is difficult to see why all this material, except a few diplomatic and military secrets, should not be open to the scholars of the country. It is here that the political scientist would find the real nuts to crack and the real researches for his students to make. The work need not all be done in Washington, but it could be done in reference to Washington. *The central agency would, thus, have in it the making of a national university* (emphasis added).

It is then a matter, Lippmann explains in the same passage, to ensure there is a constant mutual exposure and actual circulation of personnel between government and academia – 'thus the training and the recruiting of the staff would go together … and political science in the universities would be associated with politics in America'.

Here then was a proposal to generalise the Inquiry experience into a permanent academic intelligence base by placing disciplinary social science at the disposal of the state. It involves what Gramsci theorises (1975, iii: 1551) as the process of replacing 'traditional' by 'organic' intellectuals, who are actively involved in shaping and covering ruling class hegemony. The shift involves abandoning all scholarly aesthetic and affect for the study of practical life. With their labour socialised (recall the Taylorisation of academia initiated by MIT's Pritchett), academics would become 'permanent persuaders'; passing on, through research and teaching, along with a particular set of legitimate concepts, a definite set of methodological principles applying across disciplines. Lippmann speaks (2010: 247) of the 'beginning of experimental method in social science'. Thus is put in place what Parmar describes (2002: 240) as an 'organized intellect' – 'non-partisan, disinterested and dedicated to "public service"'.

Discipline under these circumstances is ensured, paradoxically, by *inter*disciplinarity. For 'not only [is interdisciplinarity] completely consistent with disciplinarity', Menand writes (2001: 52, emphasis added): '*it actually depends on that concept*'. Indeed what is consistently pursued is the elimination of *non*-disciplinary, 'undisciplined' forms of thinking *in all fields*. 'Somewhat more cynically,' Abbott notes (2001: 135n.), 'inter-disciplinarity could also be viewed as a bind for shifting the whole university structure to a "problem-centred" one'. Wallerstein conveys the same when he writes (2001: 239) that 'the lauding of the merits of inter-disciplinary work in the social sciences has so far not significantly undermined the strengths of the organizational apparatuses that shield the separate disciplines. Indeed, the contrary may be true.' The discipline first of all serves to discipline the academics themselves, narrowing their claim to expertise; an IR student introduced to the field via the antinomy of idealism and realism, will hesitate to have a view on, say, psychoanalysis versus behavioural psychology, and vice versa for a psychology student. Hence 'in most substantive areas there is what to outsiders seems like an amazing lack of reciprocal knowledge' (Abbott 2001: 142). But this is just how interdisciplinarity keeps experts corralled in for functional problem-solving. For anything not part of the standard curriculum, ask an expert! It all begins at the teaching stage with what Collins calls (1998: 521) 'rote learning, narrow technique, and a routine of exercises and exams', even though it is only 'among intersecting factions at a focus of attention that creativity exists'.

The academic intelligence base that class strategists like Root and Lippmann were calling for was already being shaped through research projects financed by the large foundations, beginning with the Carnegie network. The Carnegie Endowment study of the causes of the Balkan wars begun in 1911 in Berne, Switzerland, was the first of these. The project's members, including the former Austrian finance minister and economist E. von Böhm-Bawerk, the Fabian journalist H.N. Brailsford, Samuel T. Dutton of Columbia University, and others, toured the region to find those guilty of atrocities and recommended that these might have been prevented by Western intervention (Tournès 2010: 42–3, cf. 20). By adopting a political-justice perspective instead of a political-economy one, the Carnegie project pointed the way for the emerging discipline. After the Great War it was continued by Shotwell, of the Inquiry and the CFR, now under the heading *The Economic and Social History of the World War*. Between 1921 and 1937, this project, with its 14 national secretariats, some of which had already been recruited before the war, produced more than 300 monographs. There were other important studies, like Charles K. Webster's comparison, commissioned by the Foreign Office, between Vienna and Versailles on boundary changes, reparations, colonial redistribution and the creation of new international organisations, but nothing that compared with the Carnegie project.

The Rockefeller charities had meanwhile taken their place too in the structure of socialised science. In 1892 Rockefeller began the project of building the University of Chicago from a small Baptist college into one of the key centres of learning in the nation (Nielsen 1985: 84). To evade taxation and streamline their philanthropy, Rockefeller and his son, J.D. Rockefeller Jr., in 1913 launched the eponymous foundation. A massacre among striking workers at a Rockefeller mine the next year led the younger Rockefeller to plead for class compromise. Briefly thereafter, as Ryan and Scott document (1995: 443–4), he became involved in ecumenical Christianity, establishing the Institute of Social and Religious Research and the Laymen's Foreign Mission Inquiry, both devoted to 'practical Christianity as the key to harmonious relations between capitalists and labour'. Foreign affairs entered into the Rockefeller purview via medical research. The sanitation campaign it financed from 1910 in Latin America (where US troops had died of yellow fever) or the anti-TB campaign the Foundation mounted from 1917 when Wilson declared war on Germany and began shipping troops to France, signalled that the Rockefellers fine-tuned their concerns to US foreign policy (Tournès 2010: 11–12; this still holds for its role in the International HIV/AIDS Alliance; Elbe 2009: 121). The General Education Board established in 1912 was the final component of the pre-war Rockefeller network, highlighting the importance of teaching and curriculum development – in brief, discipline.

After the war, the manager of the Rockefellers' General Education Fund and the Laura Spelman Rockefeller Memorial Fund (founded in 1918), Beardsley Ruml, was instrumental in creating the first large-scale *public* funding institution of US social science. At the tender age of 26, Ruml, a psychologist, decided that the social sciences were the key to solving post-war problems. He thus geared the Spelman Fund away from humanitarian assistance and towards the social sciences, which should adopt empirical methods and focus on the application of results. The social scientist was to be an expert in the service of the running of society, not just an independent thinker (Scot 2010: 86; Fisher 1983: 209). Ruml, Ross relates (1991: 401) welded the particular interests of the foundations into a comprehensive research and method-oriented body, the Social Science Research Council (SSRC), launched in 1923, a year after Lippmann's call to arms. As Ruml claimed at its first annual conference (as in Karl 1974: 135), the aim of the SSRC was a rupture with the traditional concept of academic life and a new emphasis on a common methodological approach. 'SSRC funds and exchange were a major catalyst for the focus of social science on scientific method' (Ross 1991: 401).

The paradox explained above, that interdisciplinarity is at the heart of disciplinary organisation, was outlined by the SSRC itself in its first ten-year review. 'Concern with the inter-discipline or interstitial project', it states (as in Abbott 2001: 131, emphasis added), was meant to generate new insight and problems, 'new methods leading to advances in the scientific quality of social investigations, *cross-fertilization of the social disciplines*'. Only by adhering to compatible methods would channels be created through which each discipline could transmit its findings. This would not happen if specialisations follow their own course, since 'in the centre of established fields ... points of view and problems and methodology have become relatively fixed'. This turns discipline into a vector of control. SSRC and foundation influence, according to Ross (1991: 404), by 1925 resulted in a noticeable 'shift from understanding to control' as the strategic aim of social science in the United States. The same terminology resonates in a 1927 Rockefeller report claiming (as in Fisher 1983: 213) that social science must 'increase the body of knowledge which in the hands of competent technicians may be expected ... to result in substantial social control'.

In political science, the key figure in the transition was Charles E. Merriam (1874–1953), who worked closely with Ruml (Karl 1974: 61, 131–4). A US propaganda officer in Italy during the First World War and influenced by pragmatists G.H. Mead and Dewey, Merriam was a member of the NCF; but this organisation was no longer the progressive body that had sought to meet labour's demands halfway (Ross 1991: 458). For Merriam too (1945: v), a social science driven by 'method' and aimed at achieving 'control' was the way forward. Like Ruml he felt that social science lagged behind natural science, both in organisation and in method; 'social forces' should be studied to achieve a level of control comparable to that achieved in physics (Fisher 1983: 211). Merriam's manifesto for a new science of politics based on the empirical study of the sociological and psychological bases of politics and using quantitative methods dates from 1921. His students V.O. Key, David Truman, Herbert Simon, and Gabriel Almond would take this revolution forward after the war (Gilman 2003: 115).

Harold D. Lasswell (1902–78) occupies a special place here. 'In Lasswell,' writes Ross (1991: 457), 'Merriam found the psychological and scientific capacity he himself lacked and perhaps also found a voice for the disappointment in politics he could not quite express.' Lasswell's own interest in psychology and Freudian psychoanalysis dated from his Harvard studies with the labour relations specialist Elton Mayo; the Rockefeller Foundation supported his work early on (Parmar 2012: 282–3, n.78). In *Psychopathology and Politics* of 1930 Lasswell provides a new argument for the irrationality of the masses, which he situates in their respective cultural contexts (1960: 250–1, 262–3). In each context, 'administrators' committed to the public cause can prevent the masses from falling under the spell of emotionally blocked 'agitators'. This is Mosca all over again, this time connected to Freud and cast as a programme for training a dedicated cadre who can steer people to calmer waters. Lasswell also touched on the role of the military. In a prophetic piece he argues (1941: 455) 'that we are moving to a world of "garrison states" – a world in which the specialists on violence are the most powerful group in society'. The argument is a variation on James Burnham's *Managerial Revolution*, published later that year; like Burnham's, Lasswell's Spartan dystopia postulates a trend potentially affecting all types of society, even those like Britain and the United States committed to 'a federation of democratic free nations' (1941: 468–9). The thesis was presented as a thought experiment, exploratory like much of his writing; nothing like the method-based work that Lippmann, Merriam and Ruml had called for. After the war, however, Lasswell would become a leading figure in the disciplinary programme.

In the field of IR, the new regime was even slower in coming. IR built on what Giesen calls (1992: 14) a 'moralistic founding myth' that ascribes to all peoples of the world the innate right to the 'pursuit of happiness' – threatened by illiberal authority but protected and fostered by the West. How to put this into method-based research was not easy. Certainly the CFR working group on Anglo-American relations in the late 1920s 'ratified powerfully the strategy of many US capitalists who ... had broadly allied themselves with British expansionism' (Smith 2004: 199), but this was not a result of method-based social science. Shotwell, the most prominent figure on the academic flank of the CFR, thought that IR remained too much immersed in the study of the League of Nations and its constitutional problems; as W.T.R. Fox writes (1968:

5), as late as 1930 the majority of the 24 chairs in International Relations at US universities were held by international lawyers. In the course of the 1920s, however, Burch notes (1981, ii: 250), the CFR became increasingly dominated by men like Allen Dulles (the previously mentioned intelligence agent in the Inquiry; like his elder brother John Foster Dulles, he was a partner in the New York law firm of Sullivan and Cromwell, who were entrusted with the management of the US investments of the German chemical giant IG Farben); and Owen D. Young, chairman of General Electric. In 1930 commercial interests began to dominate the SSRC's IR section, until then composed mostly of League of Nations specialists. These were replaced by a committee of international financiers headed by Young, and Shotwell was made director (Fox 1968: 5n.).

Young was the architect of the 1929 rescheduling plan of German reparations named after him. He also sat on the board of trustees of the Rockefeller Foundation, along with Lewis W. Douglas (Morgan partner and ambassador to the United Kingdom), J.D. Rockefeller Jr., Winthrop Aldrich (the Rockefellers' banker) and the presidents of Yale, Princeton, Chicago and UCLA (Parmar 2012: 48). John Foster Dulles, advocate of ecumenical Protestantism and future secretary of state under Eisenhower, in 1935 joined the board of the Rockefeller Foundation too (Tournès 2010: 15). In the same year, the Foundation disbursed a large grant to study the role of power in international relations to the Yale Institute of International Studies (YIIS). As Parmar documents (2012: 68–9), YIIS had been identified as a centre housing the desired new type of scholarship in IR. The directors of the institute, the Dutch-born Nicholas Spykman and, from 1940, Frederick Dunn, guided it to focus on the projection of US power; with scholars such as Arnold Wolfers, W.T.R. Fox and Bernard Brodie, it was well suited to the task. 'Yale seems to be our greatest hope for an *integrated* research programme in internat'l [relations] at our Amer. Univs.', a Rockefeller Foundation official wrote in 1940 (as in Parmar 2002: 252). Yet this was still a far cry from a comprehensive disciplinary programme translated into a standard curriculum, which had to wait till after the war.

The foundations throughout were the key promoters and enforcers of discipline, that is, social discipline translated into academic discipline. The funds at their disposal outstripped federal spending on education ($200 million in 1934, 10 per cent of all US government education expenditure; state spending was also $200 million). In a study of the 20 largest US foundations for that year, the Carnegie Corporation heads the list with a capital of $157.5 million, followed by the Rockefeller Foundation. In combination, Lundberg writes (1937: 325), the two networks taken together (all Carnegie and all Rockefeller institutions) accounted for nearly 60 per cent of the capital of the largest 123 US foundations. The centrality of higher education in their disbursements (from 1921 to 1930, 60.9 per cent of educational grants, against 14.8 per cent to primary and secondary and 4.1 per cent to adult education, all of which are government concerns) highlights the disciplinary aspect, which obviously decreases in importance the further one descends to elementary skills. By denying funding to certain research programmes and rewarding others, the foundations translated their specific preferences into influence 'upon the objects, results, and methods of research' (Morgenthau 1962: 38). 'The political scientist who wants to share in these rewards and, by doing so, gain prestige and power within the profession cannot help being influenced by these positive and negative expectations.' As every academic knows today, it is through the perceived appreciation of what qualifies for funding and what doesn't that political discipline is exercised. As early as 1937, Lundberg was already citing (1937: 353) E.C. Lindeman's conclusion that 'those who live in anticipation of receiving foundation grants are the more servile'. To discourage those who have received funding from then pursuing their own objectives, the routine procedure was to make a starting subsidy dependent for its continuation on 'satisfactory progress', so as to enforce discipline throughout.

Obviously the universities themselves are relays of class discipline too, especially at the top. By the 1930s, the Ivy League universities in the United States were all under the control of big business. From Lundberg's data (1937: 375–6), we see that Harvard, with the largest endowment at the time, had a J.P. Morgan management; its largest donor was Standard Oil (including its key owner families, the Whitneys, Harknesses and Rockefellers). Yale (with the second largest endowment) had essentially the same donor base, though slightly more dispersed, and was under Morgan–Rockefeller joint management. The University of Chicago (fourth largest endowment) was of course an original Rockefeller-run institution; MIT (seventh) was under Du Pont management, with donors from the Eastman and Du Pont dynasties. Princeton (eleventh) was under National City Bank management, with a range of industry-related donors including McCormick, Dodge, and others. And so on and so forth.

With war approaching, the enforcement of discipline went hand in hand with covering the need for reliable experts. From 1939 to 1945 the Rockefeller Foundation supported the CFR's War and Peace Studies Project. It had a steering committee composed of CFR president and Wall Street banker Norman H. Davis and several old hands of the Inquiry days, such as Bowman, Allen Dulles, and Whitney Shepardson (Shoup and Minter 1977: 120). The Foundation was especially prominent in maintaining the focus on method. In the 1930s it funded CFR research using a 'study group method' bringing together experts and practitioners (Parmar 2002: 241). Those wishing to study issues that were unwelcome to the power structure were dismissed without further ado. The 1940 application by Columbia sociologist Robert S. Lynd for the American Committee for International Studies (ACIS) to investigate how democracy at home could be safeguarded from the growing military mobilisation was disqualified by Joseph Willits of the Rockefeller Foundation as not being 'real research', not 'really doable', and perhaps better treated in magazine articles. As documented by Parmar (2002: 259, cf. 2012: 90), the Carnegie Foundation for the Advancement of Teaching then weighed in (through a referee) to dismiss Lynd's approach as 'sociological fuddy-duddy', focusing too one-sidedly on Nazism whilst neglecting the communist threat. Lynd's kind of political mobilisation against fascism, it was asserted, would not help to 'prepare people to kill others'.

ATLANTIC SYNTHESIS IN INTERNATIONAL RELATIONS

For all the resources placed at its disposal, the indigenous intellectual base in the United States, certainly in IR, was still limited. It was only by mobilising scholars from across the Atlantic that it would realise its full potential. In this respect there was a difference between how British academia (with the exception of LSE) resisted the new, method-oriented social science developed in the United States, and the readiness with which German exiles embraced it. Once the Nazi regime drove many scholars out, they became the single most important source of US-style disciplinary thinking, albeit with their specific intellectual legacy a powerful ingredient.

We can be brief about the United Kingdom. British scholarship in international affairs was obviously open to US ideas and influences, but the British ruling class preferred exploring grand schemes in which the British Empire could be salvaged in the context of an

Anglo-American heartland and was less concerned about methods in social science. After the joint Institute for International Affairs had failed to materialise, the Milner Group concentrated on the RIIA, funded by Abe Bailey, who was prominent in the Group, and in the 1930s by the Astors of Cliveden. Additional funding came from the Bank of England. Quigley (1981: 190) also mentions Carnegie and Rockefeller donations. The first chair in international politics was established in 1919 at the University of Wales at Aberystwyth by the family of Clement Davies, and named in honour of Wilson (Davies, a Liberal MP and associate of Lloyd George, afterwards ran various schemes to promote the League and the Commonwealth). Its first incumbent was Alfred Zimmern, a Milner Group intellectual and the author of the UK blueprint for the League (Markwell 1986: 280; cf. vol. ii, 2010: 116–17). Zimmern, a friend of Lippmann's and Wallas', theorised the Lockean heartland as the core of a global Commonwealth constructed along functional lines, once the 'power states' (our contender states) resisting it had been subdued. As Sluga relates (2005: 11), Arnold Toynbee, Zimmern's student and the aforementioned director of the RIIA, persuaded Zimmern that the nation-state was compatible with such a scheme because it was a psychological concept to which the 'racial' contender tradition could be converted too.

Zimmern was actively involved in creating RIIA subsidiaries in the Dominions and, via the Intellectual Cooperation Organization of the League of Nations (precursor of UNESCO), beyond it. From 1928 he organised annual International Studies Conferences, in which the Carnegie institutions and the Geneva Institute for Advanced International Studies participated. G.M. Gathorne-Hardy of the RIIA and Allen Dulles for the CFR edited the conference materials. Quigley notes (1981: 193–5) that the RIIA, LSE, the Department of International Politics at Aberystwyth, and the Montague Burton Chair at Oxford were involved in these activities, all of them institutions under the influence of the Milner Group, except LSE. This latter institution, of Fabian antecedents, in the 1920s was selected by the Rockefeller Foundation as its institution of choice in Britain. As Scot documents (2010: 87–91), Ruml came to the United Kingdom in 1923 and met Sydney Webb, one of the founders, and William Beveridge, its director since 1919. Beveridge was keen on empirical methods and established a statistical research unit with Keynes in Cambridge (discontinued when Lionel Robbins and Hayek took over LSE economics). From 1919 to 1940, US foundations donated £690,000 to UK social science research centres, 95 per cent of which came from the Rockefeller Foundation; LSE got a quarter of its budget from the Foundation. Besides financing chairs and lectureships in anthropology, Rockefeller in 1926 financed a chair in international law as well as assisting in the creation of a Department of IR. In Cambridge, on the other hand, Ruml's offer of a chair in sociology and one in political science met with unexpected resistance, and the political science post, with Spelman Fund money, was eventually taken by a historian of ideas who was uninterested in 'method' (Scot 2010: 93–4; Karl 1974: 183).

The Sovereign and the State of Emergency

After the coming to power of the Nazis, the European mainland would be closed off from Anglophone influence until 1945. However, between 15 and 29 per cent of the total of around 6,000 German university professors went into exile; by 1938, a third of the entire academic corps had emigrated from Germany (Rausch 2010: 128). Ungers (1981: 1) compares the exodus to 'the waves of Hellenisation of antiquity and the migration of Greek scholars to Florence following the loss of Constantinople'. Like Hellenism, it was a synthesis, not a straightforward transplantation. As far as IR is concerned, the crucial component in this momentous transformation was the Nietzsche–Weber lineage, culminating in Weber's student Carl Schmitt (1888–1985).

The defeat of 1918 left Germany prostrate before the Allied victors and exposed to socialist revolution. Schmitt in the circumstances became the chief representative of the *Staatswissenschaften* heritage, giving it, in a regressive twist, a tribal inflection. Advocating the radical exteriorisation of the foreign from the community, Schmitt takes the Caesaristic, authoritarian potential of a contender state, in which civil society cannot self-regulate and is confiscated from above, into the domain of the rational state operating in an environment that is devoid of norms – the tribal outlaw (vol. i, 2007: 43–4). When Wilsonian universalism lost its intellectual appeal in the crisis of the 1930s and 1940s, Schmitt's critique of it, via émigré scholars or directly, would inspire the realist counterpoint to liberal global governance. In reality the link between the two was never broken: Western supremacy always remains the presupposition, even in phases in which it foregrounds the moment of force to meet a contender challenge head-on. In Schmitt it is the threat of socialism that prompts a violent reassertion of the power over life and death, and consent (in Gramsci's sense) is stripped away to reveal 'the armour of coercion'. The established order then manifests its 'dual state' structure, and power is enforced directly, as political violence.

Schmitt was a reactionary racist but not initially a Nazi (Gross 2000). He belonged to the inner circle of General Kurt von Schleicher, one of the several right-wing contestants for power at the time. Schleicher favoured a strong state guiding the people without having to rely on a party system, which Schmitt in *The Guardian of the Constitution* of 1931 (1996: 138–9) considered possible on the basis of the emergency provisions of the Weimar constitution. In his seminal *Political Theology* of 1922, he had already defined the sovereign (2005: 5) as 'he who decides on the exception'. Emergency rule was declared in 1930; three years later, the conservative bloc, unable to hold power by parliamentary means, resorted to placing power in the hands of Hitler, in spite of declining voter support. For Schmitt (1996: 45) the *decision* as such, not derived from a pre-existing norm, is the source of authority. A constitution (and law in general) can only govern those things that have been settled in the political process, not those issues that call into question this foundational act itself. So when the SS in the 'night of the long knives' in 1934, a year after Hitler's investiture by President Hindenburg, massacred the leadership of the SA Brownshirts to neutralise the working class wing of the Nazi movement and Schleicher too was assassinated, Schmitt's endorsement was no mere opportunism. 'Justice flows from the institution of the *Führer*', he argued (1989: 329); both in turn derive from the people's 'survival instinct'. 'In the supreme emergency, the supreme law is vindicated and manifests itself as the highest degree of judicially vengeful realisation of this law. All law originates in the right to life of a people'.

Schmitt's close colleague at the University of Bonn in 1925, Joseph Schumpeter (1883–1950), although equally concerned with the threat of democracy and socialism, preferred to emigrate. Born in the Dual Monarchy, Schumpeter studied with Böhm-Bawerk and served briefly as rump-Austria's finance minister in 1919 before launching a bank that went bankrupt in 1924. Whereas Schmitt is concerned with martial law and 'the armour of coercion', Schumpeter prioritises 'the moment of consent' characteristic of Atlantic liberalism. His background in the *Staatswissenschaften* allowed him to venture freely beyond economics, his paramount interest. In *Capitalism, Socialism, and Democracy* of 1942, ten years after he found refuge in the United States, Schumpeter proposes to limit popular sovereignty to a choice between alternating elites, thus providing a key component of the American panoply for global governance. Today this has become the standard for Western 'democracy promotion'; it is routinely dissociated, under the disciplinary division of labour, from economic inequality, indeed from capitalism as such.[2] Yet as William Scheuerman writes (as in Drolet 2010: 98), 'Schumpeter's "democratic elitism" simply reformed an onerous tradition of Central European authoritarianism in order to make it more palatable to an American audience'. The attempt to make Schmitt more palatable too relies on the claim (e.g. by Bendersky 1987: 91–3) that Schmitt was sidelined in 1936 following a series of attacks on him in an SS magazine. Yet in 1941–42 we still find him as a state councillor (*Staatsrat*) and member of the German Law Academy on a prestigious study group on the Nazi *Grossraum*, alongside SS intellectuals such as Reinhard Höhn and the Gestapo lawyer Werner Best (Opitz 1977: 931–2). So he consciously tied his fate to the Nazis, and his thinking predisposed him to do so in every respect.

Schmitt's theory is exclusively political. It challenges Lockean governance in the name of sovereign equality, radicalising the Nietzsche–Weber legacy discussed earlier; the irrationality of the real is the point of departure. Politics for Schmitt is about the tribal distinction between friend and foe; there is nothing in between. The Cain and Abel story of the Bible is his reference (Ramel 2012: 141; cf. vol. ii, 2010: 80). In *The Concept of the Political*, originally of 1927, Schmitt defines the enemy (1963: 27) as 'just the other, the foreigner [*der Fremde*], and it suffices for his essence that he is in a particularly intensive sense, existentially, something other and foreign'. This is not necessarily an international issue, because 'if the determining friend–foe formations arise in domestic instead of international politics civil war will result' (1996: 142). Teschke (2011: 86–7) qualifies this as a 'suppression and elimination of social relations'.

As to Weber's equation of the nation-state and power, Schmitt emphasises the concept of the 'people' as a quasi-biological entity.

---

2. To this separation Schumpeter contributed himself when he exonerated capitalism from responsibility for the First World War in an essay of 1919. Here Schumpeter argues (1951: 84) that imperialism is the atavistic reflex of the Central and Eastern European warrior aristocracies, and hence will disappear with that class.

In *Dictatorship*, originally of 1921, Schmitt argues (2006: 171, 175) that martial law with summary execution also must be applicable to citizens; if citizenship would give protection against it, declaring the state of emergency might come too late. This dovetails with his rejection of liberalism and its blurring of the dividing lines between politics and economics. Once the central political issue, the idea of sacrificing one's life, recedes into the background, society becomes depoliticised and falls prey to economic calculation (Gross 2000: 302–3). The notion of a social contract written by subjects with rights, Schmitt argued in 1931 (1996: 61, 70), undermines the idea of a constitution as the political decision of the people as a unified whole (*in sich einheitliches, ganzes Volk*). As Giesen highlights (1992: 60), Weber's charismatic leader clearly prefigures Schmitt's. There is an echo of Hegel in Schmitt's rejection of a concept of the state that sees it as one institution among others; but then, from Rousseau on (indeed from Hobbes, whom Schmitt considers the classical 'decisionist', 2005: 33), this has been a signal characteristic of the contender-state tradition.

The third element in Schmitt's theory relevant to the subsequent development of IR is the spatial ordering of world politics. Against Wilsonian universalism, considered an illegitimate extension of the Monroe Doctrine beyond the Western hemisphere, Schmitt posits the right of contender states to erect their own 'Grand Areas' (*Grossräume*). He envisioned a titanic struggle between sea powers and land powers, both preyed on by Jews, who were neither one nor the other (Gross 2000: 274, 282). This displaces the notion of the sovereign state per se to a state commanding such a *Grossraum*. It was also a geopolitical inflection of the concept of international law, a *nomos* instead of the *cosmos* of global governance – a 'geopolitical pluralism' (Teschke 2011: 81). Yet Schmitt's juridical approach is distinct from the geopolitical tradition that runs from Kjellèn and Ratzel to Haushofer. It conceptualises spatial constellations in terms of law and sovereignty, not as boundary adjustment to topography or territory necessary for autarky. Conquest, the violent occupation of space (the root of the Greek *nomos*), according to Teschke (2011: 75; cf. Ramel 2012: 148–9) is the extra-legal form to which this higher sovereignty gives entitlement, even in the international sphere – 'Might generates right'.

In 1932 Schmitt explained his concept of a state carving out its own space in this way, a 'total state' (Gross 2000: 96–7), to the *Langnam-Verein* (the 'association with the long name' – the coal and steel industry organisation of Rhineland–Westphalia). It was the political triumph of this (economically bankrupt) bloc of heavy industries over the competitive, world-market-oriented fractions of German capital that would secure Hitler's rise to power and drive out the core of the nation's scholarship – to the United States.

Recruiting Central European Scholarship for Atlantic Social Science

US foundations played a prominent role in accommodating intellectuals who fled Germany on account of their political views or on account of Nazi racism. The Rockefeller Foundation had prior experience: in the 1920s it had rolled out a programme to assist the emigration of scholars from the Soviet Union, for which its Paris bureau served as the headquarters (Dosso 2010: 109; Krige 2006: 79). The massive and sustained support of the Carnegie Endowment and the Rockefeller Foundation to the 'technical sections' of the League of Nations (hygiene, economic and financial organisation, and the International Institute of Intellectual Cooperation), gave them access to the heart of the League's European operations in key areas (Tournès 2010: 17). Eligibility for funding presumed the usefulness of research for a 'stable social and international order' as defined by the foundations and the SSRC; 'method' was valued too, as in the case of the behavioural research of Charlotte Bühler and her husband in Vienna, supported by the Rockefeller Foundation (cf. Jahoda, Lazarsfeld and Zeisel 1975: 10).

US readiness to welcome the European refugees after 1933 was not just a matter of charity. Certainly there was an authentic openness and solidarity – unlike Britain, where Germans were often held collectively responsible for the rise of Hitler (Shain 1989: 35). However, US bodies like the Rockefeller-funded Special Research Aid Fund for Deposed Scholars of 1933, the Emergency Committee in Aid of Displaced German Scholars created in the same year by the Institute of International Education, and others (including one based in Switzerland) were instructed to be selective in granting support. As the president of the Rockefeller Foundation, Raymond B. Fosdick, put it in a report of July 1940, the aim was 'to save a small part of what [the Foundation] considered the most productive and potentially the most useful part of the population'. Dosso (2010: 112) concludes from this that the prime intention was to enrich American intellectual life. In a prior memorandum entitled 'If Hitler Wins', the Foundation's social-science director proposed to Fosdick the idea of bringing to the United States 100 of the best minds from Britain, 75 from France, and smaller contingents from the other countries; but 'the best' were to be selected in light of their potential as intelligence assets. Obviously many refugees were keen to demonstrate their loyalty to the United States by accepting work as propagandists or intelligence officers in the Office of Strategic Services (OSS), the wartime precursor of the CIA: Hajo Holborn, whose chair in Berlin had been sponsored by Carnegie before he fled, became assistant to the head of the OSS research division, the historian William L. Langer; Franz Neumann, of *Behemoth* fame, became the division's most prominent researcher (Walther 1991: 142–3; Söllner 1990: 645).

However, the project of recreating a German social science in exile never got off the ground. Attempts by Alfred Vagts (who in 1932, while in London, decided not to return to Germany), and M. Sommerfeld to try and bring together the German social science émigrés into a separate structure, not dependent on US foundation funding and control, foundered in spite of the support of Charles Beard, Vagts' father-in-law (Walther 1991: 139–41). Even the New School of Social Research in New York (founded in 1919), according to Walther, remained first of all part of the East Coast academic landscape. Thus the émigré scholars were incorporated in the United States into a political science that Lippmann, Lasswell, and others claimed should be approached from a psychological angle (substituting for political economy). Yet this was a choice welcome to many of them. As Paul Lazarsfeld, who had worked with the Bühlers in Vienna, put it later (1975: 20), 'the lost revolution had changed us into social psychologists'. Hence culture, but also propaganda and public opinion, emerged as key areas the newcomers were recruited for. In May 1938, the State Department announced the creation of a special division dedicated to international cultural relations, intended to counter the ideological influence of the USSR and Nazi Germany. This also drew the large foundations closer to the war effort (Krige 2006: 76).

Lazarsfeld, funded by the Rockefeller Foundation, meanwhile became a pioneer of US market research and media studies on account of his ability to apply quantitative methods to social-psychological concepts. In 1944 he published *The People's Choice*, the path-breaking work on voter analysis (Abbott 2001: 21; Parmar 2012: 282–3, n.78). Lazarsfeld also acted as a patron of the members of the Frankfurt *Institut für Sozialforschung* in exile (many of them at the New School, some in California). Since the Frankfurt School had explained the rise of Hitler 'by joining Marxist and Freudian ideas to an analysis of the new cultural techniques for controlling public opinion and human behaviour', Pells writes (1985: 217), its members were seen as qualified for social-psychological research too. One of their leading lights, Theodor Adorno, was given a job by Lazarsfeld to work on the Rockefeller-financed Princeton Radio Research Project. But what came out in 1940 was not the empirical study on media influence that had been commissioned, but a critical analysis of the US culture industry, later elaborated into the *Dialectic of Enlightenment* of 1944, co-authored with Max Horkheimer. The latter, like his associate and fellow émigré Herbert Marcuse, was a fierce critic of positivist empiricism, arguing (as in Reisch 2005: 122) that its supposed rejection of metaphysics was just an endorsement of the existing order. For these critical scholars it was difficult to accept a culture in which, as Söllner writes (1990: 637), 'democracy, belief in science, and progress' were seen as identical, and from which any sense of contradiction had been removed. The business logic permeates everything – or as Horkheimer and Adorno conclude in their 1944 study (1990: xii), 'public opinion has reached a stage in which thought inevitably becomes a commodity, and language the means of promoting that commodity'. Today we can read the same in a postmodern writer like Lyotard (1984), albeit uncritically.

At the other end of the political spectrum, German exiles in international politics and law brought the Nietzsche–Weber–Schmitt legacy to the United States. The key exponent of this tendency was the émigré Hans J. Morgenthau (1904–80). Morgenthau was influenced by legal scholars such as Hugo Sinzheimer and Schmitt's nemesis, Hans Kelsen, who had supervised Morgenthau's doctoral thesis in Geneva, where they found temporary refuge before moving on to the United States. Yet Morgenthau's original inspiration was Weber's concept of power (he had been a student of K. Rottenbücher's, a friend of Weber's, at the University of Munich). Scheuerman observes (2008: 47) that both Schmitt and Morgenthau grounded their 'arguably bleak visions of political life in pessimistic versions of political anthropology'. As Morgenthau himself confirmed later (as in Giesen 1992: 53n.), the idea of the irrationality of the real, which is expressed in the tension between juridical norms and actual power relations (nowhere more so than in the international sphere) was borrowed from Schmitt, with whom he had a meeting before leaving Germany in 1934. Morgenthau used Schmitt's title, the *Concept of the Political*, for a book of his own published in Paris in 1933 with the added subtitle 'and the theory of international disputes'. Unlike other disciples of Sinzheimer's, such as E. Fraenkel and Sigmund Neumann, who saw Schmitt's critique of law as an illustration of the authoritarian tendency of capitalism, Morgenthau 'responded to the collapse of Weimar democracy and left-wing reformism by implicitly integrating some of the least tenable views of its most prominent rightist critic into his own brand of realism' (Scheuerman 2008: 48).

Morgenthau was only one of a predominantly German-speaking contingent among the foreign-born scholars of international studies (IR and comparative politics/area studies). In Table 2.1 I have listed 30 who came as adults to the United States and were still active as academics in the 1960s, with their connection with the federal government and other affiliations as given in the respective sources (not the intelligence connections). Besides the foundations already mentioned, this includes the Ford Foundation and the RAND Corporation to which I return in the next chapter, and the Guggenheim Foundation, spun off from the non-ferrous metal empire of that name. Through Bernard M. Baruch it controlled the important War Industries Board, precursor of the post-war military–industrial complex of which RAND was the key think tank (Burch 1981, ii: 224, 240).

Although the list is not exhaustive (notably, Franz Neumann, who taught at Columbia and the FU in Berlin, is not on it because he died in a car accident in Switzerland in 1954), it illustrates the degree to which the post-war IR and comparative politics professions owe their profile to the transatlantic exodus – which would be even greater if we included those who came to the United States as youngsters (Table 2.2). Their eventual inclusion into the socialised academic structures is also given to remind us of the imbrication of intellectual work with the foundations and the US state (on the APSA list both the adults and those who came as youngsters were proportionally more involved with state institutions than the average for the IR/comparative politics group of 174 names). Of the later arrivals, the proportion of German-speakers is only half of those listed. Even so the bulk of the 1960s US IR and comparative politics elite was still imported from Europe.

The Europeans brought with them an understanding of the primacy of the state over society characteristic of the contender-state experience; the tradition of organic nationality; and the tendency to situate themselves in a scholarly, philosophical tradition. IR

Table 2.1 IR and comparative politics scholars resident in the United States in the 1960s and born in Europe before 1918 with (semi-)government and/or foundation affiliations (as listed in American Political Science Association membership or in *Who's Who in America*).

Name	Country and Year of Birth	Name	Country and Year of Birth
Hannah Arendt R, Gug	Germany 1906	David Mitrany* FO, C	Rumania 1888
Reinhard Bendix* C	Germany 1916	H.J. Morgenthau SD	Germany 1904
Karl W. Deutsch Gug	Austria–Hungary 1912	S. Neumann* DD	Germany 1904
Heinz Eulau F	Germany 1915	J. von Neumann* Rand	Austria–Hungary 1903
Werner Feld SD	Germany 1910	Guy J. Pauker F, Rand	Rumania 1917
Carl J. Friedrich DD	Germany 1901	Anatol Rapoport*	Russia 1911
John H. Herz R	Germany 1908	Joseph A. Schumpeter*	Austria–Hungary 1883
H. Holborn* R, C, SD	Germany 1902	Pitirim A. Sorokin	Russia 1889
Bert F. Hoselitz *F	Austria–Hungary 1913	Hans Speier* Rand	Germany 1905
S.D. Kertesz R, Gug	Austria–Hungary 1904	Nicholas J. Spykman*	Netherlands 1893
K.E. Knorr* SD, DD, Rand	Germany 1911	R. Strauss-Hupé DD	Austria–Hungary 1903
Hans Kohn* Har, Moore	Austria–Hungary 1891	I. Szent-Miklosy	Austria–Hungary 1909
George A. Lanyi R	Austria–Hungary 1913	Alfred Vagts*	Germany 1892
K. Loewenstein R, C, Gug	Germany 1891	Karl A. Wittfogel	Germany 1896
Roy C. Macridis R, F	Turkey 1918	Arnold O. Wolfers SD	Switzerland 1892

SD: State Department; *DD:* Defense Department; *FO:* Foreign Office (UK); *Rand:* RAND Corp.
Foundations: *C:* Carnegie; *F:* Ford; *Gug:* Guggenheim; *Har:* Harris; *R:* Rockefeller.

Sources: APSA 1968; names with * added from *Who's Who in America 1964–65*.

Table 2.2 IR and comparative politics scholars resident in the United States in the 1960s and born in Europe after 1918 with (semi-)government and/or foundation affiliations (as listed in American Political Science Association membership or in *Who's Who in America*).

Name	Country and Year of Birth	Name	Country and Year of Birth
V.V. Aspaturian *R, Rand*	USSR 1922	Henry A. Kissinger *SD*	Germany 1923
Gerhard Braunthal *USAF*	Germany 1923	R. Kolkowicz *Rand*	Poland 1929
Z. Brzezinski *Gug, SD*	Poland 1928	Juan Linz	Germany 1926
F.S. Burin *Maxwell, SD*	Germany 1922	George Liska *R*	Czechoslovakia 1922
Alexander Dallin *SD*	Germany 1924	George Modelski	Poland 1926
Harry Eckstein	Germany 1924	J.P. Nettl	Germany 1926
Ivo K. Feierabend	Czechoslovakia 1927	A.F.K. Organski *C, F*	Italy 1923
Ernst B. Haas *R, SD*	Germany 1924	U. Ra'anan *For. min. Israel*	Austria 1926
M. Halpern *SD*	Germany 1924	S.H. Rudolph *F, Howard*	Germany 1930
John F. Harsanyi *R*	Hungary 1920	D.A. Rustow *Gug, SD, Rand*	Germany 1924
Stanley Hoffmann*	Austria 1928	Dusan Sidjanski	Yugoslavia 1926
F.C. Iklé *USAF, SD, Rand*	Switzerland 1924	J.G. Stoessinger*	Austria 1927
John H. Kautsky *R, SD*	Austria 1922	J.K. Zawodny *F*	Poland 1921

SD: State Department; *DD*: Defense Department; *FO*: Foreign Office (UK); *Rand*: RAND Corp.
Foundations: C: Carnegie; F: Ford; *Gug*: Guggenheim; *Har*: Harris; R: Rockefeller.

Sources: APSA 1968; names with * added from *Who's Who in America 1964–65*.

realism made landfall with them, first settling in Yale, from where it spread to UCLA, Northwestern, Princeton, the University of North Carolina, and the University of Pennsylvania; although by Nicolas Spykman's own account (as in Parmar 2012: 72), it required an effort to overcome Christian reservations against the centrality of power instead of morality.

In 1940–41 the Wilsonian ideal of an open world was unattainable. The United States had to settle for an avowedly temporary regional formation, the Grand Area, given the extent of Nazi conquests. Shoup and Minter (1977: 135–40) discuss how a CFR working group that included Ivy League economists Jacob Viner and Winfield Riefler (whom we will encounter again in the next chapter) drew the contours of the minimum area that the United States would have to defend in order to survive a parallel German *Grossraum*. Yet Viner and Riefler also expected that the Grand Area would serve as the 'organised nucleus' of a post-war world economy. This demonstrates how the 'realist' perspective is always premised on a return of the conditions favouring its 'idealist' opposite – a limited sphere-of-influence is only the temporary substitute for the projection of global governance. In that respect the ideas of refugee scholars from Europe arrived just in time. Edward Earle's research seminar at Princeton, run with Rockefeller, Carnegie and US Army support, was one of the nodes through which their ideas were fed into the academic intelligence base. 'Such was the European outlook and ethnic composition of Earle's seminar that [Carnegie Corporation] trustee Arthur W. Page referred to it as a "refugee colony"'; but, as Parmar comments (2012: 75), to Earle 'scholars from the more statist European tradition were an essential part of the reformation of American attitudes to international relations'.

Compared to the Germans, the other continental European nationalities eligible for US support were less inclined to merge into the academic infrastructure across the Atlantic. Before the Nazi occupation of France, Raymond Aron was among those supported by the Rockefeller Foundation as part of a strategy of reforming French social science along the preferred lines (Tournès 2010: 22). Aron, a socialist in the 1920s, became an assistant at the University of Berlin in the early 1930s. There he made the acquaintance of the Lithuanian-born Shepard Stone, a Ph.D. student and future director of International Affairs at the Ford Foundation. After the collapse of France in June 1940, Louis Rapkine, a French citizen of Russian birth, became the key figure in helping French scientists escape the country. As Krige recounts (2006: 82), Rapkine set himself up at the New School in New York, entrusted by the Rockefeller Foundation with passing on funding to émigrés. After the fall of France, the Rockefeller bureau in Lisbon became the nerve centre of organising the exodus.

The French on the Rockefeller list of the 'best' 75, compiled by Hamilton Fish Armstrong (executive director of the CFR and editor of the journal *Foreign Affairs*), included Julien Benda, author of *Treason of the Clerks*; the philosopher Henri Bergson; the anthropologist Marcel Mauss, and the political scientist André Siegfried (Dosso 2010: 113). Other French scholars who found refuge in the United States included the anthropologist Claude Lévi-Strauss, who was among the beneficiaries of dedicated Rockefeller programmes, as well as composers and philosophers. With few exceptions they would all return to France after the war, not least because the United States considered the French as 'enemy aliens' – first, Dosso explains (2010: 121–3), because of Vichy; then because of Roosevelt's personal hostility towards De Gaulle (motivated of course by political differences concerning the future of French colonial possessions); and finally, because France during the war considered communists as fellow citizens. French nuclear scientists were not allowed to work in the Manhattan Project, and six of them worked instead on the Anglo-Canadian atomic programme, including Bertrand Goldschmidt, a key figure in France's post-war nuclear effort.

Italians, finally, included philosophers such as Max Ascoli, who obtained a Rockefeller scholarship in 1931 and moved to the New School, as well as the historian Gaetano Salvemini, who was recruited by Harvard after he had been fired from his chair at Florence in 1926 (Attal 2010: 144). Salvemini was associated with the Paris-based Concentrazione Antifascista of Carlo Rosselli, established in 1927 and merged with Iustizia e Libertà three years later. Rosselli, who had led his own Garibaldi Battalion in the Spanish Civil War under the slogan, 'Today in Spain, tomorrow in Italy', was assassinated by Mussolini agents in 1937. His group, transformed into the Action Party, would play an important role in the post-war transition (Shain 1989: 42, 108–9). The most important Italian under US protection was Luigi Einaudi, the economist who through his extensive contacts with the Rockefeller Foundation was able to tour the United States and yet survive the fascist era in his home country (his son Mario, a professor at Messina, did emigrate). After the war Luigi Einaudi became governor of the Bank of Italy and economics minister; in the meantime he propagated the empirical approach to social science in Italy (Attal 2010: 145–6). Bruno Foa, a collaborator of Einaudi's, in 1927 moved to LSE and to Princeton in 1940. Otherwise Italians and French (with the exception of Aron) would remain, if not politically suspect, outside the Atlantic synthesis that shaped the IR discipline.

3

Cold War Discipline in International Relations

The atomic bombardment of Hiroshima and Nagasaki ushered in a new era of world politics in which, paradoxically, Western supremacy was no longer secure. Certainly a draft NBC newscast about the bomb that spoke (as in Boyer 1985: 4–5) of 'the history of man' was changed into the claim that 'Anglo-Saxon science has developed a new explosive 2,000 times as destructive as any known before'. But the attacks raised profound anxieties and put to the test established concepts of security. To mobilise US society behind a fresh contest with the new contender state, the USSR, at this level of potential carnage and destruction, anti-communism had to be articulated in ways catering to the fear of strangers that Lipschutz (2001: 36) traces back to early European settlement and Puritan notions of 'possession' by evil forces, alien or even extra-terrestrial.

This chapter argues that the scholarly community in the United States, now prominently including the IR profession, volunteered by a large majority to play its part in the effort. In a climate of regimentation in which, as Reisch has documented (2005: 154), the fear of nuclear war was only mitigated by the knowledge that 'neighbours, co-workers and friends were uniformly united against communism', the discipline placed itself at the service of the newly reorganised national security state and the economic system it was set up to defend. From a Lockean perspective, a society not based on private property is already irrational; the notion of the irrationality of the real that European refugee intellectuals brought with them only added to the sense of vulnerability felt by broad layers of the population. Carl Schmitt's idea of imposing authority in a climate of terror thus acquired new relevance. It transmuted, in Teschke's words (2011: 72–3), 'the politics of the exception ... into the politics of fear as a socially integrative device'. In IR it produced a combative 'realism', and, at the RAND Corporation, an autistic quasi-social science that would later blossom into 'rational choice'. The deep politics operating behind the façade of public institutions, or what the crown prince of the Nietzsche–Weber–Schmitt legacy among German émigrés, Hans Morgenthau, would later call the 'dual state', was a force in both. Cold War strategists doubling as scholars and academics reporting directly to Allen Dulles at the CIA ensured that the discipline remained imbricated with the national security state.

The foundations meanwhile supervised the evolution of IR as a 'normal science', including the quantitative analysis of war and the study of the Lockean heartland as a core zone of peace ('security community'). However, when President Eisenhower made his famous farewell speech about the military–industrial complex in 1961, his specific warning about the corruption of scholarship signalled the degree to which the academic intelligence base had by then been colonised by US militarism. The chapter concludes with how the Congress for Cultural Freedom worked to adjust European intellectual traditions and sensibilities to the need for expert knowledge and its insertion into the anti-communist crusade.

COMPROMISE AND CONFRONTATION IN THE NUCLEAR AGE

The disquiet over the atomic bombardment of the Japanese cities, with hundreds of thousands of civilians incinerated, was not easily dispelled. A Dutch psychologist touring the United States in 1946 traced the anxieties he encountered to repressed guilt over the bombing (Boyer 1985: 183). Certainly the official reason given for it, that it would shorten the war ('save lives'), carried weight in light of expected casualty figures in an assault on the mainland. Yet the Dutch judge on the Pacific war crimes tribunal, B.V.A. Röling (1970: 167–9), concluded from the minutes of the Japanese Imperial Council of 10 August that discussion at the time centred on the post-war status of the emperor, not on the atom bombs. Nagasaki, devastated the day before with some 150,000 dead on impact, was not even mentioned.

Sensational accounts such as John Hersey's book-length report on Hiroshima, first published in the *New Yorker* a year after the attack and serialised in more than 50 US newspapers, and military assessments (as in Boyer 1985: 66) that in an atomic bombardment of New York, the city's skyscrapers 'would fly apart as though they themselves were bombs and someone had lighted their fuse', made the public receptive to the idea of world government, called for by the nuclear physicists Albert Einstein and Leo Szilard. With wartime 'Uncle Joe' sentiment about Stalin still around, many thought that the USSR would voluntarily submit to it too. But the often-quoted statements by Secretary of State Byrnes that 'rattling the bomb might make Russia more manageable' and that it would 'put us in a position to dictate our own terms at the end of the war' point to an interpretation of global governance more in the spirit of the 'American Century' proclaimed by *Time–Life* publisher Henry Luce. Indeed, on closer reading many world government proposals explicitly rule out dictatorships from participating. Thus in his bestselling *Anatomy of Peace*, journalist Emery Reves warned (1947: 249, emphasis added) that to avoid 'the apocalypse of an atomic world war', only a world federation modelled on Hamilton's original design would 'prevent the next war and … *stop our drifting towards totalitarianism*'. The British philosopher and future nuclear pacifist Bertrand Russell (as in Easlea 1983: 121) even claimed that for world government to work, a preliminary atomic bombardment of the USSR was necessary, since 'communism must be wiped out' first.

Christian Ethics Against Totalitarianism

To provide the social sciences with an ethical codex for the nuclear age, the Rockefeller Foundation in December 1945 convened a dedicated committee chaired by New Jersey Bell president Chester I. Barnard (later himself president of the Foundation) and including Foundation trustee John Foster Dulles. Dulles from his experience with the World Council of Churches hoped religion would point the way forward (cf. vol. ii, 2010: 183). However, as Ryan and Scott record (1995: 445–8, emphasis added), Barnard was advised that US citizens had become too reliant on 'the altruistic, or "soft," side of Christianity *to the detriment of the "harder" virtues of pugnacity and self-assertion*', and recommended instead that academic experts be mobilised for authoritative guidance. Gabriel Almond, a wartime student of Nazi Germany and the dean of post-war modernisation studies, considered the public mentally unstable; he reckoned (as in Gilman 2003: 53, emphasis added) that it was 'in the social sciences in the universities that a democratic ideological consensus can be fostered and *a democratic elite discipline encouraged*'.

During the war US academic life experienced what Abbott calls (2001: 132, 133n.), 'a blast of interdisciplinarity', producing 'the enormous culture and personality literature of the 1930s and 1940s'. Restoring disciplinary surveillance and adjusting it to the needs of a new age was an urgent task. Ivy League economist Jacob Viner, a US government consultant, director of one of the Morgan group's international utilities, and mentioned in the last chapter as an architect of the CFR's wartime Grand Area plan, proposed to cover the ethical side of nuclear weapons by incorporating philosophy into university curricula; Joseph H. Willits, director of the Rockefeller Foundation's social sciences division and a former dean of Wharton business school, insisted that liberal economic principles remain central (Ryan and Scott 1995: 450–3). Another trustee of the national security state, Chicago sociologist and Psychological Warfare Division veteran Edward Shils, involved himself in the *Bulletin of the Atomic Scientists* to prevent the physicists from venturing into world government fantasyland again (Gilman 2003: 51). Yet John Rockefeller Jr. did not want Christianity left out of the equation. He saw on the horizon an imminent struggle between the Christian West and atheist powers, and preferred to follow the lead taken by the elder Dulles.

Dulles was also on the board of Union Theological Seminary (UTS), affiliated with Columbia University. Nicknamed the 'Red Seminary' in the New Deal years, UTS would be investigated in the McCarthy period, but not because of Reinhold Niebuhr (1892–1971), the theologian of second-generation German immigrant background later crowned the founder of post-war IR realism (George Kennan famously called him 'the father of all of us'). Niebuhr during the war embraced the project of a global governance by the allies, including the USSR. So did the Rockefeller Foundation, which in 1943, as Richard Fox relates (1985: 211, 217), dispatched him to Britain to propagate the idea. Visiting occupied Germany in September 1946, however, Niebuhr joined the chorus of those detecting a Soviet design to subjugate the whole of Europe. This earned him an introduction from Allen Dulles to the Council on Foreign Relations and an advisory position to the US State Department. In the climate of guilt and fear of the immediate post-war years, Niebuhr's conclusion that communism was even more dangerous than Nazism because of its atheism, propagated through the pages of *Time*, *Life* and *Reader's Digest*, worked to galvanise a mass public. Later in 1946 Niebuhr chaired the founding meeting of Americans for Democratic Action (ADA), an initiative of Roosevelt's widow Eleanor to salvage the New Deal welfare state in the Cold War context (Pells 1985: 109; Fox 1985: 227–9). In 1949 he quashed the 'Illusion of World Government' in *Foreign Affairs*, but also warned (1966: 180) against moral self-righteousness.

The Yale Institute for International Studies in the course of the war consolidated its position at the centre of the academic intelligence base. Avoiding 'abstract schemes of a new world order' (no world government ideas) or 'ivory tower speculation' (Parmar 2002: 248, 250, citing the Institute's own assessment), it worked closely with the War Department to ensure 'quick mobilization of academic knowledge and its application to practical questions of policy'. The Institute's W.T.R. Fox, agreeing that atomic issues should not be left to the physicists, arranged with Edward Shils for social scientists to take part in the first dedicated conference at the University of Chicago in the autumn of 1945. There Viner surprised the audience by calling the atomic bomb a 'weapon of peace', because states would always be able to retaliate (Kaplan 1984: 25–7). This idea, deterrence by retaliation, would be taken further by Viner's protégé, YIIS scholar Bernard Brodie (1910–1978). Brodie by then enjoyed the confidence of the US defence establishment. As chairman of an APSA panel on politico-military relations he won acceptance for the idea of scholars collaborating with the War and the State Departments (Parmar 2002: 250). When the YIIS decided to put together a collection of papers, *The Absolute Weapon*, the editorial role went to Brodie. Published in 1946, it elaborated on the theme of deterrence and also dealt with issues such as arms control. Authors included Dunn, Wolfers, Fox, and Percy Corbett, a Canadian Rhodes scholar and fellow of All Souls, who came to Yale towards the end of the war as chairman of the Politics Department and edited *World Politics* when it was launched in 1948 (Quigley 1981: 306).

With the Princeton economist Winfield Riefler (a Grand Area strategist alongside Viner) and the Chicago sociologist William Ogburn, Brodie also sat on a dedicated SSRC committee which according to Boyer (1985: 176–7) succeeded in supplanting the world-government idea by civil defence (for which Ogburn thought the Pueblo Indian model of dispersing across the countryside might provide the model). The next step was to reinsert the new weapon of mass destruction into a Clausewitzian framework as a legitimate means of coercion. This Brodie did in an article in *Foreign Affairs* entitled 'The Atomic Bomb as Policy Maker'. The bomb, he claimed (1948: 24, cf. 29), should not be seen as the 'visitation of a wrathful deity', but 'as an instrument of war – and hence of international politics'. And whilst the US nuclear monopoly was a temporary advantage, maintaining superiority over the Soviet Union was both feasible and worth the effort since the atomic bomb was the decisive weapon – even if the military had obviously not fully realised it yet. Air Force commanders continued to plan for city bombing campaigns in Second World War style, which, as Brodie warned in an August 1950 magazine piece (as in Kaplan 1984: 37), misrecognised the qualitative novelty of the atom bomb, and anyway would be a waste of bombs.

The assumption of the irrationality of the real that German émigrés brought to the United States in the 1930s implies a fixation on one's own agency and a neglect or even dismissal of the possibility to communicate or negotiate. Carl Schmitt's references to the 'survival instinct' thus acquired a new pertinence; as Radhika Desai writes (2001: 394), the threat of nuclear annihilation removes any 'calculus of proportions' from thinking about and preparation for war. Hans Morgenthau's version of Schmitt in these circumstances 'effectively became the determining influence for the entire realist ethic' (Giesen 1992: 59), which Morgenthau underscored by a disciplinary intervention of his own. This took the form of an attack on Edward Hallet Carr's *Twenty Years' Crisis* of 1946 (originally 1939) in the first issue of *World Politics* – thus clearing the ground for Morgenthau's own *Politics Among Nations* in the same year (1948).

To disqualify Carr's analysis, which articulates the relationship between liberal global governance and realism in a way that removes the ideological gloss from the role of the Anglophone West, Morgenthau (1948: 130–1, 134) mocks the Briton's argument that the liberal powers too should make sacrifices in order to avoid war. He also dismisses the claim that a planned economy is progressive. Carr's suggestion that democracy should include the economy and that communism has a moral content too, made Morgenthau declare *The Twenty Years' Crisis* a 'failure', its author a 'Machiavelli without *virtù*'. Thus Carr was written out of the script to make way for Morgenthau's own tome, which instead postulates (1967: 10) that every state, irrespective of time and place, is driven by a Nietzschean will to power. Compared to Carr's 'ironic and polemical' subtleties, Stanley Hoffmann would comment later (1977: 45), Morgenthau's realism offered a non-controversial starting point for academic careers. More sophisticated approaches like Carr's or later, Raymond Aron's (with whom the Austrian-born Hoffmann had worked in Paris before leaving for Harvard) were not suitable for that purpose. The same holds for the work of Morgenthau's predecessor at Chicago, Charles Merriam. Although he too wrote a book inspired by Schmitt in the 1930s (Giesen 1992: 58n.), he grew critical of the pessimism of the German immigrants in the course of the war. Merriam's own idea of politics as a fluid process of seeking the 'consent and assent of the governed' (1945: v), would not, however, survive the frenzy of McCarthyism.

Schmitt's legacy thus became part of the arsenal of the West. Of his original critique of the universalisms of both Anglo-American liberalism and Soviet communism, only that of the latter remained. Denounced as 'totalitarianism' (another term coined by Schmitt; G. Schwab in Schmitt 2005: xxxvii), Soviet state socialism was equated with Nazism by Hannah Arendt, who defined it in 1951 (1968: 155) as a populist response to dissolving community bonds in modern society. By claiming that in both its Nazi and its Stalinist versions totalitarianism is inclined to 'radical evil', Arendt and other European émigrés, such as Carl Friedrich and Zbigniew Brzezinski (see their 1963), thus impart a friend–foe matrix on Morgenthau's realism again, whilst transferring the association with wars of aggression, surprise attack and genocide from the group of contender states that had actually committed all of these to the Soviet Union.

This only added to the ferocity of the communist witch-hunt that also played a role in enforcing academic discipline. The advice given to President Truman to 'scare the hell out of the American people' in order to obtain support for foreign intervention entailed a loyalty review programme for government employees in 1947. In turn it unleashed the exorcism of evil in which Senator Joseph McCarthy made his name. Besides actual communists, McCarthyism primarily had the East Coast internationalists in its sights. Their understanding of Western supremacy was Wilsonian, whereas the red-baiters adhered to what is today called 'homeland security'. This put them on the trail of men like Alger Hiss, general secretary of the founding conference of the United Nations and from 1946 president of the Carnegie Endowment for International Peace. In 1949 Hiss was forced to step down to face the House Un-American Activities Committee; eventually he was condemned to a five-year prison sentence for perjury. As Pells relates (1985: 270–2), Harry Dexter White, undersecretary of the Treasury, architect of the Bretton Woods agreements and director of the IMF, died of a heart attack the day after a humiliating appearance before the Committee; William Remington, a top Department of Commerce official, was murdered in prison.

Compared to this the persecution of dissident academics was a sideshow, albeit one with long-lasting consequences. It worked, Reisch comments (2005: 20), to discipline US academia to the point where no further surveillance beyond peer review was necessary. Nearly all state and some Ivy League universities implemented loyalty oaths; 150 faculty members at the University of California alone were fired in 1949 for refusing to sign one (ibid.: 249; Boyer 1985: 103). Many academics became turncoats and informers, following the sad example of the historian Daniel Boorstin, who had in fact been a party member but retained his post by a pathetic repentance. Since the average US citizen associated 'social science' with socialism and 'international' with un-American activities, the IR profession was soon in the firing line too. The University of Chicago scholar Frederick Schuman, a student of Charles Beard's, had already been investigated by the Illinois state legislature in the 1930s. He was attacked again by the American Legion in 1949, but fought back with the support of his combative university president, Robert M. Hutchins. Owen Lattimore, on whose work I rely extensively in Volume I, was targeted, along with the Institute for Pacific Relations and its journal *Pacific Affairs*, because, in the paranoiac imagination of the inquisitors, he had colluded in the 'loss of China'. Testifying for the prosecution, communist-turned-Cold Warrior Karl Wittfogel cited as proof of Lattimore's treason the *absence* of Marxism in the latter's work (Reisch 2005: 256, 259–60). Johns Hopkins decided the matter by closing Lattimore's school of International Relations, forcing him to spend the remainder of his career at the University of Leeds in England. Chicago's Hutchins was an exception; as R.C. Lewontin writes (in Schiffrin 1997: 20), 'the greatest direct enemy of the Left in the academy was not the coherent policy of the state, but the opportunism and cowardice of boards of trustees and university administrators'.

In this respect, the foundations were no better. Lindsley Kimball, vice-president of the Rockefeller Foundation, in 1951 sketched a grim picture (as in Krige 2006: 142) of how communists, using 'a protective coloration, and a genius for disguise', had created 'a twilight zone between war and peace' in which they were almost impossible to track down and be defeated. In the same year, Guggenheim president Henry A. Moe ruled out members of the Communist Party from funding; the Association of American Universities in 1953 declared that membership 'extinguishes the right to a university position' (as in Schiffrin 1997: 76, 42).

Yet in 1952 a Congressional Select Committee was tasked with investigating whether the foundations were not in fact 'using their resources for un-American and subversive activities or for purposes not in the interest or tradition of the United States'. Luckily, Krige recounts (2006: 140–1), it was found that broadly speaking they had been supportive of 'the American system of free enterprise'.

Academic Intelligence for Covert Action

In the New Deal, Roosevelt's response to the Depression, the social basis for the 'American system of free enterprise' had been enlarged by including organised labour. One aspect of McCarthyism was to discipline labour again, but class collaboration could not be suspended altogether. The unions were certainly intimidated, yet without their consent, the Fordist–Keynesian compromise, based on redistributing the benefits of productivity rises in the mass-production industries, would not hold. Niebuhr's role in the ADA was part of the adjustment of this class compromise to the new Cold War context, and so was his IR realism – both were based on the recognition that capitalism in its prevailing, 'corporate liberal' form allows its constitutive social forces to be organised according to their own principles (see my 2012: 90–106). So whatever the vitriol of his anti-Soviet stance, Niebuhr's realism (and the same holds for Morgenthau's, or even Schmitt's) did not deny the right of the USSR to exist on its own terms. Only in the 1980s transition from corporate liberalism to neoliberalism (neoconservatism in the United States) would this implicit recognition be withdrawn.

Yergin (1980: 11) labels corporate liberal realism the 'Yalta axiom', after the February 1945 conference dividing post-war Europe. The counterpoint, *denying* legitimacy to the Soviet Union, would then be the 'Riga axiom', a reference to the capital of Latvia in which the United States maintained an observation post to monitor developments in Soviet Russia as long as diplomatic recognition was in abeyance. George F. Kennan (1904–2005) was among the young US diplomats whose outlook on the Soviet Union was shaped by exposure to and identification with White émigrés in Riga. Working with the University of Chicago Russia specialist Samuel N. Harper (appointed to a State Department post in 1918) and fellow diplomat Charles Bohlen, Kennan laid the foundations for the uncompromising attitude that would resonate in early post-war 'Russia' scholarship at Columbia, Harvard, and elsewhere, and which resurfaced in the Reagan era for what we now know was the final run.

Stationed at the embassy in Moscow at war's end, Kennan was in a position to push home his long-standing conviction that no concessions should be made to the USSR. Expressing the frustration over the Soviet rejection of IMF and World Bank membership in February 1946 that dashed any hopes of its submission to Western global governance, his 'Long Telegram' painted the Soviet Union in alarmist terms. Recommending, as Yergin recounts (1980: 174), that the conflict with the USSR be dramatised, it was duly leaked to the media, with *Time* magazine publishing excerpts accompanied by suggestive cartography of areas soon to fall into Soviet hands. Even so, Kennan in the notorious 'X' article in *Foreign Affairs* in July 1947 confined himself (1951: 105) to painting the Soviet threat in the darkest possible hues. Evoking its 'particular brand of fanaticism ... unmodified by any of the Anglo-Saxon traditions of compromise', his assessment of the USSR fitted into the Niebuhr paradigm; Kennan merely hoped (1951: 141) that whilst being 'contained', the USSR would not stand the test of time and disappear in due course.

If in his public stance Kennan accepted the hegemonic Yalta position, in his role as director of policy planning at the State Department he initiated what would evolve into the NATO underground – responsible for such bloody episodes as the strategy of tension in 1970s Italy or the successive coups and massacres in post-war Turkey (Ganser 2005). In an early memo Kennan proposed that the United States should follow the lead of the British Empire in setting up 'organized political warfare' and it was at his request, Wilford records (2008: 31, cf. 25–6), that Secretary of State Acheson asked the veteran anti-Bolshevik Joseph Grew to head a Free Europe Committtee. A May 1948 memo signed by Grew advocated the use of (public) 'liberation committees' to attract recruits for private undercover networks in target countries. This built on prior experience with preventing a communist election victory in Italy, for which the National Security Council in its first session in December 1947 had created an undercover unit. Kennan took this further by proposing the creation of an Office of Political Coordination (OPC), which would handle all psychological and economic warfare, as well as sabotage. Its remit included subversion, support of armed resistance and liberation of prisoners (Müller 1991: 63–4; Lucas 1996: 281, 284).

This gets us one step closer to the ruling class, and more particularly, to the fraction most directly involved in the dual state at that juncture: the bankers and corporate lawyers in the orbit of the Dillon, Read investment bank and the Brown Brothers Harriman group associated with the intelligence world. BBH was one of the last big private banks in the United States, and, through Harriman, Ripley, the banker of Boeing and United Aircraft, two top defence contractors. Averell Harriman held office in several Democratic administrations, always prominently dealing with the USSR, where the Harrimans had lost their manganese deposits to revolution. Dillon, Read was one of the key US investment channels to pre-war Germany. Paul H. Nitze, its vice-president at the outbreak of the Second World War, was Kennan's successor as director of the State Department's Policy Planning Staff. His advocacy of a roll-back policy (notoriously in NSC-68 of 1950 and the Gaither Report of 1957) also influenced the IR discipline in that period, in which Nitze took a direct interest. In 1943 he co-founded the Washington-based School of Advanced International Studies (SAIS) of Johns Hopkins University, today named in his honour.

The OSS, though officially disbanded, at war's end had been kept alive as a dual state structure, over the fierce opposition of FBI chief J. Edgar Hoover – another struggle between the homeland security forces and the East Coast upper class. As Phillips documents (2004: 194, 198; cf. Scott 2010: 27–8, 55), BBH partners Robert A. Lovett and David K.E. Bruce (OSS head in wartime London and connected by marriage with the Mellon dynasty), former OSS director William J. Donovan, Allen Dulles, and the latter's protégé, the Wall Street lawyer Frank Wisner, in various ways worked to restore a unified foreign intelligence service; yet it took until 1947 before Hoover's resistance was overcome. Dillon, Read bankers James Forrestal (secretary of the Navy) and Ferdinand Eberstadt (vice-president of the War Production Board) were the architects of that year's National Security Act. In their preliminary report they claimed (as in Rothkopf 2005: 52) that 'an effective national security policy calls for active, intimate and continuous relationships not alone between the military services themselves but also between the military services and many other departments and agencies of government'. The Act, then, established a unified Department of Defense, a National Security Council (NSC), and the CIA. A year later the OPC was established as a covert action organisation, officially outside this framework. Kennan, who had come up with the idea, and Allen Dulles, then deputy CIA director, selected Wisner as its head.

Academics, and IR scholars in particular, were close to the OSS–CIA–OPC lineage all along. When the OSS was founded in 1941, Roger Hilsman notes (as in Trumpbour 1991: 13), 'one of the basic ideas behind it was the novel and almost impish thought that scholars could in some respects take the place of spies'. In the last chapter we saw that émigré IR scholars had joined in force – for good reasons of course. As the president of the International Studies Association, John Gange, recalled later (as in Windmiller 1968: 120), the OSS 'was like a big university faculty in many respects – sometimes, staff meetings were just like faculty meetings'. Nicknamed the 'chairborne division', the OSS housed eight future presidents of the American Historical Association and five future presidents of the American Economic Association (Engerman 2003: 85). In international and adjacent academic studies, the OSS was equally important. From fewer than ten dedicated IR degree programmes in the United States before the war, the discipline expanded to 191 such programmes in 1968; most of them, according to Harvard's McGeorge Bundy (as in Trumpbour 1991: 13), 'manned, directed, or stimulated by graduates of the OSS'. That this did not mean that the discipline merely shifted to a peaceful stance is brought out by Project Troy, a psychological warfare plan to undermine the Soviet order in Eastern Europe that ran parallel with other covert operations under OPC and CIA auspices.

Project Troy began as an inquiry into Soviet jamming of the Voice of America radio broadcasts in 1950, after the outbreak of the Korean War. For the project, commissioned by the State Department, the MIT president, James Killian, and the dean of humanities and social studies, John Burchard, assembled a group including participants from Harvard and other universities. Out of it emerged MIT's Centre for International Studies (CIS, officially established in 1952), initially funded, according to the Centre's own website, by the CIA and later by the Ford Foundation (cf. Hulnick 1987: 42). Actual roll-back plans were ambitious, heralding the global governance project. Thus the parallel Psychological Strategy Board outlined a five-year programme (as in Lucas 1996: 289), beginning with a no-holds-barred propaganda offensive ('a high-hearted crusade … to let people everywhere choose how they wish to be governed'), and culminating in the collapse of communism 'through uprisings supported by United Nations resolutions and bombing of Soviet railroads and communications'. Radio Free Europe, set up by Grew's committee mentioned earlier, would assist the Voice of America in the propaganda war (Scott-Smith 2002: 65).

Academics working for psychological warfare included Paul Lazarsfeld and his Bureau of Applied Social Research at Columbia (funded by the US Army and the CIA; Boneau 2004) and Hadley Cantril, the pioneer of academic public opinion studies at Princeton. Cantril had been supported by the Rockefeller Foundation during the war and as Parmar documents (2002: 256), the US Army's Psychological Warfare Research Bureau in Cantril's office also dates from that time. James Burnham, Trotskyite-turned-Cold Warrior and author of *The Managerial Revolution* of 1941, was prominent in political warfare too. A protégé of Henry Luce and ally of William Donovan, in mid 1949 Burnham got his security clearance from the OPC to operate under cover of a sabbatical from the philosophy department at New York University. Together with his colleague Sydney Hook, he was involved in preparatory work for the Congress for Cultural Freedom, to which we turn below (Wilford 2008: 78, cf. 74–5; Scott 2010: 75).

Both Troy and the psychological strategy offensive subsided after Eisenhower assumed the presidency, but the recruitment of social scientists by the national security state continued. The German émigré Hans Speier, whom we will meet again as social science director of the RAND Corporation, was also director of Project Troy. Afterwards he chaired a committee composed of Troy alumni (Shils, Ithiel de S. Pool, Lasswell and others; Gilman 2003: 158) that disbursed Ford money for CIS. Lasswell, as we saw, was a creative scholar before the war, whose originality owes much to his readiness to step over disciplinary boundaries – politics and psychology, notably. In 1950 however he became one of the most vocal advocates of mobilising social scientists for the academic intelligence base. In *Power and Society* of 1950, co-authored with the Ukrainian-born RAND Corporation philosopher Abraham Kaplan, the authors speak (as in Pielke 2004: 216–17) of 'the *intelligence division*' of the social sciences as 'the subgroup making available to the leadership facts and analyses, and clarifying goals and alternatives'. A year later, in his introductory chapter to *The Policy Sciences*, co-edited with Daniel Lerner of CIS, Lasswell specifies this as (1951: 3–4) 'the findings of the disciplines making the most important contributions to the intelligence needs of the time'. This was a Cold War version of the original Lippmann design, including the emphasis on method.

Henry Kissinger, future national security adviser and secretary of state under Nixon and Gerald Ford, also began his career under OPC auspices. Kissinger served in US Army counterintelligence in Europe during the war and from 1946 to 1949 taught German history in the European Command Intelligence School at Oberammergau in the Bavarian Alps (Müller 1991: 65). After his return to the United States, the veteran IR scholar William Y. Elliott, his mentor and doctoral supervisor at Harvard, got him working for the OPC as organiser of the International Summer School Seminar. It was intended, as Kissinger put it in a memo to Elliott (as in Wilford 2008: 124) to create 'a spiritual link between a segment of foreign youth and the U.S.' Funding was through personal grants, from 1953 by the Farfield Foundation (a CIA front), and a year later by the Ford Foundation. In 1952 Kissinger had become an adviser to the Psychological Strategy Board of the Joint Chiefs of Staff, recommending the mobilisation of West German public opinion against the Soviet Union by using clubs of former prisoners of war (Müller 1991: 65–6). For the Harvard Seminar, Kissinger selected the theme of self-realisation through freedom, avoiding topics that might activate disdain for the United States among foreigners (Parmar 2012: 103–4). With alumni such as future leaders Y. Nakasone (class of 1953) and Valéry Giscard d'Estaing (1954), the money, one would think, was not wasted. Certainly the OPC had meanwhile become embroiled in scandal. But when CIA director Walter Bedell Smith merged it into the CIA in 1952 with the aim of bringing its activities under proper oversight, the result, Scott writes (2010: 28), 'was the opposite. Instead of the CIA absorbing and taking over OPC, OPC, especially under Allen Dulles, effectively took over the CIA.'

Dulles, who from 1948 doubled as president of the Council on Foreign Relations, meanwhile ran an academic intelligence operation of his own, the 'Princeton Consultants'. Meeting four times a year at the university's Nassau Club, the Princeton Consultants included, as Cavanagh relates (1980: 2; cf. Wilford 2008: 128), Max Millikan of CIS, Robert Bowie (director of policy planning from 1953 to 1957 and co-founder of Harvard's Centre for International Affairs in 1958), Philip E. Mosely (then director of studies of the Council on Foreign Relations), Hamilton Fish Armstrong (editor of its quarterly, *Foreign Affairs*), along with historians and Soviet specialists. When

German-born Klaus Knorr moved to Princeton with five others in 1951–52, after the new president of Yale, Whitney Griswold, had closed down the YIIS, he also joined the Consultants. Later Knorr would become director of the Centre of International Studies, set up to accommodate the Yale arrivals at Princeton (Kaplan 1984: 49–50; Fox 1968: 54). Princeton was a 'P-source' (the CIA code word for academic intelligence), but other institutions had important intelligence links too. CIA and military intelligence supported both Harvard's Russian Research Centre (headed by veteran OSS anthropologist Clyde Kluckhohn) and Columbia's Russian Research Institute. But then, all scholars studying enemy countries, according to Bruce Cumings (as in Gibbs 2003), 'either consulted with the government or they risked being investigated by the FBI.' At Yale, Norman H. Pearson, OSS counter-intelligence officer in wartime London under David Bruce (Wilford 2008: 128), launched an American Studies programme (a key propaganda subject), whilst the historian Sherman Kent developed the analytic approach for the CIA that, as James Mann records (2004: 28), would later be attacked by neoconservatives as too realistic.

Some academics felt that the shortest route to real influence was to leave university employment and join the agency directly. Krige describes (2006: 167–8) how Richard Bissell Jr., a senior Marshall Plan official who had consulted for Project Troy while at MIT, in 1954 decamped to the CIA. Having earned his laurels with the coup in Guatemala in that year, Bissell would succeed Wisner at the head of clandestine activities in 1958 and was put in command of the Cuban operation that would end in the Bay of Pigs fiasco (O'Toole 1991: 474). Langer, too, moved from Harvard to Washington to set up the CIA Office of National Estimates, which operated until the late 1970s (Hulnick 1987: 42).

RAND and the Doomsday Ideology

At the RAND Corporation (acronym of Research and Development), the pessimistic Riga axioms were developed to their logical conclusion as a doomsday scenario of nuclear annihilation. RAND was established in 1945 in Santa Monica, California, by a group of mathematicians and engineers of the Douglas aerospace company. With the presidents of Boeing, Northrop and North American Aviation on its advisory board (the preferential link with Douglas was severed in 1948), and USAF general and head of the Strategic Air Command Curtis LeMay seconded to it, RAND became a focal point of those who wanted to ensure that there would be no demobilisation as had happened after the First World War. The Air Force–aerospace link is obvious, but the atomic arsenal itself was also a product of the top range of US industry. The uranium bomb exploded over Hiroshima had been engineered by Eastman Kodak and Union Carbide; the plutonium bomb, dropped on Nagasaki, by Du Pont de Nemours jointly with the Metallurgical Laboratory of the University of Chicago (Allen 1952: 92, cf. 75–81). The Nagasaki bomb may have been militarily superfluous in 1945, but it proved an economic hit: the first order of 400 bombs (a stockpile judged 'sufficient to achieve the "killing" of a nation'; Easlea 1983: 120) was for plutonium bombs, meanwhile produced by General Electric (Du Pont would return to the nuclear business with the hydrogen bomb).

Funding for RAND was obtained from the Ford Foundation, soon to be the largest philanthropic institution in the United States. As B.L.R. Smith relates (1966: 67–84; cf. Krige 2006: 165), San Francisco-based corporate lawyer H. Rowan Gaither (wartime administrator of the MIT Radiation Laboratory and liaison between the Air Force and the physicists involved in nuclear weapons research) convinced Henry Ford II that RAND would be vital for US security. The Wells Fargo Bank, close to the West Coast aerospace industry, soon joined in sponsoring RAND, and so did the Rockefeller Foundation and the Carnegie Corporation. At a conference in New York in 1947, Warren Weaver, then president of the Rockefeller Foundation, inaugurated a RAND social science division under Speier and an economics one under Charles J. Hitch (Smith 1966: 63). Besides MIT (through Gaither and war games specialist Philip Morse), RAND also worked closely with the YIIS; Bernard Brodie would himself move to RAND in 1951 when YIIS was closed down. Most of the work at RAND was operations research, as developed in wartime Britain by P.M.S. Blackett to investigate how new weapon systems were to be used in warfare. It also built on game theory, a mathematical innovation developed in 1930s Vienna to analyse how (economic) subjects who do not communicate other than through self-interested action can optimise their performance.

Game theory was introduced at RAND through the mathematician John D. Williams (himself the Corporation's fifth employee), who brought the Hungarian immigrant John von Neumann in as a part-time consultant (Smith 1966: 283 n.; Kaplan 1984: 63). Neumann pioneered the idea of game theory in a 1928 German journal article; in 1944, with fellow émigré Oskar Morgenstern, he published *Theory of Games and Economic Behaviour*. Neumann worked for the Manhattan Project as a mathematician and had no qualms about using nuclear weapons. At Los Alamos he was known for his extreme ideas about destroying the Soviet Union as early as possible (Easlea 1983: 120). The physicist Edward Teller in 1953 included him on the so-called 'Teapot Committee' to study the possibility of mounting nuclear warheads on ballistic missiles (Kaplan 1984: 63–4). Morgenstern was an economist who had been the head of a research institute on business cycles in Vienna; Friedrich von Hayek, his predecessor as director, had secured Rockefeller funding for it before leaving for LSE. As Leonard documents (2011: 86–93), the Hayek–Morgenstern institute interfaced with a colloquium animated by Karl Menger, one of the founders of marginalist economics; both groups in turn were interlocked with the neo-positivist Vienna Circle.

In *The Policy Sciences*, Lasswell already identifies (1951: 4–5) 'game theory and the rational theory of choice' as examples of policy science serving intelligence needs, citing two contributors to that volume, Kenneth J. Arrow and George Katona, as its representatives. Arrow, a RAND economist, in the same year published *Social Choice and Individual Values*. Of course at the time the market fundamentalism of the Viennese economists was still eclipsed by its Keynesian nemesis. Only by entrenching themselves in the Mont Pèlerin Society established in 1947 did Hayek and his neoliberal friends hold their ground, although their perspective remained part of university curricula as micro-economics, keeping alive the fiction of self-regulating markets for a second try in the 1980s (Augelli and Murphy 1997: 33; Walpen 2004). In nuclear strategy, on the other hand, the axiom that the only thing one can be sure of when pursuing one's own interest is that the 'other' is doing the same, was a direct hit. Strategic games such as the Prisoner's Dilemma prove mathematically that the only rational course to follow is to prepare for the worst. Rationality is located exclusively in the subject – the reality in which it operates is itself devoid of rationality, if not actually irrational. At the other end stands a ruthless opponent. This of course had the advantage of securing maximum military outlays whilst divorcing strategic decisions from moral considerations entirely (Rapoport 1966: 261–4). Since the assumption was a Soviet surprise attack *à la* Pearl Harbour, 'all options were on the table', including a nuclear Armageddon.

The philosophical basis for this perspective was provided by another émigré scholar, Leo Strauss. Strauss back in Europe had corresponded with Alexandre Kojève, who in the 1930s lectured at the École des Hautes Études in Paris on Hegel's *Phenomenology*. Kojève concludes (1968: 385) that since humans become historical subjects through struggle and work, these constitutive activities fall away in a future 'homogeneous universal state', when history has achieved its purpose. Strauss however had all along interpreted this sort of reasoning as a crypto-Marxist promise of reaching the realm of freedom. Rejecting Kojève's suggested escape from post-historical boredom by incidental violence, he instead argues that we should never get there in the first place. Humans exist (and thrive) in a universe of permanent danger, from which not even a Leviathan can protect them (an illusion for which he reproached Schmitt; Ramel 2012: 155; Drolet 2010: 104). Neither should we desire peace: 'Warriors and workers of all countries unite' was Strauss' 1948 rallying cry (2011: 394–5). At RAND, this slogan obtained an echo in the thinking of the nuclear strategists led by the mathematician Albert Wohlstetter, the godfather of today's neoconservatives and their dystopia of endless war.

As Fred Kaplan has documented (1984: 122–3), Wohlstetter and his wife Roberta were at the centre of an esoteric cult of self-styled nuclear 'wizards' (Roberta's dedication of her 1962 book on Pearl Harbour is to 'my favourite magician'). For the Wohlstetters and their peers, even the launch of a Soviet space satellite was a Pearl Harbour in disguise. In a 1959 article in *Foreign Affairs*, 'The Delicate Balance of Terror', Albert advocated (1974: 357) mounting hydrogen bombs on ballistic missiles in order not to doze off again into what he called 'our deep pre-Sputnik sleep'. Roberta in her Pearl Harbour study (1962: 166) likewise cautions against 'optimism about our capabilities [which in 1941] colour[ed] the perception of danger signals'. Thomas C. Schelling, a RAND analyst, US Air Force consultant, and then at Harvard's Centre for International Affairs, in his foreword to Roberta's book characterises the Japanese attack (in Wohlstetter 1962: vii) as 'a dramatic failure of a remarkably well-informed government to call the next enemy move in a cold-war crisis'. Things could only get worse: as Roberta warned (1962: 399), 'the balance of advantage seems clearly to have shifted ... in favour of a surprise attacker'. Schelling called for greater defence spending to protect the nuclear deterrent (the United States in 1941 made the mistake 'of forgetting that a fine deterrent can make a superb target'; ibid.: vii–viii). This had been Brodie's argument all along and in his RAND study *Strategy in the Missile Age* of 1959 he too called (1970: 377) for a full-spectrum rise in defence spending.

RAND in the McCarthyist years flirted with being a haven of liberal scholarship (Reisch 2005: 351). It was indeed home to a stellar cast of Soviet specialists, such as Nathan Leites, Merle Fainsod, Raymond Garthoff and Herbert Dinerstein. However, for the nuclear strategists, their work was irrelevant. The social science division was never popular, and when Speier wanted to get RAND strategist Herman Kahn interested in a study that might have raised doubts about whether the Soviet leadership was indeed hell-bent on nuclear annihilation, he was not interested. Asked to have a look at Leites' much-acclaimed *The Operational Code of the Politburo*, Kahn, the quintessential juggler with megatons and megadeaths, responded (as in Kaplan 1984: 76), 'I read *The New York Times*, what the hell should I read Nathan Leites for?' Remaining ignorant about what possibly motivated the opposite number in the nuclear standoff (let alone the actual geophysical consequences of nuclear war) was a precondition of the strategists' doomsday calculations. In that sense today's dismissal of any inquiry into the motives of 'terrorists' is not different from, say, Schelling's ruminations (1966: 112–13) about turning nuclear war into a 'war of nerve, of bargaining, of demonstration', in which the nuclear destruction of targets would serve to convey messages to a Soviet leadership with whom no dialogue was possible otherwise.

This was never just abstract thinking. In July 1961, as Scott documents (2010: 196), the chairman of the Joint Chiefs of Staff, Lyman Lemnitzer, agreed with the CIA director, Dulles, to begin to raise tension with the USSR through a series of calculated provocations, eventually entailing a surprise nuclear attack. According to subsequent testimony to the National Security Council it would have led to at least 140 million fatalities on the Soviet side. The schedule was meant to come to a head in 1963, but the Cuban missile crisis, the closest the world has come to a nuclear holocaust to date, cut planning short. Also the balance of forces between the different branches of the military had shifted in the meantime; the other services were beginning to catch up with the hitherto privileged US Air Force as new challenges emerged from the decolonisation process. Kahn, the self-styled Clausewitz of the nuclear age, who had worked for three different aerospace defence contractors, decided to explore new grounds. A year after the publication of *On Thermonuclear War* of 1960, the man who inspired the mad eponymous hero of Stanley Kubrick's satirical film *Dr Strangelove* left RAND to set up his own Hudson Institute on the East Coast (Smith 1966: 83n).

THE IDEOLOGY OF WESTERN SUPREMACY AS NORMAL SCIENCE

Rational Choice, game theory, and the Straussian thesis of endless war would all resurface in the 1980s along with US neoconservatism. In between, pragmatic moderation prevailed. Dewey's exhortations that American intellectuals should shun the extremes of left and right and occupy 'the vital centre' (a phrase used as the title of Arthur Schlesinger's 1949 book, one of the period's most influential works according to Scott-Smith 2002: 42) envisioned a routine process of academic research and teaching. This was to proceed on the methodological basis provided by empiricist pragmatism, to which émigré neo-positivists added a set of explicit procedural rules.

When the SSRC under Ruml began the process of placing the social sciences under the regime of method in the 1920s, the neo-positivists of the Vienna Circle were also engaged in a process of scaling back philosophy to method. 'Through philosophy, hypotheses are clarified, through the sciences, they are verified', Moritz Schlick (1930: 8), the successor of Ernst Mach as chair of philosophy at the University of Vienna, famously summed up their programme. However, the neo-positivists also included leftists like the Berlin-born Otto Neurath, a philosopher of language who played a role in the short-lived Munich Council Republic and later made his 'isotype' pictogram script available for Soviet propaganda purposes. As early as 1939, at a conference at Harvard, Reisch recounts (2005: 14–15, 169), a student of Dewey's denounced Neurath's 'Unity of Science' movement as 'totalitarian'. In Britain, where he found refuge, Neurath soon came under attack by Hayek and his fellow refugee Karl Popper, a philosopher of science also from Vienna but outside the 'Circle'. Hayek and Popper shared an abhorrence of the growing state role in corporate liberal capitalism. The two men corresponded when Hayek was writing *The Road to Serfdom*, published in 1944 (Pasche and Peters 1997). Hayek's argument that planning leads to totalitarianism (a thesis based on a theory of knowledge that rules out the possibility of centrally collecting the information required if planning is to succeed) complements Popper's in *The Open Society and Its Enemies* a year later, which claims that 'totalising philosophies' (especially those emboldening intellectuals to become a political force, i.e. Plato, Hegel and Marx) pave the way for dictatorship.

Although Popper too was a founding member of the Mont Pèlerin Society (Walpen 2004: 101), his version of neo-positivism has a sociological, investigative aspect lacking in Hayek's market fundamentalism, which uses mathematics, but only for the deductive elaboration of the axioms of rational choice. And whereas Hayek's neoliberal economics had to wait till the 1970s to be adopted as a practical proposition, Popper's method was immediately welcome. The Keynesian, corporate liberal economy so much detested by Hayek had little use for his solipsistic utilitarianism; Popper's version of the neo-positivist legacy on the other hand was congenial to a society organised around the progressive redistribution of productivity gains through class compromise. It also helped that Popper remained in Britain – the neo-positivist émigré philosophers who landed in the United States, were often mistrusted as radicals. Rudolf Carnap found himself on Hoover's list of suspects for having signed a call for peace and having declined a visiting professorship at UCLA in protest over the loyalty oath requirement (Reisch 2005: 105, 119, 277). Carnap eventually consulted for RAND, which had in-house philosophers of the same stripe (fellow émigré Carl Hempel and Lasswell's co-author Abraham Kaplan among others). Still according to Reisch, they were basically busy pruning neo-positivism of any leftovers of 1920s bourgeois radicalism; this chimed with the concerns of the Rockefeller Foundation, which also funded work at the University of Chicago to sanitise Neurath's philosophy of signs into semiotics.

Pragmatism meanwhile, unlike the highly formalised neo-positivism, is characterised by the negative attitude to systematic philosophy that was part of the US intellectual tradition. It was occasionally mocked by the more sophisticated Europeans for its lack of sociological self-consciousness. Certainly Dewey indignantly rejected Bertrand Russell's characterisation of his approach as an expression of 'the age of industrialism and collective enterprise'; but Russell insisted and defined it more precisely (1961: 781) as 'a power philosophy, though not, like Nietzsche's, a philosophy of individual power; it is the power of the community that is felt to be valuable'. At bottom though, neo-positivism only makes explicit a fundamental characteristic of bourgeois society, formal equivalence, that is also implied in the unreflected empiricism of the Pragmatists.

In neo-positivism, equivalence transpires in the one-on-one relation between concept and empirical reality, word and thing/'fact'. As Goldmann argues (1977: 11), in bourgeois society 'the access to all values [is conceived] from the point of mediation', so 'the mediating value becomes an absolute value'. In scientific practice, the medium (rules specifying valid claims or hypotheses) thus becomes the criterion for validity rather than merely a tool 'that provides access to other values of a qualitative character'. William James even makes the comparison with market exchange when (as in Sahakian and Sahakian 1965: 394) he identifies 'truth' with a 'credit system' through which thoughts and beliefs pass 'so long as nothing challenges them, just as bank-notes pass so long as nobody refuses them'.

Popper would then add the notion of a progressive accumulation of established fact, identifying sound method as the precondition for such a cumulative process – like sound money for capital accumulation. This variety of neo-positivism, in which the form of the language becomes all-important (it must restrict itself to statements that can be falsified), was further popularised by A.J. Ayer (*Language, Truth and Logic*, first published 1936, reissued in 1946). Together with Popper's methodological rules it helped to remove ethics and politics from 'the accepted range of discussable subjects' in academia (G. Hough, as in Hewison 1981: 43). Or in Neufeld's words (1985: 98), the very idea of being a critic of society is ruled out by disciplinary constraints and methodological strictures. As we shall see below, Ayer, like Popper and Hayek, was firmly in the Cold Warrior camp; Popper in addition confirmed, by politically disqualifying Hegel and Marx as philosophers, the long-standing prohibition on historicising, systematic philosophy in the Anglophone West. What remained was 'method'. As Noam Chomsky recalls (in Schiffrin 1997: 173), his philosophy training at Penn State and Harvard in the 1940s and 50s was confined to recent analytic approaches – Quine and Carnap, Frege and Russell. 'Then there were the pre-Socratics, and you had to know that there was somebody named Hume'.

Even Thomas Kuhn's *Structure of Scientific Revolutions* of 1962, no doubt a serious critique of Popper's idea of incremental progress in science, does not question the separation of science from philosophy, or the disciplinary interpretation of philosophy as method. In the words of Reisch (2005: 233):

The immense success and influence of Kuhn's book helped to promote and normalize a view of the sciences as isolated from each other (in their respective paradigms) and from philosophy of science and a view of scientists and experts as properly isolated from public life.

Sticking to one's trade whilst avoiding 'ideological' commitments was thus confirmed as the high route to academic job security. What Cold War discipline did was to sanitise neo-positivism from the remaining progressive implications that ever since Comte had been associated with the growth of knowledge; Easton's idea (1985: 139–40) that the spread of 'value-free' behaviourism was a product of McCarthyism perhaps underplays the longer history. For to cite Kolko (1957: 336, emphasis added), 'the decline of American liberalism can neither be attributed to instrumentalism or some other social theory, but *to the absence of a philosophy altogether*'.

The 'Second Debate' vs. the Critique of Militarism

So how did 'method' work out in IR? This became the 'second debate'. One aspect of the operation of academic discipline in a liberal environment is the substitution of a foundational contradiction (the one necessitating the disciplinary intervention on political grounds) by subordinate antinomies. Mill claims that social reality can be interpreted differently and that in principle there is no hierarchy between claims to truth; the idea of being entitled to one's opinion is a key tenet of liberalism, certainly in academia. Once international politics was established to displace the critique of imperialism (the real debate), the antinomy between realism and Wilsonian idealism then worked to satisfy, by default, the emotional need to take sides in intellectual disputes and have a theoretical identity. Once codified as IR's 'first debate', it eclipsed the one with political economy and Marxism. Because the realism–idealism pair is a pre-Hegelian antinomy, it cannot be 'solved' either – just as it is unrelated to the development of the discipline, because nothing develops in this perspective; change is circular.

In the late 1950s, early 1960s, IR students' temperatures were raised again by the question of method. Whether international relations should be studied in terms of general laws (nomothetically, as in mathematised economics) or ideographically (the hermeneutic, neo-Kantian position exemplified by Weber), became the second debate – the one between the 'classical' approach (ideographic, as in Morgenthau, or Carr for that matter), and behavioural (nomothetic) method. Wallerstein (2001: 97) sees the foregrounding of the nomothetic–ideographic binary, originally articulated in Germany in the *Methodenstreit*, as a disciplinary mechanism in its own right. It leaves only the antinomy between positivism and hermeneutics (in IR, behavioural realism and constructivism; roughly, the first debate all over again) as the legitimate choices. In fact this debate too was a shadow-boxing match that worked to distract from another debate, referred to by outgoing president Dwight Eisenhower in his 1961 farewell speech, to which we have already referred. Both advocates and opponents of method had expressed concern about the rise of militarism, but the second debate alone was codified to be passed on to new generations of students.

Strictly speaking the second debate is not even second, since the quantitative study of the causes of war can be traced back to the very launch of the discipline. If we leave aside Schumpeter's polemical essay of 1919, a quantitative counter-argument against the association of war with capitalism emerged straight from the civil war following the Russian Revolution. Taken prisoner by the Red Army, Pitirim A. Sorokin (1889–1968), secretary of the Russian liberal politician Alexander Kerensky, narrowly escaped execution; pardoned by Lenin personally, he resumed teaching at Petrograd University and published his *System of Sociology* in 1922. Exiled to the United States in the same year, Sorokin distanced himself from Kerensky and in 1930 set up the Department of Sociology at Harvard. Sorokin's irascible character caused endless conflicts there – having withstood Lenin, he was in no mood to take orders from lesser mortals (Cot 2011: 134). War, which he measures by the strength of armies, number of casualties, and duration, according to Sorokin is not caused by capitalist competition. It is an aspect of the alternating sensate (materialist) and 'ideational' (spiritually oriented) phases that societies pass through. As he explains in his magnum opus, *Social and Cultural Dynamics* (four volumes published in 1937–41), the process, like a biological organism, obeys an 'immanent determinism'. The good news is that after a long, tortuous road, 'the Western, Euro-American, peoples were the latest in taking the creative leadership of mankind' (Sorokin 1985: xxii–xxiii). Contrary to claims by most propagandists of the Lockean heartland, these societies are not less belligerent than others; war rather is associated with transitions from the sensate or the ideational value systems.

Following a comparable method, Sorokin's contemporary Quincy Wright, occupying the chair of IR at the University of Chicago, in his monumental *A Study of War* of 1942 lists idealist, psychological, political and juridical causes of war. Wright, a consultant in matters of international law for the US Navy, the State Department, the Nuremberg Tribunal and UNESCO, also bases himself on the work of Lewis Richardson (1881–1953), a British meteorologist and pacifist who likewise developed a systems approach to arms races. It was Wright's reference to Richardson's work that got it the attention he had failed to get when writing in outlets such as the *British Journal of Psychology*. In 1960, Richardson's two books, *Arms and Insecurity* and *Statistics of Deadly Quarrels*, were published posthumously (Rapoport 1966: 258–9). Obviously none of these writers was a leftist, yet they were concerned with preventing a war, not with winning one. In addition, the 'one-sidedness' of their statistical data threatened to silence the advocates of confrontation on intellectual grounds; unless prefaced by utilitarian axioms, as in the deductive mathematics of rational choice and game theory, quantitative analysis may obey scientific necessity without paying heed to social necessity.

The IR mainstream thus had good grounds to be sceptical of a too rigid reliance on data and preferred to stick to 'pugnacious Christianity' – nothing classical here. Indeed the Rockefeller Foundation under Dean Rusk, its president from 1952 and secretary of state in the Kennedy and Johnson years, undertook to galvanise the IR profession on moral grounds first – in contrast with the stress on method in fields more easily amenable to multivariate, applied statistical analysis like sociology (or in political science and election research). As Ryan and Scott document (1995: 453), Rusk shared both Christian values and an interest in foreign affairs with his close friend J.F. Dulles, and it was under Rusk's personal auspices that a Rockefeller IR committee in 1954 convened for the first time at Columbia. In the presence of Rusk himself and Kenneth W. Thompson (a colleague of Morgenthau's at the University of Chicago and the foundation's main contact in IR), Niebuhr, Morgenthau and Wolfers (to name the most prominent participants) discussed the development of the discipline. Thompson, a devout Christian like Rusk (I follow Dunne's account, 1998: 81–2, 87 n. 66), invited his British friend, the Cambridge historian and Protestant fundamentalist Herbert Butterfield, to attend a second meeting in June 1956. With W.T.R. Fox, Louis Halle, Niebuhr, Thompson, and

Wolfers present, and Kenneth Waltz taking notes, Butterfield talked about 'morality and the historical process'. Thompson himself saw IR as arising from a Christian inspiration, something he claimed in 1959 (1966: 33) 'was so squarely at odds with Enlightenment, Darwinism, Freudianism, and Marxism'.

Whether anything is left here apart from the Bible and whether it constitutes the 'classical' approach I am not sure. What did begin to manifest itself unmistakeably now was US militarism. Paul Nitze, the aforementioned liaison between Wall Street and the national security state, also participated in the 1956 meeting of the Rockefeller IR committee. Nitze at the time was president of the Foreign Service Educational Foundation and an associate of SAIS. His alarmist Gaither Report a year later set off a flurry of calls for more military spending that resonated in the discipline, with Henry Kissinger among its most prominent advocates besides the strategic wizards at RAND. Kissinger in 1955 had been recruited for a CFR nuclear weapons group on the recommendation of the Harvard dean, McGeorge Bundy; it brought him in contact with Nitze and others in favour of projecting US power more aggressively. The thrust was in the direction of a comprehensive upgrading beyond the exclusive reliance on the Air Force's Massive Retaliation doctrine elaborated at RAND. Whilst the public was kept in a state of tension with repeated discoveries of supposed Soviet superiority (the 'bomber gap' detected in 1957 was followed in 1960 by an equally fictitious 'missile gap'), Nelson Rockefeller, head of Eisenhower's Psychological Warfare Panel, called on the president to bolster the 'will to resist' and inaugurated a programme of bomb shelter construction. He also hired Kissinger as a personal consultant. In *Nuclear Weapons and Foreign Policy* of 1957, Kissinger argued (1958: 166) that whilst nuclear war should ideally be waged as something less than a total war, it should not be ruled out either. Appointed head of a special studies project on international security in the context of the 'Rockefeller Panels' alongside Edward Teller and G. Dean, a director at weapons manufacturer General Dynamics, Kissinger even claimed (as in Collier and Horowitz 1976: 328) that 'very powerful nuclear weapons can be used in such a manner that they have negligible effects on civilian populations'.

The danger of militarism had been expressed by mainstream political scientists before – Lasswell's ruminations on the garrison state were referred to in the last chapter. By the late 1950s, this was no longer a hypothesis, as 'the top CIA and Pentagon leadership were plotting not so much with President Eisenhower as against him' (Scott 2010: 105). Hence the president's warning about a military-industrial complex in his farewell address. Eisenhower specifically identified the danger that scholarly endeavour might become subservient to it. 'The free university, historically the fountainhead of free ideas and scientific discovery', the outgoing president stated, had slipped into a danger zone where 'a government contract becomes virtually a substitute for intellectual curiosity ... *The prospect of domination of the nation's scholars by Federal employment, project allocations, and the power of money is ever present and is gravely to be regarded*' (emphasis added).

In the same period the inductive tradition pioneered by Richardson's statistical investigation of arms races was taken up again by J. David Singer and his associates at the University of Michigan. In the Correlates of War project, begun in 1963 and funded by the Carnegie Corporation and the National Science Foundation, Singer, his co-author Melvin Small and their students positioned their 'science of international relations' expressly against non-quantitative approaches based on first principles. Thus the inherent drive assumed by Morgenthau, or the aggression thesis of Konrad Lorenz were both dismissed by Singer (1980: 353) as 'not serious'. Yet their own quantitative work, although not necessarily of pacifist orientation, potentially vitiated the pluralist rule that no position can claim the truth for itself on the ground of mathematical or statistical proof. Also the 'invisible college' that Vasquez argues (1987: 110) was formed around the Michigan project (spreading across North America to Scandinavia and West-Germany, and Japan) often branched out into explicit peace research.

There is no doubt that the pretentious grandstanding about 'science' by Singer et al. provoked debate with those working in the ideographic tradition. Thus Morgenthau (1962: 28) dismissed the over-reliance on quantitative indicators as 'scholasticism'. It paradoxically removes political science ever more from empirical reality, he argued; and 'to the extent that objective reality demands qualitative evaluation, formalism either misses the point altogether or else distorts it'. Taking Lasswell and Kaplan's aforementioned *Power and Society* of 1950 as a landmark of this approach, Morgenthau does not mince his words when he identifies Lasswell as the product of a school which was 'if not hostile, indifferent to the necessary contribution of political philosophy to empirical enquiry' (1962: 32; a reference, obviously, to Merriam and the SSRC tradition); whilst in his view Kaplan, the neo-positivist, hailed from a school which sees political philosophy primarily as 'a history of errors'. Of course Morgenthau's indignation about the 'disastrous' separation of political science from political theory should not make us forget his own confusion between axiomatic first principles (the Nietzschean power drive) and a hermeneutic approach when he discusses concrete statesmanship. But this only highlights the need either to move on to a dialectical understanding or else, as Neufeld explains (1995: 85; cf. Singer 1966), to divide the field according to 'levels of analysis'. Behaviourists would then work on the 'system' level, whereas interpretive writers focus on foreign policy, looking over the shoulders of statesmen.

In the end these are minor concerns, certainly compared to the critique of militarism that animated both sides of the second debate. Kennan, who had meanwhile moved to Princeton, retreated from his earlier alarmist positions, arguing that an aggressive anti-Soviet policy would only conserve the totalitarian state. In his 1957 BBC Reith lectures he even played with the idea of a disengagement from Europe by both the United States and the USSR. Morgenthau, too, kept his distance from the Cold Warriors after the first Rockefeller meeting at Columbia. 'When the experience of totalitarianism seemed to have proved conclusively that politics is not a derivation of economics but has an autonomous realm of its own,' he wrote (1962: 328, emphasis added), 'the Second World War and its aftermath raised the issue of the autonomy of politics again. *This time, it was the military which infringed upon it.*' Not bound by restrictions of former government service, Morgenthau went further by expressing his concern (in 1955) over the dual state operative in the State Department, the officers of which, he claimed (1962: 390–1, 399–401; cf. our Preface) no longer reported to the president and the secretary of state, but to Senator McCarthy. This too was conveniently sidelined by the politically innocent and exclusively academic second debate, although it should have caused, if not a scandal, at least serious discussion. But then Morgenthau was not a radical and did not pursue his own insight further. In fact his comment in a 1961 debate (in Lanyi and Williams 1966: 538) that there seemed to be nothing between surrender and nuclear annihilation in then current strategic thinking pointed in the same direction of a limited warfare capacity that Kissinger, Brodie and other militarists were moving and which would take the United States into Vietnam.

Besides keeping IR within the confines of academic concerns, then, the function of codifying a second debate was to observe the inherent limit constituted by Kantian antinomy. This is eminently political (as was the retreat to the first debate to avoid one about capitalist imperialism), albeit not in an express sense, as the critique of militarism was or would have been. But then, there is already a risk that a too systematic reflection on an antinomy may by its own logic push beyond that boundary into the realm of Hegelian historicism or even historical materialism. Thus in his discussion of Singer's project, Vasquez provides an example (intuitive rather than learned, but intellectually honest) of where this may lead. 'Power politics', he writes (1987: 142, emphasis added),

is not so much an explanation of behaviour as it is a type of behaviour found in the global political system that must itself be explained. A more comprehensive non-realist analysis would explain when decision makers exhibit power-politics behaviour and when they do not, and *how a system that is dominated by power-politics images and behaviour could be transformed into one that is not.*

This betrays an awareness that, at bottom, foreign relations move within a contradiction, as I argue throughout this work – the contradiction between human community and common humanity. So besides conveying a mindset that is potentially at odds with preparation for war, Vasquez demonstrates that by logically reflecting on the antinomies of the first and second debates, we may recover something beyond it, which is comprehensive and historical. In turn that might raise the issue of imperialism and the establishment of equitable global governance, and of the responsibility of intellectuals in that context – something quite different from the plain ideological function of the discipline.

Theorising the Lockean Heartland

As an ideology of Western supremacy, the discipline of IR adheres to the original Wilsonian projection of liberal governance over a world of open nation-states. Realism is called for to legitimate aggression against contender states not submitting to the West's benevolent guardianship. To project a future global governance, the discipline in the 1940s and 1950s conceptualised the Lockean heartland in terms of systems theory. Systems theory was codified by Ludwig von Bertalanffy, an Austrian biologist who had survived the Nazi period with Rockefeller support and came to North America in the late

1940s. In 1954 Bertalanffy founded the Society for General Systems Theory with a group of like-minded thinkers including the critic of game theory Anatol Rapoport. The biological metaphors of systems theory (functional differentiation, auto-regulation, and others), not only serve to naturalise social relations and processes in general, as we saw in the case of Sorokin. They proved especially appropriate to the corporate liberal context with its large, self-regulating social bodies, mutually adjusting according to relations of strength (see my 1998: 143–8).

Rumanian-born David Mitrany (1888–1975) was the first to apply this theory to European post-war reconstruction. In *A Working Peace System* of 1943 (published for the Royal Institute of International Affairs), Mitrany, who served as a UK intelligence officer in the Second World War, proposes to combine planning with individual liberty on an international scale – avoiding the federalist route, which will merely reproduce state sovereignty at a new level. Taking as his model large interstate infrastructural works such as the New Deal's Tennessee Valley Authority, he advocates a system of pragmatic, technical arrangements, what he calls (1966: 27) 'the functional approach, which seeks, by linking authority to a specific activity, to break away from the traditional link between authority and a definite territory'. Entrusted to a competent managerial cadre, this would engender a 'logic of ramification' unburdened by high politics: 'technical self-determination' (1966: 72–5). Via a detour, Mitrany thus reverts to the principles of a liberal heartland, in which 'every function [is] left to generate others gradually, like the functional subdivision of organic cells' (1966: 56). One year after his book appeared, Mitrany was hired by Paul Rijkens as an adviser to Unilever. His 'functionalism' fitted the perspective of projecting the New Deal on Europe, entertained by corporate statesmen on both sides of the Atlantic and corroborating their preferences for outflanking the pre-war sovereign equality of states by rules governing property and contract transnationally.

In the United States, Mitrany's ideas resonated in discussions about the Marshall Plan. The Plan, along with the means of production of a Fordist mass-production economy, brought managerial expertise to Western European countries willing to submit to liberal governance (see my 2012: 146–66). Klaus Knorr, then still at Yale, in a paper of May 1948 warned (as in Beloff 1963: 44, emphasis added) that Marshall aid was too respectful of sovereign equality and threatened 'to reinforce the artificial *in*dependence of several economies in the region rather than their *inter*dependence. The latter would better have been achieved by assistance in reconstructing particular Western European industries rather than particular countries.' This was exactly what Mitrany had advocated (1966: 58–60). Indeed within two years the initial liberal civilian orientation of the Plan gave way to war preparation. At this juncture a project on the Atlantic community undertaken in 1951 by Princeton's Centre for Research on World Political Institutions under Richard W. Van Wagenen obtained financing from the Mellon Trust, an offshoot of the oil, aluminium and banking empire of former Treasury Secretary Andrew Mellon, the third-richest dynasty in the US capitalist class and probably the most reactionary in outlook (Nielsen 1985: 185).

Karl W. Deutsch (1912–92) was the most prominent scholar in the Van Wagenen project. Deutsch, born in Prague, joined Harvard in 1939–40 and during the war worked as a researcher for the OSS and the State Department. Developing a variety of systems theory in which the emphasis is on cybernetics (the interpretation of social systems in which information, steering mechanisms, and communication are central), Deutsch sees communities arise from a certain density in the division of labour and a parallel communication structure that makes them relatively distinct from others. Compared to *Nationalism and Social Communication* of 1953, Deutsch's approach in *Political Community at the International Level* of 1954 moves from a materialist analysis to a higher level of abstraction when he asks (1970: 27) what it is that drives communities to merge into larger ones, the 'emerging superpowers or great political communities of the present and foreseeable future'. In the world of blocs typical of the corporate liberal 1950s and 1960s, Deutsch's central concern is that the Western bloc should retain the characteristics of a Lockean state–society complex. 'If a pluralistic political community should emerge in which various functions of government were shared by several more or less autonomous units engaged in limited cooperation with each other,' he writes (ibid.), 'with the large political community mainly limited to the maintenance of peace, the comprehensiveness of political functions for each political community or unit on its own level might be lower than it is today.'

In other words, the substance of sovereignty is hollowed out by lifting the defence role to the supranational level; but unlike a federal union, this should not prejudice liberal openness if the bloc is a 'decentralized or pluralistic security community'. Deutsch defines integration in social-psychological terms, as 'the attainment of a sense of community, accompanied by formal or informal institutions or practices, sufficiently strong and widespread to assure peaceful change among members of a group with "reasonable" certainty over a "long" period of time'. A security community, then, is a bloc integrated by 'unifying habits' emerging from a certain density of transactions of various types. To become a political community, according to Deutsch (1970: 40) 'enforcement' and 'compliance' are crucial, and the latter especially has to be 'sufficiently widespread and predictable' in order 'to make successful enforcement in the remaining cases of non-compliance probable at an economically and culturally feasible cost'. In a Lockean setting, however, this will not take the form of coercion.

In this case, submission to a single command would be replaced by mutual responsiveness, communication, and cooperation, such as exist among the English-speaking members of the British Commonwealth of Nations, or among Sweden and Norway and to some extent all the Scandinavian states.

In 1957 the Princeton group published *Political Community and the North Atlantic Area*. As international affairs under the influence of decolonisation and de-Stalinisation became more fluid, the projection of global governance along Wilsonian lines acquired new urgency. Deutsch and his co-authors now interpreted the North Atlantic model as a framework for a future world order. The problems associated with the Cold War had turned out to be a relatively short-term matter compared to the far more important internal organisation of the heartland as the nucleus for 'permanent peace'. On the basis of ten prior episodes of the building of security communities, beginning with the creation of England, the merger of England and Wales, and so on, the team concludes that 'larger, stronger, more politically, administratively, economically, and educationally advanced political units were found to form the cores of strength around which in most cases the integrative process developed' (Deutsch 1957: 38). It would of course have been really striking had this been otherwise. Rapid economic development (Walt Rostow's 'take-off') likewise is seen as a threshold condition which has to be met for integration to succeed (ibid.: 83–4) – another conclusion that need not necessarily surprise.

As an exercise in 'discovering' that the English-speaking West is the sole legitimate entity on which global governance can be modelled, the work is full of such observations. Since the Lockean state–society complex is the norm, the authors can safely 'recommend' leaving separate sovereignty intact. 'Pluralistic security-communities between different peoples and countries thus appear to have had a much higher rate of survival than their amalgamated counterparts' (Deutsch 1957: 66). The North Atlantic area demonstrates the viability of this approach:

Within the [North Atlantic] area, a number of countries have already achieved pluralistic integration with each other, notably the United States and Canada. Together with the United Kingdom and Ireland, they form a group of four countries among whom the largest number of conditions favouring integration seem fulfilled already, so that one might think of them as a potential North Atlantic nucleus. (Ibid.: 199, cf. 162)

With respect to Western Europe, the problems early on identified by Mitrany and Knorr turned out to be a limiting factor in projecting liberal global governance. The Marshall Plan, as noted, soon slipped into a military track, activating the 'armour of coercion' provided by NATO, not least in the form of undercover operations in member states (Ganser 2005). From the Atlantic point of view, rearming West Germany for an impending confrontation with the USSR now became an urgent matter. It forced France to try to pre-empt steps in that direction by proposing 'European' structures to exploit the Bonn government's aspiration to restore sovereignty and gain emancipation from the Potsdam restrictions. Modernising French strategists around Jean Monnet floated successive European projects every time Anglo-American–West German agreement threatened to sideline France, a (junior) occupation power but in the long run inevitably weaker than the economic powerhouse across the river Rhine. After the Marshall Plan brought the equipment to upgrade European steelmaking for a role in a Fordist mass-consumption economy, iron and steel was the obvious first domain in which this logic became evident (coal was included for technical and ownership reasons). This would remain the underlying logic of the European integration process until 1991 (see my 2006: 39–42, 66–75).

From the liberal perspective of US integration theory, the choice of coal and steel was just that – a choice. Also, the driving forces behind French integration initiatives were not properly assessed. These included, notably, the trade-off with West Germany in the North Atlantic Cold War context, and deeper still, the strength of the Communist Party that forced French parliamentary formations to keep regrouping in successive, unstable coalitions, until De Gaulle resurrected the strong state in 1958. Ernst B. Haas (1924–2003) combined elements of Mitrany and the Deutsch group in his study on the establishment of the European Coal and Steel Community, *The Uniting of Europe* of 1958. Deutsch and his associates (1957: 81, cf. 78) found that cross-border party differences support integration, and Haas too emphasises that pluralism concerning European integration in fact helped to allow the supranational perspective to take hold across states. 'The fact that a variety of motives are dominant in each national unit actually facilitates the emergence of supranational ideologies at a later stage' (Haas 1968: 158). By leaving out the communist parties (because they were all against European integration), the author however missed the chance to understand the key driver of French politics, both pre- and post-De Gaulle. When the French president vetoed the United Kingdom's accession in 1961 because it would have strengthened the NATO axis France was trying to resist by striking its own balance with West Germany, he also acted from a domestic balance of forces underpinning a 'national interest'. Haas however could only conclude that De Gaulle spoiled the game. As he put it in the second edition of *The Uniting of Europe* (1968: xxiv), 'Incrementalism is the decision-making style of successful functionalism if left undisturbed; in Europe, however, it was disturbed by De Gaulle.'

A MARSHALL PLAN FOR THE SOCIAL SCIENCES

In the slipstream of the Marshall Plan, the Atlantic synthesis of social science consummated in the United States was projected on Western Europe. The need to develop and expand a mass consumer society modelled on Fordism fitted into the project of an impending 'American century' propagated by Henry Luce, the publisher of *Time*, *Life*, and *Fortune* magazines. Luce based his optimism on Toynbee's concept of how civilisations can rejuvenate themselves, but as Cox writes (2002: 160), his 'appropriation of Toynbee placed emphasis once again upon civilisation in the singular – the creation of a single all-embracing American-inspired world order'. Whilst the Marshall Plan provided the material elements for a Fordist economy of mass production and consumption, it was hoped that a managerial, reform-oriented empiricism was to find its way across the Atlantic as well. This opened up a vast terrain for US social science. Some of its key managers, such as Beardsley Ruml, Robert Hutchins and the advertising mogul William Benton (Hutchins' number two at the University of Chicago), were involved in the wartime Committee on Economic Development (CED) set up to study 'the future of democracy', in fact to plan for a peacetime streamlining of the corporate liberal society established in the New Deal. The CED was led by automobile manager Paul Hoffman, the eventual head of the Marshall Plan organisation in Europe.

It comes as no surprise that the key vehicle of the 'Fordist' Marshall Plan ideology was the Ford Foundation itself. As the Foundation official Peter Bell records (1973:117–19), when the inheritance of Henry Ford and his deceased son Edsel became available in 1950, it quickly rose to becoming the largest ever philanthropic institution in the United States, with between a fifth and a quarter of its budget earmarked for international issues. Gaither, mentioned already as the chairman of RAND, was entrusted with defining the foundation's aims, for which he came up with 'the establishment of peace', more specifically the 'structure and procedure by which the United States government and private American groups participate in world affairs'. The Foundation's outlook, Carew writes (1987:194–5), was rooted 'in the values of the Marshall programme'. At the request of Henry Ford II, Hoffman became president, Hutchins his assistant, and Niebuhr and other corporate liberal stalwarts became board members. The Foundation's International Affairs programme thus 'became a second home for senior Marshall Plan staff'.

The projection of global governance over a world of open nation-states was the core aim of the Ford Foundation. In fact most of the large foundations, notably Rockefeller and Carnegie, were bulwarks of forward-looking corporate liberalism, as Parmar extensively documents (2012). The Ford Foundation was merely the latest, most closely attuned to the self-confident internationalism of the post-war United States – so much so that Henry Ford II, upon his retirement in 1976, asked it to be more positive about 'our economic system'. Yet, as Nielsen reminds us (1985: 66), by that time Congress had enacted legislation limiting the range of activities eligible for Foundation support and making 'political and propagandistic gifts' illegal. So a bottom line of discipline was always maintained. Back in 1953, however, Hoffman was forced to resign and Gaither took over in order to 'streamline the foundation's overseas programs' (Krige 2006: 169). Gaither retired due to ill health in 1957 and was succeeded by John J. McCloy, US viceroy in occupied West Germany and chairman of the Rockefeller-controlled Chase Manhattan Bank. The launching of Sputnik in October 1957 led the Foundation to respond in various ways, from releasing emergency funds for top science to funding the children's television series *Sesame Street*, intended to make the hours spent in front of the television set productive for the nation's future brain power and thus to compensate for Soviet children's proficiency at chess and other pastimes in preparing them for rocket science.

The Intellectual Culture of Atlantic Fordism

North American mass culture, characterised by the naive optimism of a pioneer society, had long been obsessed with anything 'pink', and any hint of sexuality was likewise taboo. The family relations of Donald Duck and his nephews, the four of them living apart from Daisy, their 'aunt', were part of the idealised innocence of US society. For adults, the quasi-virginal Doris Day embodied what Peter Taylor calls (1996: 199), 'the everyday middle-class home life in American suburbia', as did the slightly more peppered Lucille Ball, whose *I Love Lucy* became the most popular TV soap of all time. On the serious side of mass entertainment, the Motion Picture Producers' Association (as in Krige 2006: 157) meanwhile vowed, 'We'll have no more films that show the seamy side of America … no pictures that deal with labour strikes … no pictures that deal with the banker as villain.' Art of course is always stronger than politics, and Alfred Hitchcock's oeuvre is just one towering testimony to its continuing perception of the reality of social life. Not because Hitchcock was a socialist, but, as Nicholson writes (2011: 46, emphasis added), because his dedication to his craft 'made his presentation of class conflict inevitable, simply because class conflict is a reality so powerful and so evident that it cannot easily be ignored. *It takes specialized training to ignore it.*' This training is routinely provided by US-style disciplinary social science, and its export to Western Europe in 1949–50 was a most urgent matter.

The Congress for Cultural Freedom (CCF), launched in June 1950, was a first step aimed at rallying European artists and intellectuals to the Western cause. Those commissioned for the task were agents of the dual state. In West Berlin, selected for the CCF's launch, preparations were run by Michael Josselson, head of the OPC Berlin station, and Melvin Lasky of the American Information Service. Intellectuals involved often had intelligence links, like the philosopher A.J. Ayer, who had been an MI6 operative in Paris immediately after the war and remained in close touch with the British intelligence services later; Burnham, Hook and others have been mentioned already (Scott-Smith 2002: 109; Lasch 1967: 199).

Trying to woo the non-communist left in Europe occasionally prompted a backlash at home, such as when an exhibition of abstract expressionism, an art form it was hoped would enable the United States to be seen as a contributor to avant-garde culture, was recalled from its European tour after Congress got wind of un-American art being shown abroad at the US taxpayer's expense. In Europe, on the other hand, a detached, left-leaning, middlebrow profile worked best; some of the most militant Cold Warriors, such as Burnham and the novelist Arthur Koestler, even had to be sidelined to safeguard the moderate profile (Wilford 2008: 80–1).

The CCF's main task was to translate into Atlantic loyalty the 'sense of hope and confidence' that Raymond Aron felt the Marshall Plan had instilled in Europe (as in Scott-Smith 2002: 56). Aron would become a prominent CCF member among a stellar cast of non-, anti- or ex-communist literati. The Swiss philosopher Denis de Rougemont and Ignazio Silone, co-founder of the Italian Communist Party until he broke with it in 1930, were involved in preparatory work on the European side. The CCF worldview was a blend of 'positivistic empiricism, rationalism, technocratic modernism, and a general opposition to "totalizing" philosophies' (Parmar 2012: 118–19). An array of publications were funded by the CCF: the London-based magazine *Encounter* (launched in 1953); the journal *Daedalus*, floated two years later as an interdisciplinary journal by the Academy of Arts and Sciences; the journal of Mont Pèlerin economist (and brother of Karl) Michael Polanyi, *Science and Freedom*; and *Soviet Survey*, by which Walter Laqueur made a name for himself. In most cases the CIA, the Farfield Foundation (a CIA front) or the Ford Foundation provided the actual moneys; in the case of *Daedalus*, help took the form of block subscriptions (Lasch 1967: 200; Reisch 2005: 315; Scott-Smith 2002: 90). These subsidies were unknown to most of the readership and in the case of *Encounter* caused an uproar when made public in the mid 1960s.

The idea that the complexity of industrial society itself reduces the need for unifying ideologies was a theme popularised in *Encounter* and comparable publications well before it was summed up in Daniel Bell's *The End of Ideology* of 1960 (Pells 1985: 130–1). For Edward Shils, introduced to the CCF through Polanyi, Marxism had lost all relevance for modern society for the same reason (its 'sheer unresponsiveness to the multiplicity of life itself'; as in Scott-Smith 2002: 143). 'Training' instead of education in the humanistic sense or, in Krige's words (2006: 194), 'pedagogical emphasis upon efficient, repeatable – and thereby trainable – techniques of calculation' would suffice to provide the alternative. By the mid 1950s, anti-communism was so self-evident that the CCF and its publications could adopt a detached, scholarly tone. Inevitably disagreements now arose between corporate liberals and neoliberals, between adherents of détente and unreconstructed Cold Warriors. At its 1955 Milan conference, if we follow Scott-Smith (2002: 150–3), the Harvard economist J.K. Galbraith argued that an economy should be run solely on pragmatic grounds, whilst Aron even expressed his appreciation of the planned economy. For M. Polanyi and Hayek, also attending, this was anathema from a neoliberal, market-fundamentalist point of view. The honorary chairman, Bertrand Russell, left the CCF in 1956, after having protested at the ongoing persecution of associates of the Rosenbergs, executed for spying in peacetime, and for which he had been furiously attacked in turn (Wilford 2008: 94–5). And so on and so forth.

From 1957, the CCF also sponsored the European Foundation for Intellectual Support (in French, FEIE) as an informal committee for aid to 'non-conformist' intellectuals in the East. The OPC, as will be remembered, was set up to execute a roll-back policy; undercover involvement in Eastern Europe was a key part of its remit. OSS veterans in the immediate post-war period were involved in enlisting Reinhard Gehlen, the Nazi counter-intelligence chief recruited by the US Army in 1945, linking up also with Nazi ethnic armies in Eastern Europe (Scott 2007: 12–16). The FEIE took this into the cultural sphere. It operated nominally from Switzerland to enhance its 'neutral' profile, but its real basis was in Paris, where it was close to the Polish émigré journal *Kultura* in which Burnham had been involved as an OPC/CIA liaison (Guilhot 2010: 164–5; Wilford 2008: 75). When the NATO underground in Europe was revamped into a democracy-promotion infrastructure in the 1980s to ensure that nation-states remained 'open', the preparatory work of these networks paid off handsomely (Ganser 2005; cf. my 2006: 139–46, and the present Chapter 5). However, when the CCF convened on the isle of Rhodes in 1958, roll-back began to recede into the background. 'The global struggle for cultural freedom seemed to have entered a new phase', displaying 'a new "sophistication" – about neutralism, for example – that heralded the coming of the New Frontier' (Lasch 1967: 202). Indeed in anticipation of the élan of the Kennedy years, 'a new official style was emerging ... urbane, cool and bureaucratic'. Shepard Stone, appointed in the Ford

Foundation's international programme by Gaither, in 1967 became the president of a revamped CCF, after having ended his formal association with the Foundation. However, as Krige writes (2006: 175), the organisation was too much tarnished and disappeared within a decade.

Targets and Limits of Discipline in Western Europe

The reorganisation of Western European social science along American lines was a key aim of the CCF. Melvin Lasky, concerned about the lack of political intelligence in CCF sessions, argued (as in Scott-Smith 2002: 165) the need for a 'political academy', referring to 'ideas as weapons' – 'The discipline is an ideological confidence, an intelligent awareness of what is happening and what is to be done'. The large US foundations by then were fully literate about how this discipline was to be shaped. The totalitarianism thesis once again underscored that scholarship can only flourish in a democratic context, confirming the classical liberal notion of an identity between political pluralism and a variety of opinion in scholarly matters. A truly universalistic science, Krige writes (2006: 147–8) is based on 'organized scepticism' – the agnostic tradition of Anglophone letters since Locke. The foundations thus 'sought to promote a convergence between the scientific method and the values of a liberal–democratic state'. 'Empirical realism', Scott-Smith concurs (2002: 139), was coined as the one surviving mode of thinking after the end of ideology had exhausted the reservoir of grand intellectual systems.

In 1947 the Salzburg Seminar in American Studies was launched as a European counterpart to Kissinger's Harvard Seminar. Harvard's International Affairs Committee, a body of intelligence veterans, thus aimed at neutralising 'anti-Americanism' among aspirant European elites, whilst the Ford Foundation along with the State Department and the Fulbright programme provided funding (Parmar 2012: 109–10; Wilford 2008: 129). The Seminar's alumni, among them Ralf Dahrendorf, director of LSE from 1974 to 1984, and Michel Crozier, co-author of the Trilateral Commission's *Crisis of Democracy* report of 1975 with Huntington and Watanuki, again proved worth the investment. As Attal writes (2010: 143), the motivation of foundation involvement abroad was to train future elites in modes of thought compatible with US views. Still it would take at least until the mid 1960s before the desired social science methods began to catch on in Western Europe. Outcomes in the academic sphere were intimately connected to the foreign policy postures of the different European states, and the Atlantic conjuncture I have outlined elsewhere (2012), in which, after the Marshall offensive and its spur to liberal class formation, the 1950s saw conservative retrenchment before another US offensive under Kennedy got underway, also plays out here. Even so, national differences were pronounced all along.

Britain, today an easy target for 'war on terror' discipline, was less amenable to US preferences in the original Cold War. Labour Party stalwart Harold Laski, who took over from Graham Wallas as LSE's leading political scientist, in *The Dangers of Obedience* of 1930 warned against the dependence created by private donations (Scot 2010: 90–1); publicly funded university expansion in the United Kingdom by the Labour government even had a conservative effect. The chairman of the University Grants Committee in a 1948 report complained (as in Hewison 1981: 41–2) that the original Christian inspiration of higher learning had dissipated. It was replaced by a 'morbidly exaggerated cult of neutrality', which he attributed to specialisation and departmentalisation. In IR specifically, Quigley (1981: 310) provides some striking examples of how the quality of professors declined in the immediate post-war years. It fell to Martin Wight, later baptised the founder of the 'English School', to defend the liberal imperial wisdom he assimilated when working with Toynbee at Chatham House. Exempted from military service in the Second World War as a conscientious objector, Wight studied the future of the colonies instead. C.A.W. Manning, an admirer of the League of Nations, but also a conservative racist who endorsed apartheid in South Africa (Suganami 2001: 97), brought him to LSE in 1949. In *Power Politics*, published as an RIIA pamphlet three years earlier, Wight stuck to a traditional, and as the compilers of the posthumous 1978 edition emphasise, state- and Eurocentric approach, which cannot in fact be classed even as 'realist' (Bull and Holbraad, in Wight 1986: 18–21). Neither was Wight open to the concern with 'method'. The 'behaviourist school – with its calculated exclusion of moral and ethical questions, its lack of attention to historical inquiry and its underlying utilitarianism of purpose – was one whose claims he was not able to take seriously' (ibid.: 21).

The modernisation of European universities was seen as a key element in solidifying liberal democracy and Atlantic unity. On the margins of the 1954 Bilderberg Conference, the founding event of the secretive Atlantic planning group, Shepard Stone agreed with British Labour politician Denis Healey to arrange Ford funding for a London-based International Institute of Strategic Studies; it would enhance the intellectual profile of NATO and neutralise anti-nuclear agitation. After the Suez crisis Stone was promoted by Gaither's successor, Henry Heald, to head the International Affairs Division. He had resources assigned to him that were meant both 'to strengthen ties inside the Atlantic community and to capitalise on cracks in Soviet hegemony in the Eastern bloc' (Krige 2006: 173). The Ford Foundation also focused on American studies, outstripping anything the Rockefeller Foundation had provided earlier in the United Kingdom. Manchester, Sussex, East Anglia and Hull, as well as LSE and Scottish universities, were the beneficiaries; support was based on the assumption, Parmar relates (2012: 116), that knowledge of the United States and a positive appreciation of its foreign policy went hand in hand. Stone also arranged for a Ford grant to establish a Churchill College at Cambridge.

The lineage of English-speaking IR was celebrated in *The Anglo-American Tradition in Foreign Affairs*, co-edited by Arnold Wolfers and Lawrence Martin in 1956. This anthology of classical statements from Thomas More to Wilson was meant to underpin the idea that, as Wolfers saw it (1956: xv), the 'relative island security of Britain and the United States' had allowed them to develop political institutions without taking foreign affairs into account. It endowed them with a potentially global infrastructure of democracy; the rest of the world, mired in what from the perspective of the Anglophone heartland appeared as anarchy, thus came into view as the arena of a delayed pacification along liberal lines. In fact British IR at the time was deemed retrograde and unimaginative and the Rockefeller Foundation's Kenneth Thompson, working with Butterfield, set up a British equivalent of the US Rockefeller Committee referred to earlier. As Dunne recounts (1998: 81–2, 87 n.66, 92), Manning could not be part of this enterprise on account of his racism, so Butterfield suggested Wight as their contact at LSE. Wight in turn proposed that E.H. Carr should not be invited because he would dominate the project too much; instead he brought in his own protégé, Hedley Bull. Clearly Carr's insight in *The Twenty Years' Crisis* that the supposed liberal universalism of the Lockean heartland is merely its specific format of power politics would have sat uneasily in the civilisational narrative of the English School. Wight on the other hand could be counted on to declare both Soviet communism and anti-colonialism irrational (Suganami 2001: 98). In a draft new chapter for his *Power Politics* he took care to include a stab at Carr's historical judgement (Wight 1986: 213, cf. editors' note, 215n.); whilst Bull in a 30-year retrospective duly attacked Carr's 'relativism' (Dunne 1998: 143; cf. 91, 127–9). Thanks to the prominence of religious figures, the English School project brought back Christian eschatology to what was basically a project for liberal global governance – bolstered by the participation in the British Rockefeller Committee of specialists from the Foreign Office, the Treasury, and the *Financial Times*.

Occupied West Germany should have been the showcase of remaking academia along Atlantic lines. With its contender posture defeated, the *Staatswissenschaften* effectively disappeared under the impetus of US-led restructuring (Wallerstein 2001: 195). The Neundörfer Sociographics Institute at Frankfurt on the other hand was resurrected with Rockefeller support in 1952, in spite of its association with the Nazis. An American Department was created at Frankfurt; exiled economist Eduard Heimann returned to Hamburg, and agricultural economist Karl Brandt to Heidelberg, but the key target of US involvement was West Berlin. As Rausch relates (2010: 134–6, 138), the Free University (FU), a new institution, was established as a Cold War showcase in 1948, against the background of the Soviet blockade imposed in retaliation over West German monetary reform. The State Department and the Ford Foundation poured many millions into the FU; of the 5,000 students it attracted in the first three years, 2,000 came from the Soviet zone. Subsidies were coordinated with the US High Commissioner in Germany, John J. McCloy, his assistant Shepard Stone (before he joined the Ford Foundation, of which McCloy would become president in 1966), and the naturalised political scientist Carl Friedrich, one of the theorists of totalitarianism. The Rockefeller Foundation meanwhile paid for an FU Institute for Political Science; here Ernst Fraenkel, collaborator of fellow exile Arnold Brecht, devised a federalist political regime for post-war Germany in the spirit of his critique of Schmitt when he was still a student of Hugo Sinzheimer in the 1920s (Scheuerman 2008: 48; Rausch 2010: 137).

Since the Berlin CCF conference of 1950 brought back émigré intellectuals of great stature (Scott-Smith mentions Golo Mann, Franz Borkenau, Richard Löwenthal, Franz Neumann and Eugen Rosenstock-Huessy; 2002: 103), it might have seemed that US involvement was reviving pre-war German academia – although not the *Staatswissenschaften*, which remained eclipsed. In fact, the feeling that West German social science, and IR in particular, never again found its own voice has remained (cf. Zürn 1994); a defeated contender in this respect loses more than the military contest. Horkheimer and Adorno, having returned to Frankfurt in 1949 to set up their School again, also obtained funding from the Rockefeller Foundation. Although hounded by prior FBI investigations, they were keen on retaining a link with the United States, and Rausch (2010: 140–1) argues that the Foundation thought it more important to keep transatlantic connections alive than to obtain immediate conformity with their preferred methodologies. The Frankfurt School never revived however, although Adorno and Horkheimer's student Jürgen Habermas acquired great fame and Herbert Marcuse was perhaps the single most influential thinker in the May 1968 student revolt.

In France, disdain for US mass culture had a long tradition, although resentful provincialism blended into it as well. There was a resurgence of the left upon liberation – Aron initially even joined Jean-Paul Sartre in launching *Les Temps Modernes*, although he soon switched to the right, earning a chair in sociology at the Sorbonne with his anti-left tirade, *Opium of the Intellectuals*. The Rockefeller Foundation decided as early as 1946 to fund the national science organisation, CNRS. It was determined, Krige writes (2006: 256, cf. 116), to 'remodel the [French science] community along American lines and orient it outward toward the English-speaking world'. Social science director J.H. Willetts in late 1946 singled out France as the central battleground and laboratory for the post-war struggle between the West and communism. As noted, France's powerful communist party throughout the Fourth Republic would be the main opposition, although it helped to isolate itself and scholars in its orbit by emphasising the sharp divide with bourgeois historical approaches. In science the party demanded that members side with the USSR in Lysenko's dismissal of Mendelian genetics (Krige 2006: 132–3).

Departmentalisation meanwhile was not very pronounced in French academia. Its academic structure comprised the *Grandes Écoles* training the state class and the CNRS as a comprehensive research structure; universities long remained primarily teaching institutions. French intellectuals have also traditionally avoided specialisation; and the grounding of social analysis in a broader historical and philosophical context persists too. Thus the journal

Annales in the 1920s adopted the 'historical school' approach of the German *Staatswissenschaften* (Wallerstein 2001: 195). Historians like Lucien Febvre, Marc Bloch and Fernand Braudel studied the deeper social forces that provide context to events as so many layers of temporality. Since this was the only viable alternative to Communist Party Marxism, the Rockefeller and Ford Foundations poured money into the *Maison des sciences de l'homme*, the bulwark of the social historians. But as Tournès writes (2010: 190), its success was very limited and not one of the beneficiaries in the end gave proof of any degree of 'Americanisation' in their approach. All along, US covert action remained necessary to combat the French left. In 1956, not long after the Bandung conference had created a platform for the non-aligned world, the CIA arranged for the Paris-based black writer and ex-communist Richard Wright to intervene with a carefully selected US delegation at a conference on Negro Writers and Artists to neutralise the anti-imperialist stance of participants like Frantz Fanon (Wilford 2008: 200–3).

In IR, the deep history of the *Annales* school after 1945 became a line of defence against the adoption of Americanising positivism. Pierre Renouvin's history of international relations of 1954 explicitly draws on this tradition by elaborating the 'deep forces' – cultural, social and economic structures, collective mentalities, geography and demography – into an analysis that situates interstate relations in a transnational social context (in *Foreign Affairs* of October 1934 William Langer still praised an earlier work of Renouvin's for including not only these forces but also materials made public by the Soviet Union). Aron's *Peace and War Among Nations* of 1962 too is a broad sociological work, not a theoretical treatise *within* a discipline. It remained the most quoted French IR text for many years, even though, as Giesen claims (2006: 22–3), there was no French 'IR' for at least another decade. It fell to Aron's associate Stanley Hoffman to explain (1977: 49–50) that IR is an 'American' social science not because of its scholarly achievements but as a result of 'the political pre-eminence of the United States'. Elsewhere, scholars will often tend to reflect, 'more or less slavishly, and with some delays, American fashions' for the same reason. In France, it was precisely this aspect that was most strongly resisted. In 1959, Ford Foundation officer Waldemar Nielsen reported from a CCF meeting of writers at Lourmarin, France, about what he called (as in Krige 2006: 163), the 'sickness of European intellectuals', notably the French. Often 'onetime Communists or fellow-travellers', they were still 'worrying and stewing and griping about the United States, about American domination, about the inferiority of American values, and so on'.

In Italy, finally, it was likewise a historical school of thought that profited from US concern over the prestige and prominence of communism. Against the background of undercover US support for Christian Democracy and a US naval display aimed at intimidating voters in the first general election, Benedetto Croce's philosophy of history was selected as the defence line against Marxism. Croce was an idealist and was perhaps least affected by the reformulation of European social science away from comprehensive historical social philosophy. The peculiarity of Croce's approach, Hughes writes (1958: 210), was that he 'did not impose philosophy on history, as Hegel had done – he *included* philosophy *within* history as the latter's methodology'. This was one step away from the Hegel–Marx lineage, but was obviously nothing like discarding it altogether. In spite of his past wavering on fascism, Croce's Italian Institute for Historical Studies, founded in 1946, obtained a large Rockefeller grant in 1949 (Attal 2010: 146). Gramsci's judgment of Croce's historical analysis (1975, i: 436–7; cf. Hughes 1958: 224) was that it always treats its period without analysing the prior struggle and instead concentrates on the 'ethico-political' moment, which among other things tends to glorify liberalism. It was this moral impulse that the United States wanted to bolster, given that the cultural influence of Italian communism was much more 'hegemonic' than its (materialist) French counterpart. However, as Krige relates (2006: 44), Italian academics were underpaid and demoralised, or emigrating. The lack of 'leadership' in universities was leading to 'an alarming increase in the effect of Communism upon the thinking of students as well as those in responsible positions in the universities'.

As elsewhere in Europe, Rockefeller money was used to neutralise the role of traditional scholars, whose influence on graduates was deemed 'unimaginative' (Parmar 2012: 116–17). The Ford Foundation, too, focused on 'the liberal and non-Marxist nature of the groups it financed and also their independence not just from power, but also from university structures considered inadequate, indeed archaic and bureaucratic'. But then, Attal notes (2010: 151–2), the foundations could not afford to be choosy. One of the most vocal advocates of American social science in post-war Italy, Guido Calogero, a pupil of Gentile, was actually a former fascist. Scholars like Joseph LaPalombara of Princeton, or Giovanni Sartori at Florence, who worked closely with the Ford and Rockefeller foundations respectively, were not representative of Italian political science. In the circumstances, a Cold War stance rather than 'method' was sufficient to be eligible for US funding. Carlo Cipolla, one of the continent's most eminent economic historians, was a recipient of Rockefeller money, as were the political science departments of Florence and Turin in the 1950s. When Ford decided to finance Altiero Spinelli's Institute for International Affairs (IAI) in Rome, it demanded, according to Attal (2010: 156–7), and in the spirit of the Marshall Plan counterpart funds, Italian co-funding from Giovanni Agnelli of FIAT and Olivetti (which established its own foundation in 1962).

Both in natural and social science Krige's conclusion (2006: 3) applies, that 'organizations like the Ford and Rockefeller foundations ... tried to *reconfigure* the European scientific landscape, and to build an Atlantic community with common practices and values under U.S. leadership'. Certainly in north-west Europe, including Scandinavia, the preferred social science methods and disciplinary organisation would begin to catch on during the course of the 1960s. However as late as 1967 a Ford Foundation report expressed concern (as in Gemelli 2007: 172) that Europe, 'one of the world's greatest concentrations of intellectual and educational resources', should not be left to itself and develop in ways that might turn out to be incompatible with US academic practices. One instance of how, in the absence of discipline, that concentration of intellect might lose focus was a 1961 symposium on the study of civilisations convened in Salzburg. The event illustrates that once Western supremacy is addressed expressly, it may also be questioned, especially if the participants include such producers of unabashed grand historical narrative as Arnold Toynbee and Pitirim Sorokin. The conference was supported by the Eli Lilly Foundation, an offshoot of the pharmaceutical company of that name headquartered in Indianapolis and on the way to becoming the second largest endowment of the United States, just behind Ford. By the time of the Salzburg conference it had become committed to social change, under the influence of what Nielsen sees (1985: 285–7) as a 'radicalization of American Protestantism', expressed amongst other things in the support of the National Council of Churches 'for the recognition of mainland China and its admission to the United Nations'.

In the Salzburg discussions, Sorokin's expectation (in Anderle 1964: 241) that East and West were on a path of convergence due to the West's 'progressive increase of governmental regimentation' (something he deplored) and his fear of atomic annihilation were certainly a far cry from the traditional Cold War rhetoric. Toynbee shared Sorokin's concern over nuclear weapons but also claimed (in ibid.: 230) that 'the unification of the culture of the World had to begin on a Western basis though I hardly think that it will remain so one-sidedly Western as times goes on'. Reservations of this sort highlight the fact that in the early 1960s Western supremacy was still far from self-evident, both in actual world politics and in disciplinary social science. The Vietnam War, waged in part on the recommendations of behavioural science, would turn a moment of hesitation into a veritable crisis of confidence.

4

The Pax Americana
and National Liberation

Nation-state formation assumed an unprecedented sweep in the decolonisation of the European empires after the Second World War. As in 1917–18, formal sovereign equality was seen as the defence line against internationalism, whether socialist, ethnic or religious. Certainly this time the academic resources available in the West to help formulate policy were incomparably greater. Yet to handle the hazardous transition from formal to informal empire, neither the projections of Lockean integration nor the Pearl Harbour metaphors of IR realism were of much use. Anthropology, the colonial discipline par excellence, was caught wrong-footed by decolonisation and split right across the heartland. 'Never were American and British anthropology as far apart as in the years following the war' (Vincent 1990: 272). The void, then, had to be filled by comparative politics, tailored to cover the expected modernisation process.

In this chapter, I first look at the paradigmatic episode of decolonisation that transpired in the case of British India in 1947. The transfer of power to the Congress and Muslim League leaders according to Roy (1986: 1) laid down 'a broad model for the political evolution in other dependencies', in the sense of Marx's characterisation of the English and French revolutions as instances of a broader European process. Given that colonial boundaries had been drawn by conquest and, at best, through inter-imperialist agreement, the issue was always, in the words of Easterly (2006: 255), 'which peoples got their own nation and which did not'. As the West 'imposed its map of the world on a quilt of thousands of linguistic groups, religious creeds, tribes, and racial mixtures', it fell to US political scientists to conceptualise how new states could be internally integrated in ways assisting them to get started on a Western development path.

Samuel Huntington in early 1965 articulated the critique of the optimism and compromise perspective of initial modernisation theory. Instead he called for a concentration of power in the hands of a trusted governing class, for which the military were the obvious candidates. Later in the same year, a military coup in Indonesia corrected a decolonisation that had slipped out of the control of the country's propertied classes and their Western protectors. The ensuing bloodbath among leftists highlighted the return of a coercive, neo-imperialist posture with its own advocates in US academia. The chapter concludes with a discussion of the Soviet Marxist concept of national liberation, formulated against Western neocolonialism and yet corroborating the extended reproduction of the nation-state as the governing framework.

NEW STATES AND NATION-BUILDING

The idea of an open nation-state held in trust by a friendly governing class is modelled on the Anglo-American example. It assumes that the Hobbesian transformation (summed up by Renk Özdemir as 'the forceful silencing of alternative forms of socio-political belonging'; 2009b: 150) has run its course and an assimilation of Lockean self-regulation is at least in progress. The liberal concept of 'nation', Benedict Anderson's imagined community, constitutes the norm; citizenship and the social contract ideally trump clan, tribal or other ethno-political or religious denominators. Isaiah Bowman, the pivotal figure in Wilson's Inquiry and by the early 1940s a Roosevelt adviser (as in Smith 2004: 352), characterised the US task in the emerging world as ensuring 'that they are "coming up to something such as we are"'. The United States was cast as the 'summit of modernity', to cite Berger (2006: 17), with a 'mission to transform a world eager to learn the lessons only America could teach'. The question, then, was how the United States and the Atlantic ruling classes generally would be able to identify a client governing class and certify its recruitment base.

Decolonisation by Compromise: The India–Pakistan Paradigm

British imperialists all along had seen India as a subcontinent, the part of the Orient in their possession – never as a nation-state in the making. Churchill for one considered India (as in Sarila 2006: 53) 'a geographical expression, a land that was no more a single country than the equator'. Its ethnic composition was too remote from anything resembling a 'national' entity for it to be seen otherwise and British rule only exacerbated the complexities of the ethno-religious mosaic. The Victorian enclosures worked to privatise landholding and tax-collection, whilst disrupting nomad–sedentary complementarities between dry and irrigated zones. After the Mutiny, Britain unleashed a campaign against nomads and shifting cultivators, now labelled 'criminal tribes', whilst punitive grazing taxes targeting pastoralists led to soil degradation (Davis 2002: 328). As large areas were turned over to cotton growing, starvation loomed once the Mughal infrastructure to provide for bad harvests fell into disrepair. Who would rule this fragile complex should the British Raj ever come to an end?

In the quest for a compromise with a client governing class, the Milner Group was in the forefront (Quigley 1981: 217). Recognising that the Indian National Congress could not conceivably be excluded in the long run, the Group informally began to explore grounds for a deal in the late 1920s. In 1935, the year of the Government of India Act, Lord Lothian (Philip Kerr, referred to in Chapter 2) wrote to Jawaharlal Nehru, the Congress leader, to explain to him the inherent connection between liberal global governance and the open nation-state. The world according to Lothian (in Nehru 1962: 73–4, 79) was moving 'along the lines of the ideals represented by the League of Nations, to the ending of war through the establishment of a reign of law among equal, self-governing states'. This would also end the 'hatreds, fears, suspicions, ignorances, poverty and unemployment, which are all created or stimulated by the present anarchy of sovereign states'. Whilst 'shedding the old imperialism', Britain was also 'trying to find the way to prevent the *anarchy involved in universal national self-determination* from ending in fresh wars' (emphasis added). Lothian then proceeded to point out the need to create a *two*-party system as an educational process towards a unified, constitutional state, citing the example of the United States in 1787.

Nehru in reply expressed puzzlement over the attribution of poverty and unemployment to sovereign equality. And then, what was the specific contribution of a two-party system to unification? 'Imperialism and the anarchy of sovereign states are inevitable developments of the present phase of capitalism', he wrote back (1962: 81). Britain only 'dislikes new imperialisms because they conflict with her old imperialism'. Indeed, 'ruling powers or ruling classes have not been known in history to abdicate willingly'. Lothian however warned (in ibid.: 77) that India would only remain unified if the Congress made 'concessions to communalism, to the Princes and to property', as laid down in the Government of India

Act. Nehru in turn failed to understand how that piece of legislation, which as well as dividing India into 'religious and numerous other compartments, preserves large parts of it as feudal enclaves which cannot be touched ... and checks the growth of healthy political parties on social and economic issues', could possibly contribute to unity.

Nehru's political economic understanding and occasional Marxist language should not make us forget that the Congress drive for independence was moderated by the interests of the propertied classes in India itself. As outlined in Volume II (2010: 93), Gandhi vacillated between Hindutva and all-India postures, fearing that Hindu and Muslim workers would rally to common class positions – a concern he shared with the financiers of the Congress Party such as the Birla industrial dynasty. This was also the view of British intelligence, which according to the secretary of Lord Mountbatten, the governor-general at the time of the break-up (Sarila 2006: 193, 225), saw communal violence as an antidote to a general anti-colonial uprising, and hence recommended that there should *not* be intervention to quell Hindu–Muslim disturbances. As Roy puts it (1986: 29–30), 'the bourgeois leaders of the Indian national movement ... shied away from the perspective of a revolutionary overthrow of the imperialist–colonial rule' and 'consistently worked for generating pressures for better and better compromises with the foreign overlords'. As a result (emphasis added),

The 1947 settlement was thus *the most advanced compromise* which led to the withdrawal of the British political power from India; it was at the same time a *seriously compromised advance* for the Indian national movement since the advance was circumscribed structurally ... conditioned and distorted by the very nature of the transfer of power.

British strategic interests for a possible showdown with the Soviet Union also weighed in. Thus 'the air fields in northwest India', as well as the oil routes of the Persian Gulf and in the Arabian Sea, were identified as indispensable in a report to Churchill in May 1945 (as in Sarila 2006: 22–3, 182). In case continued UK control turned out to be politically impossible, the British military command in India suggested 'Baluchistan as an alternative to India proper, on the ground that it may be relatively easy to exclude this territory from the Dominion of India'. Thus a lock was to be placed on the entrance to the Persian Gulf by subscribing to the envisaged Muslim state of Pakistan, a long-held but not really popular idea in the independence movement. Back in the 1930s, Nehru continued to insist on the unity of the Indian social formation. Yet he conceded (1962: 41–3) that 'as long as our policies are dominated by middle-class elements, we cannot do away with communalism altogether'. A federation in the sense of the 1935 Act with its religiously defined electorates was out of the question. In Roy's reading (1986: 17), Nehru considered that the struggle against the British required a reinterpretation of the Indian past, one from which communalism and tribalism would ideally be removed. 'Indian nationalists', Calhoun comments (1993: 223), 'attempted to appropriate both the rationalistic rhetoric of liberation and the claim of deep ethnic history, [emphasising] tradition almost to the point of primordiality.'

On the Muslim side, Islamists like Maududi dismissed the nation-state as a Western delusion (cf. vol. ii, 2010: 210–11). But the lawyer M.A. Jinnah in September 1939 promised the British governor general that a separate Muslim state, once cut from 'Hindu India', would side with Britain. Thus the 'Baluchistan' option began to take shape, and when the British persuaded the first minister of the Punjab to join the undertaking (important because half of the British Indian Army was recruited from that province), Jinnah in March 1940 was able to proclaim (as in Sarila 2006: 51) that 'the Muslims are a separate nation according to any definition of a nation and they must have their own homelands, their territory and their states'. In spite of his occasional lapses in matters concerning Islam, Jinnah was built up by the British as the future leader of the new state, first as the sole spokesman for the Muslims in 1940–41 and then as the trustee of the areas delineated in 1946 in a secret British blueprint of the new state's territorial layout. The incoming Labour government demanded consent from the Congress for a separate Muslim state, and minority protection in an independent India and Pakistan. Far from being solely concerned about the viability of the two new states, as Lamb maintains (1968: 105), it also had British imperial interests in mind, expecting that Pakistan would repair the damage to British prestige among Muslims over Jewish immigration into Palestine (Sarila 2006: 199, 204–5). Indeed in the words of Ernest Bevin (as in ibid.: 15), the division of India 'would help to consolidate Britain in the Middle East'. The price of course was a partition that cost the lives of at least half a million people amidst fighting and chaotic population movements which, in the Punjab alone, saw some five and a half million people change places in each direction. In addition 400,000 Hindu people fled from Sind, and more than a million from East Pakistan (today's Bangladesh) into West Bengal (Spear 1970: 238–9).

In Africa, the India–Pakistan model found few takers as long as there was an expectation that the Commonwealth model could be extended to white-minority dependencies in the British Empire. South Africa's formal independence in 1910 empowered a client governing class built around a coalition, led by Milner Group stalwart J.C. Smuts, of moderate Afrikaners and London-oriented capitalists; likewise, self-rule was given to Southern Rhodesia's 35,000 white settlers in 1923 (Hargreaves 1988: 8–9, 76–7). When Kwame Nkrumah in 1946 called for 'complete and absolute independence' for the Gold Coast, Rita Hinden of the Fabian Colonial Bureau, on the other hand, was upset over the 'misunderstanding' behind this demand (ibid.: 99). Ever since the Haitian revolution a black African claim to independence evoked honest disbelief – 'the enslaved African interpolated as the "negro"', Shilliam writes (2012: 101), had come 'to represent the absolute verso to the fullness of the civilized subject'. This sentiment was deeply rooted in the United States as well. So whilst certainly concerned that British and French colonial rule might capsize into Soviet-supported socialist departures, Washington saw this threat as acute in Asia at first.

Theorising National Integration

In the United States the independence of India and Pakistan fitted into a set of fairly naive generalisations about decolonisation as something that had already happened in North America in the late eighteenth century. In one of his many apposite observations, Tocqueville in 1840 (1990, ii: 15) noted that for an egalitarian society like the United States, 'all the truths that are applicable to [oneself] appear ... equally and similarly applicable to each of [one's] fellow citizens and fellow men'. Hence modernisation theory after the Second World War would be based on the idea that the 'assimilationist history of the United States is evidence that the basic identity of a people can be rather easily transferred from the ethnic group to a larger grouping coterminous with the state' (Connor 1972: 344).

Area studies as pursued by the OSS during the war were characterised in a report for the Smithsonian Institution of 1946 (as in Wallerstein 1997: 199) as projects 'to learn about the "funny people" of the world', not social science. Certainly the territorial committee of the Council on Foreign Relations in 1940–41 had drawn up a detailed country-by-country list of mineral and resource endowments and accessibility, but of the people who lived on top of these resources little was known except that they had to be persuaded to open up their societies to US enterprise. Neil Smith (2004: 352) cites Bowman's vision of encouraging specialisation in product groups that were complementary to existing Western production, not competitive with it; but again America's interlocutors were not identified. In 1943 the SSRC set up the Committee on World Regions which in an internal report argued (as in Wallerstein 1997: 195) that the importance of making social scientists familiar with the different regions of the world came 'second only to the demand for military and naval officers [to be] familiar with the actual and potential combat zones'. The Committee identified the 'comparative method' as the most economical way of spreading insights gained from in-depth regional analyses across the social sciences and overcoming 'the rigid compartments that separate the disciplines'. In US anthropology, according to Vincent (1990: 292), research supported by Carnegie and Rockefeller funding likewise was 'problem oriented'. Problem orientation abandons the rigidity of an idiosyncratic intellectual culture for a similarity of empirical method in each field, which as we saw is what both discipline and interdisciplinarity refer to.

International Relations as such was not included in this quest yet. Neufeld may speak (1985: 55) about the 'utility' of IR realism 'in guiding state managers in their activities of "state and nation-building"', but beyond the formal idea of sovereign equality the discipline had little to offer in this domain. The question at the end of the Second World War was how to come up with an intellectual framework for area studies from a global governance perspective, given that the pioneering work by British anthropologists on comparing African political systems had little resonance in the United States (Vincent 1990: 258, cf. 255). A purely behavioural, empirical approach would not be of much use; the educative relationship projected on the emerging countries presumes that there is an end-point to be reached that in the 'area' itself obviously cannot be in evidence yet. Hence the need for 'theory'. The most ambitious candidate in this respect, as explained by Gilman (2003: 72–112), was the structural functionalism developed by Harvard sociologist Talcott Parsons (1902–79).

Parsons upon his return from studies in Germany combined the positivism of Durkheim, marginalist economics, the economic sociology of Pareto and the interpretive hermeneutics of Weber into a grand synthesis – an amalgam of the European departures from historicising social philosophy discussed in Chapter 2. As he writes in *The Structure of Social Action* of 1937 (Parsons 1949: ix), Sorokin (his predecessor at Harvard) had still considered these authors as belonging to radically different schools, but Parsons saw them 'not simply as four discrete and different alternative theories, but as belonging to a coherent *body* of theoretical thinking' (of course Alfred Marshall, the Cambridge economist he discusses, had already done some blending of his own in this respect by extending the lineage of marginalism back to classical political economy). Thus Parsons arrived at a 'descriptive, omni-disciplinary theory of human action'. It was conceived as an alternative to empirical behaviouralism, and with the express intent of pushing back the axiomatic dominance of economics into a 'sub-system' of the overall social system. The 'development' aspect in Parsons resides in his (basically Weberian) 'action theory', subjective rationality rooted in cultural values; and secondly, in his distinction between two cultural complexes to which action is oriented ('pattern variables' constituting a social system). These are a pre-modern, or 'traditional' society (*Gemeinschaft*), and rational modernity (*Gesellschaft*) (the terms were originally coined by Ferdinand Tönnies). Parsons interprets these types in terms of Weber's idea of a pervasive rationalisation of society. This process, Parsons believed, had progressed furthest in the United States, owing to its Calvinist culture – another tenet of Weber's.

At the end of the war, when he founded the Harvard Department of Social Relations, Parsons' influence was at its peak. At an SSRC conference on area studies in 1948, he claimed (as in Wallerstein 1997: 205) that his omni-disciplinary science of society was able to overcome the lack of interdisciplinarity identified by the SSRC earlier. Area studies as an applied field would draw on insights developed in the separate disciplines, just as medicine feeds on specialised expertise from other sciences. Sponsored by the Carnegie Corporation, the Harvard group produced *Toward a General Theory of Action* (edited by Parsons and Edward Shils in 1951) as their signal work. This was the period when Parsons took part in conferences on systems theory with John von Neumann, Karl Deutsch, and others, whilst delving further into psychoanalysis; but he also drew the attention of Hoover's FBI. However, Parsonian structural functionalism was being compromised not by his politics (he had indeed campaigned against Nazism but was a fierce anti-communist too), but by its overly taxonomic character and idiosyncratic terminology (P. Nijhoff in Rademaker 1978, ii: 527–8). Yet the rationalisation perspective spilled over into 'the ethnography of political integration and bureaucracy in new nations' (Vincent 1990: 355) – in political anthropology through the work of Clifford Geertz and others, and in political sociology and comparative politics through Gabriel A. Almond (1911–2002).

Almond, an Americanist by training, star pupil of Merriam's in Chicago and veteran of the US psychological warfare apparatus, in 1954 was made chairman of the SSRC Committee on Comparative Politics. The Committee was set up by the SSRC's then president, Harvard political scientist Edward P. Herring, following a search for the most appropriate format of a large-scale research undertaking in this domain, a story told in detail by Gilman (2003). 'Few formalized academic groups', Packenham has written (1973: 225), 'have so thoroughly set the course of a segment of social science scholarship as did this Committee during that decade' (i.e. until Almond stepped down in 1963). The Committee was to replace traditional constitutional law by 'theory' – structural functionalism. Of course, as Huntington later commented (1971: 308), it was ironic that 'political scientists should have seized upon this approach in order to study political change at the same time that the approach was coming under serious criticism within sociology because of its insensitivity to … the study of change'. For the 'implied development narrative' that Gilman discerns in Parsons' thinking (2003: 87) is not a theory of development at all but a static condition in which, to cite Elias (1971: 126), 'change only results from disruptions of the normal condition of equilibrium'. This is indeed what systems theory (or the broadly identical structural functionalism) is about. Parsons said as much himself, claiming (as in Huntington 1971: 283) that 'in the present state of knowledge' (viz. in 1951) a general theory of change in social systems was 'not possible'. Since Parsons had chosen not to cross the threshold of (neo-)Kantian ontology, this was of course correct.

What counted for Herring was that Parsons' pattern variables allowed political modernisation to be quantified and statistically correlated with other variables – and thus provided the key to unlocking modernity in new nations. Following a few preliminary seminars which he considered unsatisfactory in this respect, Herring solicited the veteran student of comparative politics Rupert Emerson to assist in the quest for theory. Emerson defined the framework of political modernisation as the need to match state and society in the non-Western world. As he wrote later in the decade (1960: 96), whilst the nation represents the 'terminal community', the effectively final format of humanity's social bonding, it is the state that holds 'the greatest concentration of power'. To make the two coincident in the post-colonial world would be the 'great and revolutionary struggle' – in competition with a Soviet development model exerting its own powerful attraction. The Committee thus agreed (as in Packenham 1973: 201) to focus on 'the problem of *nationhood* (national integration, national unity, national identity) as an essential element of political modernisation', as well as on '*statehood*, or governmental capacity, authority, and power to penetrate, regulate, and draw resources from society'.

The Lockean heartland was always the norm. As Shils put it (as in Gilman 2003: 100; cf. 131), 'the modern type of society has originated only once, in the Western world'. So 'development' is the set of techniques intended to remedy the systemic malfunction of the non-Western world. To identify what the states of the English-speaking heartland actually had in common (even though they had different political systems in Parsons' sense), Almond developed the concept of political culture, by which he understands a pattern of attitudes towards political behaviour. The political culture shared by the Anglophone Western countries was 'homogeneous' (shared values) and 'secular', by which he meant something approximating the notion of a self-regulating society. Utilising the key Parsonian concept of role allocation, Almond characterises a Lockean, self-regulating society as follows (1956: 399):

A secularized political system involves an individuation of and a measure of autonomy among the various roles. Each one of the roles sets up itself autonomously in political business, so to speak. There tends to be an arms-length bargaining relationship among the roles. The political system is saturated with the atmosphere of the market.

In pre-industrial political systems, on the contrary, the clash of Western and traditional patterns may give rise to a charismatic political culture (i.e. oriented towards a strong leader, as in Weber). This culture, Almond estimates in his 1956 paper, may display a tendency towards violence, but in fact represents a step in the direction of accepting Western norms. Thus teleology replaces an assessment of how tribal or otherwise pre-modern foreign and productive relations mutate in their own right, in both the colonial and post-colonial contexts. Other authors in the same period elaborated aspects of the rationalisation process in the same social psychological framework. Thus Shils (1963: 69) argued that intellectuals in the new states had to be made 'sober, task-oriented, and professionally responsible'. David C. McClelland, one of Parsons' team at Harvard, in his books *The Achievement Motive* of 1953 and *The Achieving Society* of 1962, defined rationalisation as the replacement of the traditional understanding of social station ('ascription') by an 'achievement orientation' fed by the market and the media.

With his student Lucian Pye, a Ph.D. fresh from Princeton who worked on communist guerrillas in Malaya, and Parsons' student and OSS veteran Marion Levy, Almond formed the small core which pushed through an empirical, structural-functionalism 'light' in the Committee on Comparative Politics. In so doing they appealed, according to Gilman (2003: 129), to 'intellectuals hankering for an overarching theory of political change to rival Marxism'. Gilman also notes (ibid.: 137, 132–3) that when in 1955 Francis Sutton, who the year before had joined the Ford Foundation, participated in the work of the Committee, 'this guaranteed that as Ford began to devote its enormous resources to development, those with an inclination to social theory would find themselves favoured'. Roy Macridis on the other hand, a more traditional area specialist originally involved in the Committee, and who resisted the imposition of 'method', had his application for Ford funding turned down. Discipline was also enforced when Almond personally wrote Barrington Moore's *Origins of Dictatorship and Democracy* out of the script. First Almond points out (1967: 768–9) that this 'courageous' book was written by somebody who is 'no man's disciple, and, so far as I know, has none' (so much for career prospects). Next he rebukes Moore for denouncing imperialism but not paying attention to 'the activities of the Third International, the Stalinist subjection of Eastern Europe, and the stimulation of guerrilla warfare outside their borders by the Russian, Chinese, and Cuban Communists'. Compared to political errors of such gravity, the failure properly to identify his 'variables' or come up with 'policy alternatives' are footnote matters.

Meanwhile back in 1959 the Committee on Comparative Politics (CCP) had been broadened to include a group formed at the University of Chicago around Shils and David Apter. They jointly organised a conference at Dobbs Ferry in New York in that year, which secured massive Ford Foundation funding. Invited by

Almond, his former Chicago office mate, Shils gave the keynote address in which he defined 'the model of modernity' (as in Gilman 2003: 142) as 'a picture of the West detached in some way from its geographical origins and locus'. Almond in turn argued the thesis he also defended in his co-authored introduction to *The Politics of the Developing Areas* (with James Coleman, 1960: 57–8), i.e. that the problem for the states in the less developed world lay in the persistence of traditional 'communal' ties (lineage, caste, language) resisting the separation of powers as realised in the United States and in Britain. Of course, as Balibar points out (1991: 25), one way of dictating the necessary development path to non-Western societies is always by claiming that their social structure inhibits precisely those values abundant in the West. But then, to the question posed by Almond and Verba in *The Civic Culture* of 1963, 'How can a set of arrangements and attitudes so fragile, so intricate, and so subtle be transplanted out of historical and cultural context?' (1963: 9), British orientalist H.A.R. Gibbs (in a 1963 speech at the School of Oriental and African Studies at the University of London, as in Wallerstein 1997: 215–16) replied that 'to apply the psychology of Western political institutions to Arab or Asian situations is pure Walt Disney'. As Anglo-America is getting deeper and deeper into wars of attrition in the Middle East and Central Asia, this assessment may be confidently repeated today.

The Civic Culture even narrows the Anglo-centric focus by including West Germany and Italy (along with Mexico) in the category of societies failing to meet the Western standard set by the United States and Britain. Since class and political cleavages are more acute in these illiberal countries, the circulation of ideas and activities between civil society and the state is correspondingly less developed (Almond and Verba 1963: 143); hence they enjoy … less liberalism. In *Political Culture and Political Development*, edited by Pye and Verba in 1965, the key collection in the Princeton *Studies in Political Development Series* (funded by the Ford Foundation and the SSRC), Pye seems to open up a real comparison after all (although significantly, the only chapters on Africa – in the midst of the largest wave of state formation in history – are on Egypt and Ethiopia). Political cultures can vary on dimensions such as trust–distrust, hierarchy–equality, liberty–coercion, and national loyalty–parochialism – yet as he puts it in the introduction (Pye 1965: 22–3), 'in the United Kingdom [the United States was not included in the collection] there appears to be a unique blend in which all four values are highly emphasised'. Unique again: all others are either too much suspicion-based, hierarchical, coercive or parochial. But what about the provincialism of Almond's presidential address at the 1966 American Political Science Association (as in Gilman 2003: 154) in which he equated the step to adopt the language of systems theory with 'the ones taken in Enlightenment political theory over the earlier classical formulations'? In the end, Irene Gendzier concludes (1995: 11), all this self-congratulatory hubris only reveals that 'it was not the Third World but a particular interpretation of politics in the First World that lay at the root of this way of seeing political change'.

The dominance of the CCP was challenged, but not from an anthropologically informed foreign relations perspective. In 1965 Princeton scholars Knorr, James Rosenau and Harold Sprout asked Herring to create an SSRC committee on the linkages between national and international systems (Gilman 2003: 215–16). The pressure to connect IR back into development studies was obviously growing. Almond was still able to convince the SSRC that Rosenau's approach was too superficial for funding, but there were other forces working to integrate modernisation theory more closely with US foreign policy. Not because foreign relations other than those subsumed under sovereign equality, were ever recognised, except as obstacles. Reviewing the ten most representative monographs and edited volumes on nation-building, Connor notes (1972: 319–20, cf. 324) that 'none ... dedicates a section, chapter, or major subheading to the matter of ethnic diversity'. Yet of the 132 states then in existence, only twelve, fewer than 10 per cent, were by any standard ethnically homogeneous. When writers did recognise non-national, ethno-political subgroupings, they tended to reify them into fixed entities, failing to appreciate how colonial manipulation and the response to it, even in the process of decolonisation itself, transform them.

Stages of Growth and Polyarchy

The work in the Committee on Comparative Politics, true to the Weber–Parsons legacy, focused on rationalisation as the key to modernisation. Like so much US-style political science, it was largely an exercise in social psychology. Partly overlapping, yet with a distinct focus, were schools of thought concerned with economic development and the way in which an ideally two-party political system, recommended already to Nehru by Lord Lothian, could be grafted onto it. One strand of this was the work done by MIT's Centre for International Studies (CIS), which as we saw in the last chapter, originated in Project Troy in 1950–52. Here the key figure besides director Max Millikan was Walt Whitman Rostow (1916–2003), a Yale graduate in economics and Rhodes Scholar at Oxford before joining the OSS. Other CIS luminaries included Daniel Lerner, Pye, and Troy veteran Ithiel Pool.

Rostow authored the first Project Troy study, on 'Soviet Vulnerability'. To André Gunder Frank (1991: 17), who studied at MIT in 1958, Rostow confided that ever since he was 18 his life's mission had been 'to offer the world a better alternative to Karl Marx'. I need not repeat the well-known theory of stages that Rostow developed from the example of East European state-led industrialisation and labour mobilisation, other than that it begins with 'take-off' and ends with a US-style mass consumption society. In contrast with Almond's emphasis on the individuation of social roles and other Parsonian pattern variables, for Rostow it is technology that gave the heartland ('Britain and the well-endowed parts of the world populated mainly by Britain') its first-mover advantage in development terms. In 1954, he and Millikan composed a seminal report bringing together the conclusions of a conference at Princeton convened by C.D. Jackson, *Time–Life* vice-president and former head of the Free Europe Committee before becoming President Eisenhower's special adviser for foreign affairs (Wilford 2008: 43). From the discussions with CIA director Allen Dulles (as noted in the last chapter, both Millikan and Pye were 'Princeton Consultants'), journalists of *Time* magazine and representatives of the Chase bank and the United Steel Workers, Millikan and Rostow concluded (as in Gendzier 1995: 28; cf. Packenham 1973: 56) that the central task was to 'deny the dangerous mystique' that 'only Moscow and Peking' could transform underdeveloped countries. Hence the emphasis should be on economic development, even if this would not be immediately useful in a geopolitical, military–strategic context. The report made the rounds among academics and politicians before being deposited in the Congressional Record in 1957. A refined version, titled *A Proposal: Key to an Effective Foreign Policy*, stuck to the original argument of the 1954 report that US aid should be allocated entirely on the basis of economic criteria.

Parallel to the work done by Rostow and Millikan, studies focusing on how to discipline the working class once economic development had taken hold were undertaken under the Ford Foundation's Inter-

University Study of the Labour Problem in Economic Development, begun in 1952. The researchers who in the New Deal era had done work on the topic of 'industrial peace' for the National Planning Association ('peace' referring to the class compromise at the heart of corporate liberal capitalism) were now asked to find out, in Carew's words (1987:196), 'why, despite the huge post-war American investment of money and effort around the world, there was still resistance to the importation of American industrial relations values'. Mobilising scholars from Harvard, Princeton, MIT, Chicago and Berkeley, the project began with studying Western Europe and was geared to the periphery in the course of the later 1950s. 'If ever an academic project established intellectual hegemony by the sheer scale of its operation, this was it', Carew writes (1987:197). The programme included development sociologists Walter Galenson and Bert Hoselitz and others, but Reinhard Bendix and Seymour Martin Lipset were no doubt its most prominent scholars.

Bendix, in *Work and Authority in Industry* of 1956, addresses the different strands of managerial ideology in the process of industrialisation, basically comparing Britain and the United States with Russia. This was meant to answer the question, as formulated by his Institute director at Berkeley (in Bendix 1963: v), 'Is a prolonged period of industrial conflict an inevitable accompaniment of the process [of industrialisation] ... [and] under what conditions is industrial conflict likely to breed revolution?' In 1964, Bendix broadened this question by analysing political authority more broadly whilst expanding the comparison to include Germany, Japan and India. Using a Weberian perspective, Bendix avoids formalising this in terms of Parsons' pattern variables. Referring to Almond and Verba's *Civic Culture*, Bendix notes (1969: 358) that whilst nation-states may differ in the degree and spirit of community participation within them, 'even under optimal conditions a gulf exists between private conscience and public actions' which 'no theory of the general will has been able to bridge'. Hence Huntington (1971: 311) places him and Lipset in their own separate strand of 'comparative history', along with S.N. Eisenstadt and Barrington Moore Jr. (castigated as we saw by Almond for his politics and not properly identifying his 'variables').

Lipset co-authored several studies on social mobility and stratification with Bendix for the Ford project. He was especially concerned about the dangers posed by political participation to formal, Schumpeterian polyarchy (a term coined by Robert Dahl).

In *Political Man* of 1959 he defines democracy by reference to the *outcome* of the electoral process, not the fact that elections are held – thus identifying an important aspect of how a society becomes a legitimate member of the 'free world' of open nation-states. Taking the English-speaking heartland plus Scandinavia, the Benelux, and Switzerland as his references, Lipset argues that in a rich country inequalities decrease and durable class compromise is possible – which was true in corporate liberalism. He considers (1969: 32) that it is only in these circumstances that democracy is possible – a democracy that rests 'on the general belief that the outcome of an election will not make too great a difference in society'. As long as illiberal parties poll more than 20 per cent of the vote, however, democracy has not yet taken hold fully – so southern Europe or Peron's Argentina cannot be counted as stable democracies. Lipset too idealises the English-speaking West, especially the United States, which he casts as 'the first new nation' in his book of that title in 1963. The slogan resonated in Africa even though it became evident early on, in the words of Hargreaves (1988: 29), 'that American policy was more responsive to the needs of white business than to those of Black voters'.

In the Kennedy and Johnson administrations, the MIT approach moved into the inner sanctum of political power. Walt Rostow became policy planning director at the State Department and would be promoted to national security advisor under Johnson in 1966. President Kennedy himself inaugurated a shift in policy from 1950s-style anti-communism to economic growth and Lipset-style polyarchy. As Arthur Schlesinger Jr., special assistant to the president for foreign affairs, later put it (as in Packenham 1973: 63) 'The [MIT–Harvard] Charles River approach represented a very American effort to persuade the developing countries to base their revolutions on Locke rather than Marx'. So what if they did not follow this advice?

INTERVENTION AND REGIME CHANGE

The New Frontier of engaging Third World aspirations in a spirit of compromise never had the field to itself, nor did President Kennedy. His assassination in 1963 is one sign that the forces that his predecessor had identified as the military–industrial complex were ready to intervene to restrain any attempt to shift course (Scott 1996). Kennedy articulated the corporate liberal, managerial approach that recognised stable blocs and sovereign equality as key principles; US development aid other than military assistance grew by 30 per cent in the Kennedy years. In a conversation with leftist premier Cheddi Jagan of British Guiana, the president explained that the United States was not engaged (as in Packenham 1973: 80; cf. 59) 'in a crusade to force private enterprise on parts of the world where it is not relevant. If we are engaged in a crusade for anything, it is national independence.' As long as a state adopted such a stance (Yugoslavia being the example he quoted), he professed not to care whether it was socialist, capitalist or 'pragmatist'.

In fact this had been the line pursued by the large foundations as well. Not only did they massively underwrite 'method'-oriented research in the United States itself, but whenever a revolution occurred in a region of the Third World, they would zoom in on the 'moderate' alternative. Thus the Ford Foundation's Africa Programme followed on the heels of Ghana's independence under Nkrumah; the Latin America Programme in 1959 was inaugurated immediately after the Cuban revolution (Bell 1973: 118–20). In India, the Congress Party was supported, in Chile the governing Christian Democrats. Harvard's Development Advisory Service (DAS), a Ford-funded nation-building think tank, from 1954 served to bring Ford influence to the national planning agencies of Pakistan, Greece, Argentina, Liberia, Colombia, Malaysia and Ghana (Ransom 1974: 110). The key criterion throughout was that the dependent 'nation-state' should remain 'open' – and not only for economic exploitation. 'So-called "strong" states of the "non-West",' Pınar Bilgin writes (2008: 11), '... even when they fail to prioritise their citizens' concerns, are not considered to be a problem as long as they remain attentive to "Western" security interests.'

This is never a matter of the one-sided imposition of Western governance. The nation-state form is a structure of compromise; it is best understood as a container of popular pressures, like the compartments in a ship's hull. To remain in control, the West must continually assess the ability of a governing class to contain domestic social forces whilst ensuring that the dependent state remains 'open'. Irene Gendzier (1995: 27) cites a US National Security Council document of 1952 that laid down as a general rule that the United States should

work to associate [the] interests of [new leadership groups] with our own and, if and when they gain power, cooperate with them in working out programs that assist them to attain constructive objectives – a course of development which will tend to give a measure of moderation and stability to their regimes.

Here comparative politics comes in. An MIT report of 1960 distinguished three types of state in this respect (as in ibid.: 70): traditional oligarchies; modernising oligarchies; and potentially democratic societies. Once the oligarchies had been secured in the Cold War contest, the forces able to guide their societies towards a polyarchy compatible with US access were to be supported to finish the job. Here the academic intelligence base played a key role in identifying and rearing a properly informed governing class that would submit to Western governance.

National Security Subcontractors of the *Pax Americana*

Kennedy was impressed with Walt Rostow's *Stages of Growth* and in 1961 had him appointed deputy to his national security advisor, McGeorge Bundy. Later in the same year, Rostow became director of policy planning at the State Department. As he explained (1967: 108) in a talk to US special forces trainees in 1961, the incoming administration had inherited four major crises in the underdeveloped world – Cuba, the (Belgian) Congo, Laos and Vietnam. In line with the idea of stable blocs, Rostow interprets these four crises as breaches 'of the Cold War truce lines which had emerged from the Second World War and its aftermath'. Communism ('a disease of the transition to modernization') tried to exploit the emergence of the new nations, but Rostow was confident that if only the new societies were able to maintain their independence, they would 'choose their own version of what we would recognize *as a democratic, open society*' (ibid.: 111, emphasis added). So the establishment of sovereign nation-states was a first step to ensuring their acceptance of Western leadership of a liberal world order. The special forces were the executors of this project. 'You are not merely soldiers in the old sense', Rostow told his audience, saluting the future green berets

as I would a group of doctors, teachers, economic planners, civil servants, or those others who are now leading the way in the whole southern half of the globe in fashioning new nations and societies that will stand up straight and assume in time their rightful place of dignity and responsibility in the world community.

There was no dissimulating the direct interest of the Lockean West in enlarging its sway over other countries: 'We are struggling to maintain an environment on the world scene which will permit our open society to survive and to flourish' (ibid.: 112; cf. 115–16).

In the tumultuous decolonisation of the Belgian Congo in 1960, the United States secured lasting control for the West through a joint operation of the CIA with Belgian intelligence that deposed and brutally assassinated Patrice Lumumba, the prime minister of independent Congo who was willing to accept Soviet support. The episode, initiated under Eisenhower, ended the benign role of the United States in the decolonisation process in Africa. In hindsight, Hargreaves writes (1988: 181), 'evidence disclosed in the United States makes it clear that, under both Eisenhower and Kennedy administrations, the Central Intelligence Agency was an increasingly unscrupulous and active participant'. The US-sponsored invasion of Cuba in April 1961, on the other hand, ended in a humiliating defeat at Playa Girón. Likewise pushed into the arms of the Soviet Union, the island state was henceforth the target of a US economic blockade and the CIA's Operation Mongoose, a plan to assassinate Fidel Castro and sabotage the Cuban economy. As to Laos, the third country where Rostow claimed Cold War truce lines had been breached, the United States was drawn in by the CIA's drug-running operation (Scott 2010: 87–119; 2003: 147–66). This brings us to the fourth country, Vietnam, which the French had failed to subdue by force of arms.

In October 1961, Rostow was asked by Kennedy to accompany General Maxwell Taylor on a fact-finding mission to Vietnam, bypassing the State Department. The Rostow–Taylor mission resulted in the recommendation to increase US military presence, but president Ngo Dinh Diem simultaneously was put under pressure to execute an active programme of pacification. Taylor developed this programme together with A. Eugene Staley, a veteran Asia specialist at Stanford University. Staley, an economist by training, had a long record of international advisory roles for the State Department and the UN, and had worked with the Ford Foundation in India. In Vietnam, he led the special US financial and economics mission. The plan he worked out with Taylor foresaw the concentration of people in the countryside and the designation of so-called 'free-firing zones' where no people were supposed to be, the strategic hamlet plan (Kolko 1985: 132).

The 'action intellectuals' associated with Kennedy's 'New Frontier' followed Rostow's lead in defining the configuration of forces in the underdeveloped world in terms of military solutions. From the Second World War until well into the 1960s, 'by far the largest part of the funds for large research projects in the social sciences in the United States' were provided by 'military, intelligence, and propaganda agencies', Solovey (2001: 176) cites a review by Christopher Simpson. The Princeton Consultants discussed in the last chapter, working through Harvard historian and CIA research director Langer, constituted one of the channels feeding the agency's National Intelligence Estimates assisting a series of coups, beginning with the nationalist Mossadegh government of Iran (Cavanagh 1980: 4). Besides MIT's Centre for International Studies and Harvard, the RAND Corporation added its weight to the academic intelligence base focused on Third World state formation, and its emphasis was obviously on the contribution of the military. Hans Speier, head of social science and former Project Troy director, in his preface to the edited papers of a RAND conference on the topic in 1959 (as in Gilman 2003: 186), argued that modernisation theory faced the task of overcoming the prejudices of social scientists against a role for the military in social life. Only when this had been achieved could the functionality of military regimes be properly assessed.

In *Guerrilla Communism in Malaya: Its Social and Political Meaning* of 1956, Pye defended the thesis that political development is dependent on the personalities of leaders. This was viewed as a technical problem, which as his MIT colleague Ithiel Pool (1963: 243) argued in one of Pye's CCP Princeton volumes, could be solved by tracking down suitable candidates and then having the media bring them 'into the picture' to provide them with a following. In his chapter for the RAND collection, however, Pye claimed that it is the military who provide a 'natural focus for citizenship training'. At a 1959 conference he explained (as in Scott 2010: 98) that the military are less inclined than civilian nationalists to an anti-Western stance because they are 'more emotionally secure'. Reports from MIT in 1960 and 1962 elaborated on how the military could help back up a modern governing class, combining their 'coercive power' with the knowledge of the civilians. They also had a distinct ability, it was claimed, to win the confidence of Third World peasantries (Gendzier 1995: 65). Here, however, different histories of military involvement in politics and society were being confused. The 'historical experience of state formation in the North has created internally pacified states with outward-facing militaries', writes Anna Stavrianakis (2010: 177). The new states however had armies often disproportionately recruited from certain ethnic or ethno-religious groups and *inward-facing*, necessary to keep the multi-ethnic society together.

In Vietnam, the Taylor–Staley strategic hamlet programme was based on massive social engineering in combination with unrestrained firepower. Backed up by an MIT report co-edited by Millikan, 12,000 hamlets were designated to win over the Vietnamese for Diem's client regime by 'a curious mix of forced-labour and liberal-constitutionalist tactics', as Packenham characterises the plan (1973:83; cf. Gendzier 1995: 65–6). It called (Packenham cites the programme's own words) for the 'relocation of peasants into fortified villages, surrounded by barbed wire fences and ditches filled with bamboo spikes ... Each hamlet would elect its political representative by secret ballot.' However, 'The first element of this formula seems to have been implemented more consistently than the second.' In the autumn of 1962, disagreement arose because it seemed as if land reform previously introduced under US pressure was being rolled back through the strategic hamlet plan. The recommendations of Robert Thompson, the British theorist of the 'hearts and minds' approach who had been involved in the suppression of the communist revolt in Malaya, were now sidelined by plans to rely more on the South Vietnamese military. 'The reliance on civil authorities in the Third World after 1945 had been an error,' Kolko summarises the argument (1985: 117).

The military establishments were far better transmitters of Western values and the most promising modernizers of the traditional order. And because the United States controlled aid as well as direct training, Rostow urged much greater exploitation of these levers to advance U.S. interests. Its 'benevolent authoritarianism' would create national unity and hold power in trust for the less competent civilians.

After the assassinations of Diem and, soon afterwards, of President Kennedy himself, US military involvement was stepped up in 'response' to the 1964 Gulf of Tonkin incident, a largely fictional attack by North Vietnamese gunboats on US warships. To win the war, a torrent of social-science recommendations was unleashed, largely on the lines of the behaviourist theory, in the spirit of Watson and Pavlov. The US military were again directly involved, as they had been in 1950s strategic thinking.

In this respect there is a difference between the connections with academia of the intelligence services on the one hand and the armed forces on the other. Whilst the CIA gathers information and conducts undercover activities, global policing 'is the responsibility of the American armed forces', argues Juan Bosch (1968: 95–7; cf. Appendix I, ibid.: 133–8), the progressive Dominican politician whose country was invaded by US Marines in 1965. CIA connections with scholars focus on providing intelligence, if need be for covert action; this will not as a rule affect intellectual content in any enduring sense. Military links on the other hand do have such effects. The military, still according to Bosch, mobilise the academic intelligence base for large-scale, mid- to long-term policy, and thus actively try to mould intellectual content. This would indeed apply to the RAND Corporation and its doomsday calculations in the service of the US Air Force; it certainly applies to Project Camelot, launched by the US Army in 1962.

Camelot, named after the myth of King Arthur and the knights of the Round Table, involved large-scale behavioural research on the modalities of violent revolution and internal war in 31 countries, 'a technology of human behaviour for defense use', according to a preparatory paper. The ultimate aim, according to the US Army's chief of research and development (as in Solovey 2001: 182, emphasis added; cf. 176), was to develop *a single model* which could be used to estimate the internal war potential of a developing nation', whilst guiding 'underdeveloped countries through the modernization barrier and for countering subversive insurgency'. This is different from gathering intelligence from academics; it amounts to customising research itself and turning universities and think tanks into extensions of the American war machine. Behavioural research was funded through the Special Operations Research Organisation (SORO) at American University in Washington, DC, a campus-based contract research organisation for the Department of Defense established in 1956. It served to generate the theoretical and empirical basis from which counterinsurgency operations could be confidently designed. Latin America was the key focus, whilst major centres of Africa research, such as Northwestern, UCLA and Indiana also obtained US Army money; insights were obviously also applied in Vietnam, which was fast becoming the main laboratory of counterinsurgency. According to one of the beneficiaries, James Coleman (as in Parmar 2012: 162), there was no need to be hesitant about working for the military; the goals of government agencies are the goals of society and hence will not 'contaminate or corrupt the purity of objective scholarship'. Besides Coleman, Camelot consultants included Lewis Coser, Theodore Draper, Harry Eckstein, Shmuel N. Eisenstadt, William Kornhauser, William Riker, R.J. Rummel, Thomas Schelling, Neil Smelser, Gordon Tullock and Charles Wolf Jr., as well as some lesser-known social scientists (appendix to Solovey 2001: 198–9).

Camelot was exposed as a Pentagon operation by Norwegian peace researcher Johan Galtung, teaching in Chile at the time. The project was formally discontinued, but in fact reconstituted itself as the Centre for Research in Social Systems (CRESS; Bilgin and Morton 2002: 60). As the new channel for disbursing research money for the study of the role of the military in the Third World, the largest CRESS contract went to a group led by Morris Janowitz at the University of Chicago (Gendzier 1995: 66). Building on the Carnegie-supported Shils–Apter project there, Janowitz's intention in his programmatic *The Military in the Political Development of the New Nations* (1964: vii) was to find out how 'the armed forces can effect change … in a new nation on the basis of a minimum resort to force and coercion' (never mind that the Camelot letter of invitation, as in Schiffrin 1997: 119, asked scholars to help assist 'friendly governments in dealing with active insurgency problems'). In a critique of both the Almond and Coleman paradigm and Lipset's claims about the correlation between economic development and political pluralism, Janowitz (1964: 18–22) points out that these in fact are often negatively correlated. He also elucidates the difference between a military coup that involves closure to Western influence, such as Nasser's in Egypt (what he calls 'designed militarism'), and a 'reactive' variety, such as the one that took place in the US ally Pakistan as a response to the 'weakness of civilian rule' and popular pressure (ibid.: 83–4).

At Harvard, Samuel Huntington in early 1965 pushed the findings of Janowitz's CRESS programme to their logical conclusion by discarding the original development optimism altogether. In an article that reinserted US involvement in Vietnam into the domain of geopolitical concerns, he rejects (1965: 387–8) the idea of modernisation as rationalisation (the Weber–Parsons legacy) developed by the Committee on Comparative Politics. By raising the level of political participation, economic development and the growth of education often lead to a *reversal* of political development in the sense of a well-ordered political system (and instead to what he calls, 'political decay'). Comparing the newly independent states to the unaccompanied boys wreaking havoc in William Golding's 1954 novel *The Lord of the Flies* (and heralding his ruminations about the demand overload on *developed* states a decade later), Huntington proposes (1965: 419–21, cf. 416n.) minimising competition within the political elite, for instance by instituting a one-party system; removing hotbeds of political agitation by limiting the number of university students and keeping industrial plant size small; and enhancing social class and caste cleavages. Huntington's confidence in the military dated from *The Soldier and the State* of 1957; in 1961, in a report commissioned by the Special Studies Group of the Institute for Defense Analyses, titled 'Instability at the Non-Strategic Level of Conflict', he came up with the notion of 'preventive intervention' (Gendzier 1995: 42–3). What is needed according to Huntington (1965: 429) is a concentrated state power to keep a country in the Western camp. 'Unless that need is met with American support, the alternatives in [the developing world] remain a corrupt political system or a Communist one.' We will see below what this recommendation meant for Indonesia.

In the Vietnam War the MIT and CRESS approaches merged with IR properly speaking, social psychology being the common denominator. 'Southeast Asian countries exhibit only to a limited extent the characteristics of the modern nation-states of the West', conclude RAND counterinsurgency specialist George Tanham and Dennis Duncanson, a colonial Malayan civil servant during the communist insurrection who served on the Thompson mission to Vietnam in the early 1960s (1969: 115–16). This makes it difficult to impose authority in border areas: 'Because of the tradition of local autonomy and suspicion of outsiders, problems will arise even where officials are able and dedicated, which of course they frequently are not.' So the coercive removal of people from the land to strategic hamlets must be continued. How people felt about this was entirely secondary. 'The confiscation of chickens, razing of houses, or destruction of villages have a place in counter-insurgency efforts, but only if they are done for a strong reason: namely, to penalize those who have assisted the insurgents', wrote Camelot consultant and RAND scholar Charles Wolf in *United States Policy and the Third World* of 1967 (as in Chomsky 1969: 48). 'Whatever harshness is meted out by government forces [must be] unambiguously recognizable as deliberately imposed because of behaviour by the population that contributes to the insurgent movement.' The insights of 'science' should override any moral concerns, or to cite Tanham and Duncanson again (1969: 122, emphasis added), 'If the difficulties are not understood, they are insuperable; once they are understood they can be resolved. All the *dilemmas are practical and as neutral in an ethical sense as the laws of physics.*'

'Behaviour' thus could be projected on a linear scale. Indeed in another confident social science assessment cited by Chomsky (1969: 49), Harvard scholar Morton Halperin argued that Vietnam illustrated 'the fact that most people tend to be motivated not by abstract appeals'; rather, they follow what they think 'is most likely to lead to their own personal security and to the satisfaction of their economic, social, and psychological desires'. After the Tet offensive in 1968, which revealed to the world that an invasion force of half a million men could not secure even the main urban centres from attack (a propaganda victory for which the National Liberation Front paid a heavy price too), Huntington, chairman of the Council on Vietnamese Studies of the Southeast Asia Development Advisory Group at the time, argued (1968: 652) that even this was a US success. Tet, he claimed, was in fact a dying spasm of a guerrilla forced out of its rural milieu thanks to the US policy of driving people to the cities.

In an absent-minded way the United States in Viet Nam may well have stumbled upon the answer to 'wars of national liberation.' The effective response lies neither in the quest for conventional military victory nor in the esoteric doctrines and gimmicks of counter-insurgency warfare. It is instead forced draft urbanization and modernization which rapidly brings the country in question out of the phase in which a rural revolutionary movement can hope to generate sufficient strength to come to power.

The turn to militarisation was made in full during the Johnson presidency. Part IX of the 1966 congressional hearings on 'Winning the Cold War: The U.S. Ideological Offensive' was entitled 'Behavioural Sciences and National Security'. It argued that insights into 'human attitudes and motivations' should form the basis for the conduct of US foreign policy. Thus the insertion of decolonisation into the struggle with the Soviet contender state brought about a blending of IR and comparative politics for all but teaching purposes. The recruitment of social-science researchers for foreign policy was made mandatory, and academic research was identified (as in Gendzier 1995: 56–7) as 'one of the vital tools in the arsenal of the free societies'. In 1970 Ted Robert Gurr published a study sponsored by the Pentagon which maintained that a consequent application of violence can keep the population from resisting. Domestic dissent, too, was considered as eligible to such an approach (Gurr 1970: 256, 262).

This effectively discards the idea of a steady process of nation-building through cumulative class compromises within state borders. Such a process will take its course everywhere, except that it usually has to reverse the internal foreign relations exploited for purposes of colonial rule – which explains why it takes so much longer in such cases. One only has to think of contemporary Iraq, where the Anglo-US invasion 'in an absent-minded way' brought the Shi'a majority to power, dispossessing the ruling Sunni-led bloc, to understand how a new round of dispossession and investiture once again reverses the process of amalgamating civil society. In 1960s modernisation literature, however, the silent assumption was always that intra-state, inter-ethnic dividing lines were disappearing. In fact, ethnic consciousness was on the increase, with 'multi-ethnic states at all levels of modernity [being] afflicted' (Connor 1972: 327; cf. vol. i, 2007: 183–8). By ignoring the internal foreign relations and placing power in the hands of certain groups whilst excluding others, Connor concludes (1972: 336), nation-building turns into 'nation-destroying'.

After Camelot had been exposed, discipline over the academic intelligence base was tightened. President Lyndon Johnson decreed (as in Gough 1968: 153) that 'no Government sponsorship of foreign area research should be undertaken which ... would adversely affect United States foreign relations'. CIA involvement with US academia was unaffected by the exposure of the US Army's direction of research. Whilst Undersecretary of State Nicholas Katzenbach in 1966 intervened to limit the agency's covert funding of research and safeguard the 'integrity and independence of the educational community' (as in Hulnick 1987: 43), CIA director Admiral William Raborn in the same year prided himself on the intense traffic between academe and the agency. The State Department (which has its own intelligence agency, the Bureau of Intelligence and Research) had connections with universities that were even more extensive. Again in 1966, Deputy Undersecretary of State William J. Crockett boasted having on file more than 5,000 current IR research projects then in progress at US universities, and receiving some 200 unpublished scholarly papers each month (Windmiller 1968: 121). MIT was among the most important recipients of CIA money. Ithiel Pool, mentioned already as one of Millikan's original recruits, even proposed bringing more of US social science under the umbrella of the CIA, since the agency, 'as its name implies, should be the central social research organization to enable the Federal government to understand the societies and cultures of the world' (as in ibid.: 119). Hence, 'we should be demanding that the CIA uses us more'.

In order not to dismiss this sort of babble too easily, we should recall the scale of the destruction wrought on Vietnam, Laos and Cambodia to which mainstream academics were volunteering to devote their intellectual talents. During the Second World War, US forces dropped approximately 2.06 million tons of bombs on Europe and the Pacific. The total amount of bombs dropped on Indochina from 1965 to the end of 1972 was 7.7 million tons. With shells added, the total amount of ordnance exploded rises to more than 15 million tons, the equivalent, writes Japanese author Shingo Shibata (1973: 146; cf. Kolko 1997: 2), of more than 770 Hiroshima-type nuclear bombs. Of the forest surface of the affected region, 44 per cent had been destroyed by defoliants and other toxic chemicals by the end of 1970, along with 43 per cent of the farmland. Even by the conservative estimate of a Cornell University team, still according to the same author, more than 1 million civilians were either killed or wounded and an additional 6 million displaced, in South Vietnam alone, between 1965 and April 1971. 'Bombing and shelling by the US Forces', writes Shibata,

was carried on in a manner calculated to kill all living things on the earth and even to destroy the ecological cycle and nature itself. Air and water reserves have been polluted, with even the temperature changed in some areas. Such terms as 'biocide' and 'ecocide' were coined, and indeed even these terms still fall far short of properly describing the atrocious nature of this war.

This was what the academic intelligence base was mobilised to support, and any breach of discipline was immediately covered. When at Michigan State University the journal *Ramparts* in 1966 published an exposé of a CIA project on Vietnam, Raborn responded by ordering an investigation of the journal and those who worked for it. The incident also triggered the formation of a task force that included Katzenbach and Richard Helms (who would succeed the ineffective Raborn as CIA director), to check, in Helms' words (as in Wilford 2008: 237) on 'all of [the CIA's] relationships with academic institutions and academicians' and prevent the agency's being caught unawares by future revelations.

Yet as opposition to the Vietnam War and scepticism about the United States' world role increased, revelations about the complicity of US academics, too, multiplied. In 1967 it became public that the executive director and the treasurer of the American Political Science Association, Evron M. Kirkpatrick and Max Kampelman, were also president and vice-president, respectively, of a CIA-funded organisation called Operations and Policy Research Inc. (OPR; Windmiller 1968: 122). Kirkpatrick, whose wife Jean would later serve as Ronald Reagan's ambassador to the UN, had a background in psychological intelligence in the State Department. He was on the advisory council of Freedom Studies Centre, at the time the largest Cold War think tank, led by the counterinsurgency expert Major-General Edward G. Lansdale. As Playford tells the story (1968), when it turned out that OPR had several hundred social scientists, many of them APSA members, working for it covertly to commission and promote books favourable to US foreign policy, a committee under the Yale political scientist and president of APSA, Robert Dahl, investigated. Its report, brimming with references to the 'complexity' of ethical issues as well as to endless 'dilemmas and paradoxes', led to a walkout of critical scholars, mostly young graduates, and the formation of a Caucus for a New Political Science outside APSA.

Meanwhile the quest for an exit from Vietnam had begun in earnest with the election of Richard Nixon in November 1968. With it came a shift from Kennedy-style behaviourists to the traditional balance-of-power outlook of the earlier Cold War, a shift personified by Harvard's Henry Kissinger, Nixon's national security advisor, taking over from Walt Rostow, who had served Johnson in that capacity. On behalf of his paymaster, the then presidential hopeful Nelson Rockefeller, Kissinger had already toured Vietnam in the mid 1960s and expressed doubt about whether the war was winnable. Rockefeller translated Kissinger's advice into an early instance of active balancing by offering détente to both the Soviet Union and China. After switching to the Nixon camp, Kissinger oversaw this policy in practice, making the fates not only of Vietnam and Laos but also of Cambodia subordinate to his conception of playing the balance of power. Hitchens (2002) is of course right in calling Kissinger's policies a catalogue of war crimes. Of the aforementioned 15 million tons of ordnance dropped on Indochina between 1965 and the end of 1972, around 58 per cent was used during the Nixon administration (Shibata 1973: 148). Of course we should not forget that in many cases, what appear as 'decisions' leading to escalation, are in fact outcomes of inter-service rivalry and other bureaucratic processes. Thus the appropriation of the field of counterinsurgency by the US Army discussed earlier had left the Air Force in the cold; it only overcame its budget constraint when the bombing campaign of North Vietnam began in 1965 (Chomsky 1969: 68). By then the biggest prize in South-East Asia, Indonesia, had been secured by another murderous intervention.

Training an Alternative Governing Class in Indonesia

In Indonesia there was a violent switch from the nationalist regime of Sukarno back to military dictatorship in 1965. Sections of the Indonesian military acted with Anglo-American support to break the back of a land reform movement and the communist party, the main political force supporting it – thus averting the 'closure' of Indonesia and winning what British officials called (as in Curtis 2003: 397) the struggle 'for the commanding heights of the Indonesian economy'.

The independence movement in the Dutch East Indies never achieved 'a unity of political organisation in the spirit of the Congress Party in India' (Idenburg 1961: 130). The difference is partly explained by the Japanese occupation, which as Wertheim attests (1992: 103) 'temporarily achieved what we [the Dutch] never dared: reinforc[ing] Indonesian nationalism to make it subservient to imperialist aims'. Sukarno and his nationalists after the conquest rallied to the slogan of 'Asia for the Asians', whilst Dutch and 'Indo' (mixed) colonial personnel and their families suffered in Japanese concentration camps. This reduced any chance for a post-war decolonisation compromise, and Dutch economic interests other than those of mobile transnational capital in addition wielded great political influence at home. Granting independence to 'the more sophisticated people of Java' whilst keeping it in abeyance for others, as suggested by Owen Lattimore in 1945 (as in Friedericy 1961: 69) would have enabled a dissection of the Dutch East Indies along India–Pakistan lines. But however much the Dutch tried to contain the Sukarno nationalists' insurrection through various schemes to cut up the country along ethnic lines, decolonisation was grudgingly conceded in 1949, under pressure from the United States, which had to compete with Soviet support for decolonisation.

Even then sovereignty was transferred to 16 'partner states' and autonomous territories, whilst New Guinea remained under the Dutch until, again after military intervention had been cut short by Washington, they were forced to hand it over to Indonesia in 1963.

As I have documented elsewhere (2012: 211), Secretary of State Dulles, in a closed session of the Senate Foreign Relations Committee in 1954, argued that independence had been given to Indonesia prematurely. US social science was enlisted to groom an alternative, client governing class; not an easy task since the Dutch had left the country, then of 80 million, with only 15 Ph.Ds. One of them, the economist Sumitro Djojohadikusomo, was selected to continue his studies, funded by the Ford Foundation, at the (Johns Hopkins) School of Advanced in International Studies in Washington in 1949. As minister of trade and industry and later of finance in independent Indonesia, whilst leading a small 'socialist' party, Sumitro was an advocate of Western access (Ransom 1974: 94). When the Sukarno government, bolstered by the 1955 Bandung Conference of non-aligned states and Nasser's nationalisation of the Suez Canal a year later, began a drive to centralise state power and expel the Dutch from the economy, Sumitro joined the CIA-supported Outer Islands rebellion in 1957–58; but it was defeated.

The Ford Foundation had the leading role in grooming an alternative elite for Indonesia, as documented extensively by Ransom (1974) and Parmar (2012). The foundation's Wilsonian perspective transpires in its stated aim (as in Bell 1973: 119) of 'channelling rising nationalism into constructive purposes within a democratic framework'. Asia and the Near East in this respect 'seemed particularly important in view of major tensions that threatened world peace, in view also of proximity to the Soviet Union and Communist China and the opportunity for channelling rising nationalism into constructive human purposes within a democratic framework.' Foundation money and the national security state were on the same trail. The 1951 Stanford survey of US Asia studies funded by the Ford Foundation involved the State Department; the historian William Langer of the CIA and Clyde Kluckhohn of Harvard's Russian Research Centre were also involved. The Association for Asian Studies was set up with Ford money, with its own journal, in 1954. Given that Indonesia's Communist Party (the PKI) was the third largest in the world, the populous and resource-rich country was at the centre of US and British attention.

A series of programmes supported by the Ford and Rockefeller Foundations and run at top US universities such as MIT, Cornell, Berkeley and later Harvard, was intended to 'remould the old Indonesian hierarchs into modern administrators, trained to work under the new indirect rule of the Americans' (Ransom 1974: 96). Cornell already had a South-East Asia programme, begun in 1950 (Vincent 1990: 293) when the Ford Foundation set up the Modern Indonesia Project there. When George McT. Kahin took on the role of director of the project, Parmar records (2012: 130–5), it was cleared with Allen Dulles at the CIA in light of the intelligence it was expected to yield. Kahin worked closely with Sumitro, who by then had become dean of the economics faculty at Jakarta University. Paul Hoffman, still the president of the Ford Foundation, arranged to have Sumitro's department turned into a fully fledged graduate school with Ford money, whilst in the United States, Parsons' student Clifford Geertz and fellow Harvard graduates in this period moved to MIT to join the Ford Foundation's nation-building project for Indonesia (Schiffrin 1997: 114).

The disciplinary effect of mainstream economics, cast as technical expertise beyond politics and ideology, was at the heart of the enterprise. The 1957–58 nationalisation policy included the expulsion of Dutch economics professors from Indonesia; but Sukarno was equally suspicious of the curriculum proposed by economists at the University of Indonesia (trained under the auspices of the University of California at Berkeley). His hesitations were overcome by the Ford Foundation's threat to cut off funds if the neoclassical curriculum was tampered with – this after all is what 'discipline' is about. There was a feeling, Ransom notes (1974: 99–101), that the Ford project was training the leaders who would take over once Sukarno got out. Indeed as Parmar documents (2012: 133–5), the Ford–Cornell project had the effect of doubling the size of the indigenous social-science community, fostering and strengthening 'a strategically placed academic–political elite that was increasingly frustrated with the Indonesian government's non-aligned, independent, anti-Western, and pro-leftist orientation'. The United States also ran a training programme for trade unionists willing to oppose the WFTU-affiliated Indonesian trade union federation SOBSI (Wilford 2008: 55).

The Rumanian-born Guy Pauker of MIT's Centre for International Studies and RAND, dispatched to Indonesia to find out about the 'obstacles to economic growth', early on linked up with Sumitro and his clan of upper class 'socialists' in the tiny socialist party, the PSI. They in turn were connected with the Muslim landowner party, Masjumi, identified by the Cornell–University of Indonesia project as a potential ally against Sukarno and communism. Support for the Muslim student left, the most promising rivals of the communists, also was part of the build-up of a post-Sukarno governing class, whilst Kahin put together a guidebook on local administration that became compulsory for the Indonesian police academy (Parmar 2012: 134). Pauker, who according to Wertheim (1992: 197–8) worked hand in glove with the US intelligence services in Indonesia, in 1959 summarised his experiences in a paper entitled 'Southeast Asia as a Problem Area in the Next Decade'. Bolstering political parties (like Sumitro's PSI) would not work against the growing mass basis of the communist parties of the region, he argued (1959: 343 and passim). Given the inequality of access to land, communism would prevail unless 'effective countervailing power' were created – and those who were best equipped for this were 'members of the national officer corps as individuals and the national armies as organizational structures ... *What is most urgently needed in Southeast Asia today is organizational strength*' (emphasis added). At a RAND conference in the same year Pauker exhorted the Indonesian officers present (as in Scott 2003: 83 n. 38) 'to strike, sweep their house clean'. This of course was also the position of Huntington in the same year, and it need not surprise us that he quotes Pauker approvingly in the article cited (1965: 429–30).

At this juncture the Indonesian army's staff and command school at Bandung, SESKOAD, provided an opportunity to bring Sumitro's economics graduates and the generals in touch with each other. As Ransom documents (1974: 100–1), an Indonesian colonel whom Pauker introduced to RAND (which he himself had joined in 1958) decided to build SESKOAD into a conduit between the military and a trusted academic intelligence base. Economists from the Sumitro group along with PSI and Masjumi graduates and alumni of the Pauker and Kahin projects were cleared for lecturing at SESKOAD and thus became part of an anti-communist conspiracy around Lieutenant General Achmad Yani, the commander-in-chief. This was the group preparing contingency plans to deal with a post-Sukarno situation. The US military attaché in Djakarta, Willis G. Ethel, a close confidant of Yani and his circle, recruited Indonesian officers to study counterinsurgency at US military training schools and business administration at Syracuse and Harvard (which took over from Berkeley under the Ford Foundation programme). Five months before the coup, Lockheed and Rockwell payoffs were redirected from middlemen associated with Sukarno to new ones including Mohamed 'Bob' Hasan, subsequent financial associate of the Suharto family (Scott 2010: 147). Thus US diplomacy, business and academia became complicit in what Kolko characterises (1988: 181) as the single most bloody American intervention after 1945.

The events of September–October 1965 that inaugurated the decades-long Suharto dictatorship were triggered by the killing by a group of leftist officers of General Yani and five others of the SESKOAD brain trust. Whether or not this involved provocation, as Wertheim (1992: 195–203) and others suspect, it unleashed a well-prepared mass terror against communists and the broader land reform movement that killed hundreds of thousands, possibly more than 2 million, over the next years. In this protracted slaughter, committed whilst the Vietnam War was killing a comparable number in continental South-East Asia, both the US political authorities and the social scientists funded by the big foundations were complicit. A new US ambassador, seasoned by handling student turmoil in South Korea, took up his post a few months before the coup; the University of Kentucky's institution-building programme at the Bandung Institute of Technology had been training anti-Sukarno students who would link up with Muslim extremists in the villages in massacring PKI followers and peasants, for which the army provided them with arms (Ransom 1974: 106). The United States passed hit lists with names of thousands of PKI cadre and members of communist front organisations to the Indonesian army for execution, whilst the British even escorted an Indonesian infantry brigade from the contested Borneo boundary where the two countries' militaries had been confronting each other, back to Java to assist in the murder campaign (Curtis 2003: 392–5). Secretary Rusk cabled the US embassy in Djakarta in October (Department of State 1965) to reassure the military of IMF support to stabilise the currency, promising US small arms and equipment deliveries 'to deal with the PKI'; noting in passing that assistance by Western oil companies to the military might help postpone 'nationalization of oil industry'.

After Suharto had taken power, US-trained economists moved in to restore the 'market economy'. Harvard economist Dave Cole, who had just drafted South Korea's banking regulations, was brought in to co-author a stabilisation plan, whilst the US embassy helped with a new investment law. In 1966, the Stanford Research Institute brought 170 experts to Indonesia to oversee the transition to a privatising economy. In November, an encounter in Geneva between Indonesian economic statesmen and Western businessmen, including David Rockefeller, celebrated restored mutual confidence (Ransom 1974: 109–10, 114). A few years on and the Ford Foundation began funding a new Berkeley project to train Indonesian lawyers in handling negotiations with foreign investors. And so on. Pauker continued to defend the Suharto takeover as a last-minute stand against communism; Kahin by then had become a critic of US policy in South-East Asia. Geertz on the other hand, as Laura Nader recollects (in Schiffrin 199: 136), chose to look the other way, studying cockfighting whilst the massacres were going on. It would take 33 years of plunder and repression before the Suharto regime fell in 1998 and the country geared itself back to polyarchy, although some would say, anarchy. Continued US subsidies to the Indonesian military and arms supplies however serve to ensure that 'nothing too radical happens', whether it is independence for Aceh, economic autonomy or a nationalisation of foreign-owned business (Stavrianakis 2010: 129).

In 1973, a US-supported military coup in Chile violently removed the Allende government, an operation tellingly named Operation Jakarta. Ford Foundation officers, who had still waved away concern over the Indonesian bloodbath, were critical, however, of the repression under Pinochet – not only because the United States in the 1970s was on the defensive against progressive reform worldwide, but also because the foundations had made massive investments in Chile which could not just be written off. In Chile, 'Ford wanted … to transplant into [the country] an "American" model of the policy-oriented social scientist', writes Parmar (2012: 191): 'one who could serve any mainstream political party or administration by providing "objective" advice based on professional expertise that eschewed ideology and politics'. Not unlike the Rockefeller Foundation intending to salvage European intellectual capital in the 1930s, Ford, in what the same author calls (ibid.: 212, cf. 214–15) 'network-preservation mode', sought to preserve the skill base in Chile that it had helped to create. Its efforts were reciprocated by the willingness of leading social scientists, such as Ricardo Lagos, head of economics at the University of Chile and the country's future president, to blame themselves for indulging in ideological debates instead of sticking to technical expertise.

SOVIET AND THIRD WORLD ASSIMILATION
OF THE NATION-STATE FORM

The paradox of the Cold War as far as the struggle over control in the periphery was concerned resides in the fact that the challenge to the Lockean heartland did not extend to challenging the national state form; on the contrary. Although the USSR was a multinational state, born in a revolution led by internationalists, it soon switched to a position in which the world was seen in terms of national states, including its own constitution as a collection of republics assigned to dominant nationalities. The contender role to which it retreated in the late 1920s only consolidated this orientation.

The issue of the spread of the revolution across the existing state system slipped into the nation-state grid soon after the Russian Revolution. In March 1919, Lenin conceded that as things stood, the revolution had not ignited a truly global transformation. 'We are living not merely in a state, but in a system of states', he famously told the Eighth Party Congress, arguing for the rapid build-up of a military capacity to underpin the sovereignty of the Soviet republic (*Coll. Works*, xxix: 153). More than a year later, at the Second Congress of the Comintern in August 1920, his theses on the tasks of the communist party in 'backward countries' provoked intense debate. In response, as Hough relates (1986: 145), Lenin changed his original concept of 'bourgeois democratic movement' into 'national liberation movement', a concept much less clearly fitting the communist agenda. By now, writes Hélène Carrère d'Encausse (1979: 15), 'two concepts of revolution emerged ... that of Marx and Lenin, the revolution of the world-wide proletariat, fraternal, without borders; and the revolution of the oppressed nations'. The loss of a clear strategic focus echoed in Zinoviev's call, at a Congress of the Peoples of the East in the same year 1920 (as in Rosenstone 1982: 378), for Asians to declare a 'real holy war' and to re-create 'the spirit of struggle which once animated the peoples of the East when they marched against Europe under the leadership of their great conquerors'.

Sovereign Equality for the USSR

Nationality issues were at the heart of the predicament of the USSR and its projection of a regime of limited sovereignty in Eastern Europe. The West never failed to appreciate the potential of opening up the Soviet bloc by exploiting ethno-political fault lines. The liberal imperialist order is based on extending the open national state (hence 'liberal') by driving forward bourgeois class formation and granting sovereign equality to client governing classes. Ideally this passes through devolving power to civic nationalists whose conception of a state–society complex is modelled on the Lockean one.

In the Soviet Union, this too was the trajectory in several respects. Literacy campaigns aimed at overcoming pre-modern dividing lines, including foreign relations; but traditional social solidarities tended to be shifted to the republic, not the all-Union level. As pastoral and tribal communities were drawn into urban and modern civilisation in the non-Russian republics, traditional habits and loyalties moved upwards to the proto-nation, in the words of D.S. Carlisle (as in Roy 1994: 53), 'from a *communocentric* to an *ethnocentric* focus: from a level of kin, village, tribe to the level of ethnicity and nation'. Soviet nationality policy suffered not only from a 'legal incongruence and a spatial mismatch between its two national components – national territories and personal nationalities', Brubaker writes (1994: 55, emphasis added). It was also plagued 'by a fundamental tension ... between *two independent, even incompatible definitions of nationhood: one territorial and political, the other personal and ethno-cultural*'. This goes back to the blending of Austro-Marxist and Leninist principles of national self-determination discussed in Chapter 1. The personal, territorial and ethno-cultural identities should ultimately merge into the citizen nationality of homogeneous civil society; but in areas where different ethno-cultural communities with their own ways of life coexisted, such a transition was not easily achieved. In this respect all multinational state–socialist formations adhered to the same mixture of Austro-Marxist and Leninist interpretations of national self-determination.

Here the disciplining effect of an international order of sovereign equality hinging on nation-states must also be taken into account. Soviet legal scholars were divided about whether the USSR would have to accept this order. The initial position was that the USSR could conclude treaties with Western states but otherwise was not bound by custom and precedent, products of a bourgeois community of values. This position was sidelined, as Kubálková and Cruickshank relate (1980: 129–32) by a rival school, led by E. Pashukanis, who objected that such a community does not in fact exist and that the entire international law codex had acquired a new content by the emergence of the Soviet Union. This position in turn was discarded in the 1930s by the public prosecutor of the USSR, A. Ia. Vyshinskii. Vyshinskii held that the law in phases of rapid change had to be sidelined altogether, a position he put in practice in the show trials against the internationalist Bolsheviks in the late 1930s (Medvedev 1976: 502).

Of course Stalinism as such, as a theoretical regression from Marxism to a materialist and deterministic worldview, also played a role in the codification of the embrace of sovereign equality. By projecting a fixed historical progression of stages, any peculiarity of the non-European world, whether it concerned its class structure or its make-up in terms of foreign relations, was discarded and replaced by a teleological conception of history. Thus in 1931 V. Struve proposed to drop the concept of the Asiatic mode of production by which Marx had sought to indicate that social development had followed a multilinear track and apply the Soviet theory of stages (primitive communist, slavery, feudal, capitalist, and socialist) universally (Hough 1986: 40–1). The association of the Asiatic mode with Oriental despotism, which would later be exploited as a Cold War argument against Stalin by the communist renegade Wittfogel, was recognised in the USSR as an unattractive line of argument as the Stalin dictatorship hardened. In addition, the refugee Hungarian communist Eugen Varga, writing in 1934 (1974: 317), identified the Soviet pursuit of a collective security policy against Nazism, thus bolstering the 'camp of peace', as a strategy of normalisation of the USSR as a sovereign equal and subject of international law. Or in Hough's words (1986: 202), 'on a tactical basis, in the 1930s Soviet leaders often focused on the nation-state as the key unit, seeking to play one capitalist state off against the other'.

It was this approach that removed any scruples in the way of striking a deal with Nazi Germany in 1939 after it had become clear that the West, and Britain in particular, was trying to turn Hitler against the East by sabotaging Soviet proposals for collective security against the Nazi threat. However, in line with his disdain for the international communist movement, Stalin chose to present this manoeuvre in terms of the theory of imperialism, as a strategy instead of as a painful but inevitable tactical move. The same opportunistic elevation of tactics to strategy occurred in 1943, when he disbanded the Comintern as a sign of goodwill to the Western allies. As Claudin puts it (1975: 30), by their decision the topmost leaders of the Communist movement were spreading among the masses the illusion that equality and fraternity between nations were compatible with the survival of the principal imperialist states; the illusion that these states, by virtue of their being at war with their capitalist rivals alongside the Soviet Union, really intended to build an ideal world.

The nationalisation of the communist parties that resulted (ibid.: 313–14) paradoxically allowed the anti-fascist *inter*-nationalism of the Eighth Comintern Congress, personified by the Bulgarian party leader Georgi Dimitrov, to flourish as well. In the Spanish Civil War, as well as in the initial post-war governments of national unity in Eastern Europe, this tendency was pronounced; but a conflict with Stalinism loomed. Dimitrov, who like many in the Bulgarian party was of Macedonian extraction, in the summer of 1947 discussed the prospect of a South Balkan federation with Tito, who had his eyes on Macedonia, divided up between their two countries and Greece. As Gabriel and Joyce Kolko write (1972: 408–9), Britain supported this aspiration as a possible counterweight to Soviet influence; but Stalin wanted none of it. Dimitrov and a Yugoslav delegation including Milovan Djilas (Tito preferred not to accept the invitation) were summoned to Moscow in early 1948, where they were told off in unmistakeable terms. Nonetheless Djilas concludes from the discussions (1991: 130–1) that Stalin was not necessarily against federations, except that these obviously had to serve Soviet interests as structures of limited sovereignty. Above all, the communist revolt in Greece had to be given up in order not to provoke the United States. Bloc formation and limited sovereignty in other words were acceptable, but all within the bounds agreed with the West.

Andrei A. Zhdanov, the exponent of the most xenophobic element in the Soviet leadership, had by then mounted his campaign against any digressions from Stalinist orthodoxy. So when Varga, then the director of the Institute of World Economy and International Relations (IMEMO) in Moscow, revived Lenin's theses on state monopoly capitalism and its implication of a non-violent transition to socialism, Zhdanov went on the attack that ended with IMEMO's closure, although Varga survived. At the founding meeting of a new International, the Cominform, in September 1947, Zhdanov (1960: 155) reinterpreted the Second World War as a 'war of liberation against fascism', no longer using the wartime phrase of the 'Anti-Hitler Coalition'. The leading part played by the Soviet Union in defeating the aggressors now was seen to have 'sharply altered the alignment of forces between the two systems – the Socialist and the Capitalist – in favour of Socialism'. For all the anger over the Marshall Plan and the West German money reform, the Soviet response thus in effect reciprocated Western corporate liberalism, the international compromise agreed at Yalta. For both East and West, this compromise implied limited sovereignty of the nation-states within their respective blocs.

Henceforth, Soviet and East European thinking about national statehood and national liberation developed on the margins of a basically defensive, conservative posture. Academic commentary, as in the case of the paradigmatic decolonisation of India, might produce real insight; but this did not alter Moscow's highly conventional diplomatic practice. Thus Yuri Zhukov of the Soviet Academy of Sciences at an Inter-Asian conference in New Delhi in March 1947 (as in Sarila 2006: 309–10) characterised the British offer of Dominion status for India as a postponement of independence motivated by fear of the Indian working class, a fear shared by the Indian bourgeoisie. Gandhi's non-violence was dismissed as a ploy to keep the people disarmed. Rejecting the Pakistan solution as a British imperial strategy, Zhukov underscored the Indian Communist Party call for a Soviet-style nationality policy including the right of secession and the option of rejoining India. In practice, however, the USSR supported India from a standpoint of rivalry with China–Pakistan throughout.

With de-Stalinisation, IMEMO, Varga's old institute, was resurrected under Khrushchev against the background of new openings to Third World states (Kubálkova and Cruickshank 1980: 160). In the resulting liberalisation of academic debate, L. Vasil'ev in 1957 unearthed the concept of the Asiatic mode of production again, and later expanded this to what he calls the state mode of production (Hough 1986: 51; cf. Lefebvre 1977). The Cuban revolution, led by bourgeois democrats who then embraced Marxism, caused considerable debate as to the possibility of non-capitalist development; G. Mirsky of IMEMO wondered whether Third World countries necessarily had to follow the heavy-industrialisation road pioneered by the USSR (Hough 1986: 81, cf. 131). Mirsky's idea that a Third World state can be virtually independent of its economic base was interpreted by Iskenderov (1972: 20–2) as a temporary stage of non-capitalist development, pursued by a national bourgeoisie interested in the development of the productive forces independently from the imperialist West and its local supports. Given that the working class was politically weak in that transition, not too much should be expected in terms of socialist orientation. Iskenderov's claim (1972: 85) that 'the logic of the national liberation movement, which initially is aimed at national liberation [alone], in the end will compel the movement to turn against capitalism as a social system, which brings about colonial oppression', however, was contradicted in many cases.

In the 1970s, Soviet international thought had reached the stage where it began to merge into Western discourse altogether. The International Political Science Association was invited to hold an international meeting in Moscow in 1978, a sign of the degree to which a separate discipline of political science in the USSR was taking shape. F. Burlatsky and G. Shakhnazarov were the leading figures in this movement; by the 1980s, in Hough's estimate (1986: 255; cf. 123), Soviet academia had taken its distance from the imperialism tradition to such an extent that many of its IR specialists held views 'similar to that of such representatives of the "realist school" as Hans Morgenthau'. Especially once Soviet thinking adopted the US theory that the Third World military were the natural proponents of sovereign equality, because the army, as a modernising force, by nature adopts a competitive attitude to the outside world (Mirsky, as in Hough 1986: 161; Iskenderov 1972: 129), class analysis receded further behind the concepts of nation-state and sovereign equality. Only when Yuri Andropov took over in 1982 did a more attentive and theoretically sophisticated attitude towards the nationality issue emerge as well.

As KGB chief, Andropov had addressed the cadres of his organisation on this matter back in 1972. In 1975, a panel of specialists was set up in the Academy of Sciences by the Soviet establishment to begin the serious study of national and ethno-politics – with ethnographers like Yulian Bromley prominently involved. Andropov's own statements, after he had assumed the post of general secretary, reflect this work and confirm his late conversion to a moderate, reformist position (Roy 1994: 51). At this point, the historical materialist approach to foreign relations that I develop in this work was evident in writings by R. Kosolapov (as in Hough 1986: 203), who in 1979 stressed the social nature of international relations, which 'have their beginnings in contacts between clans, tribes, and so forth'. At IMEMO, the thesis was developed that dependent development follows a different route in different countries: each represents (as in Hough 1986: 93) 'an integral and evolving social organism with its own logic and social-genetic "code" for this evolution'. This obviously dovetails with the concept of ethnogenesis and its connections to foreign relations as developed by Bromley, Gumilev and, further back, Shirokogorov (cf. vol. i, 2007: 4–9, 19–29). All this tragically went down with the USSR once Andropov died and, after a short interregnum by Chernenko, Mikhail Gorbachev, Andropov's choice as his successor, took over to preside over what became the act of capitulation. It entailed the break-up of the USSR into 15 nation-states, each with unsolved minority problems once the socialist autonomy policy was abandoned along with any remaining internationalism.

National Statehood as a Revolutionary Goal in the Third World

The national liberation perspective formulated by Lenin broke with the stagist calendar, but its implications were far from clear. From the Soviet point of view, the consolidation of its own sovereign equality was an absolute priority, and when the defeat of the Chinese revolution in the late 1920s postponed the prospect of world revolution even further, Stalin lost interest in the Third World (Hough 1986: 37). As a result little attention was paid to Mao Zedong's analysis of the classes in Chinese society from which he derived a new revolutionary doctrine, one that accorded the peasantry a much more central role. In Wang Hui's *Empire or Nation-State* (2009) Mao's ideas on China's future status as a sovereign equal are contrasted with the lineage of the Han nationalists around Sun Yatsen. Sun embraced the Han ethnic nationalism of Zhang Taiyan, who interpreted the rule of the (Manchu) Qing dynasty (from 1644 to 1912) as an epoch of foreign domination from which the Han 'race' should emancipate itself (ibid.: 56n). Although he also admired the Russian Revolution, for Sun it was Japan that would spearhead the rebirth of Asia. It had shown the way by abrogating the unequal treaties imposed by Europe and establishing the first independent Asian state. For China to join this revolution (and in our terms, adopt a contender posture) implied that it must establish a nation-state too. Sun imagined this would be a Han-Chinese state which, like Japan, would adopt Western means to free itself from imperialist dominance (ibid.: 62).

The Communists under Mao Zedong and Zhou Enlai instead followed the lead, on the one hand, of Marxist nationality policy (autonomy and internationalism), and on the other, of the framework of the integral imperial state, articulated by Kang Youwei and his pupil Lian Qichao. Kang (like Sun) had been forced to seek refuge in Japan after the coup against the short-lived reform of Qing emperor Guangxu in 1898, to whom Kang had personally explained the need for modernising the country along the lines of the Meiji revolution from above 30 years earlier. In Japan he wrote a book on how nationality, along with the abolition of class and ethnic differences, would be overcome (ibid.: 61n.). The combined Marxist–statist approach became the lodestar for the policy, building on a liberated zone (the area around Yenan in Northern Shensi province) that Mao, whose leadership had been put to the test by initial defeats, had reached after the Long March along the Tibet border to the north in 1934–35. In the resistance to the Japanese invasion, the party then adopted the strategic goal of national liberation, unifying the nation's energies in the struggle with imperialist aggression. 'The one and only policy for overcoming difficulties, defeating the enemy and building a new China', Mao wrote in 1938 (1971: 143), 'is to consolidate and expand the Anti-Japanese National United Front and mobilize the dynamic energy of the whole nation.'

This 'nation' was conceived as a multinational entity under a single state. To mobilise the non-Han ethnic groups for the fight against the Japanese invaders the use of non-Chinese languages and the Chinese dialects was being encouraged (Wang 2009: 146–7; Zhang 2010: 63). Because the nationalist Guomindang under Chiang Kai-shek was more concerned with fighting the communists than with resisting Japanese aggression, the communist party became the symbol of the struggle for national independence. Mao now filled in the gap between 'bourgeois democracy' and 'national liberation' by baptising 'national democracy' as the transitional form on the road to socialism. This also worked to consolidate the imperial boundaries as 'national' in an expanded sense. Löwy interprets this (1981: 117) as an incomplete break with Stalinism, or, in other words, with the revolution from above for which the sovereign state provides the framework. When Mao's armies took control of China in 1949, he had to overcome pro-Soviet forces in the communist party, concentrated in Manchuria, the most developed part of China. Here the Japanese army had applied modern planning methods to develop the infrastructure of its puppet state Manchukuo and industrialise it. Thus, through the back door, the anti-Manchu legacy of Zhang Taiyan and Sun Yatsen seeped in again, blending with the policy of a broad class alliance into a subliminal nationalism potentially directed against the USSR.

Via the 1955 Bandung Conference and the Non-Aligned Movement this eventually contributed to the Sino-Soviet split, in which the two faced each other as rival sovereign states. Already in 1960 Zhou Enlai spoke about Sino-US relations in a way that, according to Edgar Snow (as in Schurmann and Schell 1968: 299), owed everything 'to the logic of nationalism, quite apart from communism'. Through the ensuing twists and turns, from the 'Third Worldism' articulated by defence minister Lin Biao, with its emphasis on economic self-reliance at home and abroad (ibid.: 338), to the termination of the Cultural Revolution by Deng Xiao Ping and the turn to capitalist practices in 1979, China consolidated as a nation-state. This made it liable to being 'balanced' by the West, first against the Soviet Union, and then, as a contender state itself, via the siege of an Asian alliance ranged against it under US auspices. Western balancing also dealt the final blow to the internationalism professed by both the USSR and China. If, in the former, internationalism in the 1920s had already degenerated into obligatory support for its own survival as a state, China, by subordinating its international engagements to its anti-Moscow stance, also gave up any adherence to principled internationalism.

This was acutely felt in Vietnam. Suffering from aggression by the United States, the country was being sacrificed to the national interests of both the USSR and China as these two were played off against each other by the Nixon–Kissinger triangular diplomacy. 'To achieve détente in certain concrete conditions in order to push forward the offensive of the revolutionary forces is correct', the newspaper *Nhan Dan* wrote in an editorial on 17 August 1972 (as in Shibata 1973: 152). 'But if in order to serve one's narrow national interests, one is to help the most reactionary forces stave off dangerous blows, one is indeed throwing a life-buoy to a drowning pirate.' This was what Lenin had attacked Kautsky for – not seeing that alternating peaceful and warlike policies ultimately rest on the same imperialist basis and that this basis must be focused on, and eventually dislodged, by revolution. But then, Ho Chi Minh had been a founding member of the Third International. He was able to develop Marxist theory in ways that neither the bureaucratised academia of the Soviet bloc, nor the Chinese communists, for whom theory was often a tool in intra-party struggles, could achieve any longer. In a 1957 article on the October Revolution and the liberation of the peoples of the East, Ho argued (1980: 232–3) that 'the national movement, if it is truly directed against imperialism, is an objective support of the revolutionary struggle; [and] that national demands and movements must not be judged by their narrow political and social character, but by the role they play in relation to the international imperialist forces'. Ho went on to explain that the revolution in the colonial and semi-colonial countries is a 'national democratic' one, in which the national bourgeoisie, the peasants and the workers constitute a 'national front against the feudal landowning classes'.

This conforms to Mao's notion of national democracy. True, the Vietnamese had based their declaration of independence from France in 1945 on the United States Declaration of Independence; but where the US Declaration spoke of 'all men', etc., Vietnam's added the concept of the 'nation'. The text, writes Shibata (1973: 15), was 'not a socialist document, but a declaration of a democratic nature'. This democracy in Vietnam was not a formal matter. Given its exposure to colonial and neo-colonial aggression, the Vietnamese nation had a decentralised make-up related to defence needs which in turn reflected the Asian village structure of the past. So the Vietnamese in the 1960s began work on Marx's notion of the Asiatic mode of production, which Soviet China scholars in the 1920s had intensively discussed but which was rejected for political reasons by Stalin and Mao alike (Hough 1986: 47). In Vietnam, however, the concept of a non-historical and stagnant village community that is implicit in the assessment of the Asiatic society as unchanging, was challenged in practice. According to Jean Chesneaux (as in Shibata 1973: 183), the ability of Vietnam to resist in the face of unprecedented bombing and to repair damage to its infrastructure is to be explained by the resilience of the village communities inherent in the Asiatic mode. But as Shibata explains (ibid.: 184–7), even under fire, important social changes had been wrought in Vietnam (like the 1954 land reform during the war with the French), which mutated traditional village self-sufficiency into what Ho Chi Minh, as early as 1945, called 'self-reliance' – but on a superior level of development of the productive forces.

Thus between 1960 and 1965, when US bombing of North Vietnam began in earnest, the ratio of agricultural to industrial output changed, from 58.3 to 41.7 per cent in 1960, to 46.3 to 53.7 per cent in 1965 (ibid.: 190). So there was a specific, decentralised development during conditions of war that ultimately brought the country (at least the North) to a specific form of nation-statehood that can no longer be reduced to the Asiatic mode of production, but that represents a peculiar form of the state mode of production. However, this success in achieving nation-statehood, however heroic, had a downside, especially once internationalist connections with Soviet and Chinese state socialism atrophied. For in the end, the result is an independent nation-state like all others; and formal sovereign equality, once consolidated (if need be with minority protection), works to throw a state back on itself facing Western supremacy and its claim to global governance. Indeed, 20 years after having militarily defeated the United States and its clients in Saigon, Vietnam came sixth in the cumulative liberalisation index of 28 (ex-)communist states compiled by the World Bank (Kolko 1997: 34). Whether such a fate also awaits the Stalinist nationalism of Korea remains to be seen. Its *Dzhu'che* ideology, originally formulated by Kim Il Sung, the communist partisan leader in the war against Japan, prescribes the creation of a culture that is, in the words of his son, Kim Jong Il (Kim 1982: 44), 'national in form and revolutionary and socialist in content'.

Perhaps the only Third World region where national liberation was consciously geared to internationalism on a secular basis (so not counting Muslim resistance to the national state form, discussed in vol. ii) was Latin America. The continent also did not have a regional socialist 'superpower' to monopolise internationalism for its own interests. A Latin American concept of foreign relations not subsumed under state nationality was formulated by José Carlos Mariátegui in the 1920s. Mariátegui distinguishes between the ability of the indigenous Amerindian population to assimilate socialist ideas, and the (white and mestizo) bourgeois sensitivity to the 'nationalist myth'. 'A revolutionary indigenous consciousness will perhaps take time to form', Mariátegui wrote in 1929 (2011: 325, cf. 272 on the bourgeoisie), heralding the contemporary surge of radical democracy and socialist ideas in the ethnically diverse countries of Latin America. 'But once Indians have made the socialist idea their own, they will serve it with a discipline, a tenacity, and strength that few other proletariats from other milieus will be able to surpass.' This optimistic assessment might be dismissed as wishful thinking were it not for a second source of internationalism, originally supported by the progressive white and mestizo bourgeoisie: the aspirations of the heroes of Latin American independence – Bolívar, San Martín, José Martí and others – for continental solidarity. Fidel Castro's conclusion that a national bourgeoisie in contemporary imperialism can no longer play a progressive role (Castro 1969: 103) here has worked to complement the internationalism of the late Hugo Chávez, Moráles in Bolivia, Correa in Ecuador, and others in whom we may recognise the connection to indigeneity that Mariátegui spoke about.

In practice, Cuba's internationalism, exemplified in the figure of Ernesto 'Che' Guevara, linked up with a series of progressive struggles in Africa. None was more dramatic than the military intervention on the side of the Angolan MPLA that covered the period 1975–1991 and included a defeat of the invasion by Apartheid South Africa in 1987–88. Of course both Angola and South Africa have meanwhile become regular nation-states too, with all that that implies – but Africa in that sense still has the future in front of it and may surprise the world in many ways. As to Cuba, its extension of medical frontline services to Venezuela in exchange for oil, and the ALBA free trade zone, may further consolidate the attempts to transcend the nation-state grid in Latin America – in the spirit of global governance, but from the angle of internationalism.

5
The Crisis of International Discipline

The explosion of the universities in May 1968 for a time seemed to dislodge both the disciplinary division of labour and the taboo on Marxism. 'What 1968 did', Wallerstein writes (2001: 100), 'was to break the total control over the world university system by the heirs of nineteenth-century thought and restore the university to its role as an arena of intellectual debate.' The counter-movement was not long in coming. Lewis F. Powell, future Supreme Court justice, was one of many conservatives denouncing the university campuses as bastions of the left (I follow Giroux 2007: 142–3), 'the single most dynamic source for producing and housing intellectuals who are unsympathetic to the free enterprise system'. In a 1971 memo Powell called for a conservative renaissance to 'nourish a new generation of scholars who would inhabit the university and function as public intellectuals actively shaping the direction of policy issues'. A series of New Right think tanks was launched at this juncture to ensure a concerted roll-back of the left surge in the universities and society at large. They included the Heritage Foundation, established in 1973 by beer magnate Joseph Coors and Christian neoconservative Paul Weyrich, the Olin Foundation, to which I come back below, and others.

The mainstream Trilateral Commission, established at the same time, had a different perspective on the establishment of a world order; it did not really have a different view of the role of the academic intelligence base. Columbia IR scholar Zbigniew Brzezinski, who assisted David Rockefeller in setting up the TC, characterised the desired type of intellectuals (as in Chomsky 1969: 28) as 'generalists–integrators who become in effect house-ideologues for those in power, providing overall intellectual integration for disparate actions'. So how was the restoration of discipline, coming from these two angles, achieved?

In this concluding chapter we first look at how IR was enriched with an ethics compensating for the crisis of Vietnam-era behaviourism. Also, an international political economy was floated to incorporate themes raised by the student movement – transnational corporations and international inequality. After the collapse of the Soviet Union, celebrated as the 'end of history', the West only really faced assorted Islamists recruited as auxiliaries against the left over half a century. Deprived of the Cold War contender, both theoretically and in practice, neoconservative ideologues enlarged this enemy out of all proportion to justify a life-and-death struggle, dramatised in Huntington's 'clash of civilisations' – against Islam, but also against China and Russia, as long as record US defence expenditure was secured. As we shall see below, the outlines of a 'war on terror', including domestic surveillance and indefinite detention, had been elaborated already in the early 1980s, whilst policy intellectuals were falling over each other announcing an impending new Pearl Harbour as the 1990s drew to a close. By selling out to the self-fulfilling fiction of Islamic terrorism, the discipline of IR today has itself largely degenerated into a mercenary, 'embedded' auxiliary force.

GLOBAL ETHICS, IPE AND THE POSTMODERN QUANDARY

The war in Vietnam gravely undermined the moral posture on which Western supremacy is premised. The indiscriminate bombing and defoliation campaigns and the accompanying domestic turmoil, culminating in the assassinations in 1968 of civil rights leader Martin Luther King Jr. and anti-war presidential primary candidate Robert Kennedy, exposed the criminal war machine to the full glare of publicity. Behavioural positivism, with its confident predictions of 'victory', was effectively bankrupted in the war; an ethical revival had to come from outside disciplinary social science. Since the moral counterpart to pragmatism (given the absence of systematic philosophy in the United States) was always the Social Gospel movement, it comes as no surprise that the chief figure in the emergence of a 'normative' theory that found its way into IR was a man long attracted to theology and who at one point even considered entering the Episcopalian priesthood, John Rawls (1921–2002).

After having served in the Pacific war, Rawls during a fellowship at Oxford in the 1950s came under the influence of Isaiah Berlin, the liberal commentator invited to All Souls and the Milner Group in the 1930s (Quigley 1981: 314). Back in the United States Rawls taught at Cornell before moving to Harvard in 1962. In his *Theory of Justice* of 1971 he develops a liberalism with a social democratic bottom line, but otherwise anchored in the self-interested pursuit of justice – provided that the 'less favoured' are given a minimum share in the liberal order (1973: 542). Rawls even radicalises the utilitarian idea of the isolated, solipsistic subject by situating it behind a 'veil of ignorance'. This allows one to develop an intuitive concept of justice, not from judging the social order, but from an imaginary 'original position' irrespective of one's actual assets and endowments. Giesen rightly characterises this (1992: 170) as logically equivalent to game theory (and, by implication, rational choice). But then, Rawls' aim (1973: 11, emphasis added) is 'to present a conception of justice which generalizes and carries *to a higher level of abstraction* the familiar theory of the social contract as found, say, in Locke, Rousseau, and Kant'. It begins with 'one of the most general of all choices which persons might make together, namely, with the choice of the first principles of a conception of justice' (ibid.: 13). We are looking, in other words, at an aestheticised liberalism, for which Rawls was awarded the National Humanities Medal in 1999. His work, the accompanying tribute states, 'helped a whole generation of learned Americans revive their faith in democracy itself'.

Resurgent Idealism?

A Theory of Justice appeared amidst considerable uproar in the North American philosophy profession. This began, if we follow Giesen's account (1992: 154–9), when the *Journal of Philosophy* in early 1967 carried a resolution denouncing, on moral grounds, the quest for a military decision in Vietnam; to which philosophers on the US West Coast responded by giving the floor to Noam Chomsky, who denounced the war in the clearest of terms. This did not fail to mobilise the 'moderates', who rushed to reject Chomsky's 'political fantasies' and 'strident moralism'. Veteran Cold Warrior Sydney Hook weighed in to warn that professional philosophers should never take sides in political matters; IR scholar Charles Kegley on the other hand urged that US philosophy abandon its 'exaggerated professionalism' and tackle real questions. Here Rawls was of little help, because his solitary 'individual' (solely concerned with rights and justice, and apparently unconcerned with material matters) is not a territorial animal, but a cosmopolitan. Calhoun in this connection speaks (2002) of 'the class consciousness of frequent travellers'; indeed the subject in *A Theory of Justice* is a hotel guest rather than the occupant of a real home (Ramel 2012: 159).

Rawlsian cosmopolitanism inevitably calls forth its opposite, communitarianism. Communitarianism one-sidedly highlights the human community, understood in antinomy with common humanity; its main proponent, Michael Walzer, emerged from the quest for political relevance in philosophy. In the first issue of the new journal *Philosophy and Public Affairs*, Walzer, then also at Harvard, raises the question, under what circumstances is violent intervention in another sovereign state warranted. Initially presented at the September 1970 APSA convention, the paper argues (1971: 19) that British terror bombing of the working-class neighbourhoods of German cities was justified by the exceptional evil of Nazism. Although Vietnam is mentioned only once in this text, Walzer, following Kant's categorical imperative (only commit those actions worthy of constituting a universal principle) implies that bombing Vietnam was *not* warranted, and hence does not fall within the 'just war' tradition. After he published *Just and Unjust Wars* in 1977 and returned to Princeton, Walzer specified his understanding of the right to intervention further. In his view the liberal West, held together by a 'high density pluralism', may intervene with force of arms (ideally through a UN with military muscle, and backed up by the Bretton Woods institutions and the International Criminal Court) if tyranny, ideological zeal or ethnic hatred violate effective self-determination. Kosovo in 1999 for Walzer was a case in point (Ramel 2012: 167–71, 176–8).

Paradoxically, cosmopolitanism does not really contest this interventionist stance. But then, the disciplinary demarcation line is not between cosmopolitanism and communitarianism, but between them as legitimate alternatives and others that lead to really different conclusions (such as, no intervention). Thus for Falk's and Mendlovitz's world order project, war should be outlawed on the grounds of public international law; it should also be dealt with (1966: vii) by 'an autonomous academic discipline of world order', which is 'synthetic, cutting across such established educational divisions as law, political science, sociology, economics [and] history'. This obviously was a bridge too far. Falk was duly attacked by his erstwhile follower Hedley Bull, who in the 1970s turned against his former patron, reproaching him (as in Dunne 1998: 140–1) for drifting to advocacy and 'global salvationism'. Once again we see how a fundamental contradiction is sidelined by a subordinate antinomy, and the substantive problem declared out of bounds.

Actually Falk and Mendlovitz are closer to Kant's original peace project than are the new humanitarians. Kant, Giesen reminds us (1992: 175), considered peace a preliminary condition, necessary to allow the reign of reason and freedom to take hold in the first place. Cosmopolitans and communitarians on the other hand both proceed from the assumption of Western (moral) supremacy, whether as a high-density pluralism or, in Rawls' case, as an accomplished liberal democracy separate from the rest. 'A democratic society is complete in that it is self-sufficient and has a place for all the main purposes of human life', Calhoun (2002: 877) cites the inimitable Rawlsian prose of *Political Liberalism*, published in 1993. 'It is also closed, in that entry into it is only by birth and exit from it is only by death.' This closure cannot refer to the nation-state; here cosmopolitans differ from communitarians. Thus when Walzer and (with explicit reference to Hegel) Mervyn Frost in Britain were seen to assign a moral value to the state as such, Rawls' student Charles Beitz (as in Giesen 1992: 233) declared this inappropriate, because it 'conceived of the state as an arena relatively closed in on itself in which processes of change transpire without significant outside influence'. States must be 'open', otherwise the guidance of the West will not work. In the English School, Manokha (2008: 35–6) reports a comparable quibble resulting from Bull's hesitation to allow humanitarian intervention to subvert international order and peace; something the 'solidarist' current of John Vincent and others were less inhibited about. But the principle is common to all: states that violate self-determination and human rights, or simply lack 'justice', are liable to punitive action.

Resurgent idealism was also evident in Michael Doyle's 'democratic peace' thesis. Funded in 1979–82 by the Ford and MacArthur Foundations, Doyle's writing is another example of how a bland, self-congratulatory idea continues to be rehashed. From Hakluyt to the 'pluralistic security community' of Deutsch and his associates, from Hume to the English School, Rawls and Walzer, the idea is the same – the liberal heartland is entitled to project its global governance on the basis of its superior civilisation, which (among Western allies at least) includes the absence of open warfare (Barkawi and Laffey 1999: 420–2; Parmar 2012: 231). This aesthetics of Western supremacy, and the new normative theories generally, are not really contradicted by their 'realist' opposite either. Thus Kenneth Waltz's *Theory of International Politics* of 1979 at first sight provides a behavioural model (albeit with almost no operational empirical aspect to it). Yet on reflection Waltz turns out to be especially concerned with avoiding equitable global governance. 'The influence behind my preference [for realism] is partly Immanuel Kant and partly Reinhold Niebuhr', he explains (1986: 341).

Kant feared that a world government would stifle liberty, become a terrible despotism, and in the end collapse into chaos. Niebuhr drew the conclusion from his dim view of human nature that domestically and internationally the ends of security and decency are served better by balanced than by concentrated power.

Despite its apparent rejection of all normative assumptions, Waltz's agnostic neo-realism hence ends up sharing the 'pluralist' position of the communitarians, who in turn share with the cosmopolitans 'our' right to intervene.

An IR Niche for the World Economy

The war in Vietnam that pushed the United States into effective bankruptcy and forced the Nixon administration in 1971 to suspend the gold cover of the dollar confronted the mainstream with the need to allow a measure of economic understanding back into IR. Of course this was a delicate operation when one recalls that the discipline had been established to sideline the theory of capitalist imperialism. Yet the dollar crisis and the challenge to state sovereignty by transnational corporations (dramatised by Atlantic tensions with Gaullist France and the overthrow of Allende in Chile) required an explicit inclusion of the role of transnational business and money flows, not just interventions by relative outsiders, such as the former financial journalist Susan Strange (1972), then teaching at LSE, or business economists like Harvard's Raymond Vernon (1973). As early as 1968 Charles P. Kindleberger (1910–2003), who worked for the State Department preparing the Marshall Plan before moving to MIT as Ford International Professor of Economics, categorically declared (1969: 207) that 'the nation-state is just about through as an economic unit. General De Gaulle is unaware of it as yet, and so are the Congress of the United States and right-wing know-nothings in all countries.' Was this then the end of a discipline?

In 1970 Robert O. Keohane and Joseph S. Nye Jr., both of Harvard's Centre for International Affairs, reclaimed the terrain for IR by convening a conference on transnational relations. Coining it a new 'paradigm' in the then fashionable nomenclature of Thomas Kuhn's critique of Popper (Keohane and Nye 1973: xii–xiii), they conveniently generalised the theme of transnational relations away from its most contentious forms. Thus papers published in the Summer 1971 special issue of the leading liberal IR journal *International Organization* included 'case studies' of the Roman Catholic church, revolutionary movements, the Ford Foundation and the labour movement. The formal definition of transnational relations used by the editors is less important here than their attempt to allow a new set of subjects ('actors') to be identified at and between the 'levels of analysis' of IR, although Robert Gilpin in his contribution ensured that state-centric, 'realist' analysis retains a place of its own in the newly defined sub-discipline. In their conclusion Keohane and Nye (1973: 396–7) also refer to Kindleberger's proposal to establish a general agreement for investment (along the lines of GATT for trade), which the MIT economist hoped would apply anti-trust regulation now that the national state was a thing of the past. Indeed in *American Business Abroad* Kindleberger had argued (1969: 11–14) that foreign direct investment is primarily about securing monopolistic advantages, a thesis for which he referred to the work of Stephen Hymer. From the range of proposals made in that period to subject transnational corporations to a code of conduct enforced by the United Nations, in the end only anti-trust provisions would survive (see my 2006: 132).

To the often-raised objection that what is presented as transnational investment was in fact US neo-imperialism, Kindleberger replied (1969: 72) that the United States indeed fostered foreign investment through various measures, but that it did so 'in the interest of the economic recovery of foreign countries … and with their concurrence'. So when the Nixon administration devalued the dollar in 1971, the question arose how this benign liberal order would survive the decline of the state that had overseen its establishment at Bretton Woods. In *The World in Depression* of 1973, Kindleberger deduces from an analysis of the 1930s economic crisis that the world economy requires the active leadership of the most powerful country. This shifts the emphasis from a purely self-interested economic role to a 'hegemonic' one as a disinterested guardian of the global political economy. The Depression had occurred in the interval between Britain's and the United States' assumption of this role; 'hegemonic stability', the label given to Kindleberger's argument, would thus be required for the period following the uncoupling of the dollar from gold, or a Depression might result. As Radhika Desai argues (2013: 125), 'hegemonic stability theory' effectively displaces the thesis of US imperialism by a theory of benign leadership. She also demonstrates that paradoxically, world systems theory, as articulated by Immanuel Wallerstein and Giovanni Arrighi, lent a measure of plausibility to HST by arguing that the Netherlands or even Genoa in the past had played comparable roles as 'hegemons'; and that the two strands, incompatible in so many other respects, share a lineage to the thinking of French political economist François Perroux (see my 2009: 151).

Perroux in the 1950s and 1960s formulated his concern from the vantage point of a contender state. Kindleberger (as in Desai 2013: 128) wants to turn Perroux's 'peculiarly French idea, with its overtones of resentment at alleged domination by the United States' into an argument for a benign US role in shaping liberal global governance. Thus the leading state, with a global, 'systemic' role, is posited between the straightforward cosmopolitan idea of a post-national world market, and nation-states which cannot exist without that one state's leadership. This safely corrals international political economy (IPE) as a *sub*-discipline of IR. Certainly its origins in a crisis of discipline initially left the field more open than perhaps intended. As Katzenstein, Keohane and Krasner note (1998: 645, cf. 656), the (sub-)disciplinary boundaries of IPE 'have been set less by subject matter than by theoretical perspectives'. In hindsight however, IPE has proved equally committed to barring any incursion of Marxist (or Marxist-inspired) work dealing with imperialism. Keohane even claims (2009: 35) that there was no IPE to speak of – 'around 1970 ... there was no field. Very little research was being done'. Never mind, apparently, the voluminous writings of André Gunder Frank, Harry Magdoff's *The Age of Imperialism* of 1969, or the works of materialist historians such as William Appelman Williams or Gabriel Kolko, to name only a few in the English language.

Indeed the so-called 'third debate' in IR, which supposedly allowed different theoretical frameworks back in, was radically curtailed almost from its inception. It was never allowed to call into question, as a comprehensive global political economy does, the disciplinary boundaries themselves. By the operation of mechanisms such as journal editorial policy, IPE in the United States, according to Maliniak and Tierney (2009: 26, Fig. 7), is even more monoculturally positivist (especially after 1985) than IR overall. Since US academic practice is followed elsewhere with ever greater stringency to meet 'international standards', the trend is not confined to North America either. 'Just as IR was constructed as a discipline both for and about the "great powers", and an "American social science",' writes Nicola Phillips (2009: 92), 'IPE has crystallized as a field ... for the principal purpose of analyzing the political economy of advanced capitalism that knits together [the advanced industrial powers].' This was certainly the remit of the '1980s Project' launched by the Council on Foreign Relations in 1974.

The 1980s Project involved several US members of the Trilateral Commission that had been formed the year before. It provides a comprehensive blueprint based on the work of a study group led by the economist and former State Department Policy Planning Staff official Miriam Camps, and with Stanley Hoffmann and his Harvard colleague Joseph Nye as its most prominent IR participants. Camps' pilot study, *The Management of Interdependence* of 1974, argues that the desired international order, not US national interest in a narrow sense, would have to guide US foreign policy. This order must be underwritten by the Trilateral partners – the United States and Canada, the member states of the European Community, and Japan – just as they will manage it collectively. The study recommends that the 'Trilateral World' develop the capacity 'for anticipating problems, sounding early warnings, seeing inter-connections between issue-areas, deciding which of a half-dozen possible agencies should act, pushing for needed new codes and other institutional reforms'. Indeed in Camps' words (as in Shoup and Minter 1977: 265–6, emphasis added), the Trilateral partners would have to see to it that

the rules, goals and procedures that the advanced countries adopt to govern economic relationships with one another *should be the norms of the global system*. In other words, the arrangements among the advanced countries would be the central core of the wider system; *other countries would be expected in time to join the central core.*

Thus the Anglo-centric idea of a liberal epicentre of global civilisation is spelled out once again. Hoffmann in 1978 summarised the conclusions of the Camps group in *Primacy or World Order*, warning that a Democratic president should abandon the illusion that the international order would have to be an American order, and thus avoid slipping into imperial adventures again. Rather than leading a new moral crusade (his book appeared during Carter's human rights offensive), Hoffmann recommends (1978: 200) to work solely towards consolidating the collective interests of the West. Nye in turn provided, again in a joint enterprise with Keohane, a key concept denoting the norms arising from these collective interests: the *regime*. Following up their investigation of transnational relations with a new collection entitled *Power and Interdependence* published in 1977, the editors borrow this term from Easton's systems analysis of the 1960s. In addition to a set of authorities and a political community in every political system, Easton distinguishes (1965: 157) 'some kind of stability in the rules and structures through the use of which demands are converted into outputs, an aspect that will be designated as the regime'. From the perspective of the Lockean heartland, regime theory provides an overall frame specifying, for each functional area separately, the relationship between the rules under which Western global governance operates and the nation-states it seeks to discipline.

Incorporating European Scholarship after May 1968

The 1970s saw another push by the large foundations to incorporate Western Europe into the realm of US social science. By funding empirical social and political science abroad, Giuliana Gemelli records (2007: 175), the Ford Foundation hoped to generate a 'habitus-forming force', an organisational synthesis that would link research to political decision making, whilst stimulating cooperation between academia, business and the public sector. This chimes with the definition of the ideal intellectual of the Trilateral Commission, who is likewise 'policy-oriented, well-connected to the key centres of national policy planning and associated with elite universities' (Gill 1990: 161). Yet the production of policy-oriented 'house ideologues' of Trilateral stripe succeeded much better along the North Atlantic axis than in France, where the impact of May 68 provoked both postmodern departures and far right intellectual crossfire. Generally in southern Europe political class conflict continued to resonate intellectually to a much greater extent.

The Ford Foundation had by then abandoned any Cold War relics and adopted a technocratic posture; its international director,

Shepard Stone, throughout opposed the frontal approach to the USSR (Guilhot 2010: 173–4). This could only help in making US-style social science more attractive. The establishment of the European Consortium for Political Research (ECPR) in 1970, funded by a large Ford grant with additional support from the Volkswagen Stiftung, aimed to overcome the national particularities of intellectual life in Western Europe and find a common language and methodology, focused on quantitative techniques and deductive mathematics. But even if the driving force of first generation ECPR work, Jean Blondel, was a Frenchman, its impact would remain confined to north-west Europe for quite a while. The idea of an academic intelligence base means that, as Lippmann put it in the 1920s, intellectuals take their place 'in front of decision instead of behind' and forget about 'historical riddles' (cf. our Chapter 2). Indeed if 'intellectuals [are] not being forced to test ideas constantly with the establishment of our world', Max Kohnstamm, the first European director of the Trilateral Commission, maintained (as in Gill 1990: 152), they 'will tend to become abstract and therefore useless'. The ECPR should organise this on a European scale by 'discovering new means by which to bring more closely to all the value of collaborative action across various cultures', as Blondel put it in 1976 (as in Gemelli 2007: 179; cf. 173). Collaboration also implied 'interdisciplinary' research, which, as will be remembered, is code for *enhancing* disciplinary demarcation whilst using common research methods – not a *post*-disciplinary social science as understood by Jessop and Ngai-ling Sum (2001).

In France, and the Mediterranean countries generally, the traditional intellectual, who straddles the disciplines in a pre-disciplinary sense, was not easily dislodged. French intellectuals ever since the Dreyfus trial or Julien Benda's *Treason of the Clerks* of 1927 had sought to decide big ethical–political issues by dramatic interventions, developing a style that relies on literary aesthetics to make their case. For the Trilateral Commission, these are 'value-oriented' intellectuals, whose views are largely irrelevant to the 'Commission's major discourses, which are liberal and functionalist' (Gill 1990: 159). A European research programme in the field of experimental social psychology under the auspices of the US Office of Naval Research and funded with Ford money was instructed (Gemelli 2007: 184, citing S. Moscovici) 'to keep out the descriptive, literary, essay-type practitioners who "masquerade in France as social researcher"'. Still today, disciplinary specialisation as developed in the United States and adopted in northern Europe is not popular in France. Here a professor of IR may also be a novelist or an actor, as the intellectual culture remains governed 'by the spirit of the *aggregation*, of the institutionalised, encyclopaedic tradition ... the cult of the manifold, all-round intellectual' (Giesen 2006: 20).

Certainly the Americanisation of social science also affected France. But in the transition its tradition of scholarly aesthetics produced a politically hybrid, postmodern body of thought which uniquely implanted itself on the other side of the Atlantic again, eventually being tolerated by the mainstream. This improbable trajectory was premised on many circumstances, one of them the sterilisation of French historical materialism. Marxism in the Popular Front years in the 1930s had 'forced open the doors of the university', Debray writes (1981: 59). But they closed again immediately after it had entered, trapping it in 'a learned theoreticism and a formalism from which it will have difficulty in recovering'. In the 1960s, Louis Althusser was the main exponent of this 'learned theoreticism', actually a revamped version of the anti-dialectical, anti-historical materialism of the Second and Third Internationals. In *For Marx* of 1965 and the collective *Reading Capital* of the same year, Althusser introduced an anti-voluntarist Marxism which was static and academic, divorced from any real movement. A year later Michel Foucault joined Althusser in his attack on 'humanism', albeit inspired by Nietzsche rather than by Marx. Althusser presents the movement of history as an objective process in which subjects act out roles defined ultimately by the economic structure; Foucault, although rejecting the term structure later, in *The Order of Things* (originally *Les mots et les choses*) of 1966 and the *Archaeology of Knowledge* three years later analyses the history of thought in terms of discursive structures characteristic of historical epochs, likewise reducing the role of historical initiative by 'decentring the subject' from its supposed sovereignty (Foucault 1969: 23).

The French Communist Party and the trade union under its influence, CGT, shared the materialism of the academic Marxists and the economism it legitimates. They interpreted May 68 as a repetition of the 1930s Popular Front, when mass strikes blocked the breakthrough of fascism in France, whilst securing wage rises and paid holidays. Anxious not to see the potential rewards of disciplined strike action squandered as a result of issues such as full workers' control or sexual liberation, the party went out of its way to denounce as *groupuscules* (tiny little groups) the rival left formations that sprang up everywhere around it to articulate these demands and many others. Posters depicting Communist militants joining hands with the riot police under the slogan 'They won't get through' capture the resulting perception of the Party as part of the old order. This pushed intellectuals on the left but outside the Party into often radical opposition to it. What was the point of combating the discipline of capital, if only to exchange it for the discipline of the party–state? Thus psychoanalyst Félix Guattari coined the slogan (1976: 7, 22 n.1), 'We are all *groupuscules*', whilst others resisted the overly teleological reading of history as a 'grand narrative' to which individual aspirations were unduly subordinated. In fact this was also a rebellion against Althusser and Foucault, in that it celebrated a radical individualism, surprisingly compatible with the neoliberalism that raised its head in the 1970s.

In line with the overall political balance in southern Europe, scholarly–literary interventions had mostly been launched from the left, but now this changed. A barrage of heavy-handed far right tracts, such as J.-F. Revel's on the 'totalitarian temptation' of 1976 or Alain de Benoist's two-volume *View from the Right* of 1977, allowed the 'New Philosophers' – notably, André Glucksmann and Bernard-Henri Lévy (who became an institution in his own right as 'BHL') – to present neoliberalism as a progressive intervention again. Glucksmann's and Lévy's books, in which they denounced Soviet totalitarianism whilst identifying the united 'old' left as its extension to France, became best-sellers. Foucault surprisingly gave enthusiastic support to Glucksmann, although his theory of diffuse social power is the opposite of Glucksmann's focus on the state. Foucault also denied ever having been a structuralist, instead priding himself (as in Christofferson 2009) on having waged 'a struggle against the coerciveness of a unitary, formal and scientific theoretical discourse'. Not long afterwards, Jean-François Lyotard, in a study of knowledge commissioned by the provincial government of Québec, argued that in the post-industrial epoch not truth, but *performance* becomes the criterion of the effectiveness of knowledge. Postmodernism according to Lyotard (1984: xxiv) refers to an 'incredulity towards meta-narratives', in the place of which he expects the ascent of 'a pragmatics of language particles'. This effectively enlisted postmodernism into US-style pragmatism – a most useful approach, of course, in the highly commodified environment in which academics must find employment.

The explosion of post-1968 new thinking, both postmodernism and the formalistic materialism of Althusser, had a huge resonance outside of France as well. Not since 1950s existentialism had French *littérateurs* commanded such a public abroad. Foucault and Lyotard – as well as Gilles Deleuze, co-author with Guattari of *Anti-Oedipus* of 1972, Jacques Derrida and his 'deconstructionism', and others – became icons of the new, politically hybrid cult. When President Giscard, no doubt pleased with the neoliberal twist that Glucksmann and BHL gave to their anti-totalitarianism, invited the 'New Philosophers' to the Elysée palace for lunch, he expressed his satisfaction (as in Debray 1981: 167) with the fact that 'in ideas and philosophy, France's trade balance is positive'. In combination with another strand of the May 1968 revolt, Herbert Marcuse's and André Gorz's dismissal of the working class as a revolutionary force, all this worked to make the wooden materialism of Soviet Marxism, faithfully reproduced by the French Communist Party, look retrograde. Konstanty Jelenski, an anti-communist Polish exile in Paris, in 1977 reported to the Ford Foundation's international affairs director Francis Sutton that the left had lost its self-confidence and that he was trying to get anti-Marxist articles published in left journals (Guilhot 2010: 177–8). The anti-totalitarian campaign, as Duménil and Lévy highlight (2010: 7), also prepared the ground for the conversion of the Communists' nominal allies, Mitterrand's Socialists, to neoliberalism. This in turn worked to convince broad layers of France's managerial cadre class to subscribe to the ideology of the market as the sole arbiter of social life.

Postmodernism (or post-structuralism) remains a hybrid politically, evading easy classification. Foucault in 1977–78 raised the alarm about the West German anti-left *Berufsverbote*, interpreting them in a tradition of state control of the population (2004). Yet the attack by Lyotard and others on historicising social philosophy ('meta-narratives') obfuscates 'second-dimension' time, which, as argued in Volume II (2010: 12–13), lends meaning and purpose to human action. By rejecting as totalitarian any explicit 'all-embracing representation' (the term used by Jean Piaget for second-dimension time, as in ibid.), human existence is reduced to meaningless, repetitive gestures. In this spirit Harvey analyses (1995: 292) postmodernity as a cultural by-product of the 'time–space compression' inherent in finance-led accumulation, of 'futures markets in everything … coupled with the "securitization" of all kinds of temporary and floating debts, [all] techniques for discounting the future into the present'. The loosening up of encrusted social roles once the shackles on capital movements have been removed evokes a sense of fluidity and indeterminacy; postmodernism and post-structuralism appear to articulate this best. This created an 'oppositional' niche in the human sciences that yet was completely divorced from any practical struggle, ubiquitous references to 'resistance' notwithstanding. The career of the Italian political philosopher Antonio Negri may serve as a reminder that this particular lineage of 'resistance' paradoxically may work to consolidate the forces it supposedly contests, in this case with a resonance in IR, an area not covered by French postmodernists.

Negri studied in the United States on a Rockefeller grant and in spite of his nominal leadership of the extreme left *Potere Operaio* (later *Autonomia Operaia* – Workers' Power/Autonomy) regularly visited the United States afterwards, at a time when members of the mainstream Communist Party could not obtain visas. Willan records (1991: 186–8, 352) Negri's involvement in US and Italian secret service 'false flag' operations in his country, among others by providing weapons to the Red Brigades who abducted and assassinated Christian Democrat politician Aldo Moro in 1978. Imprisoned in Italy, Negri achieved fame in Anglophone IR with *Empire*, co-authored with Duke University literature professor Michael Hardt (2000). The first of a trilogy and undoubtedly a fascinating collage of political philosophy, *Empire* concludes with a eulogy about an insurrection of the masses, the 'multitude'. 'Autonomous movement is what defines the place proper to the multitude ... the cities of the earth will at once become great deposits of cooperating humanity and locomotives for circulation', Hardt and Negri assure us (2000: 397). Identifying the masses, in the spirit of the Italian *Operaista* school, as the 'real productive force' unmediated by capital, they continue: 'Everywhere [these movements] create that wealth that parasitic postmodern capitalism would otherwise not know how to suck out of the blood of the proletariat.'

Hailed as a 'sweeping neo-Marxist vision of the coming world order' by *Foreign Affairs*, the house organ of the Council on Foreign Relations, *Empire* shares with other postmodern accounts its failure to identify 'which social forces might lead in the struggle to effect those far-reaching changes' (Neufeld 1995: 113) – thus exposing the innocence behind the insurrectionist grandiloquence. This has slowly won it the role of a tolerated playground for young academics, even in IR. Keohane's presidential address at the 1988

International Studies Association in Steve Smith's words (2000: 380–5) still 'disciplined the discipline' by declaring postmodernism illegitimate, along with other 'reflectivist' approaches. However, writing with Katzenstein and Krasner a decade later, Keohane not only consented to giving constructivism a legitimate presence beside 'rationalism' (covering both rational choice and positivism). Postmodernism too was now partially legitimated (Katzenstein, Keohane and Krasner 1998: 678, cf. 646) as a breeding ground for 'critical constructivism', giving it one foot in the discipline.

THE TURN TO COERCIVE GLOBAL GOVERNANCE

Whilst a new ethics was being formulated and IPE absorbed themes raised by the student movement, the militarists whose influence on the IR discipline dates from the 1950s were mobilising against détente. They were reinforced by a segment of the liberal Jewish intelligentsia of New York, which switched to the right in response to the anti-Zionism that was an element in 1970s anti-Western mobilisation. As neoconservatives, or neocons (see my 2006: 160–1, 232), they were among the most vocal in the drive to abrogate the corporate liberal recognition of the Soviet bloc and its allies in the Third World; the Helsinki Accords of 1975 confirming the division of Europe agreed at Yalta would turn out to be the final concession made to Soviet security concerns. When Secretary of State Kissinger flew to Moscow in January 1976 for SALT arms control negotiations, Richard Perle, one of the neocons from the entourage of the 'senator for Boeing', Henry Jackson, leaked details of the trip to the press. In the so-called Halloween Massacre, managed by Dick Cheney and Donald Rumsfeld from the Ford White House, CIA director William Colby (who had fired the paranoid counter-intelligence chief J.J. Angleton in the wake of public revelations about CIA misconduct), was replaced by George H.W. Bush, whilst Rumsfeld went to the Pentagon as the new Secretary of Defence (Scott 2010: 153; 2007: 57–8). In the course of 1976, a series of major reshuffles set the stage for an aggressive restoration of Western supremacy.

Refocusing the Academic Intelligence Base

The militarist Committee on the Present Danger (CPD) in its original form dates from the 1950s. In 1976 it was reconstituted as a neocon bulwark to campaign for a more aggressive US posture towards the Soviet bloc and the progressive Third World coalition. The author of the 1950 Cold War manifesto NSC-68, Paul Nitze, who led the original Committee, was again among the leading figures in 1976, along with Eugene Rostow of Yale. Edward Teller, political scientists Jeanne Kirkpatrick of Georgetown University, Seymour Martin Lipset, R.L. Pfaltzgraff Jr., U. Ra'anan and others, as well as William J. Casey, future CIA director, and Ray S. Cline, former deputy at the CIA, also joined the new CPD (Scott 2010: 173). A subsidiary European–American Workshop chaired by veteran nuclear strategist Albert Wohlstetter aimed at winning over European politicians for a confrontation strategy (Adler and Haas 1992: 387). Funded by David Packard of Hewlett-Packard and by charities spun off from the Mellon dynasty, the CPD's first concern was to get President Ford to allow a 'Team B' to assess CIA estimates of the 'Soviet threat', judged as too conservative (Scheer 1982: 53–65).

With Casey, Teller, and Robert Galvin (CEO of Motorola and the American Security Council) on the president's Foreign Intelligence Advisory Board, and Colby replaced by Bush, Team B, headed by red-baiting Harvard historian Richard Pipes, duly concluded there was a 'window of vulnerability' that exposed the United States to nuclear surprise attack – a familiar theme from 1950s RAND theorising (Scott 2007: 60). Team B included Nitze, Foy Kohler (former US ambassador to Moscow and professor of IR at the University of Miami), William R. van Cleave (professor of IR at the University of Southern California and fellow of the Hoover Institution at Stanford), Lieutenant General Daniel O. Graham, former head of the Defense Intelligence Agency, Thomas Wolfe of RAND, and others. The presidential election in November was won by Jimmy Carter, the candidate of the Trilateral Commission and the CFR '1980s project', so it looked as if the CPD confrontation strategy would be sidelined. In fact, the grip of the neocons on the academic intelligence base was reinforced. When Carter drafted moderate Trilateralists like Cyrus Vance and Michael Blumenthal into his cabinet, their places on the board of the Council on Foreign Relations were taken by Nitze, Pipes, the Rostow brothers Walt and Eugene, and other CPD and Team B activists (Silk and Silk 1981: 220).

For the neocons, the integrity of the Soviet bloc had been respected for too long. As Wolfowitz argued in the 1970s (as in Mann 2004: 75–6, cf. 24), Kissinger, the realist, did not understand 'the country he is living in': the United States 'is dedicated to certain universalistic principles', to which other states must submit. As noted in the last chapter, Kissinger's crimes in South-East Asia and his support for assassinations and torture in Latin America followed from a consistent 'power politics' in which war and repression are the continuation of US policy by other means – but *within* its own bloc. Kissinger, then, was a 'realist' in the Yalta sense; Carter's national security adviser, Zbigniew Brzezinski, on the other hand, shared the neocon mindset out of his desire to dislodge Soviet control over Eastern Europe. In 1978–79 he directed the CIA to begin funding the resistance in the conservative Muslim countryside to the communist Afghan regime. The ensuing Soviet intervention, Brzezinski boasted to a reporter of the *Nouvel Observateur* in 1998, had been his aim all along. 'On the day the Soviets officially crossed the border, I wrote to President Carter, saying in essence: "We now have the opportunity of giving to the USSR its Vietnam War"' (as in Scott 2010: 176–7; 2003: 35 n. 17). Asked by the interviewer whether he did not regret in hindsight that this had given the country to the Taliban, he laughed it off, dismissing the threat posed by 'some agitated Muslims' as negligible compared to 'the liberation of Central Europe and the end of the Cold War'. A year before the interview, Brzezinski had laid out his own version of Mackinder's heartland theory in *The Grand Chessboard*, a work in which he reiterates (1997: 31 and passim) the belief that whoever controls central Asia holds the keys to world power.

At the time this triumphant outcome was far from evident. The Iranian revolution in 1979, combined with the Sandinista victory in Nicaragua and armed rebellion across Central America, were severe blows to Western supremacy and to US leadership in particular. The occupation of the American embassy in Teheran in November 1979 and a botched rescue operation humiliated the United States. The CIA's access to academia just then suffered from congressional investigations. Frank Church, who chaired the Senate committee on the subject, was especially concerned (as in Wilford 2008: 253) over the 'operational use' of individual academics in 'providing leads and making introductions for intelligence purposes, collaboration in research and analysis, intelligence collection abroad, and preparation of books and other propaganda materials'. When the Iranian revolution was further seen (as in Ege 1984: 5) as a *research failure*, not an intelligence failure – 'a persistent failure to analyse or appreciate the precariousness of the Shah's rule' – Carter commissioned an outside review of the CIA so that this deficiency might be overcome. Hence among his 'three wise men' was the IR scholar (and former member of Allen Dulles' 'Princeton Consultants') Klaus Knorr. Admiral Stansfield Turner, Carter's director of the CIA, then appointed Robert Bowie of Harvard, another former Princeton Consultant, to head a Foreign Assessment Centre. Consultations with universities were also undertaken, with mixed results; Harvard's Derek Bok refused to sign a comprehensive agreement with the CIA (Cavanagh 1980: 7; Hulnick 1987: 44).

All this changed with Reagan's election victory, achieved by banging the drum of a restoration of US military strength. Thirty-two CPD members in all joined the new administration (Brownstein and Easton 1983: 533; Scheer 1982: 145–6). At the CIA, Casey was first of all concerned with overcoming the decline of covert action (from about half the CIA budget in the 1950s to 4 per cent when Colby left; Woodward 1987: 44), but the intelligence collaboration with universities was intensified too. It was the conviction of Bush, the vice president and former CIA director, that US intelligence had always depended more 'on a community of scholars than on a network of spies' (as in Trumpbour 1991: 13), and as Ege documents (1984: 3–4), 250 universities and colleges had Pentagon contracts in 1980–81, with MIT and Johns Hopkins accounting for half of the total. There was the occasional scandal, as when IR scholar Richard Mansbach and a Rutgers colleague were reprimanded by their school officials for depositing students' papers in a CIA-funded research project without their knowledge (ibid.: 2, 6), or when Nadav Safran, director of the Centre for Middle Eastern Studies at Harvard, was censured for using CIA money for a conference in 1986 without informing the attendees (Wilford 2008: 253). Not everybody was on the take: Africa was a key arena in the strategy of 'low intensity warfare' against progressive governments, but twelve Africa Study centres in 1981 refused to accept Defence Intelligence Agency money. In IR, Robert Keohane, whilst acknowledging that working for government bodies brings rewards, likewise made the choice of keeping his distance (Mooney 2000). But then, the academic intelligence base is a layered structure with differential roles, of which maintaining discipline is as important as serving in government.

The Dual State and the Origins of the War on Terror

Reagan's election campaign among other things received a boost from the refusal of the occupiers of the US embassy to release the American hostages before November 1980. The media coverage of this event heightened the 'pervasive cultivation of mistrust, apprehension, danger, and exaggerated "mean world" perceptions' of the preceding period (Gerbner et al. 1980: 25). As it turned out later, the delay in releasing the hostages had been arranged in secret talks in Paris between William Casey and representatives of Iran and Israel in the summer of 1980 (Scott 2010: 170). The agreement also laid the foundations for a bold plan to obtain the release of other US hostages, held by Lebanese Shi'ite militias, which in turn became part of a covert financing scheme for the Nicaraguan Contras. This created a triangular web of clandestine connections between the National Security Council in Washington, Israeli arms traders and the Likud government elected in 1977, and Saudi Arabia. Casey acted in a private capacity when he established contact with the Pakistani dictator, Zia ul-Haq, and the chief of Saudi intelligence, Prince Turki al-Faisal, to supply arms to the jihadists fighting the Soviet army in Afghanistan. As Scott documents (ibid.: 10–11), a subsidy of $1 billion from Turki and matching funds from the CIA, distributed through the Pakistan-based Bank of Commerce and Credit International (BCCI), allowed the operation to remain outside congressional oversight. At the National Security Council, Marine Colonel Oliver North was entrusted with coordinating these myriad covert dealings, eventually exposed as 'Iran–Contra'. There was a second aspect to this triangular structure, also under North's operational supervision: the domestic shadow government structure held in reserve for an emergency.

The Reagan administration, building on Nixon-era emergency plans for dealing with the domestic repercussions of Vietnam and the black emancipation movement, in tandem with the turn to an aggressive foreign policy, also ratcheted up homeland security. In its Reagan-era version, this was the Continuity of Government (COG) project, an ultra-secret enterprise to impose the surveillance and mass detention of political dissenters, as well as the emergency appointment of military commanders ruling under martial law (Scott 2007: 23). James Mann records (2004: 138–9) how Donald Rumsfeld and Dick Cheney were recruited as team leaders in exercises preparing for nuclear-war management, as were James Woolsey, later CIA director, and others. Supervised by Casey and Vice-President Bush, Rumsfeld and Cheney became 'principal figures in one of the most highly classified programmes of the Reagan administration', although neither of them held any office at the time. The shadow apparatus thus put together is characterised by Mann (2004: 145) as 'the permanent, though hidden, national security apparatus of the United States, inhabitants of a world in which presidents may come and go, but America always keeps on fighting' – in other words, the covert element in Morgenthau's 'dual state'. In the hearings on the Iran–Contra scandal, Oliver North, who had handled money, weapons and drugs transfers from the White House basement, was asked (as in Scott 2007: 23) whether he had worked on 'a contingency plan ... that would suspend the American constitution', but he declined to answer.

In fact North's boss, Vice-President Bush, was present at the first of a series of high-level conferences at which, long before '9/11', the need for imposing a domestic state of emergency as part of a comprehensive war on terror was explored. Menachem Begin, Likud prime minister and himself a former operative of the Irgun terror gang (cf. vol. ii, 2010: 198–202), in 1979 officially opened the Jerusalem Conference on International Terrorism. Bush at the time was still a Republican hopeful looking for a rallying theme; his tenure at the CIA had been discontinued when Carter assumed office, but a shadow 'CIA-in-exile', including Bush and Casey, then Reagan's campaign manager, kept contacts with British and Saudi and other friendly Middle Eastern intelligence services alive. Bush through his oil interests had many links to Saudi Arabia; Casey's close friend and business associate, oilman Bruce Rappoport, in turn had intimate ties with Israeli intelligence and with BCCI, which funnelled money to the Afghan insurgency (Scott 2010: 163; 2003: 47–8, cf. 19–20n.). Henry Jackson and two terrorism specialists, Yonah Alexander of the State University of New York and Ray Cline, already mentioned as former deputy CIA director and then a professor of IR at Georgetown, also participated in the Jerusalem event (Callahan 1990: 5; Garthoff 1994: 23n.). Garthoff mentions a follow-up conference in Washington ('under expanded auspices') in April 1980. It featured Henry Kissinger, Reagan's national security adviser Richard Allen, Pipes, and a host of neoconservatives from the United States. Here I concentrate on the third conference in the series, held in Washington in June 1984.

Convened by the then Israeli ambassador to the UN, Benjamin Netanyahu, this event is the clearest, most detailed announcement of a comprehensive war on terror in the public domain. Its participants included foreign policy dignitaries such as George W. Schultz, US secretary of state after the ouster of Alexander Haig, and Yitzhak Rabin, the Israeli defence minister, as well as top-level officials in the homeland security domain, such as US Attorney General Ed Meese and FBI Director William Webster. The journalists Claire Sterling, Arnaud de Borchgrave, George Will and Bob Woodward, and the scholars Bernard Lewis of Princeton, Michael Ledeen of Georgetown, Eugene Rostow (director of the US Arms Control and Disarmament Agency at the time), and several others also participated. As in the earlier conferences, the terrorism theme was deployed to suggest a continuity between the 'Soviet threat' and Third World national liberation struggles, between the Cold War and its aftermath, in much the same way that the totalitarianism thesis had allowed the projection onto the Soviet Union of Axis wars of aggression and genocide.

Netanyahu defines the 'worldwide network of terror' (1986: 3, cf. xi) as being composed of the 'two main antagonists of democracy in the post-war world', communist totalitarianism and Islamic radicalism. Israel's strategy of blaming the mainstream Palestinian resistance in the territories occupied in the 1967 war for the terrorism of fringe groups was to be expanded into a general strategy for the West. The conference developed the notion of pre-emptive attack on states 'supporting terror', especially if they were armed with weapons of mass destruction. The renegade British Labourite Paul Johnson and Eugene Rostow both praised the Israeli invasion of Lebanon in 1982 as setting an example for terrorists worldwide. It sent a message to 'the master killers of Tehran and Tripoli' (Johnson), whilst Rostow claimed that intervention should be recognised as a right (in Netanyahu 1986: 36–7, 148). Secretary Shultz identified a 'league of terror' composed of Libya, Syria, Iran and North Korea, recommending that if intelligence warranted it, pre-emptive attack to disarm a terrorist state must be an option (in ibid.: 16). For as Republican senator Paul Laxalt put it (in ibid.: 187), 'if we learned that Libya or Iran had obtained ... a nuclear weapon, would we really be obliged to wait until that weapon was used?'

Of course the question was how to mobilise society for campaigns of such proportions. Here Netanyahu himself volunteered what is perhaps best called a 'supply-side' approach by indicating that a systematic approach to terror would only work if, somehow, an event beyond the routine plane hijacking or bombing were to occur. Thus he argues (ibid.: 218, emphasis added) that

Terrorism follows an inexorable, built-in escalation. To be effective, it must continually horrify and stupefy. Yet once we have become accustomed to a particular level of violence, *a new outrage is required to shock our sensibilities*. It used to be enough for terrorists to hijack a plane to attract international attention; next it became necessary to kill a few hostages; in the future, more violence will be required.

It was only after a truly mighty blow that 'a successful war on terrorism ... not just erratic responses to individual terrorist acts' could be launched, and that the United States would be able to build 'an anti-terrorist alliance ... with two or three or possibly more countries' (ibid.: 221). Since no country but the United States 'has the capacity to align the West in this matter, [it] alone can credibly threaten the offenders, and [it] alone can impel the neutrals to shed their neutrality', Netanyahu argued (ibid.: 225–6). 'The more America resorts to action, such as punishing terrorists and their backers, the greater the number of states which will join the effort to combat terrorism.'

So, 17 years before 9/11, a scenario had been laid out that left little to the imagination. When the attacks on the Twin Towers in fact happened, the provisions of the shadow government – the Patriot Act and the declaration of the state of emergency – were enacted with lightning speed. This is the dual state aspect of the War on Terror. At the Jerusalem conference in 1979, Bush had still worried (as in Ralph 2008: 265) that in a terror emergency, 'the legitimate exercise of state power' might be frustrated by the liberal conscience of 'the open society'. In 1984, however, Netanyahu was confident (1986: 225–6) that given a major outrage that would shock the world, the 'citizens in a democracy', united in fear, would accept being 'soldiers in a common battle'. People would then be 'prepared to endure sacrifice and even ... immeasurable pain', and the 'war against terrorism' could be won. Rallying the population requires depicting 'terror' as an *absolute evil*, as Italian analysts of the 1970s strategy of tension had already noted (Sanguinetti 1982: 53–5); approaching it analytically, in its true proportions, is best avoided. At the 1984 conference, John O'Sullivan, deputy editor of *The Times* of London, in this respect favourably compared the way the tabloids publicise only the horrors of a terror incident with the tendency of the quality press to try to explain its causes (which he claimed works *for* the terrorists). Television moderator Ted Koppel, however, expressed confidence that once a war had been declared (which President Johnson had failed to do in Vietnam), 'then all kinds of societal pressures, and indeed legal pressures, [would] come to bear on the media *to play a different role from the one they play right now'* (in Netanyahu 1986: 235, 239, emphasis added). It would indeed come to depend on the Mannings, Assanges, and Snowdens of this world to reveal what the mainstream media no longer report, or only selectively.

Within a year after the Jerusalem conference, Reagan's first secretary of state, Vietnam veteran and former NATO commander Alexander Haig Jr., gave the new narrative the official stamp of approval when, in a State Department current policy document, he characterised terrorism as the greatest threat to world peace on account of its reliance on Moscow, the global nerve centre. Haig re-baptised national liberation movements as 'terrorists', just as he dismissed the concept of a 'Third World' (Hippler 1986: 43). That Claire Sterling's *The Terror Network*, supposedly exposing a worldwide terror operation managed by the KGB, and on which Haig relied, was based on prior CIA disinformation (Woodward 1987: 92) did not matter; the terrorism theme had already received an academic stamp of approval. Cline and Alexander based their 1984 book, *Terrorism: The Soviet Connection* (1986), on PLO materials captured by the Israeli army in its incursion into Lebanon to support the claim that Palestinian resistance to occupation was directed from Moscow. In a study for the US Senate Subcommittee on Security and Terrorism, *State-Sponsored Terrorism*, they argue that the illegality of international terror would remain beyond the reach of international law as long as the term 'national liberation' went unchallenged.

The terrorism theme quickly spread from the fringes of the IR discipline to the mainstream. The International Security Council (ISC), a project of the Moon Sect of South Korea and its front organisation, CAUSA, for its pamphlet series recruited William R. Van Cleave, Eugene Rostow, Arnaud de Borchrave (editor-in-chief of the *Washington Times*, launched by Moon as a counterweight to the supposedly liberal press in the United States), as well as assorted generals and admirals. An ISC pamphlet of 1986 thus established that 'Soviet client states ... are today confronting national liberation struggles directed at them' (International Security Council 1986: 8), a reference to the Contra terror and sabotage operations in Nicaragua, Angola and Mozambique, as well as the Afghan insurrection, unified under the Reagan Doctrine of intercontinental counterrevolution. Ray Cline was made the editor of a *Terrorism* book series; Yonah Alexander directed his own Institute for Studies in International Terrorism at SUNY. If this was still on the far right of the political spectrum, the editorial board of the journal *Political Communication and Persuasion*, also under Alexander's direction, already included Leonard Binder (UCLA), James N. Rosenau (University of Southern California), as well as representatives of think tanks such as the Heritage Foundation and RAND. Samuel Huntington, Lipset and a number of political figures, including Margaret Thatcher's mentor Lord Chalfont, Helmut Sonnenfeldt of the Brookings Institution, and journalist George Will, sat on the advisory board. This array of names, and events such as the 1985 conference on Islamic fundamentalism at Harvard (Bilgin and Morton 2002: 61), make clear the extent to which academia in the Reagan period was already being enlisted in the elaboration and propagation of the theme of (Islamic) 'terror'.

Limited Sovereignty and Democracy Promotion after the Soviet Collapse

The counterpart to Western supremacy, exercised through liberal global governance, is the open nation-state. The obligation of 'openness' implies that we are looking at limited sovereignty, not sovereign equality, which is only formal. The Monroe Doctrine and the 'open door' forced on China come to mind as examples, but if we think back to Lord Lothian's advising Nehru on having a *two*-party system, it is obvious that openness limits sovereignty not just in respect of foreign policy or trade and capital movements; it also does so by prescribing a polyarchic electoral democracy. There must be a viable opposition available to derail any contender-state posture – ideally one that can be openly supported from abroad.

Within the IR discipline, Stanford scholar Stephen D. Krasner has most consistently argued the case for limiting sovereignty, eventually taking his recommendations to the State Department as policy planning director in the aftermath of the Iraq invasion. In *Structural Conflict: The Third World against Global Liberalism* of 1985, Krasner theorises how sovereign equality and international organisation based on it allowed the non-aligned bloc to try to dislodge the global political economy from its Lockean moorings. The project for a 'New International Economic Order', adopted by a majority in the United Nations General Assembly, thus came close to changing the world economy to what Krasner calls, using another Eastonian term, a regime of 'authoritative allocation'. As long as formal sovereignty and state-based voting are left to operate without restraint, he warns (1985: 81), a global contender coalition might fatally compromise the 'market-oriented' regime in which 'allocation of resources is determined by the endowments and preferences of individual actors who have the right to alienate their property' – in brief, liberal capitalism. Once state sovereignty is restricted, the quest is then for the basis of a self-regulating society supporting polyarchy. Joel Migdal's *Strong Societies and Weak States* of 1988, cited in both my previous volumes, has been identified (Bilgin and Morton 2002: 62) as the sort of work investigating the 'civil society' potential in target states.

When the Soviet bloc began to crumble and the signs indicated that the USSR might soon follow, the focus on opening up dependent societies returned as well. Francis Fukuyama, a member of the State Department Policy Planning Staff under Paul Wolfowitz and a resident RAND Corporation consultant, captured the neocons' triumphant mood with his 'End of History' article in *The National Interest*. Announcing the 'unabashed victory of economic and political liberalism' (1989: 3), on a scale that has left only a handful of rogue states (and liberal academics) committed to Marxism, Fukuyama declares that with the collapse of Soviet state socialism, all systematic historical alternatives to liberal capitalism have exhausted themselves. Along with Wolfowitz, who in 1976 recruited him as an intern, Fukuyama had been groomed in neoconservatism as a member of the Telluride Circle at Cornell, convened around the political philosopher Allan Bloom. Bloom in turn was a pupil of Leo Strauss, but Fukuyama bases his argument on the idea of the universal homogeneous state of Strauss' interlocutor, Kojève. Bloom's *Closing of the American Mind* of 1987 restates the superiority of pragmatism over philosophically grounded European social thought (which he sees as a corrupting influence on the American intelligentsia; Reisch 2005: 371); Fukuyama however treads where few US scholars have dared when he engages with Hegel and (in the book version) Nietzsche.

Whether Hegel can be called as a witness for the triumph of Lockean liberalism is one thing. But the propagandistic impact of Fukuyama's intervention cannot easily be overstated. Capitalism is the endpoint of economic development; Schumpeterian polyarchy, the climax of political development. Multiparty elections are about selecting a government, but given that 'the economy' has already reached the best of all worlds, its management cannot be tinkered with. Any remaining states not submitting to Western supremacy lack legitimacy; they are 'mired in history' and can no longer assert sovereign equality against the heartland, which alone is entitled to write the rules for the international order. In this respect Fukuyama's role is not that of an original thinker (most of what is interesting is already in Kojève and other sources), but as a neocon propagandist. The Olin Foundation, spun off from gunpowder manufacturer Olin Mathieson, funded Fukuyama's book project; it has played an important role in restoring intellectual hegemony for neoconservatism by intellectual activism (rather than entrenching behind established values). As one of its managers stated in the mid 1980s (as in Nielsen 1985: 43), 'Ideas and intellectuals count enormously ... The things the Reagan Administration is doing now were perked [sic] in a small circle of intellectuals.'

Taking the battle to the realm of ideas now that the Soviet contender state (still nominally committed to a socialist society) was beginning to lose its grip in Eastern Europe also had profound implications for the nature of Western intervention. Here the work of Gene Sharp of the Albert Einstein Institute helped restructure the NATO underground into an apparatus for 'democracy promotion', especially in those state socialist countries where the transition to polyarchy remains incomplete. Sharp's ideas about removing dictators by civil disobedience fit into a tradition that goes back to the 1960s. As Mowat relates (2009: 247), Fred Emery, director of the psychological warfare branch of the British military, the Tavistock Institute (which has its own journal, *Human Relations*), in 1967 came up with the idea of deploying 'swarming adolescents' against unwanted governments and state classes. Two years later the resignation of De Gaulle, destabilised by the events of May 1968, demonstrated the viability of the principle. Since the May movement targeted not only capitalism, but also state socialism, this made it all the more interesting to psychological warfare strategists.

In the 1960s and 1970s, an offshoot of the Congress of Cultural Freedom, the European Foundation for Intellectual Assistance (FEIE), with the aforementioned Konstanty Jelenski in Paris as the driving force, and funded by the Ford Foundation, had been awarding travel grants to East European intellectuals to come to the West, whilst supplying literature to the East. Hungary and Poland were easiest to access; the institutes of social studies in Warsaw and Lodz were key centres of the revision of Marxism and the turn to sociology. As Guilhot records (2010: 171), the philosopher Leszek Kołakowski studied and taught at both institutes before becoming an FEIE contact. Books by Bernard-Henry Lévy and his fellow New Philosophers were hand-delivered to an eager readership. When

Ford funding dried up under Reagan, the Hungarian political exile and neoliberal LSE graduate George Soros kept the network afloat. By 1988 his Swiss-based Karl Popper Foundation provided 80 per cent of FEIE's running costs. The Open Society Institute, named after the polemical work of Soros' revered teacher, would take over the FEIE office in Paris; the Central European University in Budapest would eventually serve as a key transmission belt of Western academic discipline in the region (Guilhot 2010: 181–2; Moody 2010: 8–10).

With Gorbachev in charge in Moscow, covert intervention, as with the Gdansk strikes and the Solidarnosc trade union, became obsolete. Leaving matters to the Catholic Church and the CIA (as in Poland) could lead to the United States 'losing the war of ideas with the Soviet Union if Reagan did not align [himself] clearly with the forces of democracy' (Drolet 2010: 98). This triggered a rethink of undercover involvement, which explains the paradoxical continuity between the NATO 'stay-behind' networks like Gladio in Italy, that in the 1970s were used for US-orchestrated terror campaigns, and what became the 'democracy promotion' campaign. Robinson (1996: 92–3) highlights this when he discusses how the new civil society and NGO engagement emerged from the establishment in 1981 of Project Democracy, attached to the National Security Council. It was supervised by Walter Raymond Jr., CIA propaganda specialist and collaborator of Oliver North. Two years later the National Endowment for Democracy (NED), formally incorporated by Congress in November 1983, was instituted as the 'overt', public arm of Project Democracy, of which the CIA and the NSC continued to handle the 'covert' arm. Here Gene Sharp's concept of withdrawing consent from authoritarian governments and creating open nation-states held in trust by client governing classes obtained the channels for its practical application.

Sharp, a former aide to A.J. Muste, the Trotskyite labour activist and pacifist, studied at Oxford in the 1960s and held various research positions in the Centre for International Affairs at Harvard. He was appointed to a chair in political science at the University of Massachusetts in 1972 and in 1983 set up the Albert Einstein Institution in Boston (Helvey 2004: 10). This aligned him with the democracy promotion drive which through the NED would later provide funding for the training of democracy activists deployed against authoritarian or otherwise undesirable rulers. Sharp's theory of power is based on the notion that since government cannot be exercised by force alone, citizens can change it by actively withdrawing consent. Because of his non-theoretical language, Martin writes (1989: 213–14), Sharp won his greatest following among grassroots activists, not in the academic community. For the activists, he 'has a higher profile ... than any other living political theorist'. The idea of capturing the energy unleashed in the fight for democracy, critically mobilising the fervour of new generations arriving on the political scene, gives his 'withdrawing consent' its 'May 68' quality of a liberating youth festival. In 1985 Sharp published *Making Europe Unconquerable: The Potential of Civilian-Based Deterrence and Defense*, with a foreword by George Kennan (an earlier book of Sharp's had a foreword by RAND veteran Thomas Schelling). As Mowat relates (2009: 249–50), the idea for a civilian defence infrastructure in Europe had been suggested to Sharp by General Edward Atkeson, former intelligence chief of the US Army in Europe. Atkeson in the mid 1980s gave seminars at Harvard on 'civilian-based defence and the art of war', before joining the Einstein Institution advisory board in the 1990s.

US academia was quick to pick up the scent of democracy promotion as a vector of bringing open nation-states under Western global governance. 'By the mid-1980s,' Robinson writes (1996: 16), 'the intellectual community had joined [the democracy promotion shift in the US policymaking establishment]. University presses churned out a whole new class of "democratization" literature and democratization courses sprang up on campuses.' Case Western Reserve University in Cleveland in 1989 began a series of conferences under its Program for Social Innovations in Global Management. Howard Perlmutter, professor of social architecture at the University of Pennsylvania's Wharton School and a follower of Fred Emery's, under the heading of 'rock video in Kathmandu', argued in *Human Relations* of 1991 (as in Mowat 2009: 247) that unwanted rulers in states with a traditional society can be dislodged by exposing them to aggressive forms of Western culture, or 'global civilisation', such as rock concerts. The civil society narrative is crucial here. It speaks to a liberal mindset which rejects state authority and thus chimes with anti-authoritarian inclinations among the young. A discredited state then faces an insurrectionary movement with evident Western cultural overtones (rock and dance). Close on the heels of the pop concert revolution come the cohorts of the NED network: the international operations of the Democratic and Republican parties, the Centre of International Private Enterprise (the international arm of the US Chamber of Commerce) and the Free Trade Union

Institute (AFL-CIO), all disguised as NGOs. In combination they can deliver the complete inventory of a functioning 'civil society' (Robinson 1996: 95).

The removal in 1986 of Philippines dictator Ferdinand Marcos was the first activist operation run by the NED jointly with Freedom House and the Soros Foundation. The US-based dual state displaced Marcos' own repressive apparatus by death squads no longer operating under state auspices. The (partial) transformation of the transnational covert action network into one of democracy promotion was never a matter of a change of mind; it represents a broadening of the means available to Western supremacy. The need to keep the democracy movement from moving beyond polyarchy is reason enough to have a residual covert action capability in place. Thus US Army Colonel Robert Helvey, a veteran of the Defense Intelligence Agency, upon his retirement attended Sharp's classes at Harvard and learned (2004: xii) that 'strategic non-violent struggle is about seizing political power and denying it to others. It is not about pacifism, moral or religious beliefs.' As US military attaché in Myanmar from 1983 to 1985 Helvey worked to organise Karen minority insurgents and followers of Aung San Suu Kyi. He also trained Beijing student leaders in Hong Kong in techniques that would be deployed in the Tiananmen revolt of June 1989, and subsequently advised the Falun Gong sect in China (Mowat 2009: 248).

The CIA by then was firmly focused on the 'youth factor' in target countries. 'The youth of a growing population may very well play a major role in pressing for change', Helvey records (2004: 15). 'They are among those who are actually disproportionately disadvantaged; they have less at stake in the existing structure of authority, more idealism, more impatience.' For the same reasons, because they are impetuous and daring, they should be properly guided to avoid committing violence themselves. Yet Tavistock Institute director Fred Emery (as in Mowat 2009: 247) claimed that recalcitrant states could now be brought down by 'swarming adolescents' assembled at rock concerts, turning their 'rebellious hysteria' into a force for good. From the 1989 Velvet Revolution in Prague, via Lithuania, where Sharp provided training to rebels against the USSR in 1990, to Albania, there has followed a whole series of US-managed 'civil society revolutions'. Under the auspices of the International Republican Institute (IRI) in 1998–2000, Helvey and Sharp travelled to Belgrade to train Otpor ('resistance'), after which followed Georgia, Ukraine and Kirgizstan (see my 2006: 351–2). In Belarus and Iran, on the other hand, the limits of the civic road were brought to light. The same is true in Venezuela, where Sharp and Helvey met wealthy citizens after the failed coup against Hugo Chávez (who in his political career won 15 of the 16 elections in which he stood as a candidate, but nonetheless was considered authoritarian; Rosenberg 2011).

Helvey was not the only security figure in the democracy promotion infrastructure. The junk bond financier Peter Ackerman, author of *Strategic Nonviolent Conflict* of 1994, became the founding chairman of the Washington-based International Centre on Nonviolent Conflicts, with the former US Air Force officer Jack DuVall as president. Jointly with the former CIA director James Woolsey, DuVall also directs the Arlington Institute, another Washington outfit, created in 1989 by the former Chief of Naval Operations advisor John L. Petersen, 'to help redefine the concept of national security in much larger, comprehensive terms' (as in Mowat 2009: 246). It does so by introducing 'social value shifts into the traditional national defence equation'. Ackerman, along with Gene Sharp, supported Helvey in writing *On Strategic Nonviolent Conflict*, a practical handbook of people's-power takeover; in it, the chief case officer for youth movements in the Balkans and Eastern Europe in the 1990s identifies (Helvey 2004: x) Burma, Iran, Tibet and Zimbabwe as future targets of non-violent struggle. Since Anglo-American political science, and IR in particular, have not shown much interest in covert action (surveying five top journals in the field for the 1991–2000 period, Gibbs in 2003 found not a single article dealing with the topic), democracy promotion was not systematically connected to it either (see Cox, Ikenberry and Inoguchi 2000).

The dissemination of Western-style political science under the auspices of the NED includes the *Journal of Democracy*, a pseudo-academic publication with articles commissioned by the NED. It was edited by the Hoover Institute scholar Larry Diamond, who is also associated with the Democrats' Progressive Policy Institute. As Parmar recounts (2012: 232–3), Diamond would influence thinking in the Clinton administration about threats coming from non-integrated, non-democratic states and eventually served on the Provisional Authority in occupied Iraq. *Democracy in Developing Countries*, of 1988–89, in four volumes, edited by Diamond, Juan J. Linz and Seymour Martin Lipset, and *Transitions from Authoritarian*

Rule: Prospects for Democracy, of 1986, also four volumes, edited by Guillermo O'Donnell, Philip C. Schmitter and Laurence Whitehead, were both commissioned with the intent of informing US policy and policymakers. Diamond, Linz and Lipset define democracy (as in Robinson 1996: 54, emphasis added) as a 'political system, *separate and apart from the economic and social system ...* A distinctive aspect of our approach is to insist that issues of so-called economic and social democracy be separated from the question of governmental structure.'

Bracketing off the economy from politics and entrusting it to (neoliberal) 'experts' had been Huntington's recommendation in the *Crisis of Democracy* report to the Trilateral Commission of 1975. It would figure again in Fukuyama's 'end of history' argument – indeed it is inherent in Schumpeterian polyarchy. Projecting Lockean global governance rules out economic sovereignty. So much was made clear by the Harvard IR don Graham Allison, to whom I return below, in his preface to *Window of Opportunity* (1991: xi), co-authored with the Russian liberal politician Grigory Yavlinsky and published when Gorbachev was still in power. Allison explains that the political economy of the Soviet Union is beyond reform; 'it must be replaced' via 'a program for speeding its replacement by a market-oriented democracy'. This project, 'Strengthening Democratic Institutions', sponsored by the Carnegie Corporation and the Getty Foundation, became mired in corruption, with Harvard's Andrei Shleifer acting as an adviser to vice-premier Anatoly Chubais under a USAID contract. It led to a US government lawsuit against Harvard, Shleifer, and others that was only settled with Harvard paying $31 million – and Shleifer remaining at his post (Trumpbour 1991: 15; McClintick 2006). The episode shows that propagating a system in crisis increases instability on an extended scale, ultimately bolstering a resurgence of contender states.

WESTERN SUPREMACY IN CRISIS

In his analysis of imperialism, Schumpeter in 1919 defined the phenomenon as an atavism traceable to the continued military predilections of aristocratic warrior elites whose economic role had expired. Imperialism therefore was an 'objectless disposition' (1951: 6; cf. our Chapter 2, note 2), a meaningless, pathological feature carried over from the past. The collapse of the Soviet Union and the New World Order pronounced by George H.W. Bush upon the victorious conclusion of the Gulf War of 1991 has turned United States militarism into such an 'objectless disposition'. Concern among US militarists that the appetite for oversized defence budgets might be subsiding had by then been mounting. At the time of publication of the best-selling *The Rise and Fall of the Great Powers* of 1987 by Yale historian Paul Kennedy, Assistant Secretary of Defense Richard Armitage warned that the book was being used (as in Mann 2004: 161) 'by many who want to roll back our defense commitments around the world'. Concerned about ideas such as Senator Edward Kennedy's proposals to reduce defence spending and use $200 billion over a number of years to invest in health, education and jobs programmes, Paul Wolfowitz, then undersecretary of defense under Dick Cheney, in 1991 commissioned a Defense Planning Guidance for 1994–99 that argued the case for continued military outlays. Wolfowitz too had been a student of Allan Bloom at Cornell and wrote his Ph.D. for RAND strategist Albert Wohlstetter at the University of Chicago; Fukuyama was one of his protégés (Mann 2004: 23–30). He would be a key member of the group that by launching the invasion of Iraq in 2003 pushed the world a step deeper into the epoch of endless war that Leo Strauss had called for.

The eventual DPG recommended that the United States should ensure that its allies would not feel inclined to develop a military capacity outside US command structures (thus European integration should not undermine NATO), whilst echoing the recommendations of the Netanyahu papers that pre-emption and punishment were legitimate forms of dealing with the threat, real or imagined, of weapons of mass destruction. Western supremacy was articulated in the recommendation that the United States should remain a generation ahead of all others in the decisive technologies of the future (DPG 1992: 18, 46); NATO should be expanded into Eastern Europe whilst Russia should be prevailed on to reduce its forces and presence unilaterally (DPG 1992: 21, 48). This strategy, in James Mann's summary (2004: 200), sought to ensure that 'no future adversary with whom anyone could suggest the need for détente, would ever emerge'. There was one problem with the DPG strategy – there might be no credible enemy any longer. This brings us to Samuel Huntington's 'clash of civilisations' argument, first published in a *Foreign Affairs* piece in 1993 and subsequently in a book of 1998.

Huntington replaces the ambivalent 'end of history' thesis (with its implication of residual, basically mop-up operations) with the notion of an era of existential struggles – Strauss instead of Kojève. Funded, like Fukuyama, by the Olin Foundation and the CIA (Trumpbour 1991: 13), Huntington's thesis identifies China and Islamic terrorism as the twin challenges facing the West. This claim, rather more tenuous of course than postulating a connection between the USSR and national liberation, is corroborated by the designation of Islam and Confucianism as inherently foreign civilisations. Huntington also takes a leaf from Oswald Spengler's *Decline of the West* of 1918, emphasising that the possibility of a Western demise cannot be ruled out and that the projected confrontation will not be one of choice. One may object of course, as Robert Cox does (2002: 142), that Huntington's 'residual Cold War focus on civilizations distracts attention from the socially polarizing consequences of globalizing market economics, the true generator of chaos'. But the social necessity that Huntington articulates is to keep the heartland on a war footing – something on which 'globalizing market economics' and certainly the United States at its heart have come to depend.

China, the new contender state after 1991, has no transnational revolutionary network like that of the USSR, its predecessor. So the Middle East and the Muslim diaspora must fill the void. Islamic terrorism according to Huntington (1998: 265) has its roots in a 'demographic explosion in Muslim societies', turning 'large numbers of often unemployed males' into a 'natural source of instability and violence'. Israeli author Martin van Creveld's thesis in *The Transformation of War* of 1991, that most wars in the nuclear age have been low-intensity conflicts in which guerrilla or otherwise irregular forces defeated far more powerful states, offers another angle on this phenomenon, equally highlighting the West's vulnerability. The transparency of borders actually raises the spectre of a collapse of the state system itself, suspending the constitutional container role of the state and creating 'failed states', 'rogue states' and the like. In a magazine piece for *The Atlantic*, Robert Kaplan argues (1994, emphasis added) that this opens up 'an epoch of themeless juxtapositions, in which *the classificatory grid of nation-states* is going to be replaced by the jagged-glass pattern of city-states, shanty-states, [and] nebulous and anarchic regionalisms'.

The nation-state, Kaplan maintains, has historically functioned as 'a place where everyone has been educated along similar lines, where people take their cues from national leaders, and where everyone (every male, at least) has gone through the crucible of military service, making patriotism a simpler issue'. In the 'coming anarchy', however, states would fall victim to only partially controlled population movements, which tear up the 'national' fabric of state–society complexes and exacerbate insecurity and anomie. Indeed in the absence of a generally accepted source of evil, Lipschutz comments (1999: 418), 'the polity is threatened by internal disorder and indiscipline arising from the collapse of a cohesive self'.

Under the Spell of the War on Terror

The Clinton administration focused on a neoliberal globalisation offensive that initially sidelined the recommendations of the Defense Planning Guidance. In his second term, however, the president took the militarists' concerns on board in his NATO enlargement policy and the intervention in Yugoslavia (for details, see my 2006: 261–81). The neocons meanwhile hibernated in academia in between Republican administrations. Cheney went to the American Enterprise Institute, before becoming CEO of Halliburton; Wolfowitz was appointed dean of the Johns Hopkins School of Advanced International Studies in Washington. Condoleezza Rice, a leading critic of Clinton's foreign policy and later Bush's national security adviser and secretary of state, in 1991 returned to Stanford. There she became provost and joined George Shultz, former secretary of state, who was at the Hoover Institution, on the board of Chevron, besides accepting directorates at Transamerica, Hewlett-Packard, Charles Schwab, and a position on the advisory council of J.P. Morgan (Mann 2004: 225–6). In 1995 Rice co-authored a study on German reunification with the University of Virginia IR scholar Philip Zelikow.

Zelikow may be considered the key figure in the academic intelligence base as far as the War on Terror is concerned. In the spirit of the Netanyahu assessment of 1984, that 'a new outrage is required to shock our sensibilities' (see above), he argues in a 1999 paper for the Miller Institute that historical periods are defined by what he calls (as in Sacks 2008: 223) 'moulding events' or series of events that 'become etched in the minds of those who live through them'. Pearl Harbour was such an event; for an entire generation it lent a self-evident quality to the notion of defence. It is not enough that it happens: the 'moulding event' and its implications must resonate among a receptive, mediating cadre. As Zelikow explains (as in ibid.), the 'creation and management of "public myths" or "public presumptions"' is not just a matter of beliefs 'thought to be true (although not necessarily known to be true with certainty)'. They must also be 'shared in common within the relevant political community'. This is the disciplinary aspect that a war on terror following a 'moulding event' would entail. It institutes the 'complex triangle of sovereignty, discipline, and governmental management' that allows a state to invoke security concerns, and as Elbe explains (2009: 13, 15), to remove social issues 'from routine democratic deliberation procedures by pushing them into the higher echelons of the state's inner circles of power'. In other words, a major security crisis will activate the dual state structure and keep it in place indefinitely, as a constitutional feature of the social order.

That the security crisis, the 'moulding event', would be a major terrorist attack, was by then a commonplace. President George H.W. Bush in 1988 had already switched the threat warning from impending Soviet atomic attack (I quote Mann 2004: 144) to 'terrorists carrying nuclear weapons attack[ing] the United States'. After a delay, Clinton issued a presidential directive (in 1995) that gave priority to preventing terrorists from obtaining weapons of mass destruction, if only to contain the consequences of the Soviet meltdown. This was followed by a rise in funding, triggering not only the familiar bureaucratic infighting, but, in the neoliberal setting, also the privatisation of security under the doctrine of 'new public management' (Ortiz 2010: 115–31). CIA director John Deutch in 1996 testified that terrorists would attack US information systems, prompting Senator Sam Nunn (as in Lipschutz 1999: 420, cf. 427) to speak of an 'electronic Pearl Harbour'. Deutch soon afterwards became a director of Science Applications International Corporation (SAIC), a private intelligence company founded back in 1970, and of which former CIA Director Robert Gates was also a director. As Scott documents (2010: 183–4; cf. Ortiz 2010: 114, 160), in 1997 SAIC established a Centre for Counterterrorism Technology and Analysis. In the same year, the neocons regrouped in the Project for a New American Century (PNAC), established by Cheney, Rumsfeld, Wolfowitz, Armitage, Perle and others, with IR scholars such as Fukuyama, Amitai Etzioni, Fred Iklé, Stephen Rosen, Henry Rowen and Morton Halperin, signing up as well.

Continuing the drumbeat, Richard Betts of Princeton in 1998 warned in *Foreign Affairs* (as in Lipschutz 1999: 423) that a 'radical Islamic group' might launch a biological attack, or that 'enemies' 'might attempt to punish the United States by triggering catastrophes in American cities'. Yielding to pressures to raise the nation's temperature, Clinton in May 1998 established the position of National Coordinator for Security, Infrastructure, and Counter-Terrorism in the NSC. Zelikow in an article on 'Catastrophic Terrorism' in *Foreign Affairs*, co-authored with Deutch (then deputy secretary of defense) and the former assistant secretary of defense and Harvard IR scholar Ashton B. Carter, speculated on the impending 'transforming event' that would, 'like Pearl Harbour … divide our past and future into a before and after'. Referring to the World Trade Centre bombing attempt of 1993, the authors effectively spell out the combination of a war on terror and the imposition of the surveillance state and suspension of civil rights. Indeed, had the 1993 event succeeded,

The resulting horror and chaos would have exceeded our ability to describe it. Such an act of catastrophic terrorism would be a watershed event in American history. It could involve loss of life and property unprecedented in peacetime and undermine America's fundamental sense of security … The United States might respond with draconian measures, *scaling back civil liberties, allowing wider surveillance of citizens, detention of suspects, and use of deadly force.* (Carter, Deutch and Zelikow 1998: 81, emphasis added)

The PNAC in 2000 rehearsed the themes of the Defense Planning Guidance again in its study *Rebuilding America's Defenses*. Conceding that 'at present the United States faces no global rival', it recommended that 'America's grand strategy should aim to preserve and extend this advantageous position as far into the future as possible'. In advocating a revolution in military affairs to ensure US pre-eminence, the document notoriously contained the phrase that this would most likely be a protracted transformation, 'absent some catastrophic and catalyzing event – like a new Pearl Harbour'.

Still in 2000, Carter, Deutch and Zelikow were also participants in the high-level Aspen Strategy Group, directed by the PNAC signatory, Goldman Sachs adviser and research scholar at Harvard's Belfer Centre Robert Zoellick. The group in August volunteered advice for the incoming president (Bush Jr. as it turned out) in a series of edited collections, thus coming one step closer to actual policymaking. After Zoellick became a foreign policy adviser for the Bush campaign, Zelikow took over and edited the papers. Here Ashton Carter (in Zelikow 2001: 37–8) identifies the dangers facing the United States as the rise of China; the possible descent into chaos of Russia; proliferation of weapons of mass destruction, especially those of the defunct USSR; and 'catastrophic terrorism of unprecedented scope and intensity ... on U.S. territory'. Not to be outdone, Donald Rumsfeld, chairman of the commission to study the institution of a US Space Command, in its January 2001 report (as in Scott 2007: 24) predicted a 'space Pearl Harbour'. Bush had meanwhile assumed the presidency. Zelikow was on the transition team; Zoellick was chief of staff to James Baker in the Florida recount that brought Bush to the White House. In May, Vice-President Cheney was appointed to head a task force on domestic terrorism to prevent the possibility of an attack on the United States, although the task force had still not been activated in September (Mann 2004: 292). In June, Wolfowitz, deputy secretary of defense under Rumsfeld, delivered a commencement address at West Point in which he told cadets that it was 60 years since the Japanese surprise attack on Pearl Harbour. Referring to the book by Roberta Wohlstetter discussed in Chapter 3, Wolfowitz stressed the many intelligence failures that had allowed that event to take place and warned against a sense of complacency, recommending (as in Mann 2004: 291) that 'America' instead prepare for 'the unfamiliar and the unlikely'.

By that time the US intelligence services and the FBI had in fact collected ample evidence that 'the unfamiliar and the unlikely' were not far away. But with no fewer than 15 major terror and war drills in progress on 11 September (several dealing with hijacked aircraft, and one, 'Global Guardian', simulating an all-out nuclear war activating Continuity of Government provisions; Tarpley 2008: ix–xi), it would have been extremely difficult to detect the criminal twists that may have helped to turn these vast bureaucratic exercises into murderous reality.

The Embedded Discipline

'9/11' vindicated almost to the letter the scenario outlined since the mid 1980s about 'a new outrage' (Netanyahu), 'a moulding event' (Zelikow), and the many Pearl Harbours prophesied from various quarters. The War on Terror and a scaling back of democratic rights and the right of free speech (except when used to insult Muslims) were enacted with lightning speed. Before the last plane had crashed, Vice-President Cheney assumed overall command under COG provisions, whilst billionaire investor Warren Buffett and Brent Scowcroft, former national security adviser under Bush Sr., were among those spending the day at the headquarters of the

US Strategic Command, at Offut airbase in Nebraska, from where 'Global Guardian' was being directed. Buffett was supposedly hosting a business leaders' charity event; Scowcroft was on board one of the so-called 'Doomsday' planes meant to serve as nuclear war-fighting command centres. The conclusion that an integral shadow government was now in operation is hard to avoid. The Patriot Act and the Homeland Security Department's Project Endgame, with its ten-year plan to build and expand detention camps, followed. A state of emergency was proclaimed on 14 September, investing the authority to renew it in the presidency (Tarpley 2008: xi–xii; Scott 2010: 204–5). The episode made it possible to push through any policy simply by invoking 'terrorism', thus revealing 'a political technique of framing policy questions in logics of survival with a capacity to mobilize politics of fear' (Elbe 2009: 90–1, citing Jef Huysmans).

Academics working for the Bush administration led the process of ensuring that the events obtained the status of the 'public myth' or 'public presumption' that Zelikow had argued would give the moulding event its efficacy. Zelikow himself was appointed to Bush's Foreign Intelligence Advisory Board after the event and in late 2002 was made executive director of the 9/11 Commission, effectively editing the text. Zelikow and his fellow commission member Jamie Gorelick (deputy attorney general under Clinton and working for the law firm that defended Saudi Prince Mohammed al-Faisal in the lawsuit on behalf of 9/11 victims' families) were the only ones allowed to see the pre-9/11 presidential daily briefings, deemed too sensitive to be seen by other Commission members – including the chairman Thomas Kean, who was associated with the National Endowment for Democracy and president of the Carnegie Corporation (Sacks 2008: 222 and passim). Zelikow was also instructed by National Security Adviser Condoleezza Rice to rewrite a national security draft written by Richard Haass, director of policy planning, which, as James Mann relates (2004: 316, cf. 329), she thought was not bold enough on democracy promotion and regime change. The new national security doctrine should reflect the president's June 2002 idea of 'taking the battle to the enemy and ... confront[ing] the worst threats before they emerge', whilst promoting, if need be by force, 'freedom, democracy and free enterprise'.

Philip Bobbitt, who had worked for both the Bush Sr. and Clinton administrations and re-entered government on the eve of the

Kosovo adventure as director of strategic planning in the National Security Council, interprets (2002: 468) Western intervention as intended 'to vindicate market-state concepts of sovereignty'. Eventually, he claims in *The Shield of Achilles* (2002: 667), 'all the leading members of the society of market-states may come to accept … that capital markets have to become less regulated in order to attract capital investment … access to all markets has to be assured'. For if 'the nation-state justified itself as an instrument to serve the welfare of the people (the nation), the market-state exists to maximise the opportunities enjoyed by all members of society' (ibid.: 229). There is no need to dwell here on what 'less regulated capital markets' eventually led to, or whom we must think of as constituting 'society' if it is not 'the people'. The point is that no state can legitimately claim sovereign equality against the West or shield itself from neoliberal market fundamentalism. So much was made clear when Stephen Krasner took his ideas about limiting sovereignty to the State Department as director of policy planning in the wake of the Iraq invasion by the United States and Britain, replacing Haass.

Building on *Sovereignty: Organized Hypocrisy* of 1999 and *Problematic Sovereignty* of 2001, Krasner now proposed (2005: 70) formalising the class compromise with a client governing class into 'shared sovereignty', a 'voluntary agreement between recognized national political authorities and an external actor such as another state or a regional or international organization' – if need be, 'limited to specific issue areas like monetary policy or the management of oil revenues'. The former US ambassador to Ukraine Carlos Pascual actually drew up a list of countries which were liable to collapse and hence were candidates for shared sovereignty. As Pascual explained in a talk (as in Easterly 2006: 238, emphasis added), the United States envisaged writing 'pre-completed contracts to rebuild countries that *are not yet broken*'. Hence 'to create democratic and market-oriented' states it is not always just a matter of rebuilding states after they have broken up in conflict, but sometimes of actively '*tearing apart the old*'. In a joint article with Pascual in *Foreign Affairs*, Krasner further argues that the United States and others should monitor weak states in order to intervene *preventively* when conflict seemed imminent – with the CIA, the military, think tanks and universities providing information. Basically the authors propose (2005: 156–7, 162–3) that 'US or other military or peacekeeping operations' fit into a contingency planning in which the causes of internal conflict are well known in advance, so that over the longer term 'the United States will have enabled more people to enjoy the benefits of peace, democracy, and market economies'. Indeed, according to Krasner (2009), 'The international environment is too complex for any set of rules, including those regarding sovereignty, to be applied rigidly across all cases.'

Outside government the readiness of the IR mainstream to study the implications of the 'Big Bang' to which so much world politics of today can be traced, and in which so many of its elements were formed, was practically non-existent. The need for reducing civil liberties already outlined in the Netanyahu papers was underwritten by declaring it inevitable: for Keohane (2002: 39) liberalism would have to adjust to a more protective state, a sentiment echoed by Jervis (2002: 41, 49), who volunteers to sacrifice many values to 'a larger and more powerful state apparatus'. Warning that the attachment of Americans to a privileged lifestyle raises the prospect of a 'defensive and reactionary broadening of U.S. national interests', Keohane also notes (2002: 39, cf. 40) that the distinction between self-defence and humanitarian intervention may become blurred. On the whole, though, 'the response to September 11 has been comparatively muted', Brenner writes (2006: 497, emphasis added). 'It has received little sustained attention, experienced no fervent debate, and *has been largely excluded from any central focus that might have been anticipated.*' That critical scholars too will caution those trying to scrutinise the US government's conspiracy theory of 9/11 not to tread here, or will even attack them, underscores that in this domain discipline is truly hegemonic. No trespassers will be tolerated. Thus Robert Gates, in his capacity as president of Texas A&M University, censured a professor emeritus, Morgan Reynolds, for raising doubts about 9/11, since 'to suggest any kind of government conspiracy in the events of that day goes beyond the pale' (as in Reynolds 2007: 103, cf. 112–13).

Instead academics and journalists alike have become 'embedded' in the War on Terror. The CIA, after having scaled back its reliance on the academic intelligence base in the wake of the Soviet collapse, 'became a growing force on campus again', according to the *Wall Street Journal* (Golden 2002; cf. Wilford 2008: 253). In 2002, almost 350 colleges and universities conducted Pentagon-funded research; 60 per cent of defence basic research goes to universities, although the big money goes to the sciences and various branches of engineering (Giroux 2007: 53). The militarisation of research leads to classified science now being 'five to ten times larger than the open literature in US libraries' (Krige 2006 :11–12). Parmar notes (2012: 252) the shift of foundation funding in IR and comparative politics to the field of Islam, with 'radicalisation' and terrorism often taken as given.

The disciplining effect of the War on Terror and the state of emergency, which still obtains at the time of writing (August 2013), is even stronger than McCarthy era anti-communism. The percentage of respondents affirming that 'people feel as free to say what they think as they used to' in 2005 was 42.4 per cent against 55.6 in 1954 (and 52.6 in 1987); the control question inquiring about 'not feeling as free', received 45.7 per cent of affirmative answers against 30.7 in 1954 (and 39.4 in 1987) (Gibson 2008: 99). Indeed the 'McCarthyite connection that collapses democratic dissent with terrorism', according to Giroux (2007: 157, cf. 148–50), has become commonplace in the United States and increasingly elsewhere too. Overt political intimidation takes many forms, from general warnings (such as a *Wall Street Journal* editorial in 2003 about the disproportionate presence of Democrats in US universities) to individual attacks and denial of access. Mearsheimer and Walt document (2007: 180–4) the role of the Israel lobby on campus and its ability to blacklist even moderate critics of the Jewish state's warmongering and stoking up of resentment in the Middle East. In 2005, *New York Times* columnist Thomas Friedman called on the State Department to draw up a blacklist of those claiming that terrorism is an effect of US foreign policy practices. And so on and so forth.

In this climate, the liberal, Trilateral tendency in the IR discipline has shown little appetite to confront the neocon doctrine either. The strand that dubs itself neoliberal institutionalism (which holds that the Western regime may persist beyond actual US hegemony) has only timidly taken its distance from realism (cf. Jervis 1999: 43). This lineage was renewed in the Princeton Project for National Security (PPNS), organised from 2006 by Anne-Marie Slaughter and G. John Ikenberry as an attempt to revive the idea of 'an American-centred alliance ... likely [to include] the United States, United Kingdom, Australia, Canada, New Zealand, and, possibly, India'. The project, Parmar comments (2012: 249, cf. Vucetic 2011), 'is similar to an alliance centred on the English-speaking countries – an Anglosphere – the evolution of a hangover from late nineteenth-century and early twentieth-century Anglo-Saxonism'.

In other words, it is the *n*th version of the thesis of an expanding Lockean heartland. Funded by the Ford Foundation, the Carnegie Endowment, the German Marshall Fund, and David Rubinstein of the Carlyle Group, PPNS and its successor network seek to investigate the multilateral basis of liberal internationalism and salvage the Western liberal order as a rule-based system of global governance (Ikenberry 2011). Anne-Marie Slaughter was Hillary Clinton's director of policy planning from 2009 to 2011. She served on the boards of McDonald's and Citigroup and after her stint at the State Department joined the Trilateral Commission (Gill 2012: 514). Building on Joseph Nye's concepts of 'soft' and 'smart power', she proposes to exploit the potential of new developments in the social media domain. Keeping the contender state from interfering with Western global governance is crucial here. 'At a time when China is preaching the virtues and reaping many of the benefits of statism in its investment and assistance programs around the world,' her argument goes (2012: 5), 'the U.S. can model a far more pluralist approach that involve parts of the state working together with a wide range of social actors.' This would require that the West mobilise its advantages in mobile phone and other IT domains and work with Microsoft (including the Gates Foundation), Google, and others to save Africa from Chinese encroachment.

The one occasion when a senior figure from the Trilateral wing of the IR academic intelligence base spoke out about the War on Terror was when Zbigniew Brzezinski, in a testimony to the Senate Foreign Relations Committee on 1 February 2007, attacked the Bush policy – at a juncture when (as was later revealed) Vice-President Cheney, over the opposition of the Pentagon, was pushing hard for air strikes against Iran (Scott 2010: 208). Of course Brzezinski's intervention was not motivated by scholarly concern; rather the old fox saw his lifelong aspiration to target Russia sidelined by 9/11, Iraq and the ensuing destabilisation of the Middle East. Calling the invasion of Iraq 'a historic, strategic, and moral calamity, undertaken under false assumptions … driven by Manichean impulses and imperial hubris', Brzezinski (2007, emphasis added) warned against an even more disastrous involvement in Iran and the use of 'false flag' operations to kick-start 'wars of choice'. He specifically alerted the Committee to 'some provocation in Iraq *or a terrorist act in the U.S. blamed on Iran*'. Asked by a journalist (Grey 2007) whether he really meant to say that provocation including a false flag operation could in principle be the work of US officials, the following exchange suggests that the answer is 'yes'.

> Q: Dr. Brzezinski, who do you think would be carrying out this possible provocation?
> A: I have no idea. As I said, these things can never be predicted. It can be spontaneous.
> Q: Are you suggesting there is a possibility it could originate within the US government itself?
> A: I'm saying the whole situation can get out of hand and all sorts of calculations can produce a circumstance that would be very difficult to trace.

This is cryptic enough; but perhaps one cannot put it more accurately than this in one sentence. However, IR scholarship at this point was already looking at the next way station of the crusade for Western supremacy. Here the role of British academia should also be taken into account, because in the United Kingdom, the drying up of state funding has given Middle Eastern money direct access to universities to a much greater degree than in the United States. Both Oxford and Cambridge have received massive sums from Saudi sources (King Fahd and Prince Alwaleed, respectively), with the prince also being given management control (as also at the University of Edinburgh; Baehr 2011: 299). In comparison, the £1.5 million from Libya for David Held's Centre for Global Governance at LSE was small. However, this donation, accepted in spite of a negative recommendation from the school's top Middle East expert, the late Fred Halliday, was part of a complex operation, involving oil companies as well as Goldman Sachs and other investment banks, to gain access to Libya's mineral riches and its vast sovereign wealth fund. Western interest here was reciprocated by a neoliberal fraction in the country's state class around Colonel Gaddafi's son Saif.

Saif Gaddafi during his studies at LSE assimilated the gospel of Western global governance and persuaded his father and others to retool Libya as an open nation-state and pay damages for the Lockerbie bombing (although this was not Libya's doing; cf. my 2006: 340, 372n.). As Campbell documents (2013: 55–62 and passim), the Monitor group, a consultancy associated with Harvard Business School, between 2006 and 2008 signed contracts with Libya to upgrade the country's image and that of Gaddafi personally, engaging Francis Fukuyama, Benjamin Barber, Robert Putnam,

Joseph Nye and others to travel to Libya under this assignment. Nye, whose assistance was separately acknowledged by Saif Gaddafi in his LSE doctoral thesis, returned from Libya enthusiastically reporting on Colonel Gaddafi's fascination with 'soft power' (as in Campbell 2013: 59). Clearly in this case any remaining dividing lines between mainstream IR approaches had receded into the background. Nye, former chairman of the National Intelligence Council (Mooney 2000), produced a report on 'smart power' for the Obama administration prepared jointly with neocon Richard Armitage, and which Hillary Clinton and Defense Secretary Robert Gates applied as an 'operational concept for US foreign policy'. Soft or smart power in Nye's view (as in Gill 2012: 515) should include the use of NGOs as a surreptitious 'way for a government to retain control ... by covert funding through intelligence agencies'.

None of the laudatory comments on Colonel Gaddafi of course went so far as the tributes made by the sociologist Anthony Giddens, former LSE director and ideologue of the conversion of social democracy to neoliberalism (the 'Third Way') (Martins 2011: 287). The NATO-engineered regime change in Libya in 2011 threw LSE into a crisis after other aspects of its involvement were made public, but UK academia overall has tiptoed neatly in the footsteps of its big brother across the Atlantic. To name but a few in IR, Bristol University's Politics Department became involved in a Ministry of Defence project on 'Potential Generic Adversaries 2003–2033' amongst a range of defence-related activities (Stavrianakis 2006: 143); and at the author's own University of Sussex, the NATO planning director was appointed as a visiting lecturer (renamed 'visiting practitioner' following student and staff protest). As two Sussex graduate students write, this was 'part of a conscious policy designed to give [NATO] a greater academic profile and orientate research to its policy concerns' (Cooper and Pal 2011). Indeed with the book on 9/11 closed and Iraq, and now Libya, destroyed as functioning state–society complexes, sights were already set on Iran, another key project of the US neocons and the Israeli right. Within a year after Brzezinski's Senate performance the pressure group United Against Nuclear Iran (UANI) was founded by the late Richard Holbrooke, James Woolsey, Dennis Ross and Mark Wallace (its CEO at the time of this writing).

Now to claim that the atomic ambitions of Iran are military is a tall order. Challenging Israel's nuclear arsenal of 80 to 200 warheads, let alone the US stockpile of around 7,000, would obviously be suicide – even if it would make sense to have some sort of deterrence in light of crippling Western sanctions, sabotage and assassinations, and Israeli threats of attacking the Islamic Republic with the United States and NATO complicit in various ways. However, a solemn fatwa against nuclear weapons by the country's religious leader, and proposals to turn the Middle East into a nuclear-free zone instead, make clear this is not Iran's policy. Yet the UANI advisory board (I follow UANI n.d.) includes prominent members of the IR academic intelligence base nevertheless. Thus Leslie Gelb, *New York Times* writer, former assistant secretary of state, president emeritus of the Council on Foreign Relations and a member of the International Institute for Strategic Studies (IISS) in London, is on board. Gelb is a trustee of the Carnegie Endowment for International Peace and of Tufts University, a board member of Columbia University's School of International and Public Affairs, and an advisory board member for the Centre on Press, Politics and Public Policy at Harvard University's John F. Kennedy School of Government. The aforementioned Graham Allison, also on the UANI advisory board, is former dean of the Kennedy School (1977–88) and currently director of the Belfer Centre for Science and International Affairs at Harvard. The Belfer Centre's closeness to the policy world is illustrated by the presence of Robert Zoellick, William Perry, Clinton's secretary of defence, former Fed chairman Paul Volcker, historian and hedge fund consultant Niall Ferguson and General Abizaid of US CentCom as advisors or fellows (Parmar 2012: 235). It was during Allison's time as dean of the Kennedy School that it became 'heavily soaked in Department of Defense sponsorship' (Trumpbour 1991: 14). The Belfer Centre publishes the prestigious IR journal *International Security*; Olli Heinonen, former deputy director general of the International Atomic Energy Agency and a fellow of the Belfer Centre, is on the UANI advisory board alongside Allison.

Fouad Ajami, director of Middle East studies at the Johns Hopkins University School for Advanced International Studies in Washington, a board member of the Council on Foreign Relations and a member of the editorial board of *Foreign Affairs*, has also joined ranks against Iran. Others on the UANI board with IR references include Walter Russell Mead, senior fellow at the Council on Foreign Relations and author of a number of popular works on US foreign policy; Gary Milhollin, director of the University of Wisconsin Project on Nuclear Arms Control in Washington; and Henry Sokolski, of the Institute of World Politics in Washington, the National Institute for Public Policy (Heritage Foundation), and the Hoover Institution, a former assistant to Wolfowitz and a member of the Deutch Proliferation Commission and of the CIA Advisory Panel. From Britain, members with academic links include Charles Guthrie, former chief of the Defence Staff (King's College London, IISS); whilst Richard Dearlove of MI6, no doubt a venerable provider of quality intelligence for previous wars, is master of Pembroke College, Cambridge.

Of course only four or so of the above are primarily IR scholars. But then what we are looking at is not scholarship per se but the academic intelligence base and its anchorage in the national security state and transnational business, which impose a discipline that ultimately ends up as the discipline of the classroom. The UANI list indeed is particularly well connected to business, not unexpectedly of course in light of Iran's massive energy resources. Thus besides having served as an assistant secretary of defense in the Clinton administration, Allison is also (still according to UANI n.d.) a director of Getty Oil, Natixis, Loomis Sayles, Hansberger, Taubman Centers, Joule, and Belco Oil and Gas, and an advisory board member of Chase Bank, Chemical Bank, Hydro-Quebec, and International Energy Corporation. Who is applying discipline on whom in a network like this becomes a complex issue. But corruption obviously is around the corner (and not just in a pecuniary way, as in Harvard's involvement with privatisation in Russia, referred to above). Similarly, Charles Guthrie has major connections to the corporate world as director of N.M. Rothschild and Sons, Petropavlovsk PLC, Gulf Keystone Petroleum, Colt Defense LLC and Advanced Interactive Systems Inc.

The point is that none of the above, whether they are primarily academics, CFR, IISS, editorial board members, trustees of foundations, or just taking a break on campus, will tolerate, let alone initiate serious research into the backgrounds and implications of the War on Terror. They subscribe to an obvious hoax (viz. Iran's quest for nuclear weapons) – one in a series that has already featured the Tonkin Gulf incident, Lockerbie, the genocide of Kosovo Albanians, Saddam Hussein's 'weapons of mass destruction' and, today, Iran's nuclear bomb programme. So why would they want to revisit the event that started the current round?

A discipline led by scholars of this moral calibre cannot be expected to restore its intellectual integrity. Under conditions of the growing precariousness of academics at all levels, few of the rank and file can afford to take their distance from such leading scholars either. And yet, whilst both politically and economically the pre-eminence of the societies of the Lockean heartland is fast eroding, IR today is still spreading across the globe, along with economics and the rest of the Anglophone disciplinary infrastructure. The Bologna and Brisbane processes for Europe and Asia, respectively (Chao 2011), which formalise this spread by prescribing the BA, MA and taught Ph.D. structure, along with English as the academic lingua franca and editorial and visitation routines, thus lay down the academic division of labour that took shape in the United States as the universal standard of excellence. The trilogy that I conclude here is a modest proposal to liberate the study of international politics from its disciplinary, state- and Western-centred straitjacket, and anchor it in a comprehensive, philosophically informed global political economy.

References

Abbott, Andrew. 2001. *Chaos of Disciplines*. Chicago: University of Chicago Press.

Adler, Emanuel, and Haas, Peter M. 1992. 'Conclusion: Epistemic communities, world order, and the creation of a reflective research program'. *International Organization*, 46 (1). 367–90.

Allen, James S. 1952. *Atomic Imperialism: The State, Monopoly, and the Bomb*. New York: International Publishers.

Allison, Graham T., and Yavlinski, Grigory. 1991. *Window of Opportunity. The Grand Bargain for Democracy in the Soviet Union*. New York: Pantheon.

Almond, Gabriel A. 1956. 'Comparative Political Systems'. *Journal of Politics*. 18 (3). 391–409.

—— 1967. 'Review: *Social Origins of Dictatorship and Democracy: Lord and Peasant in the Making of the Modern World*, by Barrington Moore'. *American Political Science Review*. 61 (3). 768–70.

—— and Coleman, James S. (eds). 1960. *The Politics of the Developing Areas*. Princeton, NJ.: Princeton University Press.

—— and Verba, Sydney. 1963. *The Civic Culture: Political Attitudes and Democracy in Five Nations*. Princeton, N.J.: Princeton University Press.

Anderle, O.F. (ed.). 1964. *The Problems of Civilizations* (report of the First Synopsis Conference of the International Society for the Comparative Study of Civilizations, Salzburg, 8–15 October 1961). The Hague: Mouton.

Anderson, Kevin P. 2010. *Marx at the Margins: On Nationalism, Ethnicity, and Non-Western Societies*. Chicago: University of Chicago Press.

Anderson, Perry. 1990. 'The Nature and Meaning of the Wars of Hispanic American Liberation', in Bornschier and Lengyel 1990.

Angell, Norman. 1913 [1910]. *The Great Illusion*. New York: Putnam.

APSA 1968. *Biographical Directory* (5th edn). Washington, D.C.: American Political Science Association.

Arendt, Hannah. 1966 [1951]. *The Origins of Totalitarianism* (2nd edn). Cleveland, Ohio: World.

Armitage, David. 1997. 'A patriot for whom? The afterlives of Bolingbroke's Patriot King'. *Journal of British Studies*. 36 (4). 397–418.

—— 2000. *The Ideological Origins of the British Empire*. Cambridge: Cambridge University Press.

Arrighi, Giovanni. 1978. *The Geometry of Imperialism: The Limits of Hobson's Paradigm*. London: New Left Books.

Attal, Frédéric. 2010. 'Reconstruire l'Europe intellectuelle: les sciences sociales en Italie (1945–1970)', in Tournès 2010.

Augelli, Enrico, and Murphy, Craig N. 1997. 'Consciousness, myth and collective action: Gramsci, Sorel and the ethical state', in Gill and Mittelman 1997.

Bacon, Francis. 1942 [1597, 1612, 1625]. *Essays and New Atlantis* (introd. and ed. G.S. Haight). Roslyn, N.Y.: Walter Black.

Baehr , Peter. 2011. 'Purity and Danger in the Modern University'. *Society.* 48 (4). 297–300.

Bakan, A., and MacDonald, E. (eds). 2001. *Critical Political Studies: Debates and Dialogues from the Left.* Montreal: McGill–Queen's University Press.

Balibar, Étienne. 1991 [1988]. *Race, Nation, Class: Ambiguous Identities* (with I. Wallerstein, trans. C. Turner). London: Verso.

Barkawi, Tarak, and Laffey, Mark. 1999. 'The Imperial Peace: Democracy, Force and Globalization.' *European Journal of International Relations.* 5 (4). 403–34.

Barker, Martin. 1982. *The New Racism: Conservatives and the Ideology of the Tribe.* London: Junction Books.

Barrow, Clyde W. 1990. *Universities and the Capitalist State: Corporate Liberalism and the Reconstruction of American Higher Education, 1894–1928.* Madison, Wis.: University of Wisconsin Press.

Baudet, H., and Brugmans, I.J. (eds). 1961. *Balans van Beleid: Terugblik op de laatste halve eeuw van Nederlandsch-Indië.* Assen: Van Gorcum–Prakke.

Bauer, Otto. 1907. *Die Nationalitätenfrage und die Sozialdemokratie.* Vienna: Volksbuchhandlung Ignaz Brand.

Bell, Peter D. 1973 [1971]. 'The Ford Foundation as a Transnational Actor', in Keohane and Nye 1973.

Beloff, Max. 1963. *The United States and the Unity of Europe.* New York: Vintage.

Bendersky, Joseph W. 1987. 'Carl Schmitt at Nuremberg'. *Telos.* 72. 91–6.

Bendix, Reinhard. 1963 [1956]. *Work and Authority in Industry: Ideologies of Management in the Course of Industrialization* (foreword by A.M. Ross). New York: Harper & Row.

—— 1969 [1964]. *Nation-Building and Citizenship: Studies of our Changing Social Order.* Garden City, N.Y.: Doubleday.

Berger, Mark T. 2006. 'From Nation-Building to State-Building: The Geopolitics of Development, the Nation State System and the Changing Global Order', *Third World Quarterly.* 27 (1). 5–25.

Bernal, J.D. 1969 [1954]. *Science in History* (4 vols). Harmondsworth: Penguin.

Berndtson, Erkki. 1987. 'The Rise and Fall of American Political Science: Personalities, Quotations, Speculations'. *International Political Science Review.* 8 (1). 85–100.

Bhambra, Gurminder K., and Shilliam, Robbie (eds). 2009. *Silencing Human Rights: Critical Engagements with a Contested Project.* Basingstoke: Palgrave Macmillan.

Bilgin, Pınar. 2008. 'Thinking past "Western" IR?'. *Third World Quarterly.* 29 (1). 5–23.

—— and Morton, Adam David. 2002. 'Historicising representations of "failed states": beyond the cold-war annexation of the social sciences?' *Third World Quarterly.* 23 (1). 55–80.

Black, E.C. (ed.). 1967. *European Political History, 1815–1870: Aspects of Liberalism.* New York: Harper & Row.

Bobbitt, Philip. 2002. *The Shield of Achilles: War, Peace and the Course of History.* Harmondsworth: Penguin.

Bolton, Herbert E. 1933. 'The Epic of Greater America'. *American Historical Review*. 38 (3). 448–74.

Boneau, Denis. 2004. 'Psychological Cold War: The Science of World Domination'. Voltaire Network, 8 December. http://www.voltairenet.org/article30091.html (accessed 4 June 2013).

Bornschier, V., and Lengyel, P. (eds). 1990. *World Society Studies*, vol. i. Frankfurt: Campus.

Bosch, Juan. 1968 [1967]. *Pentagonism: A Substitute for Imperialism* (trans. H.R. Lane). New York: Grove Press.

Boucher, David. 1998. *Political Theories of International Relations: From Thucydides to the Present*. Oxford: Oxford University Press.

Bourdieu, Pierre. 1984. *Homo academicus*. Paris: Minuit.

—— 2001. *Science de la science et réflexivité*. Paris: Raisons d'Agir.

Boyer, Paul. 1985. *By the Bomb's Early Light: American Thought and Culture at the Dawn of the Atomic Age*. New York: Pantheon.

Bratsis, Peter. 2006. *Everyday Life and the State*. Boulder, Col.: Paradigm.

Brenner, William J. 2006. 'In Search of Monsters: Realism and Progress in International Relations Theory after September 11'. *Security Studies*. 15 (3). 496–528.

Brodie, Bernard. 1948. 'The Atom Bomb as Policy Maker'. *Foreign Affairs*. 27 (1). 17–33.

—— 1970 [1959]. *Strategy in the Missile Age*. Princeton, N.J.: Princeton University Press.

Brownstein, Ronald, and Easton, Nina. 1983 [1982]. *Reagan's Ruling Class: Portraits of the President's Top One Hundred Officials* (2nd edn). New York: Pantheon.

Brubaker, Rogers. 1994. 'Nationhood and the national question in the Soviet Union and post-Soviet Eurasia: An institutionalist account'. *Theory and Society*. 43 (1). 47–78.

Brzezinski, Zbigniew. 1997. *The Grand Chessboard: American Primacy and its Geostrategic Imperatives*. New York: Basic Books.

—— 2007. 'SFRC Testimony – Zbigniew Brzezinski, February 1, 2007'. http://foreign.senate.gov/testimony/2007/BrzezinskiTestimony070201.pdf (accessed 18 November 2011).

Bukharin, Nikolai. 1972 [1915]. *Imperialism and World Economy* (foreword by V.I. Lenin). London: Merlin.

Burch, Philip H. 1981. *Elites in American History* (3 vols). New York: Holmes & Meier.

Burke, Edmund. *Works* (12 vols). Gutenberg.org. (orig. *The Works of the Right Honourable Edmund Burke*, London: John Nimmo, 1887).

Byron, George Gordon. 1981 [1823–24]. *For Freedom's Battle* (vol. xi of *Byron's Letters and Journals*) (ed. L.A. Marchand). London: John Murray.

Calhoun, Craig. 1993. 'Nationalism and Ethnicity'. *Annual Review of Sociology*. 19 (1). 211–39.

—— 2002. 'The Class Consciousness of Frequent Travelers: Toward a Critique of Actually Existing Cosmopolitanism'. *South Atlantic Quarterly*. 101 (4). 869–97.

Callahan, Bob. 1990. 'The 1980 Campaign: Agents for Bush'. *Covert Action Information Bulletin*. 33. 5–7.

Campbell, Horace. 2013. *Global NATO and the Catastrophic Failure in Libya: Lessons for Africa in the Forging of African Unity*. New York: Monthly Review Press.

Carew, Anthony. 1987. *Labour under the Marshall Plan: The Politics of Productivity and the Marketing of Management Science*. Manchester: Manchester University Press.

Carr, Edward Hallett. 1964 [1939]. *The Twenty Years' Crisis, 1919-1939* (2nd edn). New York: Harper & Row.

Carrère d'Encausse, Hélène. 1979 [1978]. *Decline of an Empire: The Soviet Socialist Republics in Revolt* (trans. M. Sokolinski and H.A. La Farge). New York: Harper & Row.

Carter, A.B., Deutch, J. and Zelikow, P. 1998. 'Catastrophic Terrorism: Tackling the New Danger'. *Foreign Affairs*. 77 (6). (November–December). 80–94.

Castro, Fidel. 1969. *Fidel Castro Speaks* (ed. M. Kenner and J. Petras). New York: Grove Press.

Cavanagh, John. 1980. 'Dulles Papers Reveal CIA Consulting Network: Panel met secretly in Princeton'. *Forerunner*. 29 April. www.cia-on-campus.org/princeton.edu/consult.html (accessed 11 February 2010).

Chao, Roger Y., Jr. 2011. 'Reflections on the Bologna Process: the making of an Asia Pacific Higher Education Area'. *European Journal of Higher Education*, 1 (2–3) 102–18.

Chomsky, Noam. 1969 [1967]. *American Power and the New Mandarins*. Harmondworth: Penguin.

Christofferson, Michel. 2009. 'Quand Foucault appuyait les "nouveaux philosophes"'. *Le Monde Diplomatique* (October). CD-ROM edn 1954–2011.

Clark, Terry N. 1974. 'Die Stadien wissenschaftlicher Institutionalisierung', in Weingart 1974.

Claudin, Fernando. 1975 [1970]. *The Communist Movement: From Comintern to Cominform* (trans. B. Pearce and F. MacDonagh). Harmondsworth: Penguin.

Cline, Ray S., and Alexander, Yonah. 1986 [1984]. *Terrorism: The Soviet Connection*. New York: Crane, Russak & Co.

Colás, Alejandro. 2008. 'Open Doors and Closed Frontiers: The Limits of American Empire'. *European Journal of International Relations*. 14 (4). 619–43.

Collier, Peter, and Horowitz, David. 1976. *The Rockefellers: An American Dynasty*. New York: Holt, Rinehart & Winston.

Collins, Randall. 1998. *The Sociology of Philosophies: A Global Theory of Intellectual Change*. Cambridge, Mass.: Harvard University Press.

Connor, Walker. 1972. 'Nation-Building or Nation-Destroying?' *World Politics*. 24 (3). 319–55.

Cooper, Luke, and Pal, Maïa. 2011. 'Lectures from a Spin Doctor: A Nato strategist's position at a top British university'. *Open Democracy*. 30 June. http://www.opendemocracy.net/author/luke-cooper-and-maï-pal (accessed 12 September 2011).

Cot, Annie L. 2011. 'A 1930s North American Creative Community: The Harvard "Pareto Circle"'. *History of Political Economy*. 43(1). 131–59.

Cox, M.E., Ikenberry, G.J., and Inoguchi, T. (eds). 2000. *American Democracy Promotion: Impulses, Strategies, and Impacts*. Oxford: Oxford University Press.

Cox, Robert W. 2002. *The Political Economy of a Plural World: Critical Reflections on Power, Morals and Civilization* (with M.G. Schechter). London: Routledge.

Curtis, Mark. 2003. *Web of Deceit: Britain's Real Role in the World* (foreword by J. Pilger). London: Vintage.

Davis, Mike. 2002. *Late Victorian Holocausts: El Niño Famines and the Making of the Third World*. London: Verso.

Debray, Régis. 1981 [1979]. *Teachers, Writers, Celebrities: The Intellectuals of Modern France* (introd. F. Mulhern, trans. D. Macey). London: Verso.

Department of State. 1965. *Outgoing Telegram to Amembassy Djakarta* (Info Amembassy Tokyo, CINCPAC) (29 October; secret; declassified 1975). Original photocopy.

Deppe, Frank. 2003. *Politisches Denken zwischen den Weltkriegen* (vol. ii of *Politisches Denken im 20. Jahrhundert*). Hamburg: VSA Verlag.

Derber, Milton. 1967. *Research in Labor Problems in the United States*. New York: Random House.

Desai, Radhika. 2001. 'Fetishizing Phantoms: Carl Schmitt, Chantal Mouffe, and "The Political"', in Bakan and MacDonald 2001.

—— 2007. 'The Last Empire? From nation-building compulsion to nation-wrecking futility and beyond'. *Third World Quarterly*. 28 (2). 435–56.

—— 2013. *Geopolitical Economy: After US Hegemony, Globalization and Empire*. London: Pluto Press.

Deutsch, Karl W. 1957. *Political Community and the North Atlantic Area* (with S.A. Burrell, R.A. Kann, M. Lee Jr., M. Lichterman, R.E. Lindgren, F.L. Loewenheim and R.W. Van Wagenen). Princeton, N.J.: Princeton University Press.

—— 1970 [1954]. *Political Community at the International Level: Problems of Definition and Measurement*. Hamden, Conn.: Archon.

Dillon, Emile Joseph. 2004 [1920]. *The Inside Story of the Peace Conference* (reformatted by Blackmask Online). New York: Harper Bros.

Djilas, Milovan. 1991 [1962]. *Gesprekken met Stalin* (trans. J.F. Kliphuis and F. Stok; with 1985 interview by G. Urban). Haarlem: Becht.

Dosso, Diane. 2010. 'La Seconde Guerre mondiale et l'exil des scientifiques aux États-Unis', in Tournès 2010.

DPG. 1992. *Defence Planning Guidance, FY 1994–1999* (16 April; declassified 2008). Original photocopy.

Drolet, Jean-François. 2010. 'A liberalism betrayed? American neoconservatism and the theory of international relations'. *Journal of Political Ideologies*. 15 (2). 89–118.

Duménil, Gérard, and Lévy, Dominique. 2010. 'Alliance au sommet de l'échelle sociale: Responsabilité des cadres supérieurs'. *Le Monde Diplomatique* (July). 7.

Duncan Baretta, Silvio R., and Markoff, John. 1978. 'Civilization and Barbarism: Cattle Frontiers in Latin America'. *Comparative Studies in Society and History*. 20 (4). 587–620.

Dunne, Tim. 1998. *Inventing International Society: A History of the English School*. Basingstoke: Macmillan.

Durkheim, Émile. 1964 [1933, 1893]. *The Division of Labor in Society* (5th edn; trans. G. Simpson). New York: Free Press; London: Collier-Macmillan.

Easlea, Brian. 1983. *Fathering the Unthinkable: Masculinity, Scientists and the Nuclear Arms Race*. London: Pluto Press.

Easterly, William. 2006. *The White Man's Burden: Why the West's Efforts to Aid the Rest Have Done So Much Ill and So Little Good*. Oxford: Oxford University Press.

Easton, David. 1965. *A Systems Analysis of Political Life*. New York: Wiley.

—— 1985. 'Political Science in the United States: Past and Present'. *International Political Science Review/Revue internationale de science politique*. 6 (1). 133–52.

Eckstein, Harry, and Apter, David E. (eds). 1963. *Comparative Politics: A Reader*. Glencoe, Ill.: The Free Press.

Ege, Konrad. 1984. 'Rutgers University: Intelligence Goes to College'. *CounterSpy* (June–August). 42–4. www.cia-on-campus.org/rutgers.edu/ege. html (accessed 1 Feb. 2010).

Elbe, Stefan. 2009. *Virus Alert: Security, Governmentality, and the AIDS Pandemic*. New York: Columbia University Press.

Elias, Norbert. 1971 [1970]. *Wat is sociologie?* (trans. J. Vollers and J. Goudsblom). Utrecht: Spectrum.

Elsthain, Jean Bethke. 2001. 'Why Public Intellectuals?' *The Wilson Quarterly*. 45 (4). 43–50.

Emerson, Rupert. 1960. *From Empire to Nation*. Cambridge, Mass.: Harvard University Press.

Engerman, David. 2003. 'Review Essay. Rethinking Cold War Universities: Some Recent Histories'. *Journal of Cold War Studies*. 5 (3). 80–95.

Falk, Richard A., and Mendlovitz, Saul H. (eds). 1966. *Toward a Theory of War Prevention* (vol. i of *The Strategy of World Order*). New York: World Law Fund.

Ferguson, Niall. 2003. *Empire: How Britain Made the Modern World*. Harmondsworth: Penguin.

Fischer, Louis. 1960 [1951; 1933]. *The Soviets in World Affairs: A History of the Relations between the Soviet Union and the Rest of the World 1917–1929* (abridged edn). New York: Vintage.

Fisher, Donald. 1983. 'The Role of the Philanthropic Foundations in the Reproduction and Production of Hegemony: Rockefeller Foundations and the Social Sciences'. *Sociology*. 17 (2). 206–33.

Fosl, Peter S. 1999. 'Hume, Skepticism, and Early American Deism'. *Hume Studies*. 25 (1/2). 171–92.

Foucault, Michel. 1969. *L'archéologie du savoir*. Paris: Gallimard.

—— 2004. *Sécurité, territoire, population: Cours au Collège de France (1977–1978)* (ed. M. Senellart). Paris: Gallimard-Seuil.

Fox, Richard W. 1985. *Reinhold Niebuhr: A Biography*. New York: Pantheon.

Fox, W.T.R. 1968. *The American Study of International Relations*. Columbia, S.C.: Institute of International Studies.

Frank, André Gunder. 1991. 'The Underdevelopment of Development'. *Scandinavian Journal of Development Alternatives*. 10 (3) (special issue).

Friedericy, H.J. 1961. 'De bevolking van Nederlands-Indië en het Nederlands gezag in het decennium vóór de Japanse invasie', in Baudet and Brugmans 1961.

Friedrich, Carl J., and Brzezinski, Zbigniew K. 1963. 'Totalitarian Dictatorship and Autocracy', in Eckstein and Apter 1963.

Fukuyama, Francis. 1989. 'The End of History?' *The National Interest.* 16. 3–18.

Fülberth, Georg. 1991. *Sieben Anstrengungen, den vorläufigen Endsieg des Kapitalismus zu begreifen.* Hamburg: Konkret.

Gallagher, J., and Robinson, R. 1967 [1953]. 'The Imperialism of Free Trade', in Black 1967.

Gammon, Earl. 2008. 'Affect and the Rise of the Self-Regulating Market'. *Millennium: Journal of International Studies.* 37 (2). 251–78.

—— 2010. 'Nature as adversary: The rise of modern economic conceptions of nature'. *Economy and Society.* 39 (2). 218–46.

Ganser, Daniele. 2005. *NATO's Secret Armies: Operation Gladio and Terrorism in Western Europe.* London: Frank Cass.

Garthoff, Raymond. 1994. *The Great Transition: American–Soviet Relations and the End of the Cold War.* Washington, D.C.: Brookings Institution.

Gemelli, Giuliana. 2007. 'Networks as drivers of innovation and European scientific integration: The role of the Ford Foundation in the late Sixties and early Seventies', in B. Unfried, J. Mittag, and M. van der Linden (eds. with E. Himmelstoss). *Transnationale Netzwerke im 20. Jahrhundert/ Transnational Networks in the 20th Century.* Vienna: Akademische Verlagsanstalt.

Gendzier, Irene L. 1995 [1985]. *Development against Democracy: Manipulating Political Change in the Third World* (2nd edn). Hampton, Conn.: The Tyrone Press.

General Council. n.d. *The General Council of the First International 1864–1866. The London Conference 1865. Minutes.* Moscow: Foreign Languages Publishing House.

Gentz, Friedrich von. 2009 [1800]. *The Origins and Principles of the American Revolution, compared with the Origin and Principles of the French Revolution* (trans. J. Q. Adams, ed. and introd. P. Koslowski). Indianapolis: Liberty Fund.

Gerassi, John. 1965 [1963]. *The Great Fear in Latin America* (rev. edn). New York: Collier Books.

Gerbner, G., Gross, L., Morgan, M., and Signorelli, N. 1980. 'The "Mainstreaming" of America: Violence Profile No. 11'. *Journal of Communication.* 30 (3). 10–29.

Gibbs, David N. 2003. 'The CIA is Back on Campus'. *CounterPunch* (7 April). http://www.counterpunch.org/2003/04/07/the-cia-is-back-on-campus (accessed 14 May 2013).

Gibson, James L. 2008. 'Intolerance and Political Repression in the United States: A Half Century after McCarthyism'. *American Journal of Political Science.* 52 (1). 96–108.

Giddens, Anthony. 1985. *The Nation-State and Violence* (vol. ii of *A Contemporary Critique of Historical Materialism*). Cambridge: Polity.

Giesen, Klaus-Gerd. 1992. *L'éthique des relations internationals: Les théories anglo-américaines contemporaines*. Bruxelles: Bruylant.

—— 2006. 'France and French-speaking Countries (1945–1994)', in Jørgensen and Knudsen 2006.

Gill, Stephen. 1990. *American Hegemony and the Trilateral Commission*. Cambridge: Cambridge University Press.

—— 2003. *Power and Resistance in the New World Order*. Basingstoke: Palgrave Macmillan.

—— 2012. 'Towards a Radical Concept of Praxis: Imperial "common sense" versus the Post-Modern Prince'. *Millennium: Journal of International Studies*. 40 (3). 505–24.

—— and Mittelman, James H. (eds). 1997. *Innovation and Transformation in International Studies*. Cambridge: Cambridge University Press.

Gilman, Nils. 2003. *Mandarins of the Future: Modernization Theory in Cold War America*. Baltimore, Md.: Johns Hopkins University Press.

Giroux, Henry A. 2007. *The University in Chains: Confronting the Military–Industrial–Academic Complex*. Boulder, Col.: Paradigm.

Göhler, G. and Zeuner, B. (eds). 1991. *Kontinuitäten und Brüche in der deutschen Politikwissenschaft*. Baden-Baden: Nomos.

Golden, Daniel. 2002. 'After Sept. 11: CIA Becomes A Growing Force on Campus'. *Wall Street Journal*. October 4. http://www.mindfully.org/Reform/2002/CIA-Growing-On-Campus4oct02.htm (accessed 11 June 2013).

Goldmann, Lucien. 1977 [1964]. *Towards a Sociology of the Novel* (trans. A. Sheridan). London: Tavistock.

Gollwitzer, Heinz. 1972. *Geschichte des weltpolitischen Denkens*, vol. i. *Vom Zeitalter der Entdeckungen bis zum Beginn des Imperialismus*. Göttingen: Vandenhoeck & Ruprecht.

—— 1982. *Geschichte des weltpolitischen Denkens*, vol. ii. *Zeitalter des Imperialismus und der Weltkriege*. Göttingen: Vandenhoeck & Ruprecht.

Gough, Kathleen. 1968. 'World Revolution and the Science of Man', in Roszak 1968.

Gramsci, Antonio. 1971. *Selections from the Prison Notebooks* (trans. and ed. Q. Hoare and G.N. Smith; written 1929–35). New York: International Publishers.

—— 1975. *Quaderni del carcere*. (4 vols; ed. V. Gerratana for the Instituto Gramsci; written 1929–35). Turin: Einaudi.

—— 1977. *Selections from Political Writings 1910–1920* (trans. and ed. Q. Hoare). New York: International Publishers.

Grew, Joseph C. 1953. *Turbulent Era: A Diplomatic Record of Forty Years 1904–1945* (2 vols.; ed. W. Johnson). London: Hammond, Hammond & Co.

Grey, Barry. 2007. 'A political bombshell from Zbigniew Brzezinski: Ex-national security adviser warns that Bush is seeking a pretext to attack Iran' (2 February). www.wsws.org/articles/2007/feb2007/brze-f02.shtml (accessed 18 November 2011).

Griffin, David Ray, and Scott, Peter Dale (eds). 2007. *9/11 and American Empire: Intellectuals Speak Out*. Northampton, Mass.: Olive Branch Press.

Gross, Raphael. 2000. *Carl Schmitt und die Juden: Eine deutsche Rechtslehre.* Frankfurt: Suhrkamp.

Guattari, Félix. 1976 [1972]. *Psychotherapie, Politik and die Aufgaben der institutionellen Analyse* (preface G. Deleuze, trans. G. Osterwald). Frankfurt: Suhrkamp.

Guilhot, Nicolas. 2010. '"Un réseau d'amitiés agissantes": les deux vies de la Fondation pour une entreaide intellectuelle européenne (1957–1991)' (trans. G. Brzustowski), in Tournès 2010.

Gurr, Ted Robert. 1970. *Why Men Rebel.* Princeton, N.J.: Princeton University Press.

Haas, Ernst B. 1968 [1958]. *The Uniting of Europe: Political, Economic and Social Forces* (2nd edn). Stanford: Stanford University Press.

Habermas, Jürgen. 1971 [1962]. *Strukturwandel der Öffentlichkeit: Untersuchungen zu einer Kategorie der bürgerlichen Gesellschaft.* Neuwied: Luchterhand.

Hakluyt, Richard. 1993 [1584]. *Discourse of Western Planting* (ed. DB. and A.M. Quinn). London: Hakluyt Society.

Halliday, Fred. 1999. *Revolution and World Politics: The Rise and Fall of the Sixth Great Power.* Basingstoke: Macmillan.

Halperin, Sandra. 1997. *In the Mirror of the Third World: Capitalist Development in Modern Europe.* Ithaca, N.Y.: Cornell University Press.

Hamilton, A., Madison, J., and Jay, J. 1992 [1787–88]. *The Federalist* (introd. W.R. Brock). London: J.M. Dent.

Hardt, Michael, and Negri, Antonio. 2000. *Empire.* Cambridge, Mass.: Harvard University Press.

Hargreaves, J.D. 1988. *Decolonization in Africa.* London: Longman.

Hartmann, F.H. (ed.). 1966 [1962]. *World in Crisis: Readings in International Relations* (2nd edn). New York: Macmillan.

Harvey, David. 1995 [1990]. *The Condition of Postmodernity: An Enquiry into the Origins of Cultural Change.* Cambridge, Mass.: Blackwell.

Hegel, G.W.F. 1961 [1837]. *Vorlesungen über die Philosophie der Geschichte.* Stuttgart: Reclam.

—— 1972 [1821]. *Grundlinien der Philosophie des Rechts* (ed. and introd. H. Reichelt). Frankfurt: Ullstein.

Helvey, Robert L. 2004. *On Strategic Nonviolent Conflict: Thinking About the Fundamentals.* Boston, Mass.: Albert Einstein Institution.

Herder, Johann Gottfried. 1997 [1774]. *Auch eine Philosophie der Geschichte zur Bilding der Menschheit: Beitrag zu vielen Beiträge des Jahrhunderts* (ed. H.D. Irsmscher). Stuttgart: Reclam.

—— 2001 [1769]. *Abhandlung über den Ursprung der Sprache* (ed. H.D. Irsmscher). Stuttgart: Reclam.

Herod, Charles C. 1976. *The Nation in the History of Marxian Thought: The Concept of Nations with History and Nations without History.* The Hague: Nijhoff.

Hewison, Robert. 1981. *In Anger: British Culture in the Cold War 1945–60.* New York: Oxford University Press.

Hilferding, Rudolf. 1973 [1910]. *Das Finanzkapital.* Frankfurt: Europäische Verlagsanstalt.

Hippler, Jürgen. 1986. *Krieg im Frieden. Amerikanische Strategien für die Dritte Welt: Counterinsurgency und Low-Intensity Warfare*. Cologne: Pahl-Rugenstein.

Hitch, Charles J., and McKean, Roland N. (eds). 1974. *The Economics of Defense in the Nuclear Age*. New York: Atheneum.

Hitchens, Christopher. 2002 [2001]. *The Trial of Henry Kissinger* (rev. edn). London: Verso.

Ho Chi Minh. 1980. *Reden und Schriften: Eine Auswahl* (trans. from the Vietnamese, Russian and French; ed. W. Lulei, written 1920–69). Leipzig: Reclam.

Hobson, John A. 1968 [1902]. *Imperialism: A Study* (3rd edn). London: Allen & Unwin.

Hobson, John M. 2012. *The Eurocentric Conception of World Politics: Western International Theory, 1760–2010*. Cambridge: Cambridge University Press.

Hoffmann, Stanley. 1977. 'An American Social Science: International Relations'. *Daedalus*. 106 (3). 41–60.

—— 1978. *Primacy or World Order: American Foreign Policy since the Cold War*. New York: McGraw–Hill.

Hofstadter, Richard. 1955. *The Age of Reform: From Bryan to F.D.R.*. New York: Vintage.

Horkheimer, Max, and Adorno, Theodor. 1990 [1944]. *Dialectic of Enlightenment* (trans. J. Cumming). New York: Continuum.

Hough, Jerry W. 1986. *The Struggle for the Third World: Soviet Debates and American Options*. Washington, D.C.: Brookings Institution.

Hughes, H. Stuart. 1958. *Consciousness and Society: The Reorientation of European Social Thought 1890–1930*. New York: Vintage.

Hulnick, Arthur S. 1987. 'CIA's Relations with Academia: Symbiosis Not Psychosis'. *International Journal of Intelligence and Counterintelligence*. 1 (4). 41–50.

Hume, David. 1739–40. *A Treatise of Human Nature*, fascimile edn. (ed. A. Merivale and P. Millican). Vols i and ii. London: John Noon, 1739; vol. iii. London: Thomas Longman, 1740. www.davidhume.org (accessed 23 September 2012).

—— 1875 (1742, 1752) *Essays. Moral, Political, and Literary* (2 vols; ed. T.H. Green and T.H. Grose). London: Longmans, Green & Co.

Huntington, Samuel P. 1965. 'Political Development and Political Decay.' *World Politics*. 17 (3). 386–430.

—— 1968. 'The Bases of Accommodation'. *Foreign Affairs*. 46 (4). 642–56.

—— 1971. 'The Change to Change: Modernization, Development, and Politics'. *Comparative Politics*. 3 (3). 283–322.

—— 1998. *The Clash of Civilizations and the Remaking of World Order*. London: Touchstone Books.

Içduygu, A., and Kirişci, K. (eds). 2009. *Land of Diverse Migrations: Challenges of Emigration and Immigration in Turkey*. Istanbul: Istanbul Bilgi University Press.

Idenburg, P.J.A. 1961. 'Het Nederlandse antwoord op het Indonesisch nationalisme', in Baudet and Burgmans 1961.

Ikenberry, G. John. 2011. 'The Future of the Liberal World Order: Internationalism After America'. *Foreign Affairs*. 90 (3). 1–14.

International Security Council. 1986. *State-Sponsored Terrorism and the Threat to International Security*. New York: CAUSA International.

Iskenderov, A.A. 1972 [1970, spelled Iskenderow]. *Nationale Befreiungsbewegung: Probleme, Gesetzmässigkeiten, Perspektiven* (trans. G. Lehmann). Berlin: Staatsverlag der DDR.

Jacob, Margaret C. 1991. *Living the Enlightenment: Freemasonry and Politics in Eighteenth-Century Europe*. New York: Oxford University Press.

Jahoda, M., Lazarsfeld, P.F., and Zeisel, H. 1975 [1933]. *Die Arbeitslosen von Marienthal: Ein soziographischer Versuch*. Frankfurt: Suhrkamp.

Janowitz, Morris. 1964. *The Military in the Development of New Nations*. Chicago: University of Chicago Press.

Jenkins, Dominick. 2002. *The Final Frontier: America, Science, and Terror*. London: Verso.

Jervis, Robert. 1999. 'Realism, Neo-liberalism, and Cooperation: Understanding the Debate'. *International Security*. 24 (1). 42–63.

—— 2002. 'An Interim Assessment of September 11: What Has Changed and What Has Not?' *Political Science Quarterly*. 117 (1). 37–54.

Jessop, Bob, and Sum, Ngai-Ling. 2001. 'Pre-disciplinary and Post-disciplinary Perspectives'. *New Political Economy*. 6 (1). 89–101.

Jordan, Robert S. 1971. 'The Influence of the British Secretariat Tradition on the Formation of the League of Nations', in Robert S. Jordan (ed.). *International Administration*. New York: Oxford University Press.

Jørgensen, K.E., and Knudsen, T.B. (eds). 2006. *International Relations in Europe: Traditions, Perspectives and Destinations*. Abingdon: Routledge.

Jost, H.U. (ed.). 1997. *L'Avènement des sciences sociales commes disciplines académiques* (*Les Annuelles*, no. 8). Lausanne: Antipodes.

Kant, Immanuel. 1953 [1795]. *Zum ewigen Frieden: Ein philosophischer Entwurf*. Stuttgart: Reclam.

Kantzenbach, Friedrich Wilhelm. 1970. *Johann Gottlieb Herder in Selbstzeugnissen und Bilddokumenten*. Reinbek: Rowohlt.

Kaplan, Fred M. 1984. *The Wizards of Armageddon*. New York: Simon & Schuster.

Kaplan, Robert D. 1994. 'The Coming Anarchy: How scarcity, crime, overpopulation, tribalism, and disease are rapidly destroying the social fabric of our planet'. *The Atlantic*. February. http://www.theatlantic.com/magazine/archive/1994/02/the-coming-anarchy/304670 (accessed 13 June 2013).

Karl, Barry D. 1974. *Charles E. Merriam and the Study of Politics*. Chicago: University of Chicago Press.

Katzenstein, P.J., Keohane, R.O., and Krasner, S.D. 1998. 'International Organization and the Study of World Politics'. *International Organization*. 52 (4). 645–85.

Kautsky, Karl. 1914. 'Der Imperialismus'. *Die Neue Zeit*. 2. 908–22.

Kennan, George F. 1951 [1947]. 'The Sources of Soviet Conduct', in *American Diplomacy 1900–1950*. New York: Mentor.

Keohane, Robert O. (ed.). 1986. *Neorealism and Its Critics*. New York: Columbia University Press.

—— 2002. 'The Globalization of Informal Violence, Theories of World Politics, and the "Liberalism of Fear"'. *Dialogue IO*. 1 (1). 29–43.

—— 2009. 'The old IPE and the new'. *Review of International Political Economy*. 16 (1). 34–46.

—— and Nye, Joseph S., Jr. (eds). 1973 [1971]. *Transnational Relations and World Politics*. Cambridge, Mass.: Harvard University Press.

Keynes, John Maynard. 1920. *The Economic Consequences of the Peace*. London: Macmillan.

Kim Dschong Il. 1982. *Über die Dschutsche-Ideologie* (trans. from the Korean). Pyongyang: Verlag für fremdsprachige Literatur.

Kindleberger, Charles P. 1969. *American Business Abroad: Six Lectures on Direct Investment*. New Haven, Conn.: Yale University Press.

Kissinger, Henry A. 1958 [1957]. *Nuclear Weapons and Foreign Policy* (abridged edn.). New York: Doubleday.

Kleinschmidt, Harald. 2000. *The Nemesis of Power: A History of International Relations Theories*. London: Reaktion Books.

Kloss, Heinz. 1969. *Grundfragen der Ethnopolitik im 20. Jahrhundert*. Vienna: Braumüller; Bad Godesberg: Verlag Wissenschaftliches Archiv.

Kojève, Alexandre. 1968 [1947]. *Introduction à la lecture de Hegel: Leçons sur la Phénoménologie de l'Esprit professées de 1933 à 1939 à l'École des Hautes Études* (ed. R. Queneau). Paris: Gallimard.

Kolko, Gabriel. 1957. 'Morris R. Cohen: The Scholar and/or Society'. *American Quarterly*. 9 (3). 325–36.

—— 1985. *Anatomy of a War: Vietnam, the United States, and the Modern Historical Experience*. New York: Pantheon.

—— 1988. *Confronting the Third World: United States Foreign Policy 1945–1980*. New York: Pantheon.

—— 1997. *Vietnam: Anatomy of a Peace*. London: Routledge.

—— and Kolko, Joyce. 1972. *The Limits of Power: The World and United States Foreign Policy, 1945–1954*. New York: Harper & Row.

Krasner, Stephen D. 1985. *Structural Conflict: The Third World Against Global Liberalism*. Berkeley, Calif.: University of California Press.

—— 2005. 'The Case for Shared Sovereignty'. *Journal of Democracy*. 16 (1). 69–83.

—— 2009. 'Who Gets a State, and Why? The Relative Rules of Sovereignty'. *Foreign Affairs Snapshot*. http://www.foreignaffairs.com (accessed 12 July 2011).

—— and Pascual, Carlos. 2005. 'Addressing State Failure'. *Foreign Affairs*. 84 (4). 153–63.

Krige, John. 2006. *American Hegemony and the Postwar Reconstruction of Science in Europe*. Cambridge, Mass.: MIT Press.

Krippendorff, Ekkehart. 1982 [1975]. *International Relations as a Social Science*. Brighton: Harvester.

Kubálková, V., and Cruickshank, J.J. 1980. *Marxism–Leninism and the Theory of International Relations*. London: Routledge.

Kuczynski, Jürgen. 1977. *Gesellschaftswissenschaftliche Schulen* (vol. vii of *Studien zu einer Geschichte der Gesellschaftswissenschaften*). Berlin: Akademie-Verlag.

—— 1979 [1975]. *Wissenschaftsstrategie* (2nd edn; vol. ii of *Studien zu einer Geschichte der Gesellschaftswissenschaften*]. Berlin: Akademie-Verlag.

Lamb, Alastair. 1968. *Asian Frontiers: Studies in a Continuing Problem*. London: Pall Mall Press.

Lanyi, George A., and McWilliams, Wilson C. (eds). 1966. *Crisis and Continuity in World Politics: Readings in International Relations*. New York: Random House.

Lasch, Christopher. 1967. 'The Cultural Cold War', *The Nation*. 11 September. 198–212.

Lasswell, Harold D. 1941. 'The Garrison State'. *American Journal of Sociology*. 46 (4). 455–68.

—— 1951. 'The Policy Orientation', in Lasswell and Lerner 1951.

—— 1960 [1930]. *Psychopathology and Politics*. New York: Viking.

—— and Lerner, Daniel (eds). 1951. *The Policy Sciences: Recent Developments in Scope and Method*. Stanford, Calif.: Stanford University Press.

Lazare, Daniel. 2004. 'Deux siècles de quasi-immobilisme: La paranoïa constitutionelle contre la souveraineté populaire', in Liberman 2004.

Lazarsfeld, Paul. 1975 [1960]. 'Vorspruch zur neuen Auflage', in Jahoda, Lazarsfeld, and Zeisel 1975.

Lefebvre, Henri. 1977. *Le mode de production étatique* (vol. iii of *De l'Etat*). Paris: Union Générale d'Éditions 10/18.

Lenin, Vladimir Ilitch. *Collected Works* (39 vols; trans. from the Russian). Moscow: Progress.

—— *Werke* (39 vols; trans. from the Russian). Berlin: Dietz.

Leonard, Robert. 2011. 'The Collapse of Interwar Vienna: Oskar Morgenstern's Community, 1925–50'. *History of Political Economy*. 43 (1). 83–130.

Liberman, Jean (ed.). 2004. *Démythifier l'universalité des valeurs américaines*. Paris: Parangon.

Liebich, André. 2008. 'Minority as inferiority: Minority rights in historical perspective'. *Review of International Studies*. 34 (2). 243–63.

Lippmann, Walter. 2010 [1922]. *Public Opinion*. N.p.: BN Publishing.

Lipschutz, Ronnie D. 1999. 'Terror in the Suites: Narratives Fear and the Global Political Economy of Danger'. *Global Society*. 13 (4). 411–39.

—— 2001. *Cold War Fantasies: Film, Fiction and Foreign Policy*. Lanham, Md.: Rowman & Littlefield.

Lipset, Seymour Martin. 1969 [1959]. *Political Man*. London: Heinemann.

Locke, John. 1965 [1689]. *Two Treatises of Government* (introd. P. Laslett). New York: Mentor.

—— 1995 [1689]. *An Essay Concerning Human Understanding*. New York: ILT Digital Classics. www.ilt.columbia.edu (accessed 20 July 2012).

López-Alves, Fernando. 2000. *State Formation and Democracy in Latin America 1810–1900*. Durham, N.C.: Duke University Press.

Löwy, Michael. 1981. *The Politics of Combined and Uneven Development: The Theory of Permanent Revolution*. London: Verso.

—— 1998 [1974–1993]. *Fatherland or Mother Earth? Essays on the National Question*. London: Pluto Press, for the International Institute for Research and Education.

—— 2004. 'Les affinités électives étatsuniennes entre libéralisme et social-darwinisme', in Liberman 2004.

Lucas, Scott. 1996. 'Campaigns of Truth: The Psychological Strategy Board and American Ideology, 1951–1953'. *International History Review*. 18 (2). 279–302.

Lundberg, Ferdinand. 1937. *America's 60 Families*. New York: The Vanguard Press.

Luxemburg, Rosa. 1966 [1913]. *Die Akkumulation des Kapitals: Ein Beitrag zur Ökonomischen Erklärung des Imperialismus*. Frankfurt: Neue Kritik.

—— 1970. *Politische Schriften*. Leipzig: Reclam.

Lyotard, Jean-François. 1984 [1979]. *The Postmodern Condition: A Report on Knowledge* (foreword by F. Jameson, trans. G. Bennington and B. Massumi). Manchester: Manchester University Press.

Mackinder, Halford J. 1904. 'The Geographical Pivot of History'. *The Geographical Journal*. 23 (4). 421–37.

Macpherson, C.B. 1962. *The Political Theory of Possessive Individualism: Hobbes to Locke*. Oxford: Oxford University Press.

Maliniak, David, and Tierney, Michael J. 2009. 'The American School of IPE'. *Review of International Political Economy*, 16 (1) 6–33.

Mann, James. 2004. *Rise of the Vulcans. The History of Bush's War Cabinet*. New York: Penguin.

Mann, Michael. 1987. 'Ruling Class Strategies and Citizenship'. *Sociology*. 21 (3). 339–54.

Manokha, Ivan. 2008. *The Political Economy of Human Rights Enforcement*. Basingstoke: Palgrave Macmillan.

Mao Zedong. 1971. *Selected Readings from the Works of Mao Tsetung* (trans. from the Chinese). Peking: Foreign Languages Press.

Mariátegui, José Carlos. 2011. *José Carlos Mariátegui: An Anthology* (ed. and trans. H.E. Vanden and M. Becker; written 1923–30). New York: Monthly Review Press.

Markwell, D.J. 1986. 'Sir Alfred Zimmern Revisited: Fifty Years On'. *Review of International Studies*. 12 (4). 279–92.

Martin, Brian. 1989. 'Gene Sharp's Theory of Power'. *Journal of Peace Research*. 26 (2). 213–22.

Martins, Hermínio. 2011. 'Dear LSE: Notes on an Academic Disaster'. *Society*. 48 (4). 286–9.

Marx, Karl. 1973. *Grundrisse: Introduction to the Critique of Political Economy (Rough Draft)* (introd. and trans. M. Nicolaus; written 1857–58). Harmondsworth: Pelican.

Mayall, James. 1990. *Nationalism and International Society*. Cambridge: Cambridge University Press.

Mayer, Arno J. 1967. *Politics and Diplomacy of Peacemaking: Containment and Counterrevolution at Versailles 1918–1919*. New York: Alfred J. Knopf.

McCarney, Joseph. 2000. *Hegel on History*. London: Routledge.

McClintick, David. 2006. 'How Harvard Lost Russia'. *Institutional Investor Magazine*. 24 January. http://www.institutionalinvestor.com/Article/1020662/How-Harvard-lost-Russia.html (accessed 7 August 2013).

Mearsheimer, John J., and Walt, Stephen M. 2007. *The Israel Lobby and U.S. Foreign Policy*. New York: Farrar, Straus & Giroux.

Medvedev, Roy A. 1976 [1971]. *Let History Judge: The Origins and Consequences of Stalinism* (trans. C. Taylor, ed. D. Joravsky). London: Spokesman.

Menand, Louis. 2001. 'Undisciplined'. *The Wilson Quarterly*. 45 (4). 51–9.

Merriam, Charles E. 1945. *Systematic Politics*. Chicago: University of Chicago Press.

MEW (*Marx-Engels Werke*; 35 vols). Berlin: Dietz, 1956–71. (Vols. xxiii–xxv contain *Capital*, vols i–iii.)

Milios, J., and Sotiropoulos, D.P. 2009. *Rethinking Imperialism: A Study of Capitalist Rule*. Basingstoke: Palgrave Macmillan.

Mill, John Stuart. 1929 [1859]. *On Liberty*. London: Watts & Co.

Mitrany, David. 1966 [1943]. *A Working Peace System*. Chicago: Quadrangle.

Molnár, M. 1975. *Marx, Engels et la politique internationale*. Paris: Gallimard.

Moody, George. 2010. *Transnational Dissemination of the Anglo-American International Relations Discipline in Central and Eastern Europe*. Final Report on British Academy small grant (SG-50186). Mimeo.

Mooney, Chris. 2000. 'For Your Eyes Only: The CIA will let you see classified documents – but at what price?' *Lingua Franca*. November. 35–42. http://www.cia-on-campus.org/mooney.html (accessed 11 June 2013).

Morgenthau, Hans J. 1948. 'The Political Science of E.H. Carr'. *World Politics*. 1 (1). 127–34.

—— 1962 [1940–1960]. *The Decline of Democratic Politics* (vol. i of *Politics in the Twentieth Century*, 3 vols). Chicago: University of Chicago Press.

—— 1967 [1948]. *Politics among Nations: The Struggle for Power and Peace* (4th edn). New York: Knopf.

Mosca, Gaetano. 1939 [1923, 1896]. *The Ruling Class* (2nd edn; ed. and introd. A. Livingston; trans. H. Kahn). New York: McGraw–Hill.

Mowat, Jonathan. 2009. 'The New Gladio in Action? "Swarming Adolescents" and "Rebellious Hysteria"', in Tarpley 2009.

Müller, Leo A. 1991. *Gladio: das Erbe des Kalten Krieges*. Reinbek: Rowohlt.

Nehru, Jawaharlal. 1962 [1936]. *India's Freedom*. London: Allen & Unwin.

Netanyahu, Benjamin (ed.). 1986. *Terrorism: How the West Can Win*. London: Weidenfeld & Nicolson.

Neufeld, Mark. 1995. *The Restructuring of International Relations Theory*. Cambridge: Cambridge University Press.

Nicholson, Mervyn. 2011. 'Alfred Hitchcock Presents Class Struggle'. *Monthly Review*. 63 (7). 33–50.

Nicolson, Harold. 1961 [1946]. *The Congress of Vienna: A Study in Allied Unity, 1812–1822*. New York: Viking.

Niebuhr, Reinhold. 1966 [1949]. 'The Illusion of World Government', in Hartmann 1966.

Nielsen, Waldemar A. 1985. *The Golden Donors: A New Anatomy of the Great Foundations*. New York: Dutton.

Nielson, Jonathan M. 1992. 'The Scholar as Diplomat: American Historians at the Paris Peace Conference of 1919'. *International History Review*. 14 (2). 228–51.

Nietzsche, Friedrich. 1959 [1906]. *Der Wille zur Macht: Versuch einer Umwertung aller Werte* (ed. P. Gast with E. Förster-Nietzsche). Stuttgart: Alfred Kröner.

O'Neill, W.M. 1968. *The Beginnings of Modern Psychology*. Harmondsworth: Penguin.

Opitz, Reinhard (ed.). 1977. *Europastrategien des deutschen Kapitals 1900–1945*. Cologne: Pahl-Rugenstein.

Ortiz, Carlos. 2010. *Private Armed Forces and Global Security*. Santa Barbara, Calif.: Praeger.

O'Toole, G.J.A. 1991. *Honorable Treachery: A History of U.S. Intelligence, Espionage, and Covert Action from the American Revolution to the CIA*. New York: Atlantic Monthly Press.

Özdemir, Renk. 2009a. 'Borders of Belonging in the "Exchanged" Generation of Karamanlis', in Içduygu and Kirişci 2009.

—— 2009b. 'Population Exchanges of the Balkans and Asia Minor at the *fin de siècle*: The Imposition of Political Subjectivities in the Modern World Order', in Bhambra and Shilliam 2009.

Packenham, Robert A. 1973. *Liberal America and the Third World: Political Development Ideas in Foreign Aid and Political Science*. Princeton, N.J.: Princeton University Press.

Pannekoek, Anton. n.d. [1938]. *Lenin als filosoof*. Amsterdam: De Vlam.

Parkinson, F. 1977. *The Philosophy of International Relations: A Study in the History of Thought*. Beverly Hills, Calif.: Sage.

Parmar, Inderjeet. 2002. 'To Relate Knowledge and Action: The Impact of the Rockefeller Foundation on Foreign Policy Thinking during America's Rise to Globalism 1939–1945'. *Minerva*. 40 (3). 235–63.

—— 2012. *Foundations of the American Century: The Ford, Carnegie and Rockefeller Foundations in the Rise of American Power*. New York: Columbia University Press.

Parsons, Talcott. 1949 [1937]. *The Structure of Social Action: A Study in Social Theory with Special Reference to a Group of Recent European Writers*. New York: Free Press; London: Collier–Macmillan.

Pasche, C., and Peters, S. 1997. 'Les premiers pas de la Société du Mont-Pèlerin ou les dessous chics du néoliberalisme', in Jost 1997.

Pauker, Guy J. 1959. 'Southeast Asia as a Problem Area in the Next Decade'. *World Politics*. 11 (3). 325–45.

Peleg, Ilan. 2007. *Democratizing the Hegemonic State: Political Transformation in the Age of Identity*. Cambridge: Cambridge University Press.

Pells, Richard H. 1985. *The Liberal Mind in a Conservative Age: American Intellectuals in the 1940s and 1950s*. New York: Harper & Row.

Phillips, Kevin. 2004. *American Dynasty*. London: Allen Lane Penguin.

Phillips, Nicola. 2009. 'The Slow Death of Pluralism'. *Review of International Political Economy*. 16 (1). 85–94.

Pielke, Roger A., Jr. 2004. 'What future for the policy sciences?' *Policy Sciences*. 37 (3–4). 209–25.

Pijl, Kees van der. 1996 [1993]. *Vordenker der Weltpolitik Einführung in die internationale Politik aus ideengeschichtlicher Perspektive* (rev. edn.; trans. W. Linsewksi). Opladen: Leske+Budrich.

—— 1998. *Transnational Classes and International Relations*. London: Routledge.

—— 2006. *Global Rivalries from the Cold War to Iraq*. London: Pluto Press; New Delhi: Sage Vistaar.

—— 2007. *Nomads, Empires, States* (vol. i of *Modes of Foreign Relations and Political Economy*). London: Pluto Press.

—— 2009. *A Survey of Global Political Economy*. PDF web-text. www.sussex. ac.uk/ir/research/gpe/gpesurvey (accessed 12 June 2013).

—— 2010. *The Foreign Encounter in Myth and Religion* (vol. ii of *Modes of Foreign Relations and Political Economy*). London: Pluto Press.

—— 2012 [1984]. *The Making of an Atlantic Ruling Class*. London: Verso.

Playford, John. 1968. 'Political Scientists and the C.I.A.' *Australian Left Review*. April–May. 14–28. http://www.american-buddha.com/politicals-cienceCIA.htm (accessed 14 May 2013).

Plekhanov, G.V. 1969 [1908]. *Fundamental Problems of Marxism* (trans. J. Katzer; ed. J.S. Allen). New York: International Publishers.

Polanyi, Karl. 1957 [1944]. *The Great Transformation: The Political and Economic Origins of Our Time*. Boston, Mass.: Beacon.

Poliakov, Léon, and Wulf, Joseph (eds). 1989 [1959]. *Das Dritte Reich und seine Denker*. Wiesbaden: Fourier.

Pool, Ithiel de S. 1963. 'The Mass Media and Politics in the Modernization Process', in Pye 1963.

Pownall, Thomas. 1971 [1768] *The Administration of the Colonies: Wherein Their Rights and Constitution Are Discussed and Stated* (4th edn; facsimile edn). New York: Da Capo Press.

Pradt, Dominique G.F. Dufour de. 1821. *L'Europe et l'Amérique depuis le Congrès d'Aix-la-Chapelle* (vol. i). Paris: Béchet ainé; Rouen: Béchet fils.

—— 1824. *L'Europe et l'Amérique en 1822 et 1823* (vol. ii). Paris: Béchet ainé.

Pye, Lucian W. (ed.). 1963. *Communications and Political Development*. Princeton: Princeton University Press.

—— 1965. 'Introduction: Political Culture and Political Development', in Pye and Verba 1965.

—— and Verba, Sydney (eds). 1965. *Political Culture and Political Development*. Princeton N.J.: Princeton University Press.

Quigley, Carroll. 1981 [1949]. *The Anglo-American Establishment: From Rhodes to Cliveden*. New York: Books in Focus.

Rademaker, L. (ed.). 1978. *Sociologische Encyclopedie* (4 vols). Utrecht: Spectrum.

Rajewsky, Christiane. 1980. 'Der gerechte Krieg im Islam', in Steinweg 1980.

Ralph, Diana. 2008 [2006]. 'Islamophobia and the "War on Terror": The Continuing Pretext for U.S. Imperial Conquest', in Zarembka 2008.

Ramel, Frédéric (ed.). 2011. *Philosophie des relations internationales* (2nd edn; with D. Cumin, C. Mallatrait and E. Vianès). Paris: Presses de Sciences Po.

—— 2012. *L'attraction mondiale*. Paris: Presses de Sciences Po.

Ransom, David. 1974. 'Ford Country: Building an Elite for Indonesia', in Weissman 1974.

Rapoport, Anatol. 1966 [1964]. 'Systemic and Strategic Conflict: What Happens When People Do Not Think – and When They Do', in Falk and Mendlovitz 1966.

Rausch, Helke. 2010. '"Allemagne, année zero"? Dénazifier et démocratiser (1945–1955)', in Tournès 2010.

Rawls, John. 1973 [1971]. *A Theory of Justice*. Oxford: Oxford University Press.

Rehmann, Jan. 1998. *Max Weber: Modernisierung als passive Revolution: Kontextstudien zu Politik, Philosophie und Religion im Übergang zum Fordismus.* Berlin: Argument Verlag.

Reisch, George A. 2005. *How the Cold War Transformed Philosophy of Science: To the Icy Slopes of Logic.* Cambridge: Cambridge University Press.

Reves, Emery. 1947 [1945]. *The Anatomy of Peace* (2nd edn; with new postscript). Harmondsworth: Penguin.

Reynolds, Morgan. 2007. '9/11, Texas A & M University, and Heresy', in Griffin and Scott 2007.

Robinson, William I. 1996. *Promoting Polyarchy: Globalization, US Intervention, and Hegemony.* Cambridge: Cambridge University Press.

Röling, B.V.A. 1970 [1968]. *Inleiding tot de wetenschap van oorlog en vrede* (2nd edn). Assen: Van Gorcum, Prakke & Prakke.

Rosenbaum, Ron. 1977. 'Last Secrets of Skull and Bones'. *Esquire*, September.

—— 2000. 'I Stole the Head of Prescott Bush. More Scary Skull and Bones Tales'. *New York Observer*, July 17.

Rosenberg, Tina. 2011. 'Revolution U: What Egypt learned from the students who overthrew Milosevic'. *Foreign Policy.* 16 February. http://www.foreignpolicy.com/articles/2011/02/16/revolution_u (accessed 24 December 2012).

Rosenstone, Robert A. 1982. *Romantic Revolutionary: A Biography of John Reed.* Harmondsworth: Penguin.

Ross, Dorothy. 1991. *The Origins of American Social Science.* Cambridge: Cambridge University Press.

Rostow, Walt W. 1967 [1961]. 'Guerrilla Warfare in Underdeveloped Areas' (address, US Army Special Warfare School, Fort Bragg), in M.G. Raskin and B.B. Fall (eds). *The Viet-Nam Reader* (rev. edn). New York: Vintage.

Roszak, Theodore (ed.). 1968. *The Dissenting Academy.* New York: Vintage.

Rothkopf, David. 2005. *Ruling the World: The Inside Story of the National Security Council and the Architects of American Power.* New York: Public Affairs.

Rousseau, Jean-Jacques. 1966 [1762]. *Du contrat social* (introd. P. Burgelin). Paris: Flammarion.

—— 1969 [1755]. *Discours sur l'origine et les fondements de l'inégalité parmi les hommes* (ed. J. Starobinski). Paris: Gallimard.

Rowse, A.L. 1998 [1966]. *Bosworth Field and the Wars of the Rose*s. Ware, Herts.: Wordsworth Editions.

Roy, Ajit. 1986 [1982]. '"Revolution" by "Consent": Indian Case Study', in Ajit Roy. *Contemporary India: A Perspective.* Bombay: Build.

—— 1994. 'National Relations in Soviet Union: Theory and Practice'. *Economic and Political Weekly.* 29 (1/2). 49–54.

Russell, Bertrand. 1961 [1946]. *History of Western Philosophy* (2nd edn). London: Allen & Unwin.

Ryan, Lori Verstegen, and Scott, William G. 1995. 'Ethics and Organizational Reflection: The Rockefeller Foundation and Postwar "Moral Deficits," 1942–1954'. *Academy of Management Review.* 20 (2). 438–61.

Sacks, Bryan. 2008 [2006]. 'Making History: The Compromised 9–11 Commission', in Zarembka 2008.

Sahakian, William S., and Sahakian, Mabel Lewis. 1965. *Realms of Philosophy*. Cambridge, Mass.: Schenckman.

Sanguinetti, Gianfranco. 1982 [1979]. *Over het terrorisme en de staat* (trans. from the French). Bussum: Wereldvenster.

Sarila, Narendra Singh. 2006. *The Shadow of the Great Game: The Untold Story of India's Partition*. London: Constable.

Scheer, Robert. 1982. *With Enough Shovels: Reagan, Bush, and Nuclear War*. New York: Random House.

Schelling, Thomas C. 1966. *Arms and Influence*. New Haven, Conn.: Yale University Press.

Scheuerman, William E. 2008. 'Realism and the Left: The case of Hans J. Morgenthau'. *Review of International Studies*. 34 (1). 29–51.

Schiffrin, André (ed.). 1997. *The Cold War and the University: Toward an Intellectual History of the Postwar Years*. New York: The New Press.

Schlick, Moritz. 1930. 'Die Wende der Philosophie'. *Erkenntnis*. 1. 4–11.

Schmidt, Brian C. 1998. *The Political Discourse of Anarchy: A Disciplinary History of International Relations*. Albany, N.Y.: State University of New York Press.

Schmitt, Carl. 1963 [1932, 1927]. *Der Begriff des Politischen* (2nd edn). Berlin: Duncker & Humblot.

—— 1989 [1940]. 'Zum 30. Juni 1934', in Poliakov and Wulf 1989.

—— 1996 [1931]. *Der Hüter der Verfassung* (4th edn). Berlin: Duncker & Humblot.

—— 2005 [1934, 1922]. *Political Theology: Four Chapters on the Concept of Sovereignty* (2nd edn; trans. and introd. G. Schwab, foreword by T.B. Strong). Chicago: University of Chicago Press.

—— 2006 [1928, 1921]. *Die Diktatur: Von den Anfängen des modernen Souveränitätsgedankens bis zum proletarischen Klassenkampf* (7th edn). Berlin: Duncker & Humblot.

Schumpeter, Joseph A. 1951 [1919]. 'The Sociology of Imperialisms', in Joseph A. Schumpeter. *Imperialism and Social Classes* (introd. P.M. Sweezy). New York: Kelley.

Schurmann, Franz, and Schell, Orville (eds). 1968. *Communist China* (vol. iii of *China Readings*). Harmondsworth: Penguin.

Scot, Marie. 2010. '"Rockefeller's Baby": La London School of Economics et la recherche économique dans l'Angleterre de l'entre-deux-guerres', in Tournès 2010.

Scott, Peter Dale. 1996 [1993]. *Deep Politics and the Death of JFK*. Berkeley, Calif.: University of California Press.

—— 2003. *Drugs, Oil, and War: The United States in Afghanistan, Colombia, and Indochina*. Lanham, Md.: Rowman & Littlefield.

—— 2007. *The Road to 9/11: Wealth, Empire, and the Future of America*. Berkeley, Calif.: University of California Press.

—— 2010. *American War Machine: Deep Politics, the CIA Global Drug Connection, and the Road to Afghanistan*. Lanham, Md.: Rowman & Littlefield.

Scott-Smith, Giles. 2002. *The Politics of Apolitical Culture: The Congress for Cultural Freedom, the CIA and post-war American hegemony*. London: Routledge.

Seaman, L.C.B. 1964 [1955]. *From Vienna to Versailles*. London: Methuen.

Shaheen, Samad. 1956. *The Communist (Bolshevik) Theory of National Self-Determination: Its Historical Evolution up to the October Revolution.* The Hague: Van Hoeve.

Shain, Yossi. 1989. *The Frontier of Loyalty: Political Exiles in the Age of the Nation-State.* Hanover, N.H.: Wesleyan University Press.

Shibata, Shingo. 1973. *Lessons of the Vietnam War: Philosophical Considerations on the Vietnam Revolution.* Amsterdam: Grüner.

Shilliam. Robbie. 2012. 'Civilization and the poetics of slavery'. *Thesis Eleven.* 108 (1). 99–117.

Shils, Edward A. 1963. 'Demagogues and Cadres in the Political Development of the New States', in Pye 1963.

Shoup, Laurence H., and Minter, William. 1977. *Imperial Brain Trust: The Council on Foreign Relations and United States Foreign Policy.* New York: Monthly Review Press.

Silk, Leonard S., and Silk, Mark. 1981. *The American Establishment.* New York: Avon.

Singer, J. David. 1966 [1961]. 'The Level-of-Analysis Problem in International Relations', in Falk and. Mendlovitz 1966.

—— 1980. 'Accounting for International War: The State of the Discipline'. *Annual Review of Sociology.* 6. 349–67.

Slaughter, Anne-Marie. 2012. 'Networked Governance'. Memorandum to the Liberal Internationalism Conference Participants, Princeton University, May 4–5. (Unpublished).

Sluga, Glenda. 2005. 'What is national self-determination? Nationality and psychology during the apogee of nationalism'. *Nations and Nationalism.* 11 (1). 1–20.

Smith, B.L.R. 1966. *The RAND Corporation.* Cambridge, Mass.: Harvard University Press.

Smith, Neil. 2004. *American Empire: Roosevelt's Geographer and the Prelude to Globalization.* Berkeley, Calif.: University of California Press.

Smith, Steve. 2000. 'The discipline of international relations: Still an American social science?' *British Journal of Politics and International Relations.* 2 (3). 374–402.

Sohn-Rethel, Alfred. 1970. *Geistige und körperliche Arbeit: Zur Theorie der gesellschaftlichen Synthesis.* Frankfurt: Suhrkamp.

Söllner, Alfons. 1990. 'Von Staatsrecht zur "political science"? Die Emigration deutscher Wissenschaftler nach 1933, ihr Einfluß auf die Transformation einer Disziplin'. *Politische Vierteljahresschrift.* 31 (4). 627–54.

Solovey, Mark. 2001. 'Project Camelot and the 1960s Epistemological Revolution: Rethinking the Politics–Patronage–Social Science Nexus'. *Social Studies of Science.* 31 (2). 171–206.

Sorokin, Pitirim A. 1985 [1957]. *Social and Cultural Dynamics: A Study of Change in Major Systems of Art, Truth, Ethics, Law, and Social Relationships* (rev. and abridged; introd. M.P. Richard; original 4 vol. edn published 1937–41). New Brunswick, N.J.: Transaction Books.

Spear, Percival. 1970 [1965]. *A History of India* (vol. ii). Harmondsworth: Penguin.

Spencer, Herbert. 1982 [1884; 1843–1891]. *The Man Versus the State, With Six Essays on Government, Society, and Freedom* (foreword by E. Mack, introd. A.J. Nock). Indianapolis: Liberty Fund.

Stalin, J.W. *Werke*. (13 vols; trans. from the Russian). Berlin: Dietz.

Stapelfeldt, Gerhard. 2001. *Der Merkantilismus: Die Genese der Weltgesellschaft vom 16. bis zum 18. Jahrhundert*. Freiburg: ça ira.

Stavrianakis, Anna. 2006. 'Call to Arms: The University as a Site of Militarised Capitalism and a Site of Struggle'. *Millennium: Journal of International Studies*. 35 (1). 139–54.

—— 2010. *Taking Aim at the Arms Trade: NGOs, Global Civil Society and the World Military Order*. London: Zed Press.

Steinweg, Reiner (ed.). 1980. *Der gerechte Krieg: Christentum, Islam, Marxismus*. Frankfurt: Suhrkamp.

Stewart, Angus. 1995. 'Two Conceptions of Citizenship'. *British Journal of Sociology*. 46 (1). 63–78.

Strange, Susan. 1972. 'The Dollar Crisis 1971'. *International Affairs*. 48 (2). 191–216.

Strauss, Leo. 2011 [1948]. 'De la Tyrannie', in Ramel 2011.

Struik, Dirk. 1977 [1948]. *Geschiedenis van de wiskunde* (rev. edn). Amsterdam: SUA.

Suganami, Hidemi. 2001. 'C.A.W. Manning and the study of International Relations'. *Review of International Studies*. 27 (1). 91–107.

Sutton, Anthony C. 1986. *America's Secret Establishment: An Introduction to the Order of Skull and Bones*. Billings, Mont.: Liberty House Press.

Szasz, Ferenc Morton. 2004. *The Protestant Clergy in the Great Plains and Mountain West, 1865–1915*. Lincoln, Nebr.: University of Nebraska Press.

Talmon, J.L. 1981. *The Myth of the Nation and the Vision of Revolution*. London: Secker & Warburg; Berkeley, Calif.: University of California Press.

Tanham, George K., and Duncanson, Dennis J. 1969. 'Some Dilemmas of Counterinsurgency'. *Foreign Affairs*. 48 (1). 113–22.

Tarpley, Webster G. 2008 [2005]. *9/11 Synthetic Terror Made in USA* (4th edn). Joshua Tree, Calif.: Progressive Press.

—— 2009. *Obama, the Postmodern Coup: Making of a Manchurian Candidate* (with chapters by Bruce Marshall and Jonathan Mowat). Joshua Tree, Calif.: Progressive Press.

Taylor, Charles. 2004. *Modern Social Imaginaries*. Durham, S.C.: Duke University Press.

Taylor, Peter. J. 1996. *The Way the Modern World Works: World Hegemony to World Impasse*. Chichester: Wiley.

Teschke, Benno. 2003. *The Myth of 1648: Class, Geopolitics and the Making of Modern International Relations*. London: Verso.

—— 2011. 'Decisions and Indecisions: Political and Intellectual Receptions of Carl Schmitt'. *New Left Review* (2nd series). 67. 61–95.

Therborn, Göran. 1976. *Science, Class and Society: On the Formation of Sociology and Historical Materialism*. London: Verso.

Thompson, Kenneth W. 1966 [1959]. 'American Approaches to International Politics', in Lanyi and McWilliams 1966.

Tocqueville, Alexis de. 1990 [1835, 1840]. *Democracy in America* (2 vols; trans. H. Reeve and F. Bowen; ed. P. Bradley; introd. D.J. Boorstin). New York: Vintage.

Tournès, Ludovic (ed.). 2010. *L'argent de l'influence: Les fondations américaines et leurs réseaux européens*. Paris: Éditions Autrement.

Trumpbour, John. 1991. 'Harvard in Service to the National Security State'. *Covert Action Information Bulletin*. 38. 12–16.

Tunander, Ola. 2009. 'Democratic State vs. Deep State: Approaching the Dual State of the West', in Wilson 2009.

UANI (United Against Nuclear Iran). n.d. List of officers and advisory board. http://www.unitedagainstnucleariran.com/about/leadership (accessed 10 November 2012).

Ungers, O.M. 1981. 'Einleitung', in *Westkunst: Zeitgenössische Kunst seit 1939*. Cologne: Aussenreferat der Museen der Stadt Köln.

Varga, Eugen. 1974 [1922–1962]. *Die Krise des Kapitalismus und ihre politischen Folgen* (ed. and introd. E. Altvater). Frankfurt: Europäische Verlagsanstalt.

Vasquez, John A. 1987. 'The Steps to War: Toward a Scientific Explanation of Correlates of War Findings'. *World Politics*. 40 (1). 108–45.

Vernon, Raymond. 1973 [1971]. *Sovereignty at Bay: The Multinational Spread of US Enterprises*. Harmondsworth: Penguin.

Vincent, Joan. 1990. *Anthropology and Politics: Visions, Traditions, and Trends*. Tucson: University of Arizona Press.

Vucetic, Srdjan. 2011. *The Anglosphere: A Genealogy of a Racialized Identity in International Relations*. Stanford, Calif.: Stanford University Press.

Walker, R.B.J. 1993. *Inside/Outside: International Relations as Political Theory*. Cambridge: Cambridge University Press.

Wallerstein, Immanuel. 1991 [1988]. *Race, Nation, Class. Ambiguous Identities* [with E. Balibar]. London: Verso.

—— 1997. 'The Unintended Consequences of Cold War Area Studies', in Schiffrin 1997.

—— 2001 [1991]. *Unthinking Social Science: The Limits of Nineteenth-Century Paradigms* (2nd edn). Philadelphia: Temple University Press.

Walpen, Bernard. 2004. *Die offenen Feinde und ihre Gesellschaft: Eine hegemonietheoretische Studie zur Mont Pèlerin Society*. Hamburg: VSA.

Walther, P.Th. 1991. 'Zur Kontinuität politikwissenschaftlicher Fragestellungen: Deutschlandstudien exilierten Dozenten', in Göhler and Zeuner 1991.

Waltz, Kenneth N. 1986. 'Reflections on Theory of International Politics: A Response to my Critics', in Keohane 1986.

Walzer, Michael. 1971. 'World War II: Why Was This War Different?' *Philosophy and Public Affairs*. 1 (1). 3–21.

Wang Hui. 2009 [2004]. *Impero o Stato-Nazione? La modernità intellettuale in Cina* (trans. and ed. G. Perini; introd. C. Pozzana and A. Russo). Milano: Academia Universa.

Watson, Matthew. 2005. *Foundations of International Political Economy*. Basingstoke: Palgrave Macmillan.

Weber, Max. 1976 [1921]. *Wirtschaft und Gesellschaft: Grundriss der verstehenden Soziologie* (5th rev. edn). Tübingen: J.C.B. Mohr.

Weingart, Peter (ed.). 1974. *Wissenschaftssoziologie 2: Determinanten wissen-schaftlicher Entwicklung*. Frankfurt: Athenäum Fischer.

Weissman, S. (ed.). 1974. *The Trojan Horse: A Radical Look at Foreign Aid*. San Francisco, Calif.: Ramparts Press.

Wendler, Eugen. 1989. *Friedrich List: Eine historische Gestalt und Pionier auch im deutsch-amerikanischen Bereich* (bilingual edn; English trans. L. Bils-Baumann and L. Bloom). Gräfelfing: Moos & Partner.

Wertheim, W.F. 1992 [1978]. *Indonesië van vorstenrijk tot neo-kolonie*. Meppel: Boom.

Wight, Martin. 1986 [1978, 1946]. *Power Politics* (2nd edn; ed. H. Bull and C. Holbraad). Harmondworth: Penguin, for the RIIA.

Wilde, Jaap de. 1991. *Saved From Oblivion: Interdependence Theory in the First Half of the 20th Century*. Aldershot: Dartmouth.

Wilford, Hugh. 2008. *The Mighty Wurlitzer: How the CIA Played America*. Cambridge, Mass.: Harvard University Press.

Willan, Philip. 1991. *Puppet Masters: The Political Use of Terrorism in Italy*. London: Constable.

Wilson, Eric (ed.). 2009. *Government of the Shadows: Parapolitics and Criminal Sovereignty*. London: Pluto Press.

Wilson, Woodrow A. 1901. 'Democracy and Efficiency'. *Atlantic Monthly*. 87 (521). 289–99. Cited from http://www.theatlantic.com/ideastour/politics/wilson-full.html (accessed 10 May 2013).

—— 1919. *Die Reden Woodrow Wilsons* (bilingual edn. published by the Committee on Public Information of the USA). Bern: Freie Verlag.

Windmiller, Marshall. 1968. 'The New American Mandarins', in Roszak 1968.

Wohlstetter, Albert. 1974 [1959]. 'Choosing Policies for Deterrence' (orig. 'The Delicate Balance of Terror'), in Hitch and McKean 1974.

Wohlstetter, Roberta. 1962. *Pearl Harbor: Warning and Decision* (foreword by T.C. Schelling). Stanford, Calif.: Stanford University Press.

Wolfers, Arnold. 1956. 'Introduction: Political Theory and International Relations', in Wolfers and Martin 1956.

—— and Martin, Lawrence W. (eds). 1956. *The Anglo-American Tradition in Foreign Affairs: Readings from Thomas More to Woodrow Wilson*. New Haven, Conn.: Yale University Press.

Woodward, Bob. 1987. *Dekmantel: De geheime oorlogen van de CIA* (trans. J. Koesen). Houten: de Haan.

Yergin, Daniel. 1980 [1977]. *Shattered Peace: The Origins of the Cold War and the National Security State*. Harmondsworth: Penguin.

Zarembka, Paul (ed.). 2008 [2006]. *The Hidden History of 9–11* (2nd edn). New York: Seven Stories Press.

Zastoupil, Lynn. 1994. *John Stuart Mill and India*. Stanford, Calif.: Stanford University Press.

Zeisel, Hans. 1975. 'Zur Geschichte der Soziographie', in Jahoda, Lazarsfeld and Zeisel 1975.

Zelikow, Philip D. (ed.). 2001. *American Military Strategy: Memos to a President*. New York: W.W. Norton.

Zhang, Yongle. 2010. 'The Future of the Past: On Wang Hui's *Rise of Modern Chinese Thought*'. *New Left Review* (2nd series). 62. 47–83.

Zhdanov, A.A. 1960 [1947]. 'Report on the International Situation', excerpts in R.V. Daniels (ed.). *A Documentary History of Communism* (vol. ii). New York: Vintage.

Zürn, Michael. 1994. 'We Can Do Much Better! Aber muss es auf amerikanisch sein?' *Zeitschrift für Internationale Beziehungen.* 1 (1) 91–114.

Index